Teacher Beware

A Legal Primer for the Classroom Teacher

Alex J. Proudfoot
Lawrence Hutchings

Detselig Enterprises Ltd.
Calgary, Alberta

Alex J. Proudfoot The University of Calgary
Lawrence Hutchings Canmore, Alberta

Canadian Cataloging in Publication Data

Proudfoot, A.J. (Alexander James), 1929-
  Teacher beware: a legal primer for the
classroom teacher

  Includes index.
  ISBN 0-920490-82-4

  1. Teachers – Legal status, laws, etc. –
Alberta.   I. Hutchings, Lawrence.   II. Title.
  KEA441.Z82P76   1988   344.7123'078   C88-091201-4

© 1988 Detselig Enterprises Ltd.
210, 1220 Kensington Road NW
Calgary, Alberta T2N 3P5

Phone: (403) 283-0900   Fax: (403) 283-6947
email: temeron@telusplanet.net
www.temerondetselig.com

Reprints: 1997, 1999

Detselig Enterprises Ltd. appreciates the financial support for our 1999
publishing program, provided by the Department of Canadian Heritage.

Printed in Canada   ISBN 0-920490-82-4   SAN 115-0324

Contents

Preface

The purpose of this text is to acquaint the classroom teacher and the potential teacher with a number of general legal principles as they are applied in the school setting. It will neither turn teachers into lawyers nor will it become a substitute for sound legal advice if they become involved in a legal action. It seeks to sensitize teachers to areas of potential danger and conflict as well as to promote an understanding and appreciation of the law and of the legal process. It is intended as a practical guide for classroom situations and therefore has become limited in its scope. It is not an exhaustive treatise on all aspects of school law; that approach would require numerous volumes. Because many legal issues are of less direct concern to the teacher in the classroom, we have tried to be critical in choosing those to be presented herein. The goal has been to be selective, and, we hope, insightful, in drawing to the attention of the teacher those legal matters which are most pressing and thus most practical for the day-to-day management of the classroom.

Although each chapter is a self-contained discussion of a particular topic, the principles discussed therein may also be dealt with from a different perspective in other chapters. To get the full view of corporal punishment issues, for example, reference should be made to the chapters on corporal punishment, child abuse, intentional torts, and student rights. The same act (or failure to act) may be viewed from a different perspective in the various chapters of this text. A reading of the entire text should provide a basic legal literacy for dealing with classroom situations and for exploring the topic further as new cases or circumstances arise.

Concrete examples drawn from reported cases and provincial legislation are used throughout this book to increase its value and relevance for the reader. The reader is provided with a variety of viewpoints in dealing with most specific legal problems and is encouraged to critically analyze each viewpoint before reaching a conclusion.

Learning Approaches Used in the Book

In a book designed for teachers we felt that its pedagogical framework would be important. We have adopted the following features to make this book a challenging and relevant reading experience.

Learning Objectives

Clearly stated learning objectives are presented at the beginning of each chapter to guide the learning experiences of the reader and to help him in understanding the materials presented.

Preview

A short preview of the material to be presented introduces each chapter and serves to highlight the key issues.

Self-Assessment

To involve the reader in the material, a series of questions concerning knowledge or attitudes and beliefs are presented at the beginning of each chapter. This allows the reader to relate his own experiences to the material covered within the chapter.

Key Terms

A list of key terms is provided at the beginning of each chapter and a glossary of these terms is included at the end of the book. When the reader is unfamiliar with a term used he should consult the glossary in order to acquire the necessary vocabulary prior to reading the textual material.

Discussion and Review Questions

At the end of each chapter, discussion and review questions are included to stimulate thought about what has been read and to encourage the reader to apply the learned concepts to the practical problems faced by the classroom teacher or administrator.

Case Studies (You Be The Judge)

Hypothetical situations are presented in order to provide the reader with a further opportunity to apply and integrate the material learned from the chapter in a realistic simulation.

Point/Counterpoint

Conflicting viewpoints on a topic covered in the chapter are presented in order to provide the reader with an opportunity to evaluate a realistic situation from at least two points of view.

References

At the end of each chapter there will be references to a variety of materials that could be used to further explore those areas covered therein.

Appendices

Certain chapters will have an appendix of lengthier materials at the end. These may serve to illustrate a concept, to provide a model of a particular document, or to provide additional background material on a specific topic.

Index

A comprehensive subject index is included at the end of the book to enable the reader to gain easy access to the textual material and references.

A.J.P
L.F.H.

Detselig Enterprise Ltd. appreciates the financial assistance for its 1988 publishing program from

Alberta Foundation for the Literary Arts
Canada Council
Department of Communications
Alberta Culture

Part One

The Legal Process

Alice had never been in a court of justice before, but she had read about them in books, and she was quite pleased to find that she knew the name of nearly everything there. "That's the judge," she said to herself, "because of his great wig."

Lewis Carroll
Alice in Wonderland

1

Introduction
to Education Law

Learning Objectives

Some of the things that you will learn from reading this chapter include the following:

(1) How law affects the daily life of a teacher.
(2) Major reasons why teachers should learn about the law.
(3) What is included in the term "education law."
(4) The relevance of American law to Canadian educational law.

Preview

There are a host of laws that affect the daily routines of the classroom. These, together with the laws establishing the structure of our educational system, are called school law or education law. Knowledge of these laws will benefit teachers both personally and professionally, make schools safer and better places for students and teachers, improve educational standards, and ultimately benefit society as a whole.

Key Terms

Statute	Regulation
Judgment	Defendant
Criminal proceedings	Civil rights
Administrative tribunal	Civil proceedings
By-laws	Constitution
Negligence	Charter of Rights and Freedoms

Self-Assessment

1. Can you list three or four laws, besides the *School Act*, which impinge upon the professional career of the teacher?
2. List two or three ways in which laws other than the *School Act* affect the teacher's conduct in the classroom.
3. How does law act as a means for the socialization of the citizenry?
4. If you were attempting to convince a friend of the value of taking a course in school law, what telling arguments would you use?
5. Why do we find conflicting judgments regarding cases which appear to have identical, or nearly identical, sets of facts?
6. Are American legal precedents generally applicable in Canadian courts? Why?

*   *   *   *

How Laws Affect the Teacher

The law affects everyone's daily life by prescribing certain rights, duties, obligations and parameters of acceptable behaviour in a variety of contexts. Teachers, in particular, have a high potential for involvement in the legal process for a number of reasons. Their professional lives are governed by a host of statutes, including: provincial school acts, education acts, teaching profession acts and many "non-education" acts. In addition there are regulations pursuant to these acts and numerous rules and by-laws adopted by teachers' associations and local school boards. Even our Constitution and *The Canadian Charter of Rights and Freedoms* contained therein deal specifically with education.

The Constitution Act, 1867 (formerly called *The British North America Act, 1867*) states:

> 93: In and for each province the Legislature may exclusively make laws in relation to education . . .

while *The Canadian Charter of Rights and Freedoms*, contained within *The Constitution Act, 1982*, provides:

> 23. (1) Citizens of Canada
>
> (a) whose first language learned and still understood is that of the English or French linguistic minority population of the province in which they reside, or

    (b)   who have received their primary school instruction in Canada in English or French and reside in a province where the language in which they received that instruction is the language of the English or French linguistic minority population of the province, have the right to have their children receive primary and secondary school instruction in that language in that province.

(2)   Citizens of Canada of whom any child has received or is receiving primary or secondary school instruction in English or French in Canada, have the right to have all their children receive primary and secondary school instruction in the same language.

(3)   The right of citizens of Canada under subsections (1) and (2) to have their children receive primary and secondary school instruction in the language of the English or French linguistic minority population of a province

    (a)   applies wherever in the province the number of children of citizens who have such a right is sufficient to warrant the provision to them out of public funds of minority language instruction; and

    (b)   includes, where the number of children so warrants, the right to have them receive that instruction in minority language facilities provided out of public funds.

29.   Nothing in this Charter abrogates or derogates from any rights or privileges guaranteed by or under the Constitution of Canada in respect of denominational, separate or dissentient schools.

From the highest to the lowest branch of government and in all levels of our courts, laws are being made that affect teachers directly. From the moment a teacher enters professional training to the moment he receives his last pension cheque, his career is governed by numerous laws related to the educational enterprise.

Many aspects of teacher education are mandated by provincial legislation. The part of the program called "student teaching" owes its very existence to laws such as the following example taken from the Alberta *School Act*:

A board shall on the request of a university under the *Universities Act* enter into an agreement to permit students enrolled in the faculty of education of that university or their instructors to attend any classroom of any school while it is in session for the purpose of observation or student teaching.

Certification as a teacher follows procedures outlined in the governing statute of the province in which the teacher intends to practice his profession. Prerequisites to certification such as citizenship status, completion of a prescribed course of study, and a period of successful teaching experience are set out in provincial law. Whether any specific individual may become a teacher is therefore a matter of law.

Upon being granted admission to the profession, the teacher encounters even more laws governing his conduct. Each province sets out, to a greater or lesser extent, the duties required of a teacher. Matters pertaining to employment conditions and labour relations are also specified by provincial statute. Local school authorities pass by-laws or enact policies dealing with their own schools and enter into contracts with teachers, thereby adding even more rules, regulations, and terms of employment to be followed by each of us. Membership in the provincial teachers' association is usually made compulsory by law. Since each organization will adopt rules dealing with professional conduct and discipline of its members, each of which carries the weight of law, there is additional legal impact upon the teacher. A compilation of all the laws, regulations, by-laws and codes that affect teachers in Canada would be an enormous task and would fill numerous volumes.

The student/teacher relationship is also subjected to various enacted laws as well as to a large body of common law or court precedents. These precedents deal with matters such as supervision of students, liability for injury to students, and matters relating to criminal conduct.

The very nature of the profession, undertaking as it does to be responsible for the safety and education of our children, provides a tremendous potential for a variety of civil and criminal proceedings on behalf of those children against teachers who fail to meet society's expectations of their role. The law has a very direct impact upon teacher conduct in the classroom, gymnasium and playground as well as in the community at large outside of school hours. Teachers may be charged with assaulting students as a result of administering corporal punishment. Teachers may be sued for negligence in supervision when a child is injured on the playground. The teaching profession is subject to constant judicial and administrative scrutiny and thus the potential for some form of legal action is ever present.

After years of faithful service, a teacher's pension becomes a matter of law. Most provinces have a specific act dealing with teacher pensions. This legislation establishes the fund, determines eligibility and details methods of payment. From cradle to grave, a teacher's life is inevitably linked to that area of study frequently referred to as "school law."

There are also strong links between law and education in a sociological sense. Education is often viewed as a process of socialization of the child and as the transmission of cultural values to future generations. The law is also a means of socialization. It is the embodiment of those fundamental values that are cherished in our society. Both law and education seek a similar goal: the well-adjusted, contributing member of society. Education is viewed by our lawmakers as a responsibility undertaken for the benefit of society as a whole not just for the benefit of the individual child.

Both education and law deal in words as the primary instrument of each profession and each has developed a specialized vocabulary. Law is concerned with the exactness of the meanings of words. Much "legalese" (with its preoccupation in form and ritual) is often viewed by laypersons as an irritation. To gain confidence in comprehending the law, we must confront the statutes and cases that are the law. Intimidation by the form of the law can be overcome by becoming familiar with it.

The law recognizes the importance of education and the responsibility that our legal system must take to ensure that an adequate education is provided for all children. This is evident in the number of laws and court cases dealing with education and is embodied in the words of the Supreme Court of the United States in *Brown v. Board of Education* 347 U.S. 463 (1954), one of the early desegregation cases, where it was stated:

> Today, education is perhaps the most important function of state and local governments. Compulsory education laws and the great expenditures for education demonstrate our recognition of the importance of education to our democratic society. It is required in the performance of our most basic public responsibilities, even service in the armed forces. It is the very foundation of good citizenship. Today it is a principal instrument in awakening the child to cultural values, in preparing him for later professional training, and in helping him to adjust normally to his environment. In these days, it is doubtful that any child may reasonably be expected to succeed in life if he is denied the opportunity of an education.

These sentiments have also been expressed by the Supreme Court of Canada in the case of *Jones v. R.* (1987) 73 A.R. 133, where Mr. Justice LaForest stated:

> Whether one views it from an economic, social, cultural or civic point of view, the education of the young is critically important in our society. From an early period, the provinces have responded to this interest by developing schemes for compulsory education. Education is today a matter of prime concern to government everywhere. Activities in this area account for a very significant part of every provincial budget. Indeed, in modern society, education had far-reaching implications beyond the province, not only at the national, but at the international level.

Thus the law takes an active role in ensuring that this "most important function" is carried out in a satisfactory way.

Need for Basic Legal Knowledge

Teachers must, therefore, acquire a basic knowledge of the laws that affect them and of the legal process inherent therein. The process or procedural aspects of the law are as much a part of the law as are the substantive parts. We often hear of someone "getting off on a technicality." Procedural rules are established to ensure fairness and must be scrupulously followed. Knowledge of the process will enable teachers to determine if they have been dealt with fairly and will help them to determine if they are dealing with others fairly. It is held that possession of this knowledge will prove to be of benefit to the teacher both personally and professionally, to the children he serves, and, ultimately, to society.

There are at least five major reasons which can be advanced in favour of teachers learning more about the law. First, the numerous statutes, regulations and by-laws (which dictate how teachers are to carry out their professional responsibilities) are to a large extent the job description for a career in education. Since no one can undertake to perform any task properly without knowledge of exactly what that task is, some legal insights are essential to the advancement of a satisfactory teaching career. Teachers must familiarize themselves with provincial statutes, school board policies, and codes of professional conduct in order to become aware of the duties and obligations placed on them by these various types of laws. They must also recognize the consequences of failing to follow these dictates. Numerous court decisions have prescribed rules of conduct and procedures to be followed by teachers. One cannot describe a teacher's duties and responsibilities without reference to the laws that define them.

Teachers face the potential threat of legal action as a part of their daily routine. Matters ranging from the videotaping of an educational television program to an explosion in the chemistry laboratory can have extensive legal consequences. To be forewarned of these possible dangers is to be forearmed in guarding against them. A little knowledge can be a valuable tool as well as a dangerous thing. Ignorance of the law will never be accepted as an adequate defence. Teachers should not adopt the complacent, "It can't happen to me," attitude. Every teacher who found himself as a defendant in a lawsuit most certainly had the same thought prior to his involvement with the legal process. Accidents can happen to any teacher just as easily as they happened to the defendants in the cases cited in this book. Knowledge of the law will provide guidance to the teacher by suggesting ways of avoiding legal conflict and suggesting ways of protecting himself and his employer should an accident occur.

Awareness of the legal implications of an action or course of conduct can be an invaluable tool for educational administrators and teachers when formulating rules and policies for the proper conduct of teachers and students. School procedures should always be formulated only after consideration of the probable legal consequences. Care must be taken to ensure that rules which are drafted do not infringe upon the civil rights of either teachers or students. Adequate procedures to ensure the safety of students in various settings must be implemented. The absence of adequate procedural safeguards are indicative of a lack of proper supervision and thus may leave the school open to findings of negligence in civil actions. Teachers and administrators must critically assess their own school policies to ensure that they are meeting the minimum standards prescribed by statute and the common law. Knowledge of the law will promote positive changes in the administration of education thus benefiting both teacher and student and resulting in schools that are safer places where the rights of all inhabitants are respected.

The law is a cornerstone upon which our society is built. This is recognized in *The Canadian Charter of Rights and Freedoms* which states:

Canada is founded upon principles that recognize the supremacy of God and the rule of law.

The concept of the "rule of law" means that governments are not above the law and can only make laws within the powers granted to them by the law. Society is thus protected from personal or political whims. In order that we all may become better citizens, we must have some understanding of this foundation. Teachers, in particular, are called upon to promote respect for our laws and to foster good citizenship in their students. This duty is often the subject of specific legislative comment such as the following provision of the Ontario *Education Act*:

235. (1) It is the duty of a teacher, . . .

> (c) to inculcate by precept and example respect for religion and the principles of Judaeo-Christian morality and the highest regard for truth, justice, loyalty, love of country, humanity, benevolence, sobriety, industry, frugality, purity, temperance, and all other virtues.

Without a broad understanding of the subject, this responsibility cannot be met effectively. To fulfill our obligations to society in this regard we must know that which we are mandated to teach.

Finally, the teacher is a role model or exemplar for his students. He is expected to conduct himself both within and outside the school in accordance with our laws. If a teacher is seen to violate any law, no matter how innocuous it may appear, what impression is created in the minds of his students? Knowledge of the law, the embodiment of society's standards of conduct, provides the teacher with a code of personal and professional conduct suitable to a teaching career. Knowledge of the consequences attending a breach of the law can serve as an effective deterrent to such conduct. For example,some teachers may view the smoking of marijuana as a harmless act and one which should not be criminalized. Would they engage in such behaviour knowing that a conviction on a possession charge will not only carry a small fine but could also result in loss of job or the possibility of being de-certified? Thus, the professional consequences of a breach of the law are frequently more severe than the legal ones.

Education Law Defined

Before discussing what "education law" is, it would be wise to define what "law" is. As teachers we are aware of the folly of presuming prior knowledge and so we will attempt to provide a basic overview of laws and lawmaking in order to help the reader gain, at minimum, an informal understanding of the material to be presented later in the book. *Black's Law Dictionary* defines law as follows:

> Law in its generic sense, is a body of rules of action or conduct prescribed by controlling authority, and having binding legal force.

Education law is not a separate recognized branch of law such as criminal law or constitutional law but rather is a study which cuts across the boundaries and encompasses many different areas of the law. Education law comprises all statutes, regulations, by-laws, policies, administrative decisions and court cases which are intended to apply to operations of the school system. It is a collection of authoritative statements about the governance of schools drawn from the various bodies having authority over such matters. Certain areas such as minority language rights and school financing legislation, while important, are of more direct concern to administrators, school boards and legislators than to teachers and thus will not be discussed herein. Teachers are, however, encouraged to become familiar with these aspects of school law since, although policies in these areas are not determined by teachers, such policies ultimately affect the make-up of the classroom and the resources available to the classroom teacher.

Education law, like all law, is not static. It changes as public attitudes and values change. What was acceptable conduct in schools a century ago is not acceptable today, nor is what we do today going to be acceptable a century from now. Education related events never happen in exactly the same way twice; each case is unique. Children seem to be able to find new and unusual ways of getting injured. This book will show how general legal principles have been applied in specific cases in the past. The reader is cautioned that its contents are not to be considered as a substitute for sound legal advice in any specific case.

The reader will note that cases which appear to have similar fact situations sometimes result in conflicting judicial interpretations. The reader is encouraged to form his own view as to which opinion he would support; further, he is cautioned to remember that because a teacher was found not to be negligent in one specific case does not mean that on apparently similar facts another court will arrive at the same conclusion. The required standards of teacher conduct are constantly becoming more demanding and thus, teachers are urged to strive to maintain the highest possible standards for themselves. Adopting practices beyond those that even the most demanding court has set will almost ensure that a teacher will never be forced to justify his actions in a courtroom.

The growing number of laws and court cases in the field of education has prompted concern and debate over the extent to which laws and the courts should become involved in the educational process. Legal intervention has become necessary to resolve the conflicts that have arisen between participants in the process. Parents may have a conflict with the school regarding their child's education; teachers may have a conflict with the administration over content of the curriculum; school boards may have a conflict with the department of education over the exercise of the powers granted to the board. Often, legal intervention becomes the only method which seems to resolve these complex issues.

All of these conflicts are subject to the overriding provisions of the Constitution and the law. The issue becomes one of how much authority each party has over the education of a child. To what extent can a parent dictate what his child will learn? How much academic freedom does a teacher have? Can boards exclude handicapped children from regular schools? Thus, the courts may be asked by one or more parties to intervene in the educational process. In some instances the courts will intervene and order changes in the system and at other times they will not. Generally, courts will only override local and provincial authorities where there has been a denial of a person's constitutional rights. On other matters they tend to uphold the local authority's powers to legislate (subject to control of the electorate), contending that where the electorate is not pleased with the policy adopted, or where there is a dispute, the local citizens have the power to make the necessary changes through the ballot box.

United States Precedent

In several segments of education law there is very little Canadian judicial authority. This is particularly true in matters pertaining to civil rights. In contrast, there are numerous United States authorities dealing with specific concerns in that area. Although these cases do not reflect the state of the law in Canada, they are useful in showing how the subject matter has been dealt with in another jurisdiction. American cases are often cited as examples for Canadian courts to follow when dealing with new areas previously not interpreted by our own courts. In matters of civil rights, Canada has only recently had an entrenched *Charter of Rights and Freedoms* whereas the United States has had a *Bill of Rights* for almost two hundred years. United States authorities are occasionally cited in this book and the reader is cautioned that they are not to be considered as representing the current state of the law in Canada but are being presented solely to show how similar issues have been defined and dealt with elsewhere.

American precedents have no binding authority in Canada although they may occasionally be referred to by our courts as "persuasive authority." Courts will tread very carefully in using American case law for authority as the following judicial quotes reveal:

> This constitutional difference has produced in the United States a judicial climate such that decisions made there should be examined with care before they are permitted to influence decisions in Canada. (*Re Zylberberg et al.* (1986) 25 C.H.R.R. 193 at 226)

> In such a field as this I think great care must be exercised in not deciding matters before our courts by an unconscious acceptance of the view taken by courts in the United States of America interpreting the effect of their Constitution on the powers of legislative and administrative bodies there. (*Ward v. Board of Blaine Lake* [1971] 4 W.W.R. 161 at 166)

> We have not a Bill of Rights such as is contained in the United States Constitution and decisions on that part of the latter are of no assistance. (*Saumer v. Quebec* [1953] 2 S.C.R. 299 at 324)

In some areas, such as negligence law, where Canada has developed a very substantial body of case law and precedents, there will be limited reference to cases from other jurisdictions. As shall be seen in the discussion of court precedent in the next chapter, decisions from other common law jurisdictions may be used to justify a finding of a Canadian court.

Discussion and Review

1. Do you think that schools and the education system are over-regulated by governments and courts? Why?
2. What areas of education should be free from legislative or court interference?
3. If you were designing a new *School Act*, what matters would you consider to be central and therefore essential for inclusion in the document?

Debate

WHEREAS the *Constitution Act, 1867* (formerly the *British North America Act, 1867*) guaranteed that each province would have sole jurisdiction over education and,

WHEREAS the purpose of the guarantees contained in Section 93 of the BNA Act was to prevent the central government of Canada (which was anticipated to be dominated by English Protestants) from interfering with the school systems of each province and especially those of the Province of Quebec, and further,

WHEREAS the Federal Government has over the years demonstrated a propensity to involve itself in Provincial matters usually basing its actions on the common good argument and,

WHEREAS language of instruction is a school matter,

THEREFORE, BE IT RESOLVED THAT: The language clauses of the Constitution (as they refer to language of instruction in schools) be struck down and that the determination of such matters be retained in the thoughtful discretion of the Provincial Legislature.

You be the Judge

A local school board has purchased science texts which teach the theory of evolution. The books are on the list of approved curriculum resources established by the provincial government. A group of parents, after appealing to their local board to remove an offending set of texts, brings legal action requesting that the books be removed from the schools or alternatively that "creation science" be taught as well. They cite the Charter provisions regarding freedom of religion in support of their position.

1. Should the courts intervene in this type of dispute and dictate what curriculum materials should be used or not used?

2. What about a teacher who chooses to teach "creation science" rather than the theory of evolution as presented in the prescribed text?

3. What if the school board had mandated the teaching of only "creation science?"

Point/Counterpoint

Below are several judicial viewpoints on whether court intervention is necessary in a given situation and on what grounds the courts will overrule the local school authorities. Try to determine what types of matters will be subject to judicial review and how the following statements could relate to the case presented above.

Opposed to Judicial Intervention:

> Professional educators – not Judges – are charged with the responsibility for determining the method of learning that should be pursued for their students. When the intended results are not obtained, it is the educational community – and not the judiciary – that must resolve the problem. For, in reality, the soundness of educational methodology is always subject to question and a court ought not, in hindsight, substitute its notions as to what would have been a better course of instruction to follow for a particular pupil. These are determinations that are to be made by educators and, though they are capable of error, their integrity ought not be subject to judicial inquiry. (*Paladino v. Adelphi University* (1982) 454 N.Y.S.2d 868)

> In matters relating to the schools under their control the defendants (the school trustees) are clothed with wide discretionary and quasi-judicial powers. Assembled at a properly constituted meeting of the Board, regularly conducted, dealing with matters within their jurisdiction, and acting in the bona fide discharge of their duties and in harmony with the laws of the Province, the regulations of the Department, and any existing judgment or order of the Court affecting them, the conclusions they reach, whether thought to be wise or unwise, cannot be interfered with by a Court. (*MacKell v. Ottawa Separate School Trustees* (1914) 18 D.L.R. 475)

> Educational institutions are concerned with the development of free inquiry and learning. The administrative officers must be free to guide teachers and pupils toward that goal. Their discretion must not be interfered with in the absence of proof of actual malevolent intent. Interference by the court will result in suppression of the intended purpose of aiding those seeking education. (*Rosenberg v. Board of Education of the City of New York* (1949) 92 N.Y.S.2d 344)

In Favour of Judicial Intervention:

In our system, state-operated schools may not be enclaves of totalitarianism. School officials do not possess absolute authority over their students. (*Tinker v. Des Moines Independent Community School District* (1969) 393 U.S. 503)

The right of a parent, therefore, to determine what studies his child shall pursue is paramount to that of the trustees or teacher. (*State ex rel. Kelley v. Ferguson* (1914) 144 N.W. 1039)

The fundamental theory of liberty upon which all governments of this Union repose excludes any general power of the state to standardize its children by forcing them to accept instruction from public teachers only. The child is not the mere creature of the state; those who nurture him and direct his destiny have the right, coupled with the high duty, to recognize and prepare him for additional obligations. (*Pierce v. Society of Sisters of Holy Names* (1925) 268 U.S. 510)

If the words of section 310 were to be read literally there could be no court review whatever of the Commissioner's decisions on appeal, for the statute states that his decision 'shall be final and conclusive, and not subject to question or review in any place or court whatever.' However, our court has determined that the Legislature did not intend that the words are to be so read . . . a narrow review of the Commissioner's decisions is available in the courts. (*Board of Education of the City of New York v. Allen* (1959) 160 N.E.2d 60)

Judicial interposition in the operations of the public school system of the Nation raises problems requiring care and restraint. Our courts, however, have not failed to apply the First Amendment's mandate in our educational system where essential to safeguard the fundamental values of freedom of speech and inquiry and of belief.

By and large, public education in our Nation is committed to the control of state and local authorities. Courts do not and cannot intervene in the resolution of conflicts which arise in the daily operation of school systems and which do not directly and sharply implicate basic constitutional values. On the other hand, 'The vigilant protection of constitutional freedoms is nowhere more vital than in the community of American schools' . . . and 'This court will be alert against invasions of academic freedom' . . . 'the First Amendment does not tolerate laws that cast a pall of orthodoxy over the classroom'. (*Epperson v. Arkansas* (1969) 393 U.S. 97)

References

The following are Canadian and English references dealing with school law and child law. There are many American references as well but we have not included them because they have limited application in Canada.

Balderson, J. and Kolmes, J. (eds.), *Legal Issues in Canadian Education: Proceedings of the 1982 Canadian School Executive Conference*. Edmonton: Xancor Canada Ltd., 1983.

Bala, N. and Clarke, K. L., *The Child and the Law*. Toronto: McGraw-Hill Ryerson, 1981.

Bala, N., Lilles, H., and Thomson, G. M., *Canadian Children's Law*. Kingston: Queen's University, 1982.

Bargan, P., *The Legal Status of the Canadian Public School Pupil*. Toronto: MacMillan, 1961.

Barrell, G.R., *Legal Cases for Teachers*. London: Methuen & Co. Ltd., 1970.

Barrell, G.R., *Teachers and the Law*. Fourth Edition, London: Methuen & Co. Ltd., 1975.

Canadian Education Association, *Education and the Law*. Toronto: Canadian Education Association, 1986.

Enns, F. *The Legal Status of the Canadian School Board*. Toronto: MacMillan, 1963.

Gilbert, V. K., Martin, R. A., and Sheehan, A.T., *A Hard Act to Follow*. Toronto: University of Toronto, 1985.

Herapath, J.N., Mitches, G.T., and Sutton, W.D., *Ontario Education and the Law*. 2nd edition, London, Ontario: Education Research Foundation of Middlesex, 1979.

MacKay, A. W., *Education Law in Canada*. Toronto: Emond-Montgomery Publications Ltd., 1984.

MacKay, A. W. and Dickinson, G. M., *Rights, Freedoms and the Education System in Canada*. Toronto: Emond-Montgomery Publications Ltd., 1987.

McCurdy, S., *The Legal Status of the Canadian School Teacher*. Toronto: MacMillan, 1968.

Manley-Casimir, M. E. and Sussel, T. A., *Courts in the Classroom: Education and the Charter of Rights and Freedoms*. Calgary: Detselig Enterprises Ltd., 1986.

Nicholls, A. C., *An Introduction to School Case Law*. Vancouver: British Columbia School Trustees Association, 1984.

OISE, *The Interaction of Law and Education*, Ontario Institute for Studies in Education, May 1974 (an extensive bibliography of legal materials of interest to educators).

Wilson, J. and Tomlinson, N., *Children and the Law* 2nd ed. Toronto: Butterworths, 1986.

Sources of Law:
Statute Law and Case Law

Learning Objectives

Some of the things that you will learn from reading this chapter include the following:

1. The degree of similarity among education laws in Canada.
2. The roots of Canadian law.
3. The functions of the legislative, administrative, and judicial branches of government.
4. The legislative jurisdiction of each level of government.
5. The influence of international treaty obligations upon the direction of Canadian education.
6. The system of common law.
7. The hierarchy of the Canadian court system.
8. The general procedures involved in initiating a civil action or conducting a criminal trial.
9. The purpose of administrative boards or tribunals in education law.
10. The rules of natural justice which guide all those who adjudicate upon or between the rights of others.
11. The definitions of constitutional, criminal, administrative, tort, and contract law.

Preview

Although the specifics of educational law vary from province to province, there exists sufficient commonalities to make it possible for the teacher to study Canadian educational law from a nation-wide perspective.

This chapter will illustrate that for the teacher who is initiating a study of Canadian educational law there are two broad areas of concern: statute law and common law. Both sources have their roots in our own particular form of government.

Statute law includes the Constitution, Acts of the Legislatures, regulations, and international treaties.

The *Constitution Act, 1867* gives each province the exclusive right to pass laws regarding education subject to the guarantees provided to Roman Catholic and Protestant separate schools. The *Constitution Act, 1982* guarantees certain language of instruction rights based upon mother tongue principles.

The heritage of the British common law is very much a presence in the daily role of the classroom teacher. Through the development of the common law principle that the teacher acts *in loco parentis*, classroom teachers enjoy certain rights to discipline and manage schools in the best interest of the child, but they have been judged to also be responsible for the safety of their young charges in all school related activities.

The two branches of law which have greatest impact upon the professional life of the teacher are criminal law and civil law. The former sets out the rules which control and govern the conduct of individuals, while the latter addresses the relationships and rights of individual citizens vis-a-vis each other.

The two essential elements which must be proven in a criminal case are guilty act and guilty mind. The standard of proof required is guilt beyond a reasonable doubt.

In civil actions standard of proof is a balance of probabilities.

The rules of natural justice provide for a hearing free from bias where each party is given the opportunity to be heard, where each party is notified of the hearing, where each is entitled to legal representation in a setting which is open to public scrutiny, and where the person hearing the facts will act fairly and with a judicious temper.

Law may be categorized as public law, those laws which affect the government in some way, and private law, which relate to rights and obligations between individual citizens.

Self-Assessment

1. How would you define education law?
2. Can you describe the major functions of the legislature, judicial, and administrative branch of government?
3. What are the essential differences between statute law and case law?
4. Are you able to describe the court hierarchy and the methods of conducting trials in the province in which you reside?
5. Within the body of the textual materials which follow it is noted that the classroom teacher receives mention in the *Criminal Code* of Canada. Do you know in what regard this mention is made?
6. Why is British common law so important to the Canadian classroom teacher?
7. Which statute provides, "Everyone has a right to education. Education shall be free at least in the elementary and fundamental stages"?
8. Are you able to recite a number of points/principles which should guide all those who make judgements upon the rights of others?

Key Terms

Codified law	Obiter dicta
Common law	Writ of summons
Statue law	Balance of probabilities
Enactment	Summary conviction
By-law	Actus reus
Minority religious schools	Mens rea
Order-in-council	Stare decisis
Ratio decidendi	Civil action

*   *   *   *

The law is not a universal or self-revealing body of knowledge but rather is one that has developed differently in each society to meet that society's particular needs and to reflect that society's morals and values. Lawful behaviour in one society may be considered a serious criminal offence in another. Consumption of alcohol, for example, is strictly forbidden in certain parts of the world and is subject to severe penalties, while in other areas the same act is socially acceptable and is often encouraged through advertising. Even within any given society, the law is found to be in a state of continual change. What may be acceptable today may not be acceptable tomorrow. For example, prohibition laws rendered a number of formerly lawful acts illegal overnight.

Across Canada education laws vary from province to province, since each provincial legislature has adopted its own view of how its schools should be run. A brief review of the various provincial School Acts and Education Acts will illustrate the vast array of differences and will also demonstrate the many similarities. The basic values of our Canadian society are the same in each province, yet the way they are incorporated into action varies widely. There is, however, a large body of law that is the same for all provinces. It consists of those court decisions relating to matters of common law.

The law is not a body of knowledge that has, conveniently, been written down in one (or even a few) places. The teacher may have to consult numerous sources in order to find all of the laws on a particular issue. These sources include legislation at various levels, court decisions, administrative procedures and decisions, and even legal textbooks. The law comes to us from many sources which may be broadly categorized as being either statute law or common law. Of these, statute law is the more important since legislatures may overrule or modify the common law by legislative enactment. Both statute and common law have their roots in our own particular form of government and therefore, in order to understand these laws we must understand the structure of our government.

Branches of Government

Canada's laws and legal system are largely based upon the British model, a circumstance which is not surprising given our historical connection with that country. The Province of Quebec, however, has a codified system of civil law, as opposed to the English common law system. The civil law in Quebec is based on the French precedent. Again this is not surprising given that province's historical, religious and cultural roots. A strong influence from the United States can be detected in certain areas of our law. Other areas are uniquely Canadian, having been developed in response to our own specific geography, history, and culture.

Our form of government, a parliamentary democracy with a constitutional monarch, bears a strong resemblance to the British system; thus many of the traditions, customs, practices and procedures of our Parliament are virtually identical to those found in the British Parliament. However, the reader is reminded that the British government is a unitary one with a central Parliament and no provincial or state legislatures, whereas Canada has a federal system of government which in certain respects resembles that of the United States with a division of powers between national and regional governments. These differences in the distribution of power have had a substantial modifying influence upon the translation of the British legal and parliamentary system into the Canadian setting.

Our government is divided into three branches: the legislative branch, the administrative branch, and the judicial branch. In theory, each has a separate distinct function, with the legislative branch having the sole power to make laws. In practice, however, each of these branches becomes involved in lawmaking to some extent.

The legislative branch, which may be either the federal Parliament or the provincial Legislative Assembly, is entrusted with the primary function of making laws by passing statutes. This is done through elected representatives of the people who thereby have ultimate control over the types of laws that they wish to see enacted. The administrative branch, or the civil service, sets up the machinery to administer the laws enacted by Parliament or the Assembly. The rules and procedures established by this branch can modify or extend the written statute as passed by Parliament. Bureaucratic red tape can significantly alter the intent of a piece of legislation. The judicial branch (the court system) is charged with the responsibility of interpreting and enforcing the enacted laws. Their interpretations are intended to clarify the meaning and extent of application of a particular law. But the court's interpretations may not always be those intended by the legislature when the law was first enacted and thus the enacted law can be modified greatly by judicial interpretation. The judiciary is also responsible for the evolution of the large body of common law or customary law which has evolved over the centuries. These laws are not found in statutes but are to be found in previous court decisions.

Thus, each branch of government (legislative, administrative, and judicial) is involved in making the laws that affect the teacher in the classroom. A simple reading of a statute or a court decision is not sufficient to fully understand how the law may affect a particular set of facts. The judiciary may have given a different interpretation of a statute than that which appears on the face of it. Also the legislature may have modified the direction taken by common law by passing a statute to amend a particular provision. For example, the common law has held teachers liable for injuries to pupils occasioned as a result of teacher negligence. In Saskatchewan, however, the Legislature has decided as a matter of public policy that teachers should not be liable for certain injuries and has enacted the following provision in its *Education Act*:

> 228. (1)Where a board of education, a principal or a teacher approves or sponsors activities during school hours or at other times on school premises or elsewhere, no teacher, principal or other person responsible for the conduct of the pupils shall be liable for damage caused by the pupils to property or for personal injury suffered by pupils during such activities.

Statute Law

Statute law consists of the numerous laws, regulations, rules, policies and procedures that have been passed by the various bodies in Canada who are empowered to enact legislation. This includes not only the federal and provincial legislatures but also local school authorities and international bodies such as the United Nations. Statute law will include, therefore, all federal and provincial legislation, the Constitution, regulations made pursuant to various statutes, local by-laws, school board policy enactments, and international treaties, conventions and declarations signed by Canada. Not all of these statute laws are of equal importance, force and effect, but each can have a considerable influence on a teacher's conduct. Frequently statute laws appear to be in conflict with each other; thus the teacher is faced with the task of deciding which law to follow. The general rule of thumb to be followed in such situations is that laws of a higher legislative authority prevail over those of an inferior one. The legislative hierarchy is, therefore: (1) the Constitution (2) federal legislation (3) provincial legislation and (4) municipal-level legislation.

The application of this general rule can be seen in the following example. The Constitution, and *The Canadian Charter of Rights and Freedoms* enshrined therein, is the supreme legislative authority in Canada. It forbids discrimination on the grounds of age. Where a local school board, a lower legislative authority, enacts a mandatory employee retirement provision for persons who have reached age sixty-five, this could be held to violate the Charter, a higher authority, and the Charter will prevail. The school by-law will be declared null and void to the extent that it violates the Charter.

This general rule is only applicable as long as the higher legislative authority is acting within its allocated sphere for passing laws. The Constitution divides legislative authority between the provincial and federal governments, giving each exclusive powers in relation to certain areas. Education is an exclusive provincial power and therefore any federal laws purporting to deal with the structure of schools are *ultra vires* or beyond the powers of the federal government and are of no force or effect. Similarly, if a province attempts to pass laws in relation to a matter exclusively federal, such as banking, those laws will also be struck down as being *ultra vires*. School authorities and municipal governments are creations of the provincial government and may only exercise legislative power in those areas delegated to them by the province. Laws made by this level of government and by administrative boards are called "subordinate legislation" because they are also subordinate to the laws of the province which created them.

There are certain areas where the exclusive jurisdiction of each legislature may appear to overlap and it is these areas, where the laws appear to be in conflict, that pose the greatest difficulty in deciding what course of conduct to follow. It may be that the lowest rung on the legislative ladder is the one that would ultimately determine the wisest course to follow. The issue of corporal punishment provides a good example of this type of conflict between different legislative bodies, each acting within its own sphere and passing perfectly valid legislation within that sphere.

When a teacher straps a pupil he is committing an act that, in any other context, would be considered to be a criminal assault, a matter that is within the federal government's legislative powers over criminal law. The Canadian *Criminal Code* specifically provides that teachers, like parents, may use force in disciplining pupils and that they will not be convicted of assault if the force used was reasonable. Thus corporal punishment, provided that it is reasonable, is acceptable to the federal government and will not be treated as a criminal assault.

Provincial legislatures, however, have exclusive jurisdiction in the field of education and may impose limits on corporal punishment or even ban it altogether. A teacher acting in violation of provincial legislation may lose his job (and perhaps his certification) even though his action is not deemed to be a criminal offence by the Federal Government. Most provincial laws are silent on the issue of corporal punishment. They simply impose a duty on principals to maintain discipline in the school. Corporal punishment is therefore tacitly approved, by default, and it is therefore left to the local school authority to decide whether to use it as a tool of discipline.

Local school boards, despite the acceptance of corporal punishment by the federal and provincial governments, may decide to ban its use in their schools. A term of employment is that a teacher will obey all lawful directives of the school board and since the matter of employment is one over which the local board has jurisdiction, it follows that the local school board can impose as a term of employment that no corporal punishment will be used. Breach of this provision will result in dismissal even though the act is authorized by higher authorities. The teacher will not be subjected to criminal penalties, will not be decertified, but will nevertheless be subjected to the harsh penalty of losing his job. If the province has banned corporal punishment throughout its schools, as has been done in British Columbia, local boards may not override such a prohibition and institute corporal punishment in their own jurisdictions.

The reader is reminded that each legislation body can make valid legislation in its own sphere and each is entitled to enforce its own legislation in that sphere despite what other authorities have said. They cannot, however, enter into an area of jurisdiction assigned exclusively to another body; for example, local school boards cannot create criminal offences, and the Federal Government cannot dictate the terms of employment contracts or set guidelines for teacher certification.

It is essential for teachers to become aware of the legislative jurisdiction of each level of government in order to determine which course of conduct to follow. Simply knowing that corporal punishment is not subject to criminal prosecution does not give the whole picture. Other, harsher consequences may follow for administering the strap. Later, we will review the legislative hierarchy in Canada in order to see what types of statutes are found within the realm of each legislative body.

As mentioned, the Constitution is the paramount statute law in Canada. All other legislation must be interpreted in accordance with its terms. The Constitution consists of two major documents, *The Constitution Act, 1867* (formerly the *British North America Act*) and *The Constitution Act, 1982* which includes as Schedule B *The Canadian Charter of Rights and Freedoms*. By definition, a constitution is that statute law which contains all of the principles and rules regarding the nature of government; the extent and limitations on the powers of that government; and which governs the legal conduct of a society.

Provincial Authority over Education

The Constitution Act, 1867 established the division of legislative power between the federal and provincial governments. Areas of exclusive jurisdiction for lawmaking are granted to each of these two levels. Municipal governments and school boards are not specifically mentioned or granted any exclusive jurisdiction. Municipal governments are creations of the province and only have such authority as may be granted by the province from time to time. A provincial legislature may decide to cease having local school boards and centralize all educational decisions within the provincial department since the existence of school boards is not a matter of constitutional right but only one of delegated provincial authorities.

Section 93 of *The Constitution Act, 1867* gave each province the exclusive right to pass laws regarding education subject to certain guarantees for denominational schools. This section reads as follows:

In and for each province the Legislature may exclusively make laws in relation to education subject and according to the following provisions:

(1) Nothing in any such law shall prejudicially affect any right or privilege with respect to denominational schools which any class of persons have by law in the province at the Union;

(2) All the powers, privileges and duties at the Union by law conferred and imposed in Upper Canada on the separate schools and school trustees of the Queen's Roman Catholic subjects shall be and the same are hereby extended to the dissentient schools of the Queen's Protestant and Roman Catholic subjects in Quebec;

(3) Where in any province a system of separate or dissentient schools exists by law at the Union or is thereafter established by the Legislature of the province an appeal shall lie to the Governor General in Council from any Act or decision of any provincial authority affecting any right or privilege of the Protestant or Roman Catholic minority of the Queen's subjects in relation to education;

(4) In case any provincial law as from time to time seems to the Governor General in Council requisite for the due execution of the provisions of this section is not made or in case any decision of the Governor General in Council on any appeal under this section is not duly executed by the proper provincial authority in that behalf and in every such case and as far as the circumstances of each case require the Parliament of Canada may make remedial laws for the due execution of the provisions of this section and of any decision of the Governor General in Council under this section.

As each province entered Confederation, these provisions were incorporated within the founding legislation with provision for variations to meet local conditions. For example, the *Alberta Act, 1905* provides:

17. Section 93 of the Constitution Act, 1867 shall apply to the said Province, with the substitution for paragraph 1 of the said Section 93 of the following paragraph:

(1) Nothing in any such law shall prejudicially affect any right or privilege with respect to separate schools which any class of persons have at the date of the passing of this Act, under the terms of Chapters 29 and 30

of the Ordinances of the North-West Territories, passed in the year
1901, or with respect to religious instruction in any public or separate
school as provided for in the said Ordinances.

The different circumstances and arrangements regarding separate
schools in each province (at the time each entered Confederation) accounts,
in large measure, for the different provisions regarding separate schools
found in each province today. Ontario, Quebec, Alberta, Saskatchewan,
Newfoundland and the Territories are all guaranteed minority religious
schools. But even these guarantees are not the same for each province since
a different form of separate school existed in each province at the date that
each entered Confederation. Ontario law did not have to provide for
separate schools beyond Grade 10 since that was the extent of public support for such schools in 1867. The other provinces have no similar guarantee that minority religious schools will be supported by public funds.

The Canadian Charter of Rights and Freedoms deals specifically with
educational rights (see Chapter 1 of this text for a printing of the provisions
regarding education) and further, affects schools through a number of other
general provisions. Since schools are agencies of the provincial government
the Charter applies to their actions as well.

32. (1) This Charter applies

    (a) to the Parliament and government of Canada in respect of all
matters within the authority of Parliament including all matters
relating to the Yukon Territory and Northwest Territories; and

    (b) to the legislature and government of each province in respect of all
matters within the authority of the legislature of each province.

The full extent of the rights and freedoms enumerated in the Charter
have not been fully tested in our courts and therefore, at this point in time,
only predictions are possible with respect to the impact and limits that will
be placed on schools as a result of the Charter. The intended meaning of the
words used will be interpreted by our courts. There are bound to be widely
differing opinions on the extent of application. How many people will be
required before the courts hold that the "numbers warrant" section of the
minority language education clause has been met? How far does the "freedom of religion" clause extend? Will prayer be banned in our schools as has
been done in the United States? It may be years before the various Charter
provisions are fully defined by our courts; however, we can declare that the
rights and freedoms granted by the Charter, whatever their extent, are
supreme and may not be infringed upon by the laws of any government,
"subject only to such reasonable limits prescribed by law as can be

demonstrably justified in a free and democratic society."

Federal Involvement in Education

Although the Constitution assigns exclusive authority over education to the provinces, there remains considerable scope for federal legislation in the field. The Yukon and Northwest Territories do not have provincial status, thus matters of education for these areas fall within the federal power. Certain groups of people also fall under exclusive federal jurisdiction: native people, children of armed forces personnel, and inmates of federal penitentiaries. Matters relating to education of these groups are also federal concerns. Schools on Indian reserves and for armed forces children are run and funded by the federal, not the provincial, government.

The federal government can have an indirect influence on education across Canada by passing legislation within certain of its own exclusive legislative spheres. Over the years the federal government has sought to encourage certain types of vocational training and has passed legislation committing federal funds to these types of programs. For example, the federal government passed the *The Technical Education Act* to promote more technical training by providing funds through a cost sharing program to any province that established approved technical training facilities in its schools. More recently, federal funds have been committed to bilingual education. Although the provinces are not required to implement these programs, they usually do so in order to take advantage of the funding provided. Ottawa therefore can indirectly cause certain types of educational programs to be implemented throughout Canada.

Another indirect federal influence on educational programs comes through materials produced by federal agencies. Both the Canadian Broadcasting Corporation and the National Film Board produce materials that may be used by educators. Specific projects may be funded with the hope that the materials will be widely used in schools. Other federal departments produce educational materials relating to their own particular area of concern such as the environment, national parks, trade, or agriculture. Although the federal government cannot mandate that these materials be used in schools, they constitute an inexpensive curriculum resource and they are often distributed in the schools. Thus the federal government has a considerable impact upon public education even though it apparently, according to the Constitution, has no power whatsoever in the field.

In many countries education is totally a federal responsibility. Great

Britain, for example, has a unitary system of government. There are no provincial or state legislatures. The educational system tends to be more uniform throughout the country. Other countries, such as the United States, have federal systems of government where education is given over to the state legislature, but where there are provisions for a federal department of education which controls certain aspects of education usually through a funding process. The Canadian government has not gone as far as the United States in using funding to control provincial education legislation but we may well see more and more federal involvement with respect to school operation and programs. There is much within the present Canadian structure which could lead towards a more American type of federal government involvement.

Each province has created its own body of statute law pertaining to education within its borders. These statutes usually include an act establishing a Department of Education, a general school act, an act regulating the teaching profession, and an act relating to the financing of schools. Some or all of these different matters may be included in one act or they may be fragmented into several shorter acts. In Appendix A to this chapter there is a list of the major pieces of education-related legislation from each province. In addition to those specifically mentioned, other legislation dealing with labour relations and municipal governments may also have a direct impact upon teachers. The teacher should consult the set of statutes for his chosen province of employment in order to fully understand the multiplicity of acts that may affect his day-to-day work environment.

Regulations

In addition to statutes, each province will have a set of regulations which are additional laws made by the Cabinet under authority of the statute. They have the same legal force as the legislation and must be consulted in order to grasp the entire picture of the statute law. Acts deal with broad general matters while regulations deal with specific details. For example, the *Manitoba Public Schools Act* provides:

Teaching month.

92 (6) For the purpose of subsection (5), a teaching month means a teaching month as defined by the minister in the regulations.

Under authority contained in the statute, the Minister has passed the following regulation dealing more specifically with the matter:

1. In this regulation, for the purposes of subsection 92 (5) of The Public Schools Act, the following definition applies:

    (a) teaching month means a calendar month in which there are at least ten teaching days as designated by the minister.

2. This regulation shall be deemed to have been in force on, from and after the day it is filed with the Registrar of Regulations.

The content of these regulations are not debated in the Legislature but are enacted by way of an order-in-council or order of the Cabinet. In effect, the Minister responsible for the Department decides what specific details should be included. This is a quick means of changing policy but it also removes many policy decisions from the scrutiny of public debate in the Legislature. The regulations themselves are usually somewhat more difficult to locate than the statute and therefore may form a body of "hidden" statute law. Merely reading an act will not give you the full text of the statute law. The regulations and the existing judicial interpretations of the statute must also be consulted, since a particular section of a specific act may have been declared to be *ultra vires* yet the section remains in the statute until an amendment can be passed.

Appendix B provides a guide on how to read and interpret an act and a regulation. The chapter on legal research illustrates how to find the acts and regulations that affect teachers as well as how to locate any judicial interpretations of those statutes.

Administration

The provincial legislature uses its power to create local school authorities and delegates certain routine functions to these boards. There is no requirement that these types of local authorities be established but it has been found to be an efficient and politically acceptable means of governing schools and so it continues. The local school board also has legislative power over matters delegated to it and it enacts policies dealing with matters such as school tax levies, use of school premises after hours, field trips, and a host of other details. These policies are often consolidated into a single volume and made available to the schools and the public. The prudent teacher familiarizes himself with board policies as well since they form part of the laws which govern his actions.

Provincial legislation also establishes other administrative tribunals such as appeal boards, certification boards, and discipline boards which are given certain powers over the teacher. These bodies are granted power to make rules regarding the conduct of proceedings before the board or tribunal. These procedural matters are often set out in by-laws passed by the particular board and will vary from board to board. Although each board will ensure a fair hearing in accordance with the principles of fundamental justice, the procedure followed by any specific board could vary widely.

International Publications

Other types of statute law which should be of interest to teachers are Canada's international obligations including treaties, international conventions and declarations. Although these may appear on the surface to be those of the highest authority, in practice they have the least binding legal force of all statute law. For example, Canada as a member of the United Nations is a signatory to a number of declarations such as the *Universal Declaration of Human Rights* which provides:

> Everyone has the right to education. Education shall be free, at least in the elementary and fundamental stages. Elementary education shall be compulsory. Technical and professional education shall be made generally available and higher education shall be equally accessible to allow the basis of merit.
>
> Education shall be directed to the full development of the human personality and to the strengthening of respect for human rights and fundamental freedoms. It shall promote understanding, tolerance and friendship among all nations, racial and religious groups, and shall further the activities of the United Nations for the maintenance of peace.
>
> Parents have a prior right to choose the kind of education that shall be given to their children.

Such declarations do not have the force of law within our own country but they do have a certain persuasive authority in that our laws are to be interpreted wherever possible so as not to conflict with our international obligations. When education is a provincial matter, federal obligations of this nature actually have little effect. Where the signatory to the declaration is also the party responsible for education, the right can be the subject of legal action in international courts. This has happened with several cases from Great Britain. The international courts are powerless to enforce their decisions and therefore a victory in such a court is often a moral victory at best. The moral force of international pressure can be persuasive, in some instances, in bringing about a change in the laws of a particular country or province. Legislators strive to keep public opinion with them and so wish to be seen honouring our international commitments and declarations rather than ignoring them.

In summary, there is a large body of statute law, from all levels of government, dealing with education. Everyday routines may be affected by the Constitution, a provincial statute and regulations, and local school policies. Teachers should make the effort to be informed about the legal expectations of each level of government.

Case Law

In addition to statute laws, there is another large body of law that affects our daily routine. It is referred to as common law or case law. These laws are those which have been established through court precedent over hundreds of years. They are not codified in a statute but are found in the decisions of judges. This body of law is also called "precedent law," "declaratory law," and "judge-made law." The roots of this law are found in the custom and precedent of ancient England where certain laws were accepted by custom throughout the land and came to be applied in a standard way to ensure uniformity and certainty. English common law has been called "the ancient unwritten law of this kingdom." Both Canada and the United States retain a large body of English common law which has, of course, been subject to local modifications. Both countries have evolved their own body of judicial precedent and interpretation of a particular rule; however judicial reference is frequently made to the ancient English cases.

An area of the common law of particular concern to teachers is tort law or legal liability for injury to another through negligent or intentional wrongdoing. Tort law is a set of legal principles imposing liability that have evolved over many years of judicial rulings in various cases. Rules of conduct have been established in certain cases and are applied to specific facts as they arise in other cases. The result is a large body of rules governing teacher conduct which cannot be found in any legislation. No statute will tell you what procedures must be followed when dealing with dangerous chemicals in the laboratory, but numerous judicial pronouncements in accident cases will tell you.

The system of common law depends upon a situation whereby the decisions of higher courts are declared to be binding on lower courts. In reaching decisions courts rely on previously decided cases, a principle known as a *stare decisis* meaning "to stand by the decision." Since it is desirable to have a common system of law there must be a standard set of legal principles that become known and accepted. There must also be a final arbiter of those principles which has become the supreme judicial authority in the country. In Canada we have established a hierarchy of courts with the Supreme Court of Canada as the final authority. This court does not hear all cases but is the guiding force behind decisions of the lower courts and is available to intervene when lower courts do not follow the standard rules.

The principle behind a decision or the reason for making that particular decision is called the *ratio decidendi* of the case. Courts are expected to identify these reasons and indicate which authority is relied upon for the principle enunciated. Judicial opinions about matters of law which are not necessary to the decision are called *obiter dicta*. For example, a case may be appealed on a number of points and the appeal court may deem it necessary to consider only one point in order to dispose of the matter. That will be their *ratio decidendi*, in the case. Often they will consider the other points raised in the appeal and make comments on them "by the way" or as *obiter dicta*. Such statements from the Supreme Court of Canada are binding on lower courts even though they were not necessary in disposing of the case.

Canadian Courts

The particulars of the court system of each province will vary slightly and further, there exist other federal courts which have specialized jurisdiction, but the following chart will give the teacher a general description of a typical provincial hierarchy of courts:

Supreme Court of Canada

Provincial Supreme Court, Appeal Division

Provincial Supreme Court, Trial Division

District or County Court

Provincial Court

Appendix D contains an outline of the court hierarchy for each province and territory. The existing court systems were established by the *Constitution Act*, 1867 and by various provincial and federal statutes.

The Supreme Court of Canada is the highest judicial authority in the land. Its decisions are final and binding on all lower courts. Whatever the Supreme Court establishes as the rule in a particular case (or says by way of *obiter*) must be followed by all other courts. The court is composed of nine justices who have the power to select the cases which they will hear. Not all nine justices hear every case. A panel of three or five justices may sit on any particular case and only on matters of great importance will all nine become involved. There is no automatic right of appeal to this court. An application must be made for permission or "leave to appeal." Leave to appeal is granted in cases of national interest or where there are important legal concerns to be addressed.

The Supreme Court of Canada is not a trial court. It does not hear witnesses or take evidence. It confines itself to hearing arguments on legal principles as presented by the particular facts of the case before it. The justices decide whether the law has been properly applied by the lower courts in the particular set of facts as determined at the trial. It relies upon its own judicial pronouncements, made in similar cases, to provide for the uniformity needed in the law yet it provides for enough flexibility to change the law when presented with new circumstances. Decisions need not be unanimous. The majority will prevails. Many cases are won or lost by a difference of one vote. Before coming to the Supreme Court of Canada, a case will have gone through the proper hierarchy within the province from which it originated.

Within each province there exists a provincial Appeal Court which is the highest court of appeal within that province. Its decisions, unless overturned by the Supreme Court of Canada, are final and binding on all lower courts in the province. Its decisions are not binding on courts in other provinces; however, they may have strong persuasive authority in similar fact situations. It too is strictly an appeal court and does not conduct trials or hear evidence. Most appeals are heard by a panel of three judges although larger panels of justices may hear a case deemed to be of importance and worthy of as much judicial interpretation as possible. Decisions of these appeal courts are not required to be unanimous. The majority decision prevails. Justices who do not agree with the majority may give a dissenting opinion which outlines their view of the law as it applies to the particular facts. Well reasoned dissenting opinions may sometimes be adopted in the Supreme Court of Canada over the majority opinion.

The next level is the Trial Division of the Provincial Supreme Court. This court may be called the Court of Queen's Bench, Supreme Court, High Court or whatever other name the province decides to adopt. It is the highest level at which trials are conducted. It also acts as an appeal court from lower court decisions in certain matters. A justice of this court may hear an appeal on a procedural matter from a lower court or may have the power to retry a case from a lower court, a procedure called a trial de novo. It is also a trial court of first instance in many (usually the more serious) criminal and civil matters. Cases may be tried by a judge alone or by a judge sitting with a jury.

Below this court, in most provinces, are district or county courts. These are trial courts whose jurisdiction to hear trials is limited in some way, either by a monetary level or by specific type of case. An appeal from this court may be taken to the Trial or Appeal Division of the Supreme Court depending upon what the particular province has decreed.

At the lowest level in the hierarchy are the Provincial Courts of each province. These are staffed by provincial court judges or magistrates and deal with minor criminal offences, small claims, family court, and youth court matters. They are the busiest of all courts and although they occupy the lowest rung in the ladder, they are not to be considered as inferior in any other way. They are staffed by qualified competent judges who must be knowledgeable in all areas of procedural and substantive law as dictated by the higher courts.

In addition to the hierarchy of courts there are numerous administrative boards and tribunals that hear matters assigned to them for adjudication. Included among such bodies are disciplinary boards, certification boards, and labour arbitration boards. Their jurisdiction is limited to specific matters and their decisions may or may not be subject to review by the courts. The statute creating a particular tribunal will state what further appeal may be taken from its decision.

The decisions of higher courts are binding on all lower courts in the province. Court decisions from other provinces have no binding authority although they may be strongly persuausive. The same is true of decisions from the higher courts of England. Decisions from other common law countries may have some moderate persuasive authority. Persuausive authority simply means that if it is a well reasoned decision, following generally accepted common law principles, a judge may be inclined to follow the reasoning even though he is not bound by *stare decisis* to do so. Appendix E shows what court decisions are binding on lower courts and which have only persuasive authority.

Many people's view of what happens in a courtroom is coloured by what they see on television and in the movies. From *Perry Mason* to *L.A. Law*, the impression gained is of a world dominated by impassioned speeches, dramatic turns of events, and high-priced lawyers wringing confessions from reluctant witnesses. In reality, most trials are a relatively dull and cumbersome procedure.

We will look at the process involved in both civil actions and criminal trials, as well as that used in administrative tribunals. Civil actions, or suits, are court proceedings between two or more parties involving disputes of a private nature, such as property, contracts, debts, or injuries sustained through negligence. Criminal proceedings are court actions commenced by the state against a party for the breach of a statute creating a criminal offence such as the *Criminal Code*, the *Narcotic Control Act*, or a provincial highway code. Administrative hearings are proceedings established under authority of a statute to determine specific types of disputes such as labour relations, certification of teachers, or internal disciplinary action within a profession.

The Civil Action

The procedure for initiating and pursuing civil actions will vary somewhat from province to province since each has the constitutional authority to create its own rules for the conduct of such actions. These rules of civil procedure are codified in each province's *Rules of Court*. To determine precisely how an action is conducted in a province, the teacher should consult these rules. Despite local differences the general procedure is fairly standard.

The parties to a civil action receive specific names or designations in the proceedings. The party initiating the action is called the plaintiff. The party against whom he is making a claim or seeking relief is called the defendant. You will encounter other descriptions of these parties as well. Some actions, such as divorce proceedings, are commenced in a special way by the filing of a document called a Petition. In such actions the party instigating the action is called the petitioner and the party against whom relief is sought is called the respondent. Actions commenced by a document known as a Notice of Motion will see the parties named as the applicant and respondent. On appeals, the party appealing the lower decision is called the appellant whether he was the plaintiff or defendant in the original action. The other party is called the respondent.

Other parties may become involved in actions as they proceed through the courts and will receive certain designations. An intervenor is a party who has an interest in a lawsuit dealing with constitutional questions although it is not a party to the original action. Intervenors are often a provincial government or a special interest group. A third party to an action is one against whom the defendant seeks relief as a result of the plaintiff's claim. For example, an insurance company may become a third party in an action involving a motor vehicle accident. The third party is one which has no relationship to the plaintiff and against whom he has no cause of action but is a party against whom the defendant can claim relief in the action.

In many jurisdictions, including Ontario, the first step in a civil action is the issuance of a Writ of Summons by the plaintiff. This document is filed at the courthouse and details the nature of the claim being made. It is served on the defendant and demands that he file a defence to the claim within a specified period, usually 15 days.

If the defendant decides to contest the claim he takes a step known as entering an Appearance. If he does not file an Appearance the plaintiff may file an Affidavit of Nonappearance which will lead to the granting of a judgment against the defendant. If the defendant does file an Appearance then the plaintiff will issue a Statement of Claim which provides further details of the claim and the basis upon which the compensation demanded was calculated.

Other jurisdictions, such as Alberta, have eliminated this first step and commence actions directly with the issuance of a Statement of Claim by the plaintiff. The Statement of Claim is served upon the defendant who must then file a Statement of Defence within 15 days. If he fails to do so, the plaintiff files an Affidavit of Default and proceeds to judgment.

Following service of the Statement of Claim, the defendant files his Statement of Defence which is a document setting out his position in the matter. He may also file a Counterclaim against the plaintiff if he feels that he is the one entitled to compensation in the matter. He may also file a Third Party Notice to add someone else to the lawsuit. The plaintiff must then file a Defence to any Counterclaim and the third party will file a Reply setting out his position.

There are numerous types of proceedings that may take place after all of these documents, collectively called pleadings, have been filed. Any party can bring applications of a procedural nature before trial of the issue. Such applications are called motions and deal with diverse matters such as ordering production of documents to other parties, posting security for court costs, or dismissal of a claim or defence as having no legal basis. The merits of the case are usually not determined at such hearings but only matters of procedure. Sometimes the merits of the case may be decided if, for example, the defendant has filed a defence for the purpose of delay only and has no real defence against the claim which can easily be established by documentary evidence such as an unpaid promissory note.

Prior to the trial each party is entitled to question the other parties to the action under oath and to see their documentary evidence. This process is known as discovery. At an examination for discovery each lawyer will cross examine the opposing parties concerning the allegations made in the pleadings. This takes place under oath in the presence of a court reporter. The evidence given may be used by the opposing party to support his case. What each party is trying to do is to gain admissions from the other that will be favourable to his case or allow him to avoid proving a time consuming matter essential to the case but not necessarily in dispute. For example, they may be seeking to gain an admission that someone is an employee of the party. This could be a cumbersome matter to prove otherwise and while it may be essential to the case is not disputed by the opposition.

The purpose of all of these preliminary procedures is to clearly define the issues that are in dispute and to save time at the trial. Most lawsuits are resolved by agreement between the parties before trial once the relative merits become clear. If the parties cannot settle the matter it will be entered for trial and a court date will be assigned. Sometimes parties bring actions to have a legal interpretation of a document or a constitutional point settled. In these cases the parties are asking the court to be a referee or make a statement as to the law. Such cases are not settled prior to trial but often the issue is clearly defined beforehand and much of the preliminary procedure becomes unnecessary.

At the trial of a civil action, the plaintiff presents his evidence first. This may involve calling of witnesses, presentation of documents, or reading in portions of the defendant's examination for discovery. Any witnesses called may be cross-examined by the opposing lawyer. At the close of the plaintiff's case the defendant will present its case in the same manner. At the conclusion of the evidence each party will present legal argument relating the evidence of the case to the law as established by precedent or statute.

Most civil actions are heard by a judge and not by a jury. In such cases the judge decides both the law and the facts of the case. If a jury is involved in the case they will determine matters of fact; that is, they will decide which version of events to believe. The jury will also decide the amount of compensation to be awarded. The judge will decide matters of law. Following presentation of argument a judgment will be given by the judge or the jury, as the case may be.

In a civil trial the plaintiff is required to prove his case to what is called a "balance of probabilities." This is a lower standard than is required in a criminal trial. The judge or jury need only be satisfied that the plaintiff's version is the more probable in case of conflicting evidence. This balance of probabilities is called the "civil burden of proof."

The civil process may often take years to get to trial and will cost thousands of dollars in legal fees and expenses. Even successful litigants may owe more in legal fees than they ultimately recover if the award is small. For this reason, there are Small Claim Courts to deal with matters of smaller monetary value in an expeditious way without the necessity of legal assistance. If a party's claim exceeds the limit established for such a court he may lower his claim to bring it within the limit, in order to save expenses. For example, if a claim is for $3,000 and the small claim limit is $2,500, the claim may be reduced to $2,500. The $500 lost may well be less than the costs involved in going through the civil process.

The Criminal Trial

The constitution grants exclusive jurisdiction to the federal government over crime but provincial legislatures can create a "quasi-criminal" offence for breach of a provincial statute or regulation. Crimes are created by statute. Unless a federal or provincial law creates a crime and establishes a penalty for it, there can be no prosecution. The procedure to be followed in criminal proceedings is set out in the *Criminal Code* and in provincial acts dealing with prosecutions for breach of provincial laws.

The Code makes a distinction between more serious crimes which are called "indictable" offences and those that are less serious which are called "summary conviction" offences. The distinction made involves not only the maximum penalty that may be imposed but also the method of procedure to be used in dealing with the matter. Provinces may only create summary conviction offences and the procedure described for dealing with such matters applies to both federal and provincial offences.

Summary conviction proceedings are commenced by the issuance of a Summons which directs the person alleged to have committed an offence, the accused, to appear before a magistrate, or a provincial court judge, to answer to the charge. The magistrate will read the charge to the accused and ask for a plea. If the accused pleads "guilty" the magistrate will hear particulars of the crime, give the accused an opportunity to speak in mitigation, and impose a sentence. The maximum term of imprisonment for such an offence is six months. Fines may be imposed as a substitute for (or in addition to) a jail term. The maximum fine will vary depending upon the statute.

If the accused pleads "not guilty," the magistrate will set a trial date, at which time he or another magistrate will hear the evidence and render a verdict. All summary conviction trials take place at the provincial court level and are heard without a jury. Certain indictable offences are also heard at this level. A magistrate has absolute jurisdiction over some minor indictable offences, such as a petty theft, and may adjudicate upon even more serious matters if the accused consents to him hearing the matter.

All criminal trials proceed with the assumption that the accused is innocent of the crime and the onus is on the prosecutor, the Crown, to prove his guilt "beyond a reasonable doubt." This criminal burden of proof is much higher than that required in a civil trial and has been described as "proof to a moral certainty." The Crown must prove all elements of the offence to this exacting standard and must do so in accordance with the rules of procedure and of evidence that have been established by statute and by precedent. The accused does not have to prove his innocence in any way. He need only raise a reasonable doubt as to his guilt in order to be acquitted. If there are flaws in the Crown procedure, the accused is also entitled to an acquittal. Guilt, in a criminal sense, is not so much that the accused did something wrong but rather that the Crown can prove, through strict adherence to a certain set of rules, that the wrong was committed by the accused.

There are two essential elements to any criminal offence which must be proved. The first is the *actus reus* or the "guilty act." The Crown must prove that the accused did the act complained of. The second element is the *mens rea* or "guilty mind-." It is not sufficient to show that the accused did a certain act, such as taking a car, but that he did it with a criminal intent. This is often difficult to prove and the law makes allowances for this by providing, in many cases, a presumption of intent unless the accused can raise a doubt otherwise. Both elements must be present in order to establish a crime. It is not sufficient to intend to steal a car if you do not commit the act. Nor is the taking of a car a crime if you believed it to be your car when you took it.

At the provincial court trial, the Crown will call witnesses and present its best case. The accused or his lawyer is entitled to cross examine any Crown witness. At the conclusion of the Crown's case, the defence may elect not to call any evidence and assert that the Crown has not met its burden of proof if the facts established fall short of establishing guilt beyond a reasonable doubt. The defence may call its own witnesses if a sufficient case has been established by the Crown in an attempt to disprove the allegation or raise a doubt. The accused cannot be forced to testify but may choose to give evidence in his own defence.

Following the evidence, each side will make a concluding argument and the judge will render his verdict and impose sentence. Sentences can be any of the following: a fine, imprisonment, both a fine and imprisonment, probation, or a conditional or absolute discharge. The discharge means that although a person has been found guilty of the offence he is deemed not to have been convicted. It is similar to a pardon. A person who receives a discharge may truthfully answer "no" if he is asked on a questionnaire whether he has ever been convicted of a criminal offence.

The procedure for trial of indictable offences is somewhat more complicated although the basic rules of evidence and burden of proof remain the same. Because these are more serious offences, the accused is given further options as to how he wishes to be tried.

The trial of an indictable offence usually begins with the laying of an "information" before a magistrate. This document states that the complainant has information and belief that the accused committed a certain offence. A warrant is issued for the arrest of the accused and he is brought before a magistrate. If the offence is not one which a magistrate has absolute jurisdiction to try, the accused will then be given an option as to how he wishes to be tried. He may elect to be tried by a magistrate, by a judge alone, or by a court composed of a judge and a jury.

If the accused elects trial by magistrate, the magistrate will then accept a plea. If a "not guilty" plea is entered, a date will be set for trial and the procedure will be the same as for summary conviction offences. The sentence imposed, however, may exceed that of a summary conviction offence and may be up to the maximum allowed for that offence.

If the accused elects trial by a judge and jury or judge alone, no plea is entered and a date is set for a preliminary inquiry. At the preliminary inquiry, the Crown is obliged to present sufficient evidence to show that it has a strong enough case to warrant a trial of the accused on the charge. It must present sufficient evidence that a properly instructed jury could convict the accused of the offence. The defendant is not obliged to call any witnesses or say anything at this point and usually will not. It gives the defence a preliminary look at the case it must meet and the opportunity to test the Crown witnesses under cross-examination. At the conclusion of the preliminary inquiry, the magistrate will either discharge the accused if there is not sufficient evidence or commit him to stand trial in the higher court.

If committed for trial, the accused will be arraigned in the higher court. This means that the formal charge, the indictment, will be read and he will be asked to enter a plea. If the plea is "not guilty" the matter will be set for trial. If it is to be a jury trial, the next step in the process is to select a panel of jurors. Once this is done the trial proceeds in much the same manner as in the lower court with the exception that it is the jury who will decide guilt or innocence. The judge will decide matters of law and instruct the jury as to what the law is concerning the offence and the burden of proof. If the accused is found guilty, the judge will impose the sentence.

The Administrative Board

There are a variety of administrative boards or tribunals which have been established to deal with a variety of matters. Among those that may be encountered by teachers are disciplinary boards, certification boards, labour arbitration boards, and boards dealing with matters of student placement. Each of these boards derives its authority from the statute creating it and each will have a different set of rules and procedures that it follows. The teacher should consult the particular statute to see what powers the board has and what procedures are mandated for it. Often such boards are allowed to develop their own set of procedures and rules of evidence.

Despite the differences in procedures, all boards are required to follow the rules of fundamental justice to ensure that each party gets a fair hearing. The formal procedures found in courtrooms are usually absent and evidence may be given under oath (or not) as the board determines. Written evidence may be received in lieu of verbal testimony. Often there is no appeal process, but a party may bring a court application to quash the board's decision if proper procedure was not followed. The courts will not substitute their judgment for that of the board but only quash the decision made if it was not arrived at fairly. The board may then re-hear the matter and follow the proper procedure as set out by the court. Sometimes, there is a provision that a judge may sit as a court of appeal from a board decision, in which case he will hear the matter following standard procedures and will render his own decision.

Although the rules of procedure and evidence for each court or tribunal will vary among jurisdictions, all of these bodies are governed by a set of general principles known as the rules of natural justice. These rules are designed to ensure a fair hearing for all disputes. Our legal system is an adversarial one wherein each party presents its own strongest case and seeks to break down the other party's case. It is felt that the truth will ultimately emerge from this process. In order to ensure that this goal is achieved certain rules of fairness must be adopted to afford each side equal opportunity to present its case. These basic rules of natural justice are as follows:

1. The person or body hearing the matter must be free from bias in favour of either party. This means that there must be no obvious bias in the sense that the adjudicator must not have a connection to either party. Everyone, of course, has his own opinions and principles that will affect his judgment to some degree and therefore no one is ever totally free from bias in that sense. Some judges are considered to be more "liberal" than others and this factor will undoubtedly affect their decisions. This rule addresses the situation where a party to a dispute is a relative of the adjudicator or where the board itself is selected by one of the parties.

2. Each party must be given the opportunity to fully present his case. This means that each party must know the case he is expected to meet and be allowed to produce all facts and evidence in his favour. This is the essence of the adversarial system. Natural justice will not be done when

only one party is heard or where one party does not know what case he must refute.

3. Each party must be notified of the hearing. Again this seems obvious in order to allow full presentation of a case, but it does not always happen.

4. Each party is entitled to legal representation, should he so desire. The rules of procedure and the substantive law are complex and may not be understood by a party. To ensure each party has an equal opportunity to present his case as fully as possible, each has the right to retain legal counsel to present his case for him.

5. The hearing must be open to public scrutiny. This does not mean that all hearings must be held in public but as rather that there must exist some form of review of the proceedings on behalf of the public to ensure that these rules are followed. Public scrutiny will include public trials or proceedings, judicial review of proceedings and appeals to higher authority.

6. The person conducting the hearing must act fairly and exercise a judicious temper. Not only must the hearing be conducted fairly; it must seem to be conducted fairly. The adjudicator must not display any feelings that would make an impartial observer think that he is biased.

One interesting case involving the concepts of natural justice is *Re Theriault* (1980) 29 N.B.R. (2d) 42, a case where these rules were abused by a Provincial Court judge causing an innocent school principal to have a warrant issued for his arrest. The case had its origins in a criminal charge against a 14 year old boy found to have 36 joints of marijuana in his possession as he left a school bus. He pleaded guilty to the offence and was remanded for sentencing.

He was sentenced to be committed to the charge of the Director of Child Welfare with a specific recommendation that he "should be moved out of that district and out of that school." The judge expressed the view that the boy was not getting proper home supervision and that it would look like a "farce" to others in the school if nothing seemed to be happening to him. The social worker assigned to the case sent the boy home for the night and made arrangements to conduct interviews with the boy, his father, and the school principal with a view to determining the best method of handling the case.

On learning that the boy had been sent home, despite his recommendation to the contrary, the judge issued warrants for the arrest of the boy, his father, the housekeeper, two social workers and the school principal. All parties appeared before him the next afternoon, at which time he conducted an inquiry into why his order was not followed and he again sentenced the boy.

The judge conducted the proceedings on his own, calling and cross-examining witnesses. He reached certain conclusions before hearing witnesses and held onto those conclusions despite contradictory evidence. One of the social workers involved, a person named Theriault, brought an application to the New Brunswick Court of Queen's Bench, Trial Division for an order quashing these proceedings. The order was granted because the hearing was conducted in breach of the rules of natural justice. The Justice hearing the appeal commented:

> A reading of the transcript of the two hearings, November 7 and November 8, leads to the inescapable conclusion that the motivation for the second, and its peremptory nature, was an effort by the Family Court Judge to bring the Child Welfare Officers to an accounting. The school principal who was also caught in the net must have wondered at the vagaries of the law that could have led to his arrest.

The decisions of courts and administrative tribunals are recorded in order that the decision may become known. More significant cases are compiled into volumes of law reports. Appendix C gives an example of such a decision from a law report showing the structure and method of interpreting such reports. The chapter on legal research will show you how to locate reported decisions on topics of concern.

At first glance this principle of *stare decisis* may seem to yield a rigid unbending system. In practice, however, case law is constantly changing and being modified. Statute law can be seen to be changed in a deliberate way by the repeal and amendment of legislation. Legislatures are not bound to follow any previously established laws other than the Constitution. Statute law can therefore break new ground or change centuries of common law by the stroke of a pen. Case law is changed by judges distinguishing precedent cases from the case before them on the facts of the case. The general principle may remain intact but the court does not apply it in a specific case because the facts are different in some material respect from those in the precedent cases. This places limits on the general principle which may ultimately be confined only to the case in which it was enunciated because all other cases will differ on the facts in some respect. No two cases are ever identical. When the Supreme Court of Canada enunciates a rule that was not previously established or overrules an existing line of cases, common law theory presumes that the law was always as is now being revealed and that previous cases were in error by believing it to be something else.

Is there then any element of predictability in the common law? Judicial decisions are based on a search for relevant cases having similar factual situations as the case before it. Equally learned judges may reach different conclusions using equally compelling reasoning and precedent for their decision. Each decision only decides the specific facts before the court but also gives some definition to the boundaries of the general principle. Because no two cases will ever be identical there will never be an exact precedent to follow and cases will be decided by analogy or similarity to existing precedent. If the outcome of all cases could be predicted with certainty, no cases would ever reach the courts since the losing party would not spend the time and money required to present his case, knowing he will lose. The general principles can be stated in many instances but whether they apply to a particular set of facts is a matter for judicial interpretation in each case and there is no certainty regarding which interpretation may prevail in the long run.

This distinction between case law and statute law is useful to some extent, but it does not show the interrelationship of the two. Statute law does not stand completely isolated from case law since the meaning of the words used in the statute are subject to judicial interpretation and the constitutionality of the law is a matter for the courts to decide. Case law can modify, extend, or declare to be invalid a statute law. Similarly, statute law can change the provisions of long standing common law traditions. If the Legislature decides that an old common law rule should no longer apply it can pass an act to that effect. There is a constant interaction between case law and statute law with each acting upon and influencing the course of the other.

Law may be divided into other types of categories besides statute and case law. That distinction is based on the source of the law; other divisions may be made according to those that the law affects or the subject matter addressed by the particular law.

Public Law and Private Law

One common way of categorizing law is dividing it into public law and private law. Public laws are those that affect the government in some way either in its relationship with other governments or in its relationship to the people it governs. Examples of public laws are criminal law, constitutional law, and administrative law. Private law, on the other hand, deals with rights and obligations between individual citizens that do not affect the government or the rest of society directly. Examples of private laws are contract law, property law, and tort law. There are blurrings of this distinction in cases where the government becomes involved with a private individual.

Where a government enters into a contract with a citizen to perform some work, the method of entering into the contract is a matter of public law since it deals with general rules between the government and citizens contracting with the government. If the individual takes action against the government for an alleged breach of contract, that is a matter of private law since the individual is enforcing a private right under the contract. It is not a matter of concern to the whole province but only to him as an individual and to the government as a party to a contract.

Certain actions may have both public and private consequences and will be dealt with under both classes of law. Public and private law may be distinguished by using the concept of "benefit." For whose benefit is the particular law? Criminal law is made for the benefit of society as a whole and is therefore public law even though a particular crime may involve a dispute between two individuals (such as an assault). These matters are deemed to be of such social importance that public intervention in the form of criminal law is necessary. The issue of damages or compensation for an injured party as a result of the assault is a matter between two individuals and is therefore private law. These laws are primarily for the benefit of the individual wronged although there may also be some broader social benefits in such laws as well. Again these distinctions are being clouded as governments intervene more and more in our daily lives. Many provinces have enacted crime compensation statutes and have established boards to determine compensation for victims of certain crimes. A matter that was previously deemed to be one for the private law has now become a matter of public law.

Much education law is in the realm of public law, since we are dealing with relationships between governments and the people on a matter that is of benefit to society as a whole. There are also areas of education law which are governed by private law, particularly in the field of negligence.

Branches of the Law

As we have mentioned previously, education law is not a distinct branch of the law but it cuts across many of the traditional branches of law. The categorization of law into branches helps us to conceptualize the nature of the problem and the principles to be invoked in the resolution of the problem. These branches deal with specific subject matters of a legal nature. Among the major branches of the law, and the types of matters that they are concerned with, we have the following:

Constitutional law – This branch of the law deals with relationships between governments and between governments and individuals as they are set out in the Constitution. The Constitution imposes limits on government action and this branch of law is concerned with defining those limits and the meaning of various constitutional documents.

Criminal law – This branch of law deals with actions that society considers to be crimes and the method of punishing those who commit such acts. In Canada, criminal law is a matter of exclusive federal jurisdiction and only the Parliament of Canada can declare an action to be a "crime." Provinces can create "quasi-crimes" for breaches of provincial statutes and these matters are dealt with under the same general principles applicable to federal crimes.

Administrative law – This branch deals with the conduct of administrative tribunals, and particularly the process involved in administrative decision making.

Tort law – This branch of the law is concerned with compensation for individuals who are injured as a result of the negligent or deliberate actions of another.

Contract law – This branch of law is concerned with the rules for making, interpreting and enforcing contracts between parties.

There are other branches and divisions of law but these are the ones that will be of primary concern to the teacher. They are useful as a means of categorizing a problem in order to find the relevant law.

Discussion and Review Questions

1. Describe how each branch of the government makes laws.

2. Does the doctrine of *stare decisis* inhibit the judiciary from changing antiquated laws?

3. Should the rules of natural justice be followed by a teacher when disciplining a student? Should they be followed by a principal or school board in suspending or expelling a student?

4. Should the provinces take more control over educational matters in order to eliminate discrepancies in school policy that exist among various local school boards?

5. Should more educational matters be dealt with through legislation rather than by regulations?

Appendix A

Provincial School Legislation

The following is a list of the major statutes in each province dealing with schools and their administration. It is not an exhaustive list for many matters pertaining to schools are included in other statutes besides these. The purpose of including this list is to assist the reader in locating relevant statutes from each province for comparison. The number of different titles used sometimes makes it difficult to find the Act of a particular province. If your province entitles its general Act as the *School Act* you may not think to look for an *Education Act* or *Public Schools Act* in another province.

Alberta

Alberta School Trustees Association Act, R.S.A. 1980 c. A-37
Department of Education Act, R.S.A. 1980 c. D-17
School Act, R.S.A. 1980 c. S-3
Teachers' Retirement Fund Act, R.S.A. 1980 c. T-2
Teaching Profession Act, R.S.A. 1980 c. T-3

British Columbia

Pension (Teachers) Act, R.S.B.C. c. 320
School Act, R.S.B.C. 1979 c. 375

Manitoba

Education Administration Act, C.C.S.M. c. E-10
Public Schools Act, C.C.S.M. c. P-250
Teachers Pensions Act, C.C.S.M. c. T-20
Manitoba Teachers' Society Act, C.C.S.M. c. T-30

New Brunswick

Schools Act, R.S.N.B. 1973 c. S-5
Teachers' Pension Act, R.S.N.B. 1973 c. T-1

Newfoundland

Department of Education Act, S.N. 1984 c. 46
School Attendance, 1978 Act, S.N. 1978 c. 78
Schools Act, R.S.N. 1970 c. 346
Newfoundland Teachers' Association, 1974 Act, S.N. 1974 c. 50
Newfoundland Teacher (Collective Bargaining) Act, S.N. 1973 c. 114

Nova Scotia

Education Act, C.S.N.S. c. E-2
Handicapped Persons' Education Act, C.S.N.S. c. H-6
Nova Scotia School Boards Association Act, C.S.N.S. c. N-23
School Boards Membership Act, C.S.N.S. c. S-6
Teachers' Collective Bargaining Act, C.S.N.S. c. T-6
Teachers' Pension Act, C.S.N.S. c. T-7

Ontario

Education Act, R.S.O. 1980 c. 129
Ontario School Trustees' Council Act, R.S.O. 1980 c. 355
School Boards and Teachers Collective Negotiations Act,
  R.S.O. 1980 c. 464
Teachers' Superannuation Act, S.O. 1983 c. 84
Teaching Profession Act, R.S.O. 1980 c. 495

Prince Edward Island

School Act, R.S.P.E.I. 1974 c. S-2
Teachers Superannuation Act, R.S.P.E.I. 1974 c. T-1.1

Quebec

Act respecting public elementary and secondary education,
  R.S.O. 1977 c. E-8.1
Act respecting private education, R.S.Q. 1977 c. E-9
Act respecting the Ministere de l'Education, R.S.Q. 1977 c. M-15

Saskatchewan

Education Act, R.S.S. 1977 c. E-0.1 (Supp)
Department of Education Act, S.S. 1983 c. D-13.01
Teachers' Federation Act, R.S.S. 1977 c. T-7
League of Educational Administrators, Directors and Superintendents Act,
S.S. 1983-84 c. L-9.01
Teachers Superannuation Act R.S.S. 1977 c. T-9

Appendix B

The Structure of an Act and Regulation

How to Read a Statute

The Title of the Act describes its subject matter

The Chapter Number is used to locate the statute

The words of enactment indicate the authority for the statute

The definition section is usually found at the beginning of the Act

Boldface numbers are called sections

Law making power is delegated to the Minister of Education

Numbers in parentheses are called subsections

Letters in parentheses are called clauses

Definitions

Regulations

SCHOOL ACT
CHAPTER S-3

HER MAJESTY, by and with the advice and consent of the Legislative Assembly of Alberta, enacts as follows:

1   In this Act,

(a) "board" means a board of trustees of a district or division;

(b) "city district" means a district situated wholly or partly within the boundaries of a city;

(c) "district" means a school district established pursuant to this or any predecessor Act or Ordinance;

(d) "division" means a school division established pursuant to this or any predecessor Act;

11 (1) In addition to his other powers specified in this Act the Minister may make regulations

(a) governing the use of English as a language of instruction;

(b) governing the use of French as a language of instruction;

(c) governing the use of any language other than English or French as a language of instruction;

(d) respecting the inspection of pupils, teachers, schools, pupil programs and courses of study;

(e) defining "resident pupil" for the purpose of sections 70 and 71;

(f) respecting the inspection of schools for the purpose of ensuring that a proper educational program is carried on and that the Act, regulations, courses of study and pupil programs are complied with;

(g) governing

(i) the examination of pupils,

(ii) the remuneration of examiners and markers,

(iii) the fees for taking examinations and in connection with re-reading examinations, remission and refund of fees,

(iv) appeals from examinations, and

(v) hourly fee rates for temporary staff,

and granting certificates to school graduates;

Roman numerals in parentheses are called subclauses

[Referred to as Section 11, subsection 1, clause g, subclause v]

PART 9
OFFENCES AND PENALTIES

Headings and marginal notes are included for quick reference

General penalty

171 Any person who contravenes this Act or the regulations is guilty of an offence and if no other penalty is prescribed liable to a fine of not more than $500 and in default of payment to imprisonment for a term not exceeding 90 days.

RSA 1970 c329 s162

Dates following each section show where it appeared in earlier version of the Act

Penalty for failure to give information

172 A person who is required by this Act or the regulations

(a) to furnish any information,

(b) to make a return or statement in writing, or

(c) to perform any act or duty,

and who refuses, neglects or fails to do so is guilty of an offence and liable to a fine of not more than $500 and in default of payment to imprisonment for a term not exceeding 90 days.

The Act may create a general penalty as well as specific penalties for any breach

RSA 1970 c329 s163

How to Read a Regulation

Regulation number
is used to locate
the regulation

Effective date of   the regulation

Act under which
it is made

Authority for
making the regu-
lation is cited

Title indicates the
subject matter

Regulations are
divided into sections,
subsections, clauses,
and subclauses

ALBERTA REGULATION 490/82

_____

(Filed on November 30, 1982)
SCHOOL ACT

_____

MINISTERIAL ORDER

I, David King, Minister of Education, pursuant to section 11 of the School Act, hereby make the regulation in accordance with the Appendix hereto being the French Language Regulation.

Dated at Edmonton, Alberta, this 26th day of November, 1982.

DAVID KING
Minister of Edu-
cation

_____

APPENDIX
SCHOOL ACT
French Language Regulation

1(1) A board shall not commence a program that uses French as the language of instruction in a school unless it has:

(a) passed and delivered to the Minister a resolution authorizing the use of French as the language of instruction, and

(b) made provision satisfactory to the Minister for the use of English as the language of instruction for all pupils who would normally attend the school and whose parents desire such instruction.

(2) The courses of study and instructional materials for the program shall be those prescribed or approved pursuant to section 11(2) of the School Act.

2 Where, pursuant to section 159 of the School Act, a board authorizes a program that uses French as a language of instruction,

(a) if the program commences in grade 1, then with respect to grades 1 and 2,

(i) the amount of time French is used as the language of instruction,

(ii) the nature and extent of English language instruction, if any, and

(iii) the point at which the English language arts program if any, is initiated

is in the discretion of the board;

(b) regardless of when the program commences, after grade 2,

(i) not less than 300 minutes per week of instruction in English language arts shall be provided for each pupil in each of grades 3, 4, 5 and 6,

(ii) not less than 150 hours per year of instruction in English language arts shall be provided for each pupil in each of grades 7, 8 and 9, and

(iii) not less than 125 hours per year or the equivalent of 5 credits per year of instruction in English language arts shall be provided for each pupil in each of grades 10, 11 and 12.

Previous regulation is repealed and is no longer in force

3 The French Language Regulation (Alta. Reg. 115/82) is repealed.

Appendix C

How to Read a Case Report

Style of cause will appear on alternate pages and in full at beginning of report

The Court and which members participated are listed

Date judgment given

Key words indicate general topic and specific topics of the case

The headnote is a summary of the facts and the court's decision. It is prepared by the editors of the particular report and is not part of the judgment

Previous cases which the Court considered are listed. Some reports will refer to digests for additional cases on the topic.

MOFFATT V. DUFFERIN COUNTY BOARD OF EDUCATION   143

MOFFATT et al. v/ DUFFERIN COUNTY BOARD OF EDUCATION et al.

Ontario, Court of Appeal, McGillivray, Kelly and Brooke, JJ.A.
October 2, 1972.

Negligence – Duty of care – Teacher asking pupil to help superintendent – Job involving lifting piano – Pupil injured – Duty of care of teacher and superintendent – Whether breach.

Public authorities – Definition of term – School teacher asking pupil to assist superintendent in school job – Whether teacher and superintendent functioning as public authorities – Whether entitled to protection of limitation – Public Authorities Protection Act (Ont.).

Defendant maintenance superintendent asked defendant teacher to provide the assistance of two boys to help him in the school auditorium. The teacher did not ask the nature of the job but called upon the infant plaintiff, who was 13 years old, and another boy to go to the auditorium to assist the superintendent. The job involved raising a piano into an upright position. In the course of the job the piano slipped on its casters and fell, injuring the infant plaintiff. *Held,* given that the standard of care required of a teacher to a pupil is that of a careful parent to a child, it was not a breach of duty for defendant teacher to allow a male pupil of the age and size of the plaintiff to respond to a request of this nature without personally inquiring as to the prupose. In any event, her action was in pursuance of a public duty and the limitation section of the *Public Authorities Protection Act, R.S.O.* 1960, c.318 (now R.S.O. 1970, c.374), ran in her favour. The maintenance superintendent, who was admitted to have been negligent, was also entitled to the protection of the Act. The statutory duty of the board of education which employed him was to provide suitable furniture and equipment for the school and to keep it in proper repair. The superintendent was acting pursuant to that duty at the time of the injury.

[Nelson et al. v. Cookson, [1940] 1 K.B. 100, apld]

A description of the nature of the case

The names of the lawyers for each party

In this case the judgment was delivered by one judge on behalf of the panel of three. Often each judge will give his own opinion.

The name of the report service and volume citation are given on alternate pages

The full text of judgment is given. Some reports only give an edited summary of the judgment.

The judge quotes from a previous decision he is relying on as precedent for his decision.

APPEAL from a judgment dismissing an action for damages for personal injuries.

G.T. Mullin, for appellants.
H.W. Snyder, for respondents.

The judgment of the Court was delivered by

Kelly, J.A.: – this action was brought to recover damages for personal injuries suffered on November 18, 1969, by Gary Edward Moffatt (Moffatt) whose date of birth was January 21, 1956, and who was at all material times a pupil at Mono-Amaranth Elementary School conducted by the Dufferin County Board of Education (the Board) pursuant to the provisions of the *Secondary Schools and Boards of Education Act,* R.S.O. 1960, c.362, and amending Acts [now R.S.O. 1970, c.425]. This action was commenced on August 18, 1970, 10 months after the injury was suffered.

146   DOMINION LAW REPORTS 31   D.L.R. (3d)

son, J. It is interesting to note that in opening his judgement he remarks that the precise point had never been argued before despite the long recognition of some duty or act that is done in the pursuance of a public authority or is carried out by a public authority through its servants or agents, that servant has the same right to the benefit of the Act as the public authority itself would have. At p. 105 he states:

> It seems to me that these two defendants were exercising what was really a public authority, because it was an authority given to the Middlesex County council to provide and maintain this hospital. The council could not exercise that authority by their own hands, but must act through other people, and on the relevant occasion their authority was being exercised by these two medical men. It seems to me idle to say that they were not acting in pursuance of a public duty and authority conferred on the Middlesex County Council. They were performing this public duty or authority, whichever you may like to call it, as agents or delegates for and on behalf of the council, and they are entitled to the benefit of the Act of 1893.

Atkinson, J., went on to say that it was hopeless to argue that the doctors in this connection were independent contractors.

I would say the same of the claim based on the alleged negligence of Robertson. The statutory duty of the Board was to provide suitable furniture and equipment and to keep it in proper repair. The defendant was exercising the authority given to the Board. The Board could not exercise that authority by its own hands but of necessity must act through others. In this case it employed the defendant Robertson as its agent. Robertson was, accordingly, performing a public duty as agent or delegate for or on behalf of the board and in so doing was entitled to the benefit of the *Public Authorities Protection Act.*

The mere fact that the servant or employee for the Board was negligent in the performance of its function did not serve to put the activity and the execution of it or its intended execution beyond the protection of the Act.

The disposition of the case

For these reasons I am of the opinion that the learned trial Judge was not in error in dismissing the action as against the defendant Robertson as well as against the other defendants. The appeal will be dismissed, with costs, if demanded.

Appeal dismissed.

Appendix D

The Court Hierarchy for Each Province

Alberta

Appellate Division of the Supreme Court (Court of Appeal)
Court of Queen's Bench (Trial Division of the Supreme Court)
District Court
Provincial Court

British Columbia

Court of Appeal
Supreme Court
County Court
Provincial Court

Manitoba

Court of Appeal
Court of Queen's Bench
County Court
Provincial Judges Court

New Brunswick

Court of Appeal
Court of Queen's Bench
County Court
Provincial Court

Newfoundland

Court of Appeal
Supreme Court (Trial Division)
District Court
Provincial Court

Nova Scotia

Appeal Division of the Supreme Court
Supreme Court (Trial Division)
County Court
Provincial Magistrates Court

Ontario

Court of Appeal
High Court of Justice (Trial court)
Divisional Court (Appeal court from county or district court)
Country or District Court
Provincial Court

Prince Edward Island

Supreme Court (Appeal)
Supreme Court (Trial)
Provincial Court

Quebec

Court of Appeal
Superior Court
Court of the Sessions of the Peace
Provincial Court

Saskatchewan

Court of Appeal
Court of Queen's Bench
District Court
Provincial Court

Yukon & Northwest Territories

Court of Appeal
Supreme Court
Courts of Justices of the Peace

Appendix E

Stare Decisis

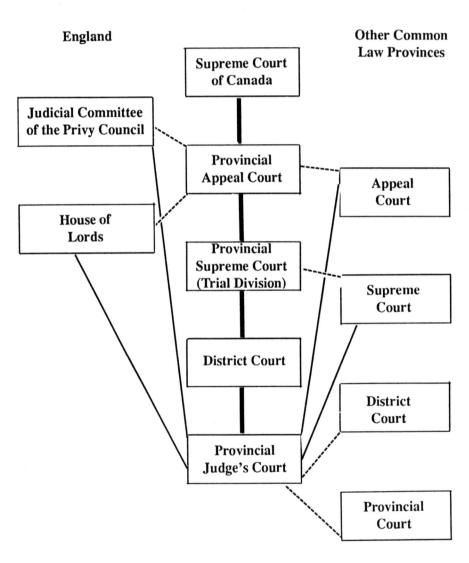

References

Gall, G. L., *The Canadian Legal System* (2nd ed.). Toronto: Carswell, 1983.

Waddams, S. M., *Introduction to the Study of Law* (3rd ed.). Toronto: Carswell, 1987.

3

Legal Research

Learning Objectives

The purpose of this Chapter is to assist the teacher in conducting his own legal research so that he may remain relatively current and knowledgeable about educational law.

After reading this chapter you will know:

1. The difference between primary and secondary sources of law.

2. How to locate a federal or provincial statute.

3. How to locate a regulation made pursuant to a statute.

4. How to locate a case.

5. How to use secondary sources to gain access to the law.

Preview

Legal materials are of two kinds, primary authorities and secondary authorities.

Primary materials are those which consist of the written law itself and include statutes, regulations and reported decisions of court cases and tribunals. Secondary materials consist of items such as legal dictionaries, statute citators, indexes, digests, periodicals, textbooks and computer software. The problem facing the teacher who wishes to undertake an updating of a statute or pursuit of a legal question, such as the degree of teacher supervision required in a chemistry laboratory, is to make efficient use of the legal library resources available locally. Nothing dampens the teacher's enthusiasm in growing professionally than an unproductive and thus frustrating research for current information. Also, the speed with which statutes sometimes change and the slowness by which cases sometimes proceed through the courts, add to teacher's uneasiness.

This chapter illustrates how primary authorities are cited and how access to them can be gained through secondary materials. It concludes with a table of abbreviations for some of the more popular reporting services.

Self-Assessment

1. Can you locate the most recent revisions to your province's labour legislation?
2. Can you locate and follow a case of purported educational negligence?
3. Do you know what the abbreviations R.S.C., C-30, and W.W.R. stand for?
4. How would you find the law pertaining to student detentions in British Columbia?

Key Terms

Citation
Report
Statute
Regulation

*   *   *   *

The process of producing law (by the legislatures and courts) results in a product: legal materials. Knowing how to use these resources will give you access to the law and answers to particular problems. Legal materials are of two kinds: primary authority and secondary authority.

Primary materials are those which constitute the actual written law itself. Included are the following:

(a) Statutes, both federal and provincial, as well as municipal by-laws,

(b) Regulations made pursuant to statutes, and

(c)   Case law, i.e. the decisions of courts and tribunals.

We have seen an example of each of these types of primary authority in the previous chapter.

Secondary sources are a means of finding and interpreting the primary materials. They are not the law itself, but are usually the starting place for finding out what the law is. Primary sources are often poorly indexed and secondary sources have been developed as a bridge to gain access to them. Imagine trying to read through every statute, regulation and judicial decision to find the law on a particular point of interest. Secondary sources point towards only those materials that are relevant to the problem and help to organize the primary sources in a meaningful way.

Secondary materials include such things as legal dictionaries, legal encyclopedias, digests of cases, textbooks, legal periodicals, and procedure manuals. Every source other than the aforementioned primary sources is a secondary source. This book is a secondary source. It is not the law but rather it is a directory that points towards the law which is contained in either statute, regulation, or case law. To learn the exact law on any point one must consult the primary source. The extracts, description and summaries contained herein represent our editing of the actual law. There is more to the law than can be found within the body of the text. Our statements should not be relied upon as being the law on any particular matter; much has, of necessity, been left out. Thus, the purpose of this chapter is to point toward some useful regal research tools.

In the previous chapter we discussed the primary sources and showed the structure of acts, regulations and cases. We will now show how to find these primary sources and how to make sure that a source is up to date, containing the most recent amendments and court interpretations. We will review first the primary sources and then the secondary sources which will give access to the former.

Primary Authority

Constitutional Documents

One of our legacies as a British colony has been that most of our constitutional documents, commencing with the *British North America Act* in 1867 and continuing through to *The Canada Act*, have been statutes of the British Parliament. Appendix II of the *Revised Statutes of Canada* (discussed below) contains thirty-eight orders, British acts and Canadian acts that are considered to be constitutional documents. More recent acts are contained in the sessional volumes of the *Statutes of Canada* (including *The Canada Act* containing as Schedule B *The Constitution Act, 1982* which was enacted for and has the force of law in Canada). Schedule 1 of *The Constitution Act, 1982* lists the constitutional statutes from 1867, and renames them. All future constitutional documents will be acts of the Canadian Parliament and thus may be found in the same manner as the other statutes.

Federal Statutes

From time to time the government consolidates all of the law currently in force and issues a set of *Revised Statutes of Canada* (R.S.C.) in several volumes. The most recent consolidation of federal statutes (as of the date of this publication) took place in 1970 and contains the full English and French texts of statutes in force as of December 31, 1969. Each act is assigned an alpha-numeric designation. The alpha designation is the first letter of the title of the act and the numeric designation is the number of the statute as it falls in alphabetic order within that letter. For example, the *Copyright Act* is chapter C-30 and the *Criminal Code* is chapter C-34. A full citation for the *Copyright Act* would be R.S.C. 1970 c. C-30 meaning *Revised Statutes of Canada*, 1970 chapter C-30. This enables us to find the text of the act in the particular volume wherein it is published.

The *Revised Statutes* has an index which is, in many ways, not very adequate. It is not a single detailed index by topic or subject matter but rather it is a set of individual indices for each statute. There is some cross-referencing by key words but one would generally need to know the name of the statute to find specific information from the index. There are also supplements and appendices to the *Revised Statutes* containing other access information such as history of the legislation and a collection of "Constitutional Acts and Documents."

Since revision took place quite some time ago, many of the acts contained therein have been repealed and amended subsequently. We must therefore have a means of getting more current information. Statutes passed since 1970 are published in sessional volumes called *Statutes of Canada* (S.C.). These are not annual publications. They are issued at the conclusion of each session of Parliament and thus may overlap several calendar years. The sessional volume following the *Revised Statutes* covers portions of three years and is cited as 1970-71-72 S.C. In these volumes each statute is assigned a numeric chapter designation within that volume. For example, the *Young Offenders Act* is cited as 1980-81-82 S.C. c. 110. When the next consolidation takes place it will be assigned an alpha-numeric designation within that revision.

These sessional volumes, the *Statutes of Canada*, also contain a "Table of Public Statutes" which show all amendments to acts up to the date of publication of that volume. The table in each volume replaces and supersedes all previous tables so that only the most recent need be consulted to give all amendments between that date and 1970. Some statutes are amended almost annually; a search through many different acts is often required to find the current wording of the particular statute. To overcome this problem the Federal Department of Supply and Services publishes periodic "office consolidations" of statutes with all amendments incorporated and all repealed sections deleted. These consolidations give the current wording of the statute without having to resort to extensive research. One need only search for amendments subsequent to the date of the consolidation, normally far fewer than the number made from the original passage of the statute.

Because some sessions of Parliament last many years and because of the delay before publication of the sessional volume, it is impractical to wait for these volumes to appear or to rely on the most recent volume as the final authority. Within a month or two of becoming law, every statute is published in the *Canada Gazette* Part III. Some issues of this publication also contain a "Table of Public Statutes" superseding that published in the last sessional volume or in previous Gazettes. Again this makes it easier to keep current.

In addition to the official publications, there are also commercially produced looseleaf versions of the federal statutes. These are continually updated to provide access to current phrasing on a timely basis. As changes are made, new pages are published for replacement and insertion. This format has also been adopted by many provincial governments and may soon become the norm for official publications as well as for commercial ones. A very useful secondary source for gaining access to the federal statutes is *The Canada Statute Citator* which is discussed later in this chapter. It outlines the current status of a statute, any judicial interpretations of the act, and any regulations made pursuant to the act.

Provincial Statutes

The mechanics of researching provincial statutes is similar to that for federal statutes. Each province has a consolidation and revision (as of a specified date) followed by sessional (usually annual) volumes of provincial statutes. The dates of the revised statutes for each province vary widely as does the system for numbering statutes. Most revisions have adopted the alpha-numeric designations for each act in the revision. Some retain this designation for subsequent statutes by using decimals. For example, a statute called the *Education Act* may have been passed after the last revision and replaces a former *School Act*. If the previous act had the same name it would be an easy matter of simply replacing the alpha-numeric designation. However, it must now be slotted into the "E" category and would fall somewhere between E-3 and E-4. It is then assigned a designation such as E-3.5. The retention of this type of designation provides some consistency in looseleaf editions and future consolidations.

Manitoba has adopted a *Continuing Consolidation of the Statutes of Manitoba* (C.C.S.M.) whereby statutes are published in looseleaf form and are continually updated and consolidated with alpha-numeric designations for each statute assigned in series. Most provinces will probably adopt this type of system in some form in the near future. British Columbia and Nova Scotia have already adopted a similar looseleaf system although these are not designated a continuing consolidation as in Manitoba.

The type and quality of indexing varies from province to province as well. Some have a comprehensive subject index while others only have an index for each individual act. Statute citators are available for each province to provide current information. Each province also publishes a form of Gazette giving current statute information prior to publication of the annual volume.

A peculiar problem exists in all provinces in that certain older English statutes, which were in force at entry into Confederation, remain in force today. Sometimes these old laws are still a primary legislative authority in the province. A comprehensive *Table of English Statutes in Force in Canada* has been published in (1964), 3 Alberta Law Review 262. The statutes themselves are found in bound editions of English statutes similar to our *Statutes of Canada*. Some statutes, such as the *Statute of Frauds,* are referred to quite frequently in judgments so this information becomes valuable to know when no act by that name is found in the provincial statutes.

The citations for provincial statutes follow the same format as federal citations, substituting the appropriate year and provincial abbreviation. Thus, R.S.N. 1970 is the *Revised Statutes of Newfoundland* 1970 and S.N.S 1983 is the *Statutes of Nova Scotia*, 1983. Following is a list of the latest statute revision for each province as of the date of this publication:

Alberta – R.S.A. 1980
British Columbia – R.S.B.C. 1979
Manitoba – R.S.M. 1970 (also C.C.S.M.)

New Brunswick – R.S.N.B. 1973
Newfoundland – R.S.N. 1970
Nova Scotia – R.S.N.S. 1967 (also a consolidated looseleaf edition)
Ontario – R.S.O. 1980
Prince Edward Island – R.S.P.E.I. 1974
Quebec – R.S.Q. (L.R.Q.) 1977
Saskatchewan – R.S.S. 1978

The Yukon and Northwest Territories do not have statutes but rather "Ordinances." The Yukon has, however, recently been designating their legislation as "statutes." An ordinance is essentially the same as a statute and the latest revisions are:

Northwest Territories – R.O.N.W.T. 1974
Yukon – R.O.Y.T. 1978

As mentioned earlier, statutes alone do not give the full story of an act, for there may be regulations made under the act which give more detail and have the same force in law as the act itself. Subordinate legislation is primary authority law made by a person or body under authority granted in a statute and includes regulations, orders, rules and by-laws. These may often be longer than the statute itself and contain much detail essential to understanding the law.

Federal Regulations

Regulations are created or amended simply by publication in the *Canada Gazette.* In 1978 the *Consolidated Regulations of Canada* (C.R.C.) was published and included all generally applicable federal regulations up to December 31, 1977. The regulations are listed alphabetically under the enabling statute with a detailed "Table of Contents" giving the location of a regulation within the 18 volumes of the publication. The regulations are designated numerically. A citation such as C.R.C. 1978 c. 427 would refer to the regulation designated as chapter 427 of the *Consolidated Regulations of Canada,* 1978.

For more current information consult the *Canada Gazette* Part II. All regulations are published in this part of the *Gazette* and a quarterly consolidated index is published in the *Canada Gazette* Part II to update the *Consolidated Regulations.* Regulations are cited by year and number as follows: S.O.R. 84-19. "S.O.R." is an abbreviation for *Statutory Orders and Regulations,* "84" refers to the year 1984, and "19" refers to regulation number 19 for that year. To find this regulation one would go the appropriate *Canada Gazette* Part II for 1984 which contains that particular number. The most recent index would show if there has been any modification of this regulation.

Provincial Regulations

Provincial regulations are also published in the official gazette for that province. Again the practice varies from province to province regarding consolidations. Some provinces have recent consolidated regulations while others do not. The same type of process is used to find a provincial regulation as that discussed above for federal regulations. Use the most current index to determine what regulations are in force under a particular statute and then go to the appropriate part of the provincial gazette or consolidation for the text of the regulation.

Municipal and School Board By-Laws and Policies

These are a form of subordinate legislation, since they are passed under enabling sections of the appropriate provincial statutes. A municipal government or school board has no inherent constitutional power to make law as do the federal and provincial governments. Their laws can only be made pursuant to a delegated authority under statute. There are a large number of these bodies and there exists no means of access to all such authority through, for example, some central clearing house. To find the text of these materials one should contact the appropriate authority who will provide the materials. Public libraries may have copies of some of the more important local by-laws but the best advice is to go to the source itself to obtain the most recent information. School board policies and by laws are often available in a manual form in each school and at the school board offices. The teacher will find that the school and district policy handbooks will answer a large number of legal questions pertaining to the operation of the school.

Case Law Reports

The primary authority for case law is found in reports of judicial decisions. Case law is based upon the establishment of general legal principles by the courts which are then followed in subsequent cases where the fact situations are similar. In order to make this a meaningful process the previous decisions must be known and must be available for consultation. Therefore, various reports of judicial and administrative tribunal decisions are published.

Although these reports are voluminous and fill huge libraries, they contain only a small percentage of all judicial decisions. Reported decisions are usually only those of appellate level courts or trial court decisions deemed to be significant. These reports are produced by private publishers whose editors determine what constitutes a significant case for that particular report.

Copies of unreported judgments may be obtained from the court issuing the judgment and from certain commercial sources. However, you must know of the existence of the case before this process can be used. There are various digests and summaries of both reported and unreported cases that point out the main topics involved and give the citation for the case. Often an unreported decision of significance to teachers is available through the teachers' association or the school board. Since they are the parties involved in the cases, they often will obtain copies of judgments for circulation among other boards and teachers.

The law reports are issued in bound volumes on a periodic basis. Many reporting services issue weekly or monthly softbound copies as well. Cases within the reports are usually listed in chronological order. Still, the particular cases reported may be several months or even a year old before publication date. Some cases (which are not thought at the time to be particularly significant) may gain significance later and thus may be reported many years after the initial decision.

The various reports may cover cases from a particular court (*Supreme Court Reports*), a geographical region (*Western Weekly Reports*), a single province (*Ontario Reports*), or a particular subject matter (*Administrative Law Reports*). Different publishers have adopted different methods of arranging their reports and so a set of rules has been established giving each report a rigid legal citation system for ease of access to the materials.

As an example to help explain the rules, consider the following citation from a leading Canadian case on negligence in the school gymnasium. One of the largest damage awards made against a school board was in the case of:

Thornton et al. v. Board of School Trustees of School District No. 57 (Prince George) et al., [1975] 3 W.W.R. 622; (1976) 73 D.L.R.(3d) 35, [1976] 5 W.W.R. 240; var'd 83 D.L.R.(3d) 480, [1978] 2 S.C.R. 267, [1978] 1 W.W.R. 607, 3 C.C.L.T. 257, 19 N.R. 552.

This collection of letters and numbers appears baffling and probably designed to discourage laypersons from pursuing the matter any further. There is, however, a strict method to this apparent madness which provides easy access to the text of the case.

Firstly, all cases are cited by the names of the parties with the plaintiff's name appearing first. In this case the plaintiff is Thornton. The abbreviation "et al." following the name is Latin for *et altera* meaning "and others" and is used because Thornton was not the only plaintiff in the case. Another student named Tanner was also injured and the parents of the students were parties to the legal action as well. Where there are numerous parties to an action only the first named plaintiff and defendant are included. Sometimes the "et al." is omitted or long names are shortened.

The "v." is an abbreviation for the Latin *versus* meaning "against." When reading a citation the word "and" is substituted for this abbreviation. The actual court pleadings use the word "and" to separate the parties and not a "v.." So *Smith v. Jones* would be read as Smith and Jones. This recitation of the names of the parties is known as the "style of cause" of an action.

Occasionally the name of the case may be followed by the abbreviation "sub. nom." and another style of cause. This means that the case is also known under a different name. The reasons for this vary but a common occurrence is that there are two or more actions commenced against one party that are at some point in time joined together for purpose of trial. Another reason is that the defendant has become the appellant and the names of the parties are now in reverse order on the pleadings.

Other Latin abbreviations also appear in the style of cause quite frequently. The one seen most often is "R." which is an abbreviation for *Rex* or *Regina*. "The King" or "The Queen" respectively. This is predominant in criminal cases which are always prosecuted in the name of the Crown. The government becomes involved in civil actions as well so do not assume that all cases using "R." in the style of cause are criminal cases. Where the Crown is the defendant in a case the abbreviation is not used and "The King" or "The Queen" is printed in full.

Certain procedural phrases are also found in the style of cause. Some cases that come before the courts do not have plaintiffs and defendants as such but are references to the court on some particular matter. "Re" is seen frequently in cases involving estates or guardianship of minors. It means "in the matter of." Another term often used is "ex p." or "ex parte" meaning "on the application of." A final abbreviation found in criminal cases is "ex rel." as in *R. ex rel. Jones v. Smith*. This means "on the information of" and indicates a privately commenced prosecution by Jones against Smith.

Following the style of cause we see an array of dates, letters and numbers. The first things to look for to make sense of these are the semi-colons. These indicate breaks in the citations for judgments from different levels of courts. In our example we may break the citation down as follows using the semi-colons:

(A) [1975] 3 W.W.R. 622;

(B) (1976) 73 D.L.R.(3d) 35, [1976] 5 W.W.R. 240;

(c) var'd 83 D.L.R. (3d) 480, [1978] 2 S.C.R. 267, [1978] 1 W.W.R. 607, 3 C.C.L.T. 257, 19 N.R. 552.

These indicate the trial court, appeal court and Supreme Court of Canada decisions in the case. The trial court decision was reported in only one regional report. The Appellate Court decision was reported in that same regional report and in a national reporter. The highest court decision is reported in a number of different types of reports. These are not different judgments but the same decision being reproduced in several different reports.

The dates in brackets are obviously the dates of the different decisions. The trial court decision was in 1975, the Appellate Court the following year, and the Supreme Court in 1978. Sometimes the date is in square brackets [ ] and sometimes in round brackets ( ). There is a reason for this. The square brackets indicate that the date is essential in the citation in order to find the case. Some reports are issued in several annual volumes, perhaps six a year. They are numbered consecutively for that year only and then over again the following year. The trial court citation means that this decision is reported in volume 3 of the *Western Weekly Reports* for the year 1975. The appeal court decision is in volume 5 of the 1976 reports and the Supreme Court decision is reported in volume 1 of the 1978 publication. Other series use a consecutive numbering system across years and one does not have to know the date to find the volume. Dates in round brackets are not essential to finding the case and are given as information only. They can be omitted and the case can still be located. Each report sets a maximum number of volumes that it will publish using consecutive numbers. When this number is reached it starts at one again and issues a new series. The series are indicated by 2d or 3d meaning "second series" and "third series." The first series will usually not have a series designation.

The commas separate different reports of the same case. Because of the numerous reporting services available, the same decision will often be reported in several different reports (especially ones from the Supreme Court of Canada which have national significance.) In our example the highest court decision was reported in five different reports. These multiple citations are given for ease of finding a decision where access to all of the reporting services is limited. If one has access only to the *Dominion Law Reports* and that citation is not given, one might assume that the case was not reported there and give up trying to locate it.

Before or after each set of citations there may an abbreviation such as "var'd.," "aff'd.," "rev'd," or "app'd." These indicate what happened to the case at that particular court level and mean that the case was "varied," "affirmed," "reversed," or "appealed."

Sometimes the jurisdiction and the court rendering the decision are placed in parentheses at the end of the citation, e.g. (P.E.I.S.C.) This indicates that it was a decision of the Supreme Court of Prince Edward Island.

Generally you will only want to look at the highest court decision since it is the one that is binding on all lower courts. Often the higher court may only vary the lower court decision somewhat, as to dollar amounts for example, or affirm it without detailed reasons of its own. In such cases you will have to consult the lower court decision to learn what principles of law were approved and applied in the case.

The same general form of citing cases is used by American and English reports. United States cases do not place brackets around the series of a report (e.g. N.Y.S.2d) and the year is given after the report citation rather than before.

Knowing this information does not enable quick access to the law unless one is able to find the citation for the case or statute dealing with the particular point of law. For this reason there are numerous secondary sources as tools to gain access to these primary authorities. Without such tools you would have to look through every volume of statutes, regulations, and law reports until you stumbled across something that was relevant to your problem.

Secondary Authority

Secondary sources not only help to locate the sometimes elusive primary source but also provide an interpretation of that source. These interpretations are not exact statements of the law; they are only the editor's or writer's opinion as to what the cases or statutes have said. For this reason the primary source should always be consulted to be certain of what the law itself says.

Secondary authorities have been developed to gain access to each type of primary source. Some have been developed specifically for case law and others for statute law. Others are more comprehensive and provide access to all primary sources. We will consider some of the general types of secondary authority with specific reference to the more popular Canadian publications. Remember, this is not an exhaustive listing of all secondary sources; rather it is a selected version of some of the more useful materials.

Statute Citators

Statute citators are publications which list statutes and provide a variety of comment on the statutes, section by section. They may include a legislative history of the section, regulations made under that section, as well as judicial interpretations of the section. These are available for both federal and provincial statutes.

For federal statutes there is the *Canada Statute Citator* which lists all federal statutes except the *Criminal Code* and *Income Tax Act* and provides summaries of cases which have dealt with any section of the act. The main text also gives any amendments to the statute. If a particular section has not been the subject of judicial comment, that section is not listed. If no part of the act has been considered by a court, the act is listed with a comment that there are no cases to report.

In addition, the *Canadian Abridgment* (discussed below) has volumes of *Statutes Judicially Considered* which are updated by *Canadian Current Law*. These serve as statute citators for both federal and provincial statutes.

There are statute citators for the provincial statutes as well, such as the *Ontario Statute Citator* or *Statutes of Saskatchewan Judicially Considered*. For the Maritime Provinces these are usually found as part of a provincial law report's index or digest volume.

Annotated Statutes

Certain federal statutes such as the *Criminal Code*, the *Income Tax Act*, and the *Divorce Act* have been the subject of much judicial comment and have separately published annotated versions which give not only the text of the statute but serve as a citator by digesting various cases that have considered under each section. Perhaps the most popular of these is *Martin's Annual Criminal Code* which includes not only the *Criminal Code* but also related statutes such as the *Young Offenders Act*.

Indexes for Law Reports

Cases are published in chronological order and not by topic; thus the only practical means of gaining access to them is through an index or digest. Each report has an index in individual volumes and also publishes a periodic comprehensive index covering a number of volumes. Key words such as "negligence" are listed alphabetically together with other limiting words. By scanning the relevant key words one will be directed to cases that can be searched for relevance to the problem.

For example, if you are looking for cases dealing with liability of a school board for accidents on the playground you may start your search under any of several key words such as "schools" or "negligence." Beside each of the key words will be listed other key words which assist in limiting the topic even further. For example you may find a listing as follows "Negligence – school board – liability – injury to pupil – playground accident – recess – duty of supervision." This may be preceded by a listing such as, "Negligence – school board – liability – injury to pupil – bus accident." Each additional word further defines the subject matter of the case to enable you to find those that are most relevant to your research.

These indexes are limited to that particular report and will not refer you to unreported cases or cases that appear only in another reporting series. To find more cases a digest or legal encyclopedia must be consulted.

Digests

Digests may consist of only a case summary digest or they may be a more comprehensive digest giving an overview of legislation as well as case summaries. These digests are arranged by legal topic. Some may be comprehensive while others are confined to specific topics such as family law.

The most comprehensive of these publications is the *Canadian Abridgment* (Second Edition) cited as Can. Abr. (2d) consisting of over fifty volumes including updating materials. It is arranged alphabetically by topic and includes a section on "Schools." Under each topic there are more specific subtopics which are easily accessed through the Table of Contents or the Index. The original thirty-eight volumes are supplemented by periodic additions called Permanent Supplements and a looseleaf current supplement. There are also volumes of words and phrases that have been judicially considered as well as case and statute citator volumes. The *Canadian Abridgment* is updated monthly by a companion publication called

Canadian Current Law (C.C.L.). One limiting factor with this digest is that it only provides information on reported cases.

Another comprehensive publication is the *Canadian Encyclopedic Digest* (C.E.D.) which is published in a Western and an Ontario edition. These deal not only with case digests but also with legislation. They are also arranged by general topics and are used in the same manner as the *Canadian Abridgment*.

Each province or region has a variety of current digests on unreported cases. On a national basis there are the *All-Canada Weekly Summaries* and *Dominion Report Service* that give digests of current cases arranged by topics on a weekly and monthly basis. Legal publishers produce a variety of provincial summaries of reported and unreported cases such as *Manitoba Decisions, Butterworth's Ontario Digest* or *British Columbia Weekly Law Digest*.

Digests are also produced for specific topics, such as criminal law or family law. One digest of particular importance to teachers is *School Law Commentary* which provides digests of recent cases dealing with all aspects of school law and provides a full text service of cases. It is available by annual subscription from *School Law Commentary*, Box 3238, Station D, Edmonton, Alberta, T5L 4J1.

Case Citators

After finding a case of relevance, it is important to know if it is still a correct statement of current law. To find out how it has been treated by other courts, there are publications known as case citators that will refer you to decisions which have considered that particular case.

These are also known as *Tables of Cases Judicially Considered*. One such service is available as part of the *Canadian Abridgment*. The *Dominion Law Reports* also publish case citators. Many reports also give listings of previous cases considered in each volume as well as in their general indexes.

These case citators indicate the manner in which the particular case was treated by the other court. The common abbreviations used are as follows: Affd. – Affirmed on appeal, Apld. – Applied by another court in reaching its decision, Dist. – Distinguished by another court as being different on points of fact or law and therefore not controlling, Folld. – Followed as a leading precedent in the area, Over. – Overruled the principle of law, Rev. – Reversed on appeal.

If the case you have found as authority has been distinguished or overruled frequently by other courts, you should look to the subsequent cases for the correct authority. If it has been followed consistently and applied by other courts you will want to look at those cases as additional authority or for extensions of the legal principles involved.

Textbooks

The term "textbook" does not necessarily mean that it is a teaching aid, although that is one use of such a publication. Textbooks are also valuable research tools for dealing with a specific topic. Texts may deal with very broad or extremely limited topics and may provide an overview of the law as of the date of publication. They can become dated and must be revised because of the rapidly changing status of the law; however, they provide a more in-depth discussion of the topic than is available in a digest.

Some law school texts are actually "casebooks" or collections of relevant cases for the subject and offer little by way of commentary. Others are collections of essays on particular topics which may be a forum for suggesting change rather than a statement of what the law is currently (although that could be a necessary part of any discussion for change.)

Legal Periodicals

These publications include law school reviews, bar association journals and special subject publications. The articles are usually current and often may be theoretical or critical of current law. Some non-legal periodicals carry legal articles of interest to their particular readers; this is especially true in the field of education.

Articles in these publications are accessed through one of the indexes to legal periodicals. The major Canadian indexes are the *Index to Canadian Periodical Literature* and the *Index to Canadian Legal Literature*. The *Index to Legal Periodicals* and the *Current Law Index* cover Canada, the United States and other common law jurisdictions. In addition to consulting these sources, teachers should also use the indexes to their own educational periodicals which cover many topics of a legal nature.

Legal Dictionaries

These are useful to helping you understand the meaning of legal phrases which will be encountered in your research. The most popular is *Black's Law Dictionary* which is an American publication. A comprehensive Canadian dictionary is *The Encyclopedia of Words and Phrase, Legal*

Maxims, Canada. The *Canadian Abridgment* also has a separate Words and Phrases volume as does the *Canadian Encyclopedic Digest.*

Computerized Research

Many of these databases of information are now accessible through computers. The researcher defines the problem in terms of essential key words that must appear in the decision or statute and the computer scans its databases for those words and provides a printed digest of all cases, statutes and regulations wherein they appear. Facilities for this type of research are available through law school and major courthouse law libraries. It is a rapid method of gaining initial information but this must be supplemented by manual research since not all reports or statutes are in the database.

This service is offered by several companies. A fee is charged for computer time as well as communication time between the terminal and the main computer. The Canadian Service is called *QUICLAW* and is run from Kingston, Ontario by QL Systems Ltd. Its database is fairly comprehensive and includes W.W.R., D.L.R., A.C.W.S., A.P., F.C.R., S.C.R., C.C.C., W.C.B., federal and provincial statutes, some regulations and some statute citators.

Other major collections of databases are *LEXIS* and *WESTLAW* in the United States and *EUROLEX* in Europe.

Table of Abbreviations

The following list of abbreviations for reporting services is by no means comprehensive. It is only a listing of the major reporting services which may be of assistance to the reader. There are more extensive lists available that should be consulted for other publications not listed here.

United States

A.	Atlantic Reporter
A.L.R.	American Law Reports
Cal. Rptr.	California Reporter
F.	Federal Reporter
F. Supp.	Federal Supplement
N.E.	North Eastern Reporter
N.W.	North Western Reporter
N.Y.S.	New York Supplement
P.	Pacific Reporter

S.	Southern Reporter
S.C.	Supreme Court Reporter
S.E.	South Eastern Reporter
S.W.	South Western Reporter
U.S.	United States Supreme Court Reports

Great Britain

A.C.	Law Reports, Appeal Cases, House of Lords
All E.R.	All England Law Reports
Ch.	Law Reports, Chancery Division Crim.
L.R.	Criminal Law Reports
E.R.	English Reports
J.P.	Justice of the Peace
K.B.	Law Reports, King's Bench Division
Q.B.	Law Reports, Queen's Bench Division
S.J.	Solicitor's Journal
T.L.R.	The Times Law Reports
W.L.R.	Weekly Law Reports

Canada

Admin. L.R.	Administrative Law Reports
A.C.W.S.	All-Canada Weekly Summaries
A.P.R.	Atlantic Provinces Reports
A.R.	Alberta Reports
A.W.L.D.	Alberta Weekly Law Digest
Alta. D.	Alberta Decisions
Alta. L.R.	Alberta Law Reports
B.C.L.R.	British Columbia Law Reports
B.C.R.	British Columbia Reports
B.C.W.L.D.	British Columbia Weekly Law Digest
B.O.D.	Butterworth's Ontario Digest
C.C.C.	Canadian Criminal Cases
C.C.L.	Canadian Current Law
C.C.L.T.	Canadian Cases on the Law of Torts
C.H.R.R.	Canadian Human Rights Reporter
C.L.L.C.	Canadian Labour Law Cases
C.L.T.	Canadian Law Times
C.P.R.	Canadian Patent Reporter
C.R.	Criminal Reports
C.R.R.	Canadian Regulatory Reporter and Canadian Rights Reporter
C.W.L.S.	Canadian Weekly Law Sheet

Can. Gaz.	The Canada Gazette
Can. L.R.B.R.	Canadian Labour Relations Boards Reports
D.L.R.	Dominion Law Reports
D.R.S.	Dominion Report Service
L.A.C.	Labour Arbitration Cases
M.P.R.	Maritime Province Reports
Man. D.	Manitoba Decisions
Man. L.R.	Manitoba Law Reports
Man. R.	Manitoba Reports
N.B.R.	New Brunswick Reports
N.R.	National Reporter
N.S.R.	Nova Scotia Reports
Nfld.&P.E.I.R.	Newfoundland and Prince Edward Island Reports
O.L.R.	Ontario Law Reports
O.R.	Ontario Reports
O.W.N.	Ontario Weekly Notes
Ont. D.	Ontario Decisions
P.E.I.R.	Prince Edward Island Reports
R.F.L.	Reports of Family Law
S.C.C.D.	Supreme Court of Canada Decisions
S.C.R.	Supreme Court Reports
Sask. D.	Saskatchewan Decisions
Sask. R.	Saskatchewan Reports
W.C.B.	Weekly Criminal Bulletin
W.D.F.L.	Weekly Digest of Family Law
W.W.R.	Western Weekly Reports

Discussion and Review Questions

1. Explain this citation in your own words:
   Thorton et al. v. Board of School Trustees of School District No. 57 (Prince George) et al., [1975] 3 W.W.R. 622; (1976) 73 D.L.R. (3d) 35, [1976] 5 W.W.R. 240; var'd 83 D.L.R. (3d) 480, [1978] 2 S.C.R. 267 [1978] 1 W.W.R. 607, 3 C.C.L.T. 257, 19 N.R. 552.

2. Try your skill at finding the answers to the following questions. First, stop and think what primary source may contain the answer and then what secondary source may help you to locate the law in that primary source.

   (a) What restrictions are placed on teachers in British Columbia regarding the length of detention that a pupil may be given?

(b) If a student picks up a piece of wire on the playground and injures his eye with it, is the school board liable to pay damages for the injury?

References

MacEllven, D.T., *Legal Research Handbook.* 2nd ed., Toronto: Butterworth's, 1986.

Roberts, Tim, *Taking the Law Into Your Own Hands: a guide to legal research.* Vancouver: Legal Services Society of British Columbia, 1981.

Part Two

Criminal Law Problems

If there were no bad people there would be no good lawyers.
Charles Dickens
The Old Curiosity Shop

4

Copyright Law

Some of the things which you will learn from reading this chapter include the following:

1. The impact of copyright legislation and its violation upon the teacher.

2. That much of the material which the teacher reads regarding copyright laws has its basis in United States legislation.

3. What the Canadian producers of copyrighted materials are seeking.

4. That the producers of copyright materials have a very legitimate legal and moral claim to the enforcement of copyright laws respecting teacher violations.

5. What the Canadian teacher needs respecting copyright.

6. What the current copyright clearance procedures are for copyrighted materials.

7. That teachers may be producers of copyrighted materials.

8. How employers may be held liable for instances where teachers violate copyright laws during their employment.

Preview

School teachers stand in grave danger of violating Canadian copyright legislation because they are unaware of the exact nature of the law, or because of the press of their daily situation. Frequently teachers are provided with insufficient or inadequate instructional materials and so they proceed to rectify the situation by making copies of commercially prepared texts, exercise books, tapes, and computer software.

When teachers violate copyright laws they do two things. First they rob the rightful owner of his income, and second they demonstrate lawlessness to their students. While motivated by the best interest of their students, they may not act in the eventual best interest of themselves or their students.

There is a great deal of false information in circulation to teachers regarding the nature of copyright legislation, what is fair use, and how approval to use copyrighted materials is obtained from the producer. This is due to a situation wherein Canadian copyright legislation which is old has been under review for a number of years without subsequent government action, and because United States legislature in this field has recently been up-dated. Since the Canadian school teacher has access to much American produced printed materials, be also has access to the American produced brochures, pamphlets and other printed materials which explain and elaborate upon recent changes.

There exists some strong legal indication that school boards could be held responsible for the copyright violations of the teachers which they employ through the principle that the employer can be held responsible for the actions of the employee if the employee is acting within the course of his employment. The Golden Rule principal of do unto others may be the most telling argument of all for the classroom teacher since teachers produce a considerable amount of instructional material some of which is copyrighted.

Self-Assessment

1. Do you know what types of materials can be copyrighted?
2. Do you know how much of a work can be produced before you have violated a copyright?
3. Do you understand what the term "fair dealing" means?
4. Do you understand the difference between "in corporeal" and "corporeal" property, and how the distinction relates to the work of the classroom teacher with regards to the production of instructional materials?
5. How does one know when a workbook, for example, has been copyrighted?

Key Terms

Fair dealing
Incorporeal property
Corporeal property
Right of integrity

*   *   *   *

Copyright laws interact with the daily activities of the classroom teacher despite the fact that many teachers never give these laws a second thought or may not be aware that their actions in the classroom might be curtailed by a strict application of such laws. Educators, as a group, may well be the major infringers of our *Copyright Act*. This is due to a general lack of knowledge concerning these laws coupled with the pressing need for readily accessible materials for teaching purposes. Even in situations where teachers are cognizant of the legal requirements to comply with copyright laws, they often deliberately infringe upon them because of the immediacy of their need for instructional material. Given the fluid nature of today's classroom, the article that is relevant for today's class may not be relevant in a few weeks or months later (the time that it may take to get copyright clearance). Because the book trade in Canada is especially concerned about the increasing number of copyright infringements which are occurring in Canadian educational institutions, it has embarked upon an active program to heighten the awareness of educators about the gravity of such infringements. Publishers feel that if all sectors of the academic community become aware of the nature of these laws and the issues and interests at stake, educators will more likely adhere to the necessary compliance procedures.

Educational infringements of copyright laws cover a broad range of activities. They include such things as making multiple photocopies of print material for classroom use, making unauthorized video or audio recordings, as well as "pirating" computer software. There appears to be an inherent conflict between the teacher's legitimate desire to make information available to students (as rapidly and inexpensively as possible) and the equally strong and legitimate desire of the copyright holder to ensure that legal requirements are followed and that he receives fair compensation for his work. A major aim of all copyright legislation is to resolve this conflict in an equitable manner. Certain jurisdictions, notably the United States, have granted educators broad immunity from the application of these laws. Other jurisdictions, including Canada, have not. Canadian copyright law does provide certain exemptions which may be applicable to educators but these exemptions are much more restrictive than those adopted by our southern neighbour.

Our present *Copyright Act* (which has remained basically unaltered since 1924) is currently the subject of much debate concerning needed reform. There have been numerous reports, inquiries and royal commissions designed to bring about reform. The interests of both educators and creators of copyrighted works have been presented clearly and forcefully. Hopefully, a reformed Act can accommodate the legitimate needs and interests of all parties concerned. Until such reform occurs, however, educators are bound by the existing law and must strive for obedience.

At the date of this publication, Bill C-60, a proposed new *Copyright Act* was before the Parliament of Canada. Despite pleas from groups of educators it contains no special educational exemptions although some form of exemption has been promised in subsequent amendments to the Act. This Bill makes specific reference to computer programs and provides for the establishment of a Copyright Board with power to make regulations. It also provides for licensing bodies in which groups of creators can band together for collective management of licensing fees and permission granting.

A note of caution is in order at this point. The United States revised and reformed its copyright law in 1976. Their act provides broad educational exemptions which have been the subject of many books, articles and pamphlets intended as guidelines for teachers. These are readily available in Canada and may be misconstrued by Canadian teachers as a reflection of the current state of the law in Canada. These materials deal only with United States law and are inapplicable in Canada. Carefully check all resource material on this subject to ensure that it reflects Canadian, not American, law. The American guidelines could, of course, be consulted as a model for reform and could serve as a basis for discussion. They should not be relied upon for authority and guidance concerning teacher conduct.

In addition to the legal considerations, broad moral and ethical questions are raised in any discussion of copyright law. The creator of any work relies on that creation for his livelihood. His job is to create and sell that particular work. Every time an unauthorized copy is made, the infringer is stealing a portion of the creator's paycheque. Publishers will no longer pay authors for books if they cannot be guaranteed exclusive rights to publication, and authors will no longer write if they are not paid. Copyright laws provide some economic security for the creator and therefore act as an impetus for further creativity. Morally, it is just as wrong to steal someone's copyright as it is to steal his car. Teachers could, in fact, contribute to a long-run decrease in the flow of information if wholesale copyright infringements are allowed to occur.

Furthermore, the teacher's position as a role model for students requires him to be seen to obey and uphold the laws of our country. This includes copyright laws. If a teacher is observed to be continually breaking these laws, what are the students to think? Are they not equally justified in stealing?

Copyright laws are easily broken with only a minimal chance of detection. In fact, no teacher has ever been sued or charged in Canada for an alleged breach of the *Copyright Act* in the classroom. It is often said that laws should not be passed that cannot be enforced, but this admission does not solve the serious problem. Some proposals for reform advocate the addition of a licensing fee to photocopiers and supplies, computer discs, video and audio tapes, and other modes of reproduction. These fees would be turned over to various author's rights societies for distribution to their members. This system is currently in force for musical works played in clubs and on radio and television. The licensing fees are paid to an association which divides them among members on a pre-determined formula. Implementation of this (or a similar proposal) would eliminate the need for enforcement and ensure compensation of copyright holders for all reproductions made.

Teachers may also be concerned at some point in their career with the *Copyright Act* from the vantage point of a copyright holder. They may author a book, produce an educational film, or design a computer program. The Golden Rule seems particularly appropriate to follow in dealing with copyright materials. Treat the works of others as you would have others treat your copyright of works.

Educators, authors, publishers, producers and others concerned will have to work together to resolve their differences. In the United States they have entered into agreements defining and authorizing educational "fair use" (see Appendix A). In Canada each group is still lobbying to promote its own position. Legislators are reluctant to act on reform in the absence of a consensus on the path such reforms should take. Rather than waiting for the imposition of laws they may not like, all sides should strive for some common ground now in the hope that reform will be implemented that much sooner.

What then is "copyright"? Quite simply, it is the right to publish, copy or reproduce any original literary, dramatic, musical or artistic work: the right to copy. This right is what the law calls an incorporeal property – one without a physical body or substance - as opposed to a corporeal property which has a physical existence. For example, when you purchase a book or a work of art you buy the corporeal or physical body of that work and the rights associated with such ownership. You may sell, give away or even destroy that physical property which you own. The purchase of the physical property does not however, give you the incorporeal rights whereby you have the right to publish your own edition of the book or produce prints of the work of art. These rights are retained by the creator who may in turn sell or transfer them to another person or company.

Specifically, the *Copyright Act* grants to the creator "the sole right to produce or reproduce the work or any substantial part thereof in any material form whatsoever." This includes the right to publish translations, to convert to another form (for example, from a novel to a play), to reproduce in another medium (for example, to produce an audio recording of a book), and to broadcast such work. No one, even for educational purposes, may copy a substantial part of such a work without the permission of the copyright holder who is entitled to charge a fee for granting such consent. This includes photocopies, mimeographs, offset prints or any other means of reprography. It also includes reproduction on audio, video, or computer tapes or discs. Further, copyrighted works may not be placed into information storage and retrieval systems without permission.

In addition to these economic rights, our copyright laws also grant moral rights to the creator. These are designed to enable the creator to protect his reputation and prevent any distortion or mutilation of his work. This "right of integrity" allows the creator to restrain any mutilation, distortion, or modification of his work that would be prejudicial to his honour or reputation. An example of the enforcement of such rights can be found in the highly publicized case of *Snow v. The Eaton Centre Ltd.* (1983) 70 C.P.R. (2d) 105 (Ont. High Ct.) which involved a Toronto artist who sued a shopping mall for placing red ribbons around the necks of his sculpture of Canada geese as part of the mall's Christmas decorations. The artist was successful and the court ordered the ribbons removed. Teachers should be aware of these moral rights and should accept and encourage respect for artistic integrity. Teachers are certainly free to criticize and comment upon artistic works but they should allow the creator to retain his artistic integrity.

Not all works are covered by copyright laws. Copyright in a work exists only for a specified period of time: usually the creator's lifetime plus an additional fifty years thereafter. Upon expiry of this period, the work falls into what is called "public domain" and may be published or produced by anyone. The works of Shakespeare for example may be published and sold by anyone so inclined to do. Caution must be exercised when dealing with publications of such works containing annotations or commentary. These annotations and comments are, themselves, original works and may be subject to copyright. They should be treated in the same manner as any other original copyrighted work.

The *Copyright Act* speaks in broad terms of literary, dramatic, musical, and artistic works. Modern technological advances are not specifically referred to in the Act. The most advanced technical terminology to be found includes reference to "perforated roll," "cinematograph film", and "radio communication"; however, this does not mean that modern advances in communication are not covered by the Act. Our courts have interpreted these broad categories to include such things as videotapes, audiotapes, photographs, and computer software, the – "contrivances" mentioned in s. 3(1)d of the Act. Proposals for reform deal more specifically with these media and in particular with computer software.

Software "piracy" is a major problem not only in schools but within the computer industry itself. It takes many hours, even years, to create certain programs which can be copied in a matter of seconds. The industry is making a concerted effort to stop such practices and there have been prosecutions of people who have sold unauthorized copies. The expense of many programs makes it almost impossible for schools to acquire adequate supplies for educational use. There are, however, many sources of "public domain" software which can be obtained and copied very economically. Many of these programs are often as good as the expensive commercial programs and preclude the possibility of being faced with breach of copyright charges.

Bill C-60 includes specific reference to "fair dealing" with computer software. The proposed law would allow someone who is in lawful possession of an authorized copy of a program to make one or more back-up copies of the program provided he uses no more than one copy at any given time and destroys all copies when he ceases to be in lawful possession of the original.

It is only the actual work itself that is subject to copyright protection and not the idea behind it. The first person to write a novel about life on Mars does not acquire the exclusive right to create all future works on the subject. Anyone else is free to create his own original work based on this idea. This accounts for the numerous books, movies and television shows based on a common idea. The idea itself may be freely used by anyone. A practical example of this principle can be seen in two court cases involving a Belgian teacher.

Georges Cuisenaire developed a system for teaching mathematics to primary school children using wooden rods of varying lengths and colours.

He wrote a book describing his system and also published tables describing the sizes and colours of the rods. His method acquired some popularity and he granted licenses to various manufacturers around the world to produce and sell his "Cuisenaire rods." Other parties began to produce their own versions of these rods and sold them without compensation to Cuisenaire and in direct competition with those manufacturers who had paid licensing fees.

Cuisenaire brought legal action against one such unauthorized manufacturer in Australia. The Supreme Court of Victoria in *Cuisenaire v. Reed* [1963] V.R. 719 held that the rods themselves were not works of "artistic" craftsmanship since no special skill was required to make them. The court went on to state that although his book and tables were subject to literary copyright there would be no infringement of that copyright unless the tables or book itself were reproduced. Since the rods did not physically resemble the book or tables, there was no infringement.

Cuisenaire also brought legal action against a Canadian manufacturer in a case which ultimately came before the Supreme Court of Canada. *Georges Cuisenaire v. South West Imports Limited* [1969] S.C.R. 208 held again that the rods themselves were not things in which copyright could be held. The court stated that although one may have copyright in the description of an art, once it has been described, the idea is given to the public for their use. The particular mode of expression of the idea is given protection but not the idea itself. Anyone may take the idea and express it in his own original fashion without compensating the originator of the idea.

The original mode of expression will be protected even where the idea upon which it is based falls into the realm of public knowledge. A particular author's history of ancient Rome will be protected even though it is based on public knowledge and facts that have been known for centuries. The "originality" lies in the manner of presenting those facts. Another case of particular interest to teachers illustrates this principle.

In *University of London Press, Limited v. University Tutorial Press, Limited* [1916] 2 Ch. 601, a private publishing firm reproduced certain university examination papers together with comments and model answers. The university's own publishing house sued for breach of copyright. The court held that the examination papers were original literary works and protected by copyright even though they were not particularly novel and were based on a body of general knowledge. It was the particular form of expression that was protected, the way the words were arranged, and not the ideas behind the words.

What then constitutes an "infringement" of copyright? Section 17(1) of the *Copyright Act* provides:

Copyright in a work shall be deemed to be infringed by any person who, without the consent of the owner of the copyright, does anything that, by this Act, only the owner of the copyright has the right to do.

An infringement is the exercise of any of the exclusive rights of the copyright owner which rights are enumerated in section 3(1) of the Act as follows:

For the purposes of this Act, "copyright" means the sole right to produce or reproduce the work or any substantial part thereof in any material form whatever, to perform, or in the case of a lecture to deliver, the work or any substantial part thereof in public; if the work is unpublished, to publish the work or any substantial part thereof; and includes the sole right:

(a) to produce, reproduce, perform or publish any translation of the work;

(b) in the case of a dramatic work, to convert it into a novel or other non-dramatic work;

(c) in the case of a novel or other non-dramatic work, or of an artistic work, to convert it into a dramatic work, by way of performance in public or otherwise;

(d) in the case of a literary, dramatic, or musical work, to make any record, perforated roll, cinematograph film, or other contrivance by means of which the work may be mechanically performed or delivered;

(e) in the case of any literary, dramatic, musical or artistic work, to reproduce, adapt and publicly present such work by cinematograph, if the author has given such work an original character; but if such original character is absent the cinematograph reproduction shall be protected as a photograph;

(f) in the case of any literary, dramatic, musical or artistic work, to broadcast by radio communication; and to authorize any such acts as aforesaid.

It should be noted that the words "or any substantial part thereof" place limits on these rights. It is not an infringement to copy less than a "substantial part." The Act provides no definition for this term and it is left to judicial interpretation to determine what constitutes a substantial part of any particular work. There is no qualitative or quantitative test that can be universally applied and each particular case will be decided on its own merits and facts. One or two paragraphs from a 500 page novel may not be a substantial part but a whole chapter could be. In the case of a short poem even a single line could be a substantial part. Factors which will be considered by a judge in determining this question include the quantity copied in relation to the whole work, the extent to which the copied material comprises the new work, the importance of the copied material in the original, and whether the new work will be competing with the original.

The *Copyright Act* does provide for some exemptions which can have a limited impact on teachers. Educators, however, would like to see broader educational exemptions similar to those existing in the United States. Creators, on the other hand, argue for no further exemptions for anyone, educators or otherwise. Each side has valid arguments to be made and it will be interesting to see how any reform of our current law will accommodate these diametrically opposed positions.

Creators view educational infringements as no different from any other copyright infringement. All infringements and exemptions have the same economic impact on the creator. They view educational exemptions as a form of subsidy they are asked to provide to schools and question why they are being asked for such concessions while others are not. Teachers do not forego their salaries, suppliers do not give up their profits, the caretaking staff is paid, so why should creators be denied their just recompense? They support education and its aims but feel that they should not be singled out to provide a special subsidy.

Educators argue in favour of such exemptions based on the delays, inconveniences, and difficulties that are encountered in obtaining permission for use of copyright materials. This, coupled with a lack of funds, makes it virtually impossible to provide relevant, timely information without resorting to infringements. School budgets simply do not allow for the purchase of 25 copies of a magazine every time it carries an article that may be educationally useful. What may be timely and necessary for the class this week may not be so in the time required to secure permission to copy. Educators argue that the greater good of an educated public outweighs the financial interests of a small segment of the population. They point out that creators would not profit by stricter rules and enforcement since educators simply cannot buy any more books, magazines, videos or films. It is felt that profits of creators are not being decreased by educational infringement in a measurable amount, so why not grant an exemption to educators?

And so the debate continues. Until it is resolved, the present exemptions for educational use are found in section 17 of the *Copyright Act* which provides:

> 2. The following acts do not constitute an infringement of copyright:
>
> (a) any fair dealing with any work for the purposes of private study, research, criticism, review or newspaper summary . . .
>
> (d) the publication in a collection, mainly composed of non-copyrighted matter, bona fide intended for the use of schools, and so described in the title and in any advertisements issued by the

publisher, of short passages from published literary works, not themselves published for the use of schools, in which copyright subsists, if not more than two of such passages from works by the same author are published by the same publisher within five years, and the source from which such passages are taken is acknowledged.

(3) No church, college or school and no religious, charitable or fraternal organizations shall be held liable to pay any compensation to the owner of any musical work or to any person claiming through him by reason of the public performance of any musical work in furtherance of a religious, educational or charitable object.

As can be seen, these exemptions are indeed limited and do not provide any blanket "fair use" or "fair dealing" privilege for educators. Copies may only be made for private study, and not for distribution to the class. Teachers may compile anthologies using copyrighted material providing that the majority of the anthology consists of original material not subject to copyright. Even this is restricted to two brief passages every five years. Wholesale reproductions of copyrighted works for school use are simply not allowed. Subsection 3 allows music classes and school concerts to function without payment of royalties to composers. Note that this only applies to musical works and does not include dramatic performances. School plays must follow the same rules that any other theatre group has to follow.

The act provides for both civil and criminal remedies on behalf of a party whose rights have been violated. On the civil side, the owner of the copyright may sue anyone who infringes upon his copyright and may recover monetary damages. In addition the court may grant other relief, including an order prohibiting further infringement or an order that all copies and plates for making them be turned over to the owner of the copyright. Criminal sanctions are in the form of creation of an offence for anyone making, selling, or distributing a protected work without authorization. The penalty is a fine for a first offence and a fine and/or imprisonment for any subsequent offences. The criminal court may also make an order for the disposition of infringing copies and of the plates for making them.

Civil liability for copyright infringement extends not only to the person actually making the copies but also to any person or corporation who authorizes such breach. In Australia, a university was held liable in damages for providing a coin-operated photocopier without exercising any control over what materials were being copied. In *Moorhouse v. University of New South Wales* (1974) 23 F.L.R. 112 the court held that by creating a facility likely to be abused, the university authorized any breaches that took place there. Thus, when teachers and students commit breaches of the Act on school copiers, the school board may also be held liable if the circumstances of the case show that the board did not exercise sufficient control over the machine to prevent abuse.

To avoid liability for infringement, the user of copyrighted material must obtain permission for use from the copyright owner. The owner may request a fee for the granting of such permission or may refuse altogether. A handbook called *Copyright Compliance* has been produced by a coalition of publishers; it sets out the recommended procedure for obtaining permission. The relevant portions are reproduced in Appendix B (with permission). Although this format is designed for printed material, it could be used with modifications for video, audio or computer software copies as well.

Teachers may also be interested in copyright law with a view to protecting their own works. The creator of any work capable of being copyrighted automatically owns the first copyright in such work. Section 12 (3) of the *Copyright Act* provides, however:

> Where the author was in the employment of some other person under a contract of service or apprenticeship and the work was made in the course of his employment by that person, the person by whom the author was employed shall, in the absence of any agreement to the contrary, be the first owner of the copyright.

When a teacher authors a book in the course of his employment by a school board, it will be the board who owns the copyright and not the teacher (unless the contract of employment provides otherwise). Most employment contracts are silent on this issue, placing the onus on any teacher who may become involved in such a situation to make sure that the contract specifies who shall own the copyright. If the book is produced on the teacher's own time, using his own facilities and materials, then ownership would remain with the teacher since it was not produced in the course of his employment but entirely outside of it.

Registration of a copyright is not compulsory in Canada nor is it required to gain the protection afforded by the Act. The Act does provide a method of voluntary registration by filing a form of notice with the Copyright Office. A copy of the work being being registered is not required. The purpose of this registration system is to give notice to the public at large as to ownership of a particular copyright. A certificate showing such registration may be produced in court proceedings as evidence of ownership. Evidence in court proceedings involving copyrighted works can be facilitated where the work has been registered. A certificate of registration can be entered in evidence to prove ownership rather than trying to prove all of the particulars surrounding the creation of the work.

An international copyright symbol has been adopted to give notice of the existence of copyright and the name of the owner. The symbol is an encircled C © followed by the year and name of the owner. The creator of any work should place this information on all copies of his work to ensure that notice is brought to the attention of anyone dealing with that work. Infringers cannot then plead that they were not aware that it was copyrighted material.

The Act places a heavy onus on the creator to ensure that his rights are maintained. Unlike other criminal offences, the police are not constantly checking for breaches of the *Copyright Act*. It is up to the owner to detect these breaches and to lay charges when warranted. As a practical matter, small scale and individual infringers are rarely detected and prosecuted. Due to the industry's growing concern with educational infringements, it would not be surprising to see a test case emerge against a large school board in the near future, particularly if reform of the *Copyright Act* is not forthcoming.

Discussion and Review Questions

1. What types of educational materials are copyrighted?
2. What is the penalty for violating copyright?
3. How much of a work can you produce before you have violated a copyright?
4. What procedures must the teacher use in order to receive approval to use materials which have been copyrighted?

You be the Judge

Bill Euclid was a mathematics teacher employed by Metropolis School Board. He developed a system for testing his students which involved the use of flash cards bearing mathematical fact problems which were to be administered in a predetermined sequence. In addition to the cards he also prepared a similar series of test sheets. Both items were designed as a diagnostic tool for determining level of ability and specific problem areas. It required years of teaching and modification before Bill perfected the sequence and the particular problems to use. He tested the system with his classes and other teachers' classes in the school and found that it was very accurate and reliable.

Bill wrote a detailed booklet outlining his theory and describing the proper procedure for administration of the tests. Being justifiably proud of his system, he approached a company called EDSYSTEMS, INC. which manufactured educational materials to see if they would be interested in publishing his system. They were and entered into a contract whereby Bill assigned his copyright to EDSYSTEMS in exchange for a lump sum payment as well as a royalty on each set sold. The company began to produce and sell kits containing Bill's booklet, a set of the flash cards and a series of his test sheets.

Tom Jones, principal of Shakespeare Elementary School, also in the Metropolis School Board, purchased one of these EDSYSTEMS kits. He was so impressed that he photocopied the entire kit on the school photocopier and distributed one to each pupil in the school to take home. He sent along a note enlisting the parents' support in monitoring their child on a regular basis using the system. He felt that this would be a good demonstration of each child's progress in math rather than just relying on report card marks.

One of the children returning home with a photocopied kit was Henry Euclid, Bill's 11-year-old son. Bill was furious. He had just been deprived of royalty payments on 475 kits. He contacted EDSYSTEMS who launched a civil action against Principal Jones and the Metropolis School Board for breach of copyright.

Issues for Decision

(1) Are mathematical fact problems, whether contained on flash cards or test sheets, capable of being copyrighted?

(2) Is Bill's system of presenting these problems in a pre-determined sequence capable of being copyrighted?

(3) Was this system created by Bill "in the course of his employment" and therefore does the school board own the copyright?

(4) Was the distribution to the students a matter of "private study" being intended for home use and therefore a fair dealing with the work?

(5) Assuming the board placed no limits or control on the use of the photocopier, would they be considered to be authorizing any breaches of copyright law that occurred on the machine?

Point/Counterpoint

We have seen how the courts in Canada handled the matter of the Cuisenaire rods in *Cuisenaire v. South West Imports Ltd.* In arriving at his decision Mr. Justice Noel of the Exchequer Court of Canada was confronted with an American decision that expressed a different point of view.

> I was also somewhat concerned when I ran across an American decision rendered in 1966 in *The Gelles-Widmer Company v. Milton Bradley Company et al.* (136 USPQ 240) where the subject matter dealt with was not too different from the one involved in the instant case.
>
> It was indeed held in that case that a flash card set that was solely utilitarian inasmuch as the cards were designed specifically for use by children in the home as educational aids, was not for that reason incapable of being the subject matter of copyright. These flash cards bore words, numbers and pictures to be shown in school drills to stimulate observation or as an aid in teaching reading and arithmetic.
>
> I should point out that in addition to these flash cards containing the arithmetic fact problems, the plaintiff, in this American case, had also drafted testing sheets which could be used for determining the development and progress the child was making as well as explanations and instructions for the child and the parents explaining the proper use of both the flash cards and the progress testing sheets . . .
>
> It is rather interesting to note, however, that the American decision held these cards "copyrightable" even if such a finding had the effect of protecting not only the expression of the author's idea or system, but also the very idea or system itself and one may wonder whether there has been an enlargement of the subject matter of copyright in that country.

This American case would have been decided differently by a Canadian court. Justice Noel seems to think that the American court went too far in its decision. How far should copyright protection be extended to educational materials such as the Cuisenaire rods or flash cards?

Appendix A

The following is the text of an agreement between representatives of the educational community and representatives of publishers and authors. It is an example of the type of guidelines for educational use that may be negotiated. See if such an agreement would meet your classroom requirements or what modifications or additions you would like to see incorporated in such an agreement.

AGREEMENT ON GUIDELINES FOR CLASSROOM COPYING

The purpose of the following guidelines is to state the minimum and not the maximum standards of educational fair use under Section 107 of H.R. 2223. The parties agree that the conditions determining the extent of permissible copying for educational purposes may change in the future; that certain types of copying permitted under these guidelines may not be permissible in the future; and conversely that in the future other types of copying not permitted under these guidelines may be permissible under revised guidelines. Moreover, the following statement of guidelines is not intended to limit the types of copying permitted under the standards of fair use under judicial decision and which are stated in Section 107 of the Copyright Revision Bill. There may be instances in which copying which does not fall within the guidelines stated below may nonetheless be permitted under the criteria of fair use.

GUIDELINES

I. SINGLE COPYING FOR TEACHERS:

A single copy may be made of any of the following by or for a teacher at his or her individual request for his or her scholarly research or use in teaching or preparation to teach a class:

A. A chapter from a book;

B. An article from a periodical or newspaper;

C. A short story, short essay or short poem, whether or not from a collective work;

D. A chart, graph, diagram, drawing, cartoon or picture from a book, periodical, or newspaper;

II. MULTIPLE COPIES FOR CLASSROOM USE:

Multiple copies (not to exceed in any event more then one copy per pupil in a course) may be made by or for the teacher giving the course for classroom use or discussion; provided that:

A. The copying meets the test of brevity and spontaneity as defined below; and,

B. Meets the cumulative effect test as defined below; and

C. Each copy includes a notice of copyright.

DEFINITIONS:

Brevity:

i. Poetry: (a) A complete poem if less then 250 words and if printed on not more than two pages or (b) from a longer poem, an excerpt of not more than 250 words.

ii. Prose: (a) Either a complete article, story or essay of less than 2,500 words, or (b) an excerpt from any prose work of not more than 1,000 words or 10% of the work, whichever is less, but in any event a minimum of 500 words. [Each of the numerical limits stated in "i" and "ii" above may be expanded to permit the completion of an unfinished line of a poem or of an unfinished prose paragraph.]

iii. Illustration: One chart, graph, diagram, drawing, cartoon or picture per book or per periodical issue.

iv. "Special" works: Certain works in poetry, prose or in "poetic prose" which often combine language with illustrations and which are intended sometimes for children and at other times for a more general audience fall short of 2,500 words in their entirety. Paragraph "ii" above notwithstanding such "special works" may not be reproduced in their entirety; however, an excerpt comprising not more than two of the published pages of such special work and containing not more than 10% of the words found in the text thereof, may be reproduced.

Spontaneity:

i. The copying is at the instance and inspiration of the individual teacher, and

ii. The inspiration and decision to use the work and the moment of its use for maximum teaching effectiveness are so close in time that it would be unreasonable to expect a timely reply to a request for permission.

Cumulative Effect:

i. The copying of the material is for only one course in the school in which the copies are made.

ii. Not more than one short poem, article, story, essay or two excerpts may be copied from the same author, nor more than three from the same collective work or periodical volume during one class term.

iii. There shall not be more than nine instances of such multiple copying for one course during one class term.

[The limitations stated in "ii" and "iii" above shall not apply to current news periodicals and newspapers and current news sections of other periodicals.]

III. PROHIBITIONS AS TO I AND II ABOVE:

Notwithstanding any of the above, the following shall be prohibited:

A. Copying shall not be used to create or to replace or substitute for anthologies, compilations or collective works. Such replacement or substitution may occur whether copies of various works or excerpts therefrom are accumulated or are reproduced and used separately.

B. There shall be no copying of or from works intended to be "consumable" in the course of study or of teaching. These include workbooks, exercises, standardized tests and test booklets and answer sheets and like consumable material.

C. Copying shall not:

a. substitute for the purchase of books, publisher's reprints or periodicals;

b. be directed by higher authority;

c. be repeated with respect to the same item by the same teacher from term to   term.

D. No charge shall be made to the student beyond the actual cost of the photocopying.

AGREED

March 19, 1976

AD HOC COMMITTEE ON   AUTHOR-PUBLISHER GROUP
COPYRIGHT REVISION LAW   AUTHORS LEAGUE OF AMERICA
                                           ASSOCIATION OF AMERICAN
                                           PUBLISHERS, INC.

Appendix B
Copyright Compliance

This material was prepared and published jointly by the Canadian Booksellers Association, Canadian Book Publishers' Council and Association of Canadian Publishers in a handbook *Copyright Compliance.*

Procedure for Seeking Permission

How does one obtain permission to reproduce copies of copyright material? We have set forth below an expeditious procedure for requesting such permission. The procedure consists of three simple steps:

Step 1: Obtain Name and Address of the publisher

The title page or the verso of the title page in most books will contain the copyright notice, the year the work was published and the name and address of the publisher. To ensure that the address is up to date, or in the event that the address does not appear, the publisher's address may be readily obtained by reference to *The Book Trade in Canada,* a reference work published annually by Ampersand Communications and found in most libraries. For the United States, consult the *Literary Marketplace.* International listings may be found in the *International Literary Marketplace.* In addition, the Canadian Book Publishers' Council and the Association of Canadian Publishers publish annual directories of members. Even if the author is the copyright owner, the first inquiry should be addressed to the publisher since it is usually the publisher who has the right to authorize reprints. If this is not the case, the publisher will be able to refer the request to the appropriate person.

Step 2: Fill Out Form A

The permission request must contain sufficient information to allow a publisher to evaluate the request. Form A, reproduced at the end of this Handbook, is provided to ensure that complete information is given. Many delays in processing permissions to date have been due to the inadequate information sent by the requesting party. If frequent requests are made by the educational institution, Form A can be freely duplicated and used as necessary.

Step 3: Send Request in Form B

A suggested letter of request, designed to accompany Form A, is set out as Form B at the end of this Handbook. It is addressed to the publisher's permissions department, and should be written on the letterhead of the requesting institution. If frequent requests of this kind are made, it is recommended that a standard form letter be made up, using the language of Form B. The letter stipulates that if permission is granted, the requesting party will ensure that any reproductions of the work are carried out in conformity with the particulars of Form A, and that each copy made carries a suitable copyright notice.

When to Send Request

Permission requests must be sent with sufficient lead time to permit the publisher the necessary opportunity to evaluate the request. For each request the publisher must carefully review the status of its rights in the work to ensure that it has the right to grant the permission requested. The requesting party should make every effort to send its request in time for the publisher to respond prior to the date when the reprints are intended to be made.

Form A   Particulars of Reproduction for Which Permission is Requested

Name of Requesting Organization:

Title of Work:

Author/Editor:

Edition:

Copyright Notice:

ISBN:

Chapters or page numbers to be duplicated:

Total number of   Number of Copies
original pages: to be made:

Use to be made of reproduced material:

Is the material to be revised and/or abridged?

If 'yes', a copy of the proposed changes is attached:

Form of distribution (classroom, newsletter, etc.):

Will the material be sold?   At what price?

Type of reprint (photocopy, offset, typeset):

Date by which reprint is to be made:

Form B   Request for Permission to Reproduce Copyright Material

---

(Use letterhead of requesting institution)

(date)

(name and address of publisher from whom permission is sought)

Attention: Permissions Department

Dear Sir/Madam:

RE: Request for Permission to Reproduce material

We are writing to request permission to make reproductions of a work (or part thereof), the rights for which we understand are owned or exercised by your firm.

In order to facilitate approval, we have attached herewith two copies of a completed form providing the particulars recommended in the Handbook on Copyright Compliance issued by CBA, CBPC and ACP in December 1985.

We would appreciate it if you could return a copy of the form along with your letter of permission.

If permission is granted, we undertake to ensure that any reproduction of the work (or part thereof) is carried out in accordance with the particulars provided on the attached form, and that a notice of copyright is included with each copy. If we reproduce the work, we also undertake to remit to you, on or before the date such reproduction is carried out, the fee if any stipulated in your letter of permission.

If in fact you do not have the authority necessary to grant permission to reprint the work in question, we would appreciate it if you could forward this request to the appropriate person.

Thank you for your attention to this matter. A self-addressed stamped envelope is included for your convenience.

Yours very truly,

(name of institution)

(signature)

(name, position)

References

A Charter of Rights for Creators. Ottawa: Supply and Services Canada, 1985.

Copyright Compliance. Toronto: Canadian Booksellers Assoc. et al., 1986.

Fox, H. G., *The Canadian Law of Copyright and Industrial Designs* (2nd ed.). Toronto: Carswell, 1967.

From Gutenberg to Telidon: A White Paper on Copyright. Ottawa: Supply and Services Canada, 1984.

Hebert, F., *Photocopying in Canadian Libraries.* Ottawa: Canadian Library Association, 1987.

Helm, V., "What Educators Should Know About Copyright," Bloomington, Ind.: *Phi Delta Kappa*, 1986. [N.B. This reflects the state of the law in the United States not in Canada]

Hopkins, R., "Copyright: Complexities and Concerns," *Canadian Library Journal,* October, 1987.

Keyes, A. A. and Brunet, C., *Copyright in Canada: Proposals for a Revision of the Law.* Ottawa: Supply and Services Canada, 1977.

Learning Objectives

This chapter will help the reader to understand:

1. The common law principal of in *loco parentis.*
2. The implications of Section 43 of the Criminal Code.
3. That the teacher's common law right to discipline students may be modified by provincial statute and school board policy.
4. The extent to which the teacher's right to discipline extends beyond the school yard.
5. The physical and emotional conditions of the child which influence judgements as to what is reasonable punishment.
6. Which parts of the child's anatomy are not suitable for receiving physical punishment.
7. The impact of the *Canadian Charter of Rights and Freedoms* upon the matter of student discipline.

Preview

The British common law principal that the teacher acts in the place of the parent or guardian extends beyond the requirement that the teacher keep the child safe from harm. It includes the teacher's right to lawfully discipline the child provided that the discipline is reasonable. Section 43 of the *Criminal Code* of Canada confirms the common law principal by providing the teacher with a statutory right to discipline.

Some provinces authorize the use of corporal punishment; others prohibit the use of the strap; and many provincial school acts are silent on the matter. Even in provinces which authorize corporal punishment some school jurisdictions have formulated policies which prohibit its use. Reasonable advice for the teacher is to review the provincial law and school board policy in the jurisdiction of his employment.

It is usual for the authority of the school teacher to discipline students to be extended by the courts to reach beyond the bounds of the school premises when the discipline is for the safety of students or the proper discipline and management of the school.

It is advisable for the teacher to consider the condition of the child, the emotional state of the teacher, the age of the child, the nature of the infraction, and the part of the anatomy to which the punishment will be applied. Application of physical punishment to a child's head for would never be considered reasonable. Turning a very young child over your knee and spanking him might be considered reasonable, but the same procedure for an older female student would surely be considered inappropriate.

Section 12 of the Charter addresses in general terms everyone's right, "not to be subjected to any cruel and unusual treatment or punishment." To date this section has not been tested in its application to school disciplinary matters.

Self-Assessment

1. Which federal law addresses the issue of the teacher's right to discipline students?

2. What is the line of demarcation which distinguishes discipline from assault?

3. May a student be disciplined by a teacher for misconduct outside of school?

4. What does the provincial school legislation in your province of residence say about the use of corporal punishment?

Key Term

in loco parentis

* * * * *

The right of a school teacher to inflict corporal punishment on a student has long been recognized in the common law. In 1765, Blackstone wrote in his *Commentaries*:

(The parent) may lawfully correct his child, being under age, in a reasonable manner; for this is for the benefit of his education . . . he may also delegate part of his parental authority, during his life, to the tutor or schoolmaster of his child; who is then in loco parentis and has such a portion of the power of the parent committed to his charge, viz. that of restraint and correction, as may be necessary to answer the purposes for which he is employed.

In addition to this delegation of parental authority, cases have held that teachers have an inherent authority to maintain discipline in the schools and may use corporal punishment to maintain order quite apart from any parental delegation of authority. Conduct which would normally be considered as a criminal assault is therefore acceptable, within prescribed limits, in the school.

Section 43 of the *Criminal Code* provides a specific defence to an assault charge for parents and teachers:

Every schoolteacher, parent or person standing in the place of a parent is justified in using force by way of correction toward a pupil or child, as the case may be, who is under his care, if the force does not exceed what is reasonable under the circumstances.

Although "Education" is a matter wholly within provincial legislative powers, this provision is a proper exercise of the federal government's criminal law power. It does not authorize the use of corporal punishment in schools but only provides a defence if such treatment should result in the laying of criminal assault charges.

Provincial legislatures have also felt compelled to make specific reference to corporal punishment on occasion. The Newfoundland *Schools Act* provides:

84. – (1) Teachers are permitted to administer corporal punishment in reason and with humanity, but they shall refrain from the use of it, until other means of discipline have been tried, and striking children on the head is forbidden, and corporal punishment shall not be administered to delicate or nervous children.

At the other end of the country, the British Columbia legislature has adopted a different approach and the has banned corporal punishment altogether by virtue of Regulation 436/81 passed pursuant to the *School Act* which states:

14. (1) The discipline in every school shall be similar to that of a kind, firm, and judicious parent, but shall not include corporal punishment.
(2) No teacher shall administer corporal punishment to any pupil.

Even if provincial legislators ban corporal punishment in schools, as has been done in British Columbia, such action will not remove the defence for criminal assault charges. There may, of course, be other consequences for a teacher who defies a provincial ban on corporal punishment but he will not be subjected to criminal charges as long as the force used was reasonable.

There have been numerous cases of teachers, charged with assault, who have invoked this protection. The judicial decisions provide guidelines to determining what has been considered "reasonable." The cases are presented in chronological order to show to what extent (if any) our concept of reasonable punishment of a student has changed over the years.

An early English case, *R. v. Hopley* (1860) 2 F & F 202, saw a boy beaten with a thick stick for two and one half hours which resulted in his death. That was going too far and the court considered it to be manslaughter. The court laid down some fundamental principles to be followed in teacher assault cases. It stated that the punishment must be reasonable and moderate, must not be protracted beyond a child's endurance, and must not be inflicted with an unfit instrument. If a child dies as a result of immoderate punishment it will be considered manslaughter, not murder.

Cleary v. Booth [1893] 1 Q.B. 465 was the earliest case to extend a teacher's jurisdiction beyond the confines of the schoolyard. In this case a headmaster punished a boy, by caning him, for an assault he committed on another student outside the schoolgrounds on the way to school. The justices hearing the case on appeal held:

> It is difficult to express in words the extent of a schoolmaster's authority in respect to the punishment of his pupils; but in my opinion his authority extends, not only to acts done in school, but also to cases where a complaint of acts done out of school, at any rate while going to and from school, is made to the headmaster.

> In my opinion the purpose with which the parental authority is delegated to the schoolmaster, who is entrusted with the bringing up and discipline of the child, must to some extent include an authority over the child while he is outside the four walls. . . It cannot be that such a duty or power ceases the moment the pupil leaves school for home; there is not much opportunity for a boy to exhibit his moral conduct while in school under the eye of the master: the opportunity is while he is at play or outside the school; and if the schoolmaster has no control over the boys in their relation to each other except when they are within the school walls, this object of the Code

would be defeated. In such a case as the present, it is obvious that the desired impression is best brought about by a summary and immediate punishment.

In 1899 a Canadian judge made the following observations on the liability of a teacher inflicting corporal punishment:

> ... the teacher who acts firmly, but kindly and mercifully, and inflicts punishment in moderation will, in most instances, and should in all, escape an investigation of his conduct in the courts. (*R. v. Robinson* (1899) 7 C.C.C. 52)

A 1904 decision, *R. v. Gaul* 36 N.S.R. 504, held that mere lack of malice or permanent injury was not the test to determine if the teacher's conduct amounted to a criminal assault. The judge is to determine if the punishment is excessive. In that case a 9-year-old boy was strapped on his back, buttocks and legs; slapped and knocked down twice; and then strapped five or six times on each hand. He was described as a "delicate boy" and the punishment brought blood, bruises, a limp, vomiting and headache. The trial judge acquitted the teacher because he had not acted out of malice nor caused any permanent injury. On appeal this was held not to be the correct test and the case was remanded back to the trial court to determine if the actions were "excessive." There is no report of the trial judge's ultimate decision on this point.

Six years later, *R. v. Zinck* (1910) 67 C.C.C. 114, determined that the following acts were not excessive. A 15-year-old boy who refused to hold out his hands was strapped on the shoulders, struck with a ruler, tripped to the floor, and then strapped on the back of his hands. This was considered to be reasonable in the circumstances.

In determining what is reasonable, courts often direct their attention towards the part of the body which has been struck. In *R. v. Metcalfe* (1927) 49 C.C.C. 260 a principal was acquitted of assault, despite bruising and welts, where the punishment was administered "on that part of her anatomy which seems to have been specifically designed by nature for the receipt of corporal punishment," namely the buttocks.

This consideration of "anatomy" was detailed in *Campeau v. R.* (1951) 103 C.C.C. 355 where it was held:

> There will be no disagreement that if a teacher strikes a pupil on the head by way of discipline his act is completely unjustified; the reason of course being that there is danger of doing permanent harm by striking a delicate part of the body such as the head. For the same reason to hit a child on the spine with a hard object such as a ruler, would in my opinion be unjustified no matter what his offence. Also, though to a lesser degree, to discipline a

9 year old child and one of 6 years by banging their knuckles on the corner of a desk is dangerous and may be unjustified. The covering over the bones on the back of the hands is very thin and the risk of permanent injury is correspondingly great.

This majority view of that case was not universally held and a dissenting opinion expressed the following sentiments:

> If corporal punishment is used, it is necessary to make it effective to a certain degree. Otherwise, far from being a measure salutory to the child, it will rather become, on his part, a cause of indifference, even more than that, of independence and defiance; hence the fault for which the punishment was intended will be repeated to satiety, since his chastisement is lenient . . . Do I need to add that in our Province (Quebec) manners and customs have always recognized corporal punishment in educational institutions? I am well aware that the tendency is to repress it more and more, but the evidence shows that the parents of the children who were chastised used corporal punishment upon them rather frequently. If such were the ways of the home, it is not at all surprising that they were the same at school. Striking a hard body like a desk with the back of the hand does not appear to me, in itself, more cruel and more dangerous than using a rod or a strap.

The principle that striking a child in the head can never be justified as set out by the majority has not been followed by other courts. The Saskatchewan Court of Appeal in *R. v. Haberstock* [1971] 1 C.C.C. (2d) 433 discharged a vice-principal who slapped a 12-year-old boy on the face and chipped his tooth. The boy was allegedly calling the teacher involved names including "short ribs." In fact it was not this pupil but another that did the actual name calling. This mistake did not affect the decision. The vice-principal had "reasonable and probable grounds" upon which he was justified in concluding that the student involved had called him these names.

> If there were such grounds, and the appellant administered the punishment in the honest belief that the boy had been guilty of conduct deserving punishment, then, if the punishment was reasonable, he would be excused from any criminal liability.

In *R. v. Bick* [1979] 3 W.C.B. 287 it was considered excessive for a vice-principal to strike a 12-year-old girl in the head in view of the possible danger of permanent harm from striking a child's head.

R. v. Kanhai [1981] 9 Sask. R. 181 involved a physical education teacher grabbing a student by the hair, taking him to his office, banging his head on the door, and having him sit in the office. Every time the student looked down the teacher "flicked" him under the chin to make him look up.

The student showed no defiance or resistance to the teacher. His offence was walking and not running during part of a running test. The student was not particularly fit. The teacher was convicted but the court granted him an absolute discharge. The court held there was no reasonable ground to believe that correction was needed since there was no challenge to his authority or hostility displayed. The pupil had committed no fault or breach of discipline deserving of any punishment.

R. v. Dimmell [1981] 55 C.C.C.2d 239 saw a classroom "brawl" between a teacher and student precipitated by the student's refusal to fill out a dismissal slip in the manner directed by the teacher. The teacher grabbed the 15-year-old boy's shirt and shook him with the result that they "traded blows." The teacher was acquitted because his actions were reasonable.

We hear or read in the newspapers of other cases involving teachers striking students more out of anger than by way of discipline. Often these teachers are acquitted and only in the most extreme cases is there a conviction. A recent case involving parental discipline set out what may become the new standard for judging such cases.

In *R. v. Baptiste and Baptiste* [1980] 61 C.C.C.2d 438 the parents of a 15-year-old girl whipped her with a belt and electrical cord. The trial judge stated:

> The concern of today's community for child abuse should be reflected in the standards to be applied. The maxim, 'spare the rod and spoil the child,' does not enjoy the universal approval it may have had at the turn of this century and indeed at the time of the various revisions of the *Criminal Code*. The formation of child abuse teams at hospitals, such as Sick Children's Hospital in Toronto, reflect the distaste of our community for corporal punishment . . . The use of force by way of correction is not a method universally approved of today . . . The use of force by way of correction of a 15-year-old girl can seldom be justified.

These sentiments met with the approval of the Saskatchewan Court of Appeal in *R. v. Dupperon* (1984) 16 C.C.C.3d 453, a case involving a father strapping his 13-year-old son on the bare buttocks. This case decided:

> In determining whether the force used has exceeded what is reasonable under the circumstances, the court must consider both from an objective and subjective standpoint such matters as the nature of the offence calling for correction, the age and character of the child and the likely effect of the punishment on the particular child, the degree of gravity of the punishment, the circumstances under which it was inflicted and the injuries, if any, suffered. Ten strokes of a leather belt on the bare buttocks is a severe beating particularly in the circumstances in which it was inflicted in this case on an emotionally disturbed boy.

It has been suggested that the passage of the *Canadian Charter of Rights and Freedoms* may have an impact on the use of corporal punishment in our schools. Section 12 of the Charter is broadly phrased as follows:

Everyone has the right not to be subjected to any cruel and unusual treatment or punishment.

The Supreme Court of the United States in the case of *Ingraham v. Wright* 430 U.S. 651 (1977) held that the cruel and unusual punishment clause in their Bill of Rights was restricted to criminal matters and did not apply to school punishment. It can be argued that s. 12 may have a different effect because it refers not to just punishment but also to "treatment." Our courts may not limit its application to criminal matters alone. It is unlikely, however, that our courts would find the use of a strap in schools to be both cruel and unusual.

Although teachers, at present, are afforded some protection from criminal responsibility for administering corporal punishment, there is a growing trend to have it banned. Other provinces may follow the lead of British Columbia and local boards may outlaw the strap in their schools. Sweden has gone so far as to remove any protection for parents or teachers with respect to striking children. There may come a day when the protection afforded by s. 43 of the *Criminal Code* is removed and anyone striking a child will face assault charges.

Point/Counterpoint

The question of whether corporal punishment should be administered is a matter of differing opinion with some vehemently opposed to the practice and others ardently in favour of it. We present some views on the issue.

Withold not correction from a child: for if thou strike him with the rod, he shall not die. Thou shalt beat him with the rod, and deliver his soul from hell. (Proverbs, 23: 13-14)

Let a routine once spring from passion, and you will presently find thousands of routineers following it passionately for a livelihood. To say that every man who beats his children and every schoolmaster who flogs a pupil is a conscious debauchee is absurd: thousands of dull, conscientious people beat their children conscientiously, because they were beaten themselves and think children ought to be beaten. The ill-tempered vulgarity that instinctively strikes at and hurts a thing that annoys it (and all children are annoying), and the simple stupidity that requires from a child perfection beyond the reach of the wisest and best adults (perfect truthfulness coupled with perfect obedience is quite a common condition of leaving a child unwhipped), produce a good deal of flagellation among people who not only do not lust after it, but who hit the harder because they are angry at having to perform an uncomfortable duty. These people will beat merely to assert their authority, or to carry out what they conceive to be a divine order ... (G.B. Shaw, *The Doctor's Dilemma*)

There are two views commonly to the fore upon this subject: one, that beating is a brutal and brutalising punishment which ought in no circumstances to be inflicted: the other, usually indicated rather than expressed by the judge or magistrate when he remarks that he was beaten at school, the implication, of course, being that the beating made him the fine fellow he is. Like most other people dealing with matters of controversy, he begs the question. He might have been a fine fellow without the whacking, and perhaps he is not a fine fellow at all. He is not alone in the exercise of the *petitio principii*, for those holding the other view willfully shut their eyes to the fact that innumerable boys have not been brutalised by caning, and that kind and reasonable people sometimes inflict that punishment. (Solicitor's Journal, June 27, 1931)

Discussion and Review Questions

1. What are the sources of the teacher's right to discipline?
2. What cautions would you recommend to a teacher who is applying physical punishment?
3. Under what conditions would it be appropriate to use corporal punishment? When is it not?

You be the Judge

Case Study #1

Bob is a high school teacher in British Columbia. He is relatively short of stature with white hair and a beard. While Bob was walking down the hall between periods one day, a 17-year-old student hailed him with "Hi, Papa Smurf." Bob slapped the student on the side of the head and sent him flying into a locker. The student was not seriously injured. The student stated that he was in a joking mood when he made the remark. Bob felt that the student was trying to embarrass him. Bob was suspended for eight days without pay and charged with assault as a result of this incident.

1) Is Bob guilty of an assault?
2) Was the board justified in suspending Bob?

Case Study #2

Carol was a grade six teacher in a school district which had adopted the following policy:

> The teacher may use force by way of correcting a pupil and maintaining order provided that the force used does not exceed what is reasonable under the circumstances.

Carol hit Junior Baker twice on the buttocks with a wooden spoon which she kept in a cupboard for such purpose. She had caught Junior bouncing a soccer ball against the heating radiator even though he and the entire class had been warned that balls were to be used only outside or in the gymnasium. The punishment was administered in a small storage room adjacent to the classroom.

Mrs. Baker had specifically requested, in writing, that corporal punishment not be administered to Junior since she was opposed to the practice as a matter of principal. Upon learning of the incident, the Bakers brought a civil action for assault against Carol, the principal, and the school board. The Statement of Claim alleged:

1. Corporal punishment was administered to Junior in violation of the parents' specific instructions to the contrary.

2. Junior Baker had not been warned that bouncing the ball in the classroom would result in corporal punishment.

3. Junior Baker was not allowed an opportunity to explain his actions.

4. The particular punishment inflicted was cruel and unusual punishment in this situation.

5. Another adult was not present during the administration of the punishment as required by school board policy.

6. Carol had not consulted with or informed Mrs. Baker regarding either the misdemeanour or the discipline used.

The Bakers sought damages for emotional distress for themselves and Junior as well as punitive damages for breach of their civil rights.

1. Identify the major issues or problems presented by this case.

2. What solutions would you offer to resolve the issues and problems?

3. At what point could the problem have been avoided?

4. Who bears the ultimate responsibility for creating the problem?

6

Child Abuse

Learning Objectives

Some of the things which the reader will learn from this chapter include:

1. The various forms of child abuse legislation, and the problems associated with some of the current legislation.
2. The types of actions which are considered to be abusive to the child.
3. The various positions respecting the solution of the problem of child abuse.
4. The problems faced by the teacher of an abused child.
5. The reporting requirements in cases of suspected abuse.
6. The moral, professional and legal obligations of the teacher.
7. Whether there is a potential for civil liability if a teacher fails to report suspected abuse.
8. Why people do not report cases of suspected abuse.
9. The legislative shields which protect those who report.
10. The problems associated with a classroom teacher as abuser.

Preview

The criminal responsibility of a parent for an assault upon a child is virtually identical with that of a teacher.

The purpose of provincial child abuse legislation is therapeutic in that treatment and rehabilitation of the offenders, while protecting the child, is the ultimate goal.

Teachers must become thoroughly knowledgeable about the criminal and civil liabilities imposed upon them with respect to child abuse and the specific reporting requirements of their province of employment and local school policies. If the latter are absent, the teacher should press for the passage of legally correct policies and procedures.

There is an educational as well as a legal side to the issue of child abuse in that teachers are often required to assume a therapeutic role in the treatment of abused children. Reporting suspected cases of child abuse, although an essential role for the teacher, is not sufficient. Teachers must take an active role in prevention education as well as assisting in the treatment of abused children.

The helping professional can face criminal and civil actions, because of failure to report, however, the more pressing issue will be the moral and professional question which must be answered.

Self-Assessment

1. Do you have a working definition of what constitutes child abuse?
2. Have you looked at the child abuse legislation for your province?
3. Do you understand what the criminal and civil law consequences are of failing to report a case of suspected child abuse?
4. Have you considered what you should do if a suspected case of child abuse appears in your classroom?
5. Have you wondered what you should do when the abused child returns to your classroom following medical,social, and legal actions?
6. Can you think of some reasons why an individual would be hesitant to report an instance of suspected child abuse?

Key Terms

Criminal law

Tort law

Administrative law

Positive legal duty

Neglected children

Children in need of protection

Necessities of life

Quasi-criminal offense

Mens rea

Strict liability

Test of reasonableness

Child abuse syndrome

The legal concept of *last chance*

*   *   *   *

Some of the legal principles involved in the matter of child abuse are closely related to those we have discussed in the issue of corporal punishment. Section 43 of the *Criminal Code* grants parents and guardians the same defence to a charge of assault that is provided to teachers. The question of criminal responsibility for a physical assault upon a child is virtually identical in both instances and courts refer to precedents involving teachers and parents interchangeably. The legal principle of what is "reasonable" in the circumstances does not change because of the family relationship.

Child abuse involves more than just physical assaults on children by parents, guardians or teachers, however. It includes sexual and emotional abuse as well. Legal issues in cases of child abuse extend beyond the parameters of the criminal law to include protective custody hearings for the child and mandatory reporting of suspected abuse. There are also civil issues of liability for failure to report (or for wrongful reporting of) suspected abuse. Child abuse is a matter of concern to both federal and provincial governments and each has legislative authority over different areas. In this chapter we will look at both criminal and civil legal issues involved in child abuse. As background for the discussion of civil law matters, the reader is directed to the chapters on tort law.

Parties involved in child abuse cases are not only parents, guardians and teachers. Although the person inflicting the abuse is often a parent, it could be another relative, a neighbour, or any other person closely involved with the child, such as a babysitter. Other helping professions, including doctors, nurses and social workers, become involved in the process of detecting abuse, protecting the child, and dealing with the effects of the abuse on the child. The issue is one that crosses many professional boundaries as well as many legal boundaries, encompassing aspects of criminal law, tort law, and administrative law.

There is an increasing awareness and concern about the extent of child abuse in our society and a concerted search for possible solutions. Legislation is the primary vehicle used by the legal profession for intervention in cases of suspected abuse. Social workers and psychologists rely on counselling as a solution to the problem while teachers see education as a useful tool in combatting abuse. It appears that no single profession will be successful in stopping or containing the incidence of abuse. A concerted multidisciplinary search for solutions will be required. Teachers and social workers must become familiar with the legal issues involved while lawyers and legislators must acquire knowledge of the psychological, social and educational issues.

Teachers may become involved in this issue from several perspectives. They must be prepared to respond in a professional and appropriate manner. Because of their daily close contact with children, teachers can play a major role in the detection and reporting of suspected child abuse cases. Beyond the unquestioned moral and professional obligations to protect children under their care, teachers have a positive legal duty to report any case of suspected child abuse to the appropriate authority. Failure to report such cases may result in prosecution under provincial legislation or exposure to a civil action for damages. In addition, professional disciplinary proceedings may be initiated against a teacher who knowingly fails to fulfill this duty.

Abused children may also present special behavioural or learning problems in the classroom. Although ways of dealing with these concerns are beyond the scope of this book, teachers are encouraged to familiarize themselves with the effects of abuse on a child (particularly how it can affect him in the learning environment) and with ways to respond to the child in the classroom setting. Recent studies have shown that instances of abuse are not rare isolated occurrences, every teacher can reasonably expect to encounter at least one abused child, and probably many more, during his career.

Information about child abuse has become a part of the school program, usually the health curriculum, in many jurisdictions. Many schools have introduced abuse awareness programs for children at all grade levels. The incidence of children reporting cases of abuse will probably increase as a result of these programs and teachers must be prepared to respond to these reports. Sound educational programs may also have a deterrent effect on potential abusers. In the past, abuse has been hidden in the closet and has not been discussed openly. Frequently, children were unaware that what was happening to them was not normal. Abusers were relatively free to conduct their activities without fear of detection. It is to be hoped that increased awareness and open discussion of the problem with children will cause abusers to have second thoughts about continuing such activity, knowing that the child and others are more likely to report the abuse. Many of the recent court cases deal with abusive actions which transpired several years earlier. This is especially true of sexual abuse.

There are numerous definitions of child abuse and much uncertainty as to which particular actions constitute "child abuse." This unhappy state of affairs has been the subject of judicial comment in the case of *R. v. Stachula* (1984) 40 R.F.L. (2d) 184 where it was noted:

> The inadequacy of the . . . definition of 'abuse' and more particularly 'sexual molestation' is most apparent and most unfortunate for those who are charged with identifying and reporting it.

Teachers are concerned with the legal definition of child abuse; however, the matter of definition is complicated because each province has adopted its own different definition for application to its own particular statute. Often these definitions go beyond what the average person may consider to be child abuse and refer to broader categories such as "neglected children" or "children in need of protection." It has been found that across Canada there are over 35 different criteria being used in provincial statutes to define this status. These range from "a child who sells newspapers or other objects in a public place" to "a child who has been assaulted or ill-treated by the custodian (of that child)." Teachers should consult the relevant legislation in the province of their employment in order to determine which specific descriptions are used in that jurisdiction.

Since there is no single legal definition of child abuse that is applicable in all provinces, we will borrow from the United States for purposes of our discussion. The *Child Abuse Prevention and Treatment Act* is a federal statute which was passed by the United States Congress in 1974. It defines child abuse as follows:

> The physical or mental injury, sexual abuse, negligent treatment or maltreatment of a child under the age of eighteen, by a person who is responsible for the child's welfare under circumstances which indicate that the child's health or welfare is harmed or threatened thereby.

The *Model Child Abuse and Neglect Reporting Law,* developed as a model for State legislatures to follow to achieve uniformity in reporting laws, uses a similar definition and draws a distinction between an "abused" and a "neglected" child. The definitions used are:

> An abused child shall mean a person under eighteen years of age who is suffering from serious physical harm, or sexual molestation, caused by those responsible for his care or others exercising temporary or permanent control over the child.
>
> A neglected child shall mean a person under eighteen years of age whose physical or mental condition is seriously impaired as a result of the failure of those responsible for his care or others exercising temporary or permanent control over the child to provide adequate food, shelter, clothing, physical protection or medical care necessary to sustain the life or health of the child.

Thus, the meaning of child abuse (as it is usually defined for legal purposes) extends beyond physical and sexual abuse to encompass mental or emotional injury caused by those who are responsible for the welfare of the child. The latter are far less easily detected. Since the identification of child abuse is a function of its definition, the broader the definition, the greater is the ease of identification. The person who is called upon to report has broader guidelines to determine what abuse is. Therefore, the teacher should become familiar with the various indicators for each type of abuse as defined by the statute in his province of employment. He cannot adequately fulfill his legal and moral obligations to the child unless he is aware of the signs indicating abuse. Identification of abuse victims is an essential first step towards the protection of an abused child and in curtailing future abuse.

In addition to provincial legislation regarding child abuse, the federal government also becomes involved through its criminal law powers. Several sections of the *Criminal Code* deal with matters that are usually considered to be child abuse. While the provinces seek to deal with the care and protection of the abused child, the criminal law deals with the perpetrator of the abuse. The *Criminal Code* does not contain a definition of child abuse but it does deal with specific acts which are usually considered as acts of child abuse under any definition of the term.

Relevant sections of the *Criminal Code* dealing with forms of sexual abuse include the following:

140. Every person who, for a sexual purpose, touches, directly or indirectly, with a part of the body or with an object, any part of the body of a person under the age of fourteen years is guilty of an indictable offence and is liable to imprisonment for a term not exceeding ten years or is guilty of an offence punishable on summary conviction.

141. Every person who for a sexual purpose, invites, counsels or incites a person under the age of fourteen years to touch, directly or indirectly, with a part of the body or with an object, the body of any person, including the body of the person who so invites, counsels or incites and the body of the person under the age of fourteen years, is guilty of an indictable offence and is liable to imprisonment for a term not exceeding ten years or is guilty of an offence punishable on summary conviction.

146. (1) Every person who is in a position of trust or authority towards a young person or is a person with whom the young person is in a relationship of dependency and who
(a) for a sexual purpose, touches directly or indirectly, with a part of the body or with an object, any part of the body of the young person, or
(b) for a sexual purpose, invites, counsels or incites a young person to touch, directly or indirectly, with a part of the body or with an object, the body of any person, including the body of the person who so invites, counsels or incites and the body of the young person, is guilty of an indictable offence and is liable to imprisonment for a term not exceeding five years or is guilty of an offence punishable on summary

conviction.

(2) In this section, "young person" means a person fourteen years of age or more but under the age of eighteen years.

150. (1) Every one commits incest who, knowing that another person is by blood relationship his or her parent, child, brother, sister, grandparent or grandchild, as the case may be, has sexual intercourse with that person.

(2) Every one who commits incest is guilty of an indictable offence and is liable to imprisonment for fourteen years.

153. (1) Every male person who (a) has illicit sexual intercourse with his step-daughter, foster daughter or female ward . . .is guilty of an indictable offence and is liable to imprisonment for two years.

166. Every one who, being the parent or guardian of a female person, (a) procures her to have illicit sexual intercourse with a person other than the procurer, or (b) orders, is party to, permits or knowingly receives the avails of, the defilement, seduction or prostitution of the female person, is guilty of an indictable offence and is liable to (c) imprisonment for fourteen years, if the female person is under the age of fourteen years, or (d) imprisonment for five years, if the female person is fourteen years of age or more.

168. (1) Every one who, in the home of a child, participates in adultery or sexual immorality, or indulges in habitual drunkenness or any other form of vice, and thereby endangers the morals of the child or renders the home an unfit place for the child to be in, is guilty of an indictable offence and is liable to imprisonment for two years.

246. (1) Every one who commits a sexual assault is guilty of (a) an indictable offence and is liable to imprisonment for ten tears; or (b) an offence punishable on summary conviction.

(2) Where an accused is charged with an offence under subsection (1) . . . in respect of a person under the age of fourteen years, it is not a defence that the complainant consented to the activity that forms the subject-matter of the charge unless the accused is less than three years older than the complainant.

These sections are relatively clear as to the type of sexual activity being prohibited with the possible exception of s. 168. There have been few cases decided under this section but one case involved a mother and her common law husband photographing an 11-year-old child in sexually suggestive poses. *R. v. E and F* (1981) 61 C.C.C. (2d) 287 held that the accused did not have to intend to endanger the morals of the child but only need intend to do the immoral act. If the act is deemed by the judge to be immoral the presumed result is that the morals of the child are endangered.

Sections 140, 141 and 146 are recent additions to the *Criminal Code* which came into effect in 1988. They are designed to deal directly with forms of sexual abuse against children. They may appear to be redundant in view of the general provisions of s. 246 concerning sexual assault. This section, however, has been interpreted in such a manner that it has afforded little protection against what may commonly be considered "sexual assault."

Chase v. R. (1984) 40 C.R. (3d) 282 involved a 40-year-old male going to the home of a neighbour and struggling with a 15-year-old girl. He grabbed her breasts and said, "Come on, dear, don't hit me, I know you want it." She testified that he tried to grab her "private" but did not succeed. The New Brunswick Court of Appeal held that although the accused was guilty of an assault it was not a "sexual" assault. The Court stated:

> The addition of the word "sexual" to the term "assault," in my opinion, suggests that it is now necessary to determine to which part of the body the unlawful force was applied. Based on the meaning of "sexual," the concept of sexual assault as being an intentional and forced contact with the sexual organs or genitalia of another person without that person's consent is rather easily understood. So would, for that matter, the forced and intentional contact of one's sexual organs with any part of another person. The problem in this case is that the contact was not with the sexual organs of the victim but with the mammary gland, a secondary sexual characteristic.
> ... In my opinion, a proper definition of "sexual assault" requires as its constituent element an application of force involving the sexual organs of another or the touching of another with one's sexual organs.

In a case annotation appearing with the case report, Christine Boyle of the Faculty of Law at Dalhousie University states:

> Judges might well be most comfortable with this kind of "shopping list" approach. The penis and vagina are on the list – the breasts and beard are not. The people who thought bottom-patting could reasonably be included are out of luck, but surprisingly, forced anal penetration with an object would also seem to be left off the list. Not even sucking or biting a woman's breast would be deemed sexual by the New Brunswick Court of Appeal. Surely this ruling and this approach are wrong on a number of levels. To be credible, the meaning of "sexual" will have to bear some reasonably close relationship to how men and women experience reality. Surely, from a woman's perspective, the touching of her breasts is a sexual act. A man might not necessarily experience the touching of his beard as sexual, but equating the beard with the breasts is an excellent example of a proposition which is abstracted to a gender-neutral level even though gender is a significant aspect of the context. Oddly, the decision does not seem to embody a particularly male perspective either.

The *Criminal Code* also deals with matters of neglect and omission as well as positive acts of physical and sexual abuse. The following sections of the Code are relevant to this form of abuse:

197. (1) Every one is under a legal duty (a) as a parent, foster parent, guardian or head of a family, to provide necessaries of life for a child under the age of sixteen years ...

(2) Every one commits an offence who, being under a legal duty within the meaning of subsection (1), fails without lawful excuse, the proof of which lies upon him, to perform that duty, if (a) with respect to a duty imposed by paragraph (1)(a) ...

(ii) the failure to perform the duty endangers the life of the person to whom the duty is owed, or causes or is likely to cause the health of that person to be endangered permanently;

200. Every one who unlawfully abandons or exposes a child who is under the age of ten years, so that its life is or is likely to be endangered or its health is or is likely to be permanently injured, is guilty of an indictable offence and is liable to imprisonment for two years.

202. (1) Every one is criminally negligent who (a) in doing anything, or (b) in omitting to do anything that it is his duty to do, shows wanton disregard for the lives or safety of other persons.

The words "necessaries of life" used in s. 197 mean such necessaries as tend to preserve life and include the provision of medical treatment. In *R. v. Tutton* (1985) 14 W.C.B. 10 it was held that it is not a lawful excuse for a parent who, knowing that a child needs medical assistance, refuses to obtain such help because to do so would contravene a tenet of his own particular religion. The guarantee of freedom of religion in section 2(a) of the *Charter of Rights and Freedoms* does not affect this issue.

In *R. v. Popen* (1981) 60 C.C.C. (2d) 232, the Ontario Court of Appeal held that a parent has a common law legal duty to take reasonable steps to protect his child from illegal violence used by the other parent towards that child. Such a parent is criminally responsible under s. 202 for failing to discharge that duty in circumstances which show a wanton disregard for the child's safety and where the failure has contributed to the physical harm or death of that child.

Every province and territory has some form of legislation which requires all suspected cases of child abuse to be reported. The Yukon Territory is the only part of the country which has adopted what may be called "permissive" legislation as opposed to mandatory reporting requirements. The relevant section of the *Children's Act* (S.Y.T. 1984 c. 2) states:

A person who has reasonable grounds to believe that a child may be a child in need of protection MAY report the information upon which he bases his belief to the Director, an agent of the Director, or a peace officer.

All other provinces use the word "shall" which makes it a legal require-ment to report and not a matter of individual choice. Prior to the enactment of this 1984 statute, the Yukon Territory also had mandatory reporting requirements; thus, their recent legislation may be considered to be a regres-sive step. The amendment was made reluctantly in response to concerns about false reports of abuse being made. At the same time the Yukon Leg-islature adopted a harsh penalty for anyone knowingly making a false report. Some suggest that false reports of abuse will continue to made whether the reporting requirements are mandatory or permissive and remov-ing compulsory reporting will do nothing to stop such incidents.

Although the provincial statutes vary somewhat in wording and in the sanctions imposed for failure to report, they all contain one essential feature. Every teacher in every part of Canada, with the exception of the Yukon, is required by law to report every instance where he has reasonable grounds for suspecting that child abuse, according to that province's definition, has occurred.

Canadian legislatures have adopted what is called the "universal" approach to the required reporting of child abuse cases. The obligation to report is imposed on everyone in the province, not just on certain profes-sional groups likely to be in a position to note such cases. Many other coun-tries and states of the United States have adopted a more restrictive report-ing requirement. They impose an obligation to report only on designated professional groups such as doctors, social workers and police officers. Teachers, however, are always included among the designated professionals required to report. New Brunswick has adopted what could be described as a hybrid approach requiring "any person" to report child abuse, but only making failure to report an offence for "a professional person" which by definition in the act includes "a school principal, school teacher or other teaching professional."

The proper approach to take in enacting this type of legislation is still the subject of much debate. Provinces are continually making amendments to their statutes and are weighing the arguments for and against different models of legislation.

People who favour a restricted approach to reporting point out that this approach will more clearly focus responsibility on those professionals whose training and position make them most likely to be aware of the prob-lem, to encounter the problem, and to recognize instances of the problem. It is felt that by restricting mandatory reporting to these individuals, they will be less likely to shirk their responsibility by assuming that someone else, such as a relative of the victim, will make the necessary report. Where everyone is required to report it is easy not to get involved and lay the blame on others who had an equal or better opportunity to observe the child and make the report. The duty is not seen as an individual one but one that somebody else will take care of. If no specific person or group is assigned the job, it will not get done.

Those who favour the "universal" approach to reporting argue that a broader net is cast which will ensure more instances or reporting. Not every abused child will come in contact with one of the designated professionals but every child will be observed by neighbours and others. They also feel that the universal approach will promote greater public awareness of the problem and consequently more public involvement in prevention of child abuse. It is contended that the problem is society's problem, not just the problem of a few professionals, and that it is society that must take action to deal with the problem.

Advocates for each approach criticize the other. The Model Child Abuse and Neglect Reporting Project in the United States favours the restricted reporting method and has this to say about the universal approach:

> While logically meaningful, it is probable that obligating everyone to report would serve to diminish the impact mandatory reporting would have on specially named professions. In addition, it would be virtually impossible to enforce a penalty for the knowing failure to report if everyone is subject to it.

The restricted approach has also been criticized:

> The degree of specification creates the danger of exonerating professionals not listed. Pharmacists, for instance, may be approached by abusive parents wanting something for their injured or distressed children.

Whatever approach is ultimately adopted in any particular province, teachers can be assured that they will most certainly continue to be among those who are required to report child abuse. Teachers should occupy a significant position in any reporting scheme because of their opportunity to observe their students in a continuing manner. Unlike a child's relationship with other professionals, a child's relationship with a teacher is not subject to parental whim or discretion. Children are required by law to attend school; the opportunity for detection of abuse is greatly enhanced in a school setting and teachers are the persons most likely to discover it.

The legal consequences for failing to report cases of suspected child abuse vary from province to province. Some provinces make failure to report a quasi-criminal offence and provide a fine and/or imprisonment for breach of this duty. Other provinces make reporting mandatory but impose no specific penalty for breach of the provision although it may be covered under a general penalty provision of the Act. Appendix A contains a summary of the reporting requirements and penalties for each province and territory.

There have been very few prosecutions for failure to report abuse and even fewer reported cases of such charges. This circumstance is not due to the fact that the majority of cases are being properly reported but rather to the tremendous legal problems encountered in detecting the offence and in proving it once it has been detected. It is feared that the lack of sanctions and the difficulty in detecting and prosecuting offenders, will render reporting requirements largely meaningless. Faced with the unsavory nature of the offence and fearful of personal retribution by offenders, people may tend to ignore their responsibilities, secure in the knowledge that they will probably never be called to account for their inaction.

One of the handful of reported cases which involve a professional charged with failure to report a case of suspected child abuse is *R. v. Cook* (1983) 37 R.F.L. (2d) 93, a decision of the Family Division of the Ontario Provincial Court which was appealed to the District Court and ultimately to the Court of Appeal. The decision of the Provincial Court in this case would seem to restrict the test for criminal liability in such cases and make the possibility of conviction for the offence less certain than the statute seems to envisage. The subsequent appeals did little to clarify the matter as they dealt with specific issues in the case and not with broad general principles that could be of guidance to practitioners. We will look first at the lower court decision and then see what happened on appeal.

The Cook case involved an Ontario doctor who was charged under that province's legislation for failing to report an instance of suspected child abuse. The particular section under which the doctor was charged reads as follows:

49. (1) Every person who has information of the abandonment, desertion or need for protection of a child or the infliction of abuse upon a child shall forthwith report the information to a society.
(2) Notwithstanding the provisions of any other Act, every person who has reasonable grounds to suspect in the course of the person's professional or official duties that a child has suffered or is suffering from abuse that may have been caused or permitted by a person who has or has had charge of the child shall forthwith report the suspected abuse to a society.

In particular, the charge against Dr. Cook alleged a violation of subsection (2) in that being a medical doctor with reasonable grounds to suspect "that a child is suffering from abuse" she failed to report such abuse.

The facts of the case may be summarized as follows. A 15-year-old girl told her mother that her step-father had been touching her in a sexual way at various times over a two year period. The following day, the mother related this story to the family doctor, Dr. Cook. Eight days later the mother returned to the doctor's office and said that her husband had admitted the acts and that they were seeking counselling. The mother indicated that matters were under control. Three months later, the step-father, as a result of another report, was arrested and charged with an offence of sexually molesting the girl. Dr. Cook was also charged with failing to report the abuse as alleged by the mother in the first instance.

In his decision, Provincial Judge Naismith made some interesting remarks concerning prosecutions for such offences. First, he pointed out that whether there had been any actual abuse or not was irrelevant to a charge of failing to report. The issue was whether there were reasonable grounds to suspect abuse and not whether there was in fact abuse. It may be taken from this remark that teachers should not have to worry about whether they can prove actual abuse in any instance where they do report, but only whether they reasonably believed that abuse had occurred.

The judge also pointed out that the offence is not one which requires the Crown to prove *mens* or a guilty mind. In other words, once the particular act which is mandated, i.e. reporting the offence, is not undertaken by the accused, a conviction must be registered no matter what the person's motives or state of mind were. The usual intent to commit an unlawful act need not be present in such cases. These types of offences are called "absolute prohibition" or "strict liability" offences. They are relatively common in provincial legislation. A typical example might be a speeding charge where the conviction does not depend on whether the accused intended to speed, or even knew he was speeding, but rather on the guilty act alone.

In reaching his decision, the judge looked at this duty to report as a two stage process. He looked first at whether the doctor had reasonable grounds to suspect abuse. He referred to that "elusive" or "vague" line that had to be crossed before reporting was required. The judge had to decide what constituted "reasonable grounds." In this instance there was only a "sketchy second-hand description" which would not put Dr. Cook over that imaginary line. The judge did not state exactly where the line could be drawn but only that in this case it was not crossed. We can assume therefore that there must be more than a "sketchy second-hand description" to raise reasonable grounds and require a report to be made. We do not know whether "detailed" second-hand descriptions are enough or whether it is sketchy "first-hand" descriptions that are required.

The second stage of the process seems to go beyond the actual wording of the statute. The judge proposed that even if reasonable grounds for reporting did exist, the courts must then inquire as to whether it was reasonable to refrain from reporting. Where a professional, exercising his professional judgment, believes that the problem can best be solved without state intervention and without further harm to the child, he should be given the benefit of a reasonable doubt as to whether he is required to report and should be acquitted.

This manipulation of the test of reasonableness seems to go far beyond the words of the statute and makes it virtually impossible to convict any professional person acting in good faith and on his professional judgment. The legislated mandatory reporting requirements become a matter for professional discretion instead of the compulsory obligation that appears to have been intended. This is not to say that professionals would have carte blanche to refrain from reporting their suspicions. But, if they do have a bona fide professional belief that the problem can be solved without reporting, they are given the benefit of that judgment and will be acquitted if they fail to report based on that belief.

The Crown appealed this acquittal to the District Court where Judge Haley set aside the acquittal and ordered a new trial to be held. She proceeded on the basis that the trial judgment disclosed an error of law and said:

> I am of the opinion that the learned trial judge erred in law when he held that the information available to the doctor on 8th February and 16th February did not constitute reasonable grounds to suspect that child abuse had taken place within the plain meaning of the words in s. 49 (2).

Dr. Cook appealed this decision further and the case was ultimately heard by the Ontario Court of Appeal. This court seized upon an issue that was not readily apparent in the previous decisions. Justice Zuber in delivering the opinion of the court (reported at (1985) 46 R.F.L. (2d) 180) stated:

> The principal issue in this case is whether or not the Crown has proved that the appellant 'who has reasonable grounds to suspect . . . THAT A CHILD IS SUFFERING' from abuse failed to report as required by the Child Welfare Act. It is significant to note that the charge did not allege, as it might have done, that the appellant had reasonable grounds to suspect THAT A CHILD HAS SUFFERED OR IS SUFFERING FROM ABUSE: see s.49(2). (emphasis added)

It is therefore not sufficient to support the charge that the material before Dr. Cook constituted reasonable grounds to suspect that child abuse had taken place at some time in the past. It was necessary to prove the charge as laid and prove that that there were reasonable grounds to suspect that 'a child . . . is suffering from abuse'. The trial judge recognized this issue in his reference to the need to prove reasonable grounds to suspect 'ongoing abuse in February, March and April'. The trial judge was not satisfied that the Crown had proved its case. I find no error in the conclusion reached by the trial judge. . .

I agree with Haley, D.C.J. in her characterization of the issue in this case as a question of law. It is apparent from her reasons that the learned District Court Judge disagreed with the trial judge because she was of the view that the information available to Dr. Cook constituted reasonable grounds to suspect that child abuse HAD TAKEN PLACE. However, as pointed out above, this was not the allegation in the charge against the appellant. (emphasis added)

Although the specific facts of the case were settled, this case does little to assist teachers to understand the scope of the obligation to report possible cases of child abuse. The issue raised by the provincial court judge as to whether a professional must report abuse even where it appears it may be detrimental to the family remains unresolved. Had the doctor been charged using the broader words of the statute we may have had a different result.

Another case dealing with a charge under this particular statute was *R. v. Stachula* cited above. In that case the defendant was again a family doctor. He had been advised by the mother that her 14-year-old daughter was pregnant and that the father was the child's 16-year-old brother. An abortion was performed but no report of child abuse was made by the doctor resulting in a charge under s. 49(2). Judge Main of the Ontario Provincial Court made the following remarks in his judgment:

No one challenges the importance of the primary focus of the Child Welfare Act in protecting and meeting the best interests of a child, particularly in a case such as this. However, it is of at least equal importance to observe the fundamental principles of criminal law when the aspect of the Act under consideration relates to a professional charged with failing to report suspected child abuse. It is unacceptable that the best interests principle ought to override the observance of the protections offered to a defendant in a criminal or a quasi-criminal proceeding . . . Faced with reasonable grounds to suspect that sexual molestation has occurred, the difficulty presented by s. 49(2) is: What then is the standard of care to be applied to the professional person having such suspicions? The words 'every person who . . . in the course of the person's professional or official duties' carry with them the implication that there is a distinction which must be made between the various classes of such professionals and that there is no universal standard of care applicable to all such persons, but rather a standard of care particular to the class in question. If the legislature had intended but one standard to apply to all professionals dealing with children, the subsection could have easily reflected that policy. In the alternative, a comprehensive and easily understood definition of the term 'abuse' could have been provided and made applicable to all professionals dealing with children regardless of their class or qualifications.

The standard of care applicable to pediatricians skilled in child abuse should not be the standard of care applicable to family practitioners or to others such as public health nurses, school teachers, family service workers or child care workers, to name but a few. The relevant standard must vary in accordance with the professional capacity of the person or persons involved in the particular case. In fulfilling its onus under s. 49(2), the Crown must lead evidence of the standard of care expected of the class of persons represented by the defendant before the court, and it has failed to do so.

In the result, I must find that the Crown has failed to lead evidence to prove all of the essential ingredients or elements of the offence. The motion is granted and the defendant is acquitted of the charge before the court.

Again, this decision introduces an element of subjectivity in the reporting requirement and also introduces a notion that different types of professionals will only be required to report if that is what an average practitioner in that profession would do. The judge introduces some negligence concepts that really have no place in the criminal law. The problem seems to be in the wording of the statute which, although its intent seems obvious, is capable of judicial interpretations beyond those that any literal reading would make apparent. Such decisions make a strong argument in favour of universal mandatory reporting in very simple terms.

Despite the many apparent barriers to a successful prosecution of a professional for failure to report a case of suspected child abuse, there may be other actions available which do not require the high degree of proof necessary to sustain a criminal conviction. Teachers work under moral and professional duties to protect their students' welfare. A teacher could, therefore, be called to account before his professional disciplinary body even when a criminal offence cannot be proven. Many professional codes of ethics address broad general duties and outline disciplinary action which is not contingent upon a criminal conviction. Some provincial reporting statutes specifically provide that the person administering the act shall report any suspected cases of non-compliance to the governing body of the professional involved in the failure to report. This certainly implies that the legislature expects discipline proceedings to be instituted against such individuals. The penalties involved in such actions may well be harsher than any criminal sanctions and could well be a stronger vehicle for ensuring that reports are made than the quasi-criminal charges. It is suggested that teachers' associations should clearly spell out that failure to report child abuse will be grounds for disciplinary action and specify the consequences.

In addition to criminal or disciplinary proceedings, there is also the potential for a civil action in damages based on the failure to report. Several such actions have been undertaken in the United States although there are no reported Canadian instances at the time of writing. The essence of such an action is that the law imposes a duty to report, such duty has been breached, and the breach has resulted in injury to the child in the form of further abuse. It is alleged that this injury could have been prevented had the professional fulfilled his obligation to report and that he is therefore liable for the subsequent harm. These United States cases have involved a variety of professionals, including teachers. Again, the threat of civil liability, like professional disciplinary action, may be a more effective means of ensuring compliance with the reporting requirements than the largely ineffective criminal sanctions which have been imposed to date.

Some states have included express statutory provisions establishing civil liability for failure to report. It can be argued that no such express authority is needed and that civil liability can be created on existing negligence law. It is a general principle of law that failure to comply with a statutory mandate in itself may establish negligence. In the case of *Landeros v. Flood* 131 Cal. Rptr. 69 (1976), the California Supreme Court held that, as a matter of law, a doctor could be liable for damages if it could be proven that he had violated the state reporting laws by knowingly failing to report his suspicions that a child's injuries were the result of abuse.

The advocacy of civil liability as a means of encouraging reporting is not motivated by a desire to impose financial burdens on teachers but rather to protect children from abuse. It is suggested as a new mechanism to make teachers aware of their legal duty and to encourage their compliance therewith. By reporting any suspected case, a teacher relieves himself from all civil liability. It is not an onerous burden to place upon teachers but only an alternate means of ensuring compliance. A few successful civil actions would do much to increase awareness and compliance, with two results: teachers will accept their duty to report; and suits alleging their negligent failure to report will disappear.

Some difficulties may well be encountered in such a civil action, however. The first is in proving that the teacher, who after all is not medically trained, had reasonable grounds to suspect child abuse. "Child abuse syndrome" is recognized medically but how many teachers are qualified to make such a diagnosis? Sadly, the realities of child abuse do not require particular expertise for recognition in many cases. On an objective test teachers would only be held to the standard of a prudent practitioner and would not be required to have any medical expertise. Only such cases as would be recognized by an average competent teacher would require reporting.

A second difficulty lies in the problem of proving that further injury was reasonably foreseeable by the teacher in the circumstances of the case. In the Cook case it may well have been that the possibility of further abuse was so remote as to preclude civil liability for failing to report. The repetitive nature of child abuse is well known, however, and it should be treated as almost obvious that further harm will come to the child if no report is made. The existence of the various reporting statutes attests to the fact that the enacting legislatures presume that repeated abuse is foreseeable.

Perhaps the most troublesome problem to overcome is whether or not the teacher's failure to report was the last chance to prevent the further injury. There may well be others who are equally (or more) to blame such as doctors, social workers and neighbours. Whose failure to report resulted in the abuse continuing? At the very least, failure to report may be viewed as a contributing cause of additional abuse (if not the only cause) and courts can impose liability to such degree as they think appropriate. Proof on a balance of probabilities, as in all other civil actions, is all that is required; there need not be certainty that this particular failure to report was the one that ultimately lead to the continuing abuse. It is not unreasonable to hold teachers liable for not reporting, since the burden placed upon them by this requirement is slight when compared to the potential harm to children.

Nevertheless, this avenue of legal redress is being pursued more often in the United States. Because of our tendency to follow the American lead in novel legal situations, it may not be long before we see Canadian cases testing the civil liability of a professional who fails to report child abuse. Even an unsuccessful civil action will cause the defendant to incur tremendous emotional and financial burdens. This possibility can be avoided entirely if the profession adheres strictly to the reporting requirements of the legislation.

Perhaps the most serious consequence for failure to report suspected child abuse lies entirely outside of the legal arena. It is the tremendous guilt that a teacher will have to bear should he fail to report and further abuse occurs. Child abuse is typically repetitive in nature, with each episode becoming more severe than the last. If a teacher fails to report a case of abuse he can be reasonably certain that the child will be subjected to even more severe abuse in the future. The anguish and guilt involved in knowing that a child may have been saved further pain by the placement of one anonymous phone call can remain for a lifetime.

Barriers to Reporting

A large proportion of child abuse cases go unreported. Some cases are only detected by police when a child dies despite previous indicators that should have been reported. Numerous reasons are given by professionals for failing to report instances of suspected abuse. The barriers to reporting can be classified as cultural barriers, administrative barriers, and personal barriers. These exist among all professions but we shall examine them in the context of educational personnel.

Cultural barriers are those which are rooted in long standing beliefs and attitudes. One of these is the notion that children are the property of their parents, who are thereby entitled to use whatever disciplinary procedures they deem appropriate. To some extent this attitude has found expression in section 43 of the *Criminal Code* which permits the use of corporal punishment which is "reasonable." This attitude is gradually changing and courts are narrowing the factual situations in which force may be deemed reasonable. In the case of *R. v. Sarwer-Foner* (1979) 8 R.F.L. (2d) 342 a judge of the Ontario Provincial Court made the following remarks concerning section 43:

> It seems to me as emphasis continues on children's rights that the application of s. 43 of the Code as a defence to assault becomes more and more delicate . . . Indeed, I would go so far as to suggest that s. 43 should not be an available defence to an assault charge where any kind of measurable injury, whether physical or mental, is shown to result from corporal punishment.

In determining reasonableness under the *Criminal Code*, a test of community standards is applied. This test may not be appropriate in child protection proceedings, however. Perhaps we should concentrate more upon the issue of whether the child's development is likely to be injured by the parent's conduct and less upon the issue of whether that particular conduct meets some vague notion of what is acceptable by community standards. If a particular course of conduct is having an adverse affect upon a child, it should be reported even though the teacher may not feel that it constitutes "abuse" under his predetermined concept of acceptable community standards. As was also pointed out in the Sarwer-Foner case:

> I realize that ideas about acceptable forms of punishment vary not only from community to community, but from person to person, and that what one accepts as normal in this regard is largely a reflection of what one has been brought up and conditioned to accept as normal.

Another culturally induced norm is our reluctance to interfere in what are perceived as the private matters of others. The existence of this cultural barrier is best illustrated in situations that have occurred where numerous onlookers refuse to intervene while someone is being murdered. In matters of child abuse, it should be obvious that protection of our students is our concern as teachers. What happens to the child outside of school affects his academic performance and behaviour in the classroom. We must not only be concerned with student welfare during school hours but also with matters that affect classroom performance outside of school hours. These are not private matters but matters that affect the teacher directly and society as a whole.

A culturally-induced barrier which contributes to non-reporting is a general lack of awareness of the nature and scope of the problem. Some of this is deliberate "I don't want to hear about it" – but much is due to neglect. As a result, many indicators of abuse go unrecognized and unreported. With more publicity surrounding the problem and more school programs being made available, teachers cannot plead ignorance as an excuse any longer. We have a duty to learn how this problem affects our students.

Found under the broad category of administrative barriers to reporting is a general lack of clearly defined policy on how such matters should be handled. In the absence of clearly defined policies and procedures, teachers may be unsure of what action, if any, is required on their part throughout the process. Again this situation appears to be changing with heightened awareness of the problem and the fact that many schools have established procedures for reporting cases of suspected child abuse. The teacher should ensure that such procedures comply with the legal requirements of his particular province of employment. It does not fulfill a teacher's legal duty to merely report the matter to a principal. The duty imposed by statute is to report it to an official responsible under the Act: usually the director of child welfare for the province, or his agent. A teacher is not protected from potential charges merely by reporting to a superior, even if that is what school policy mandates.

Another administrative barrier is concern about the image and reputation of the school when cases of this sort are reported. Principals do not want their school to be known as the one with the highest number of abused children in the province. However, it may be contended that schools with a large number of reported abuse cases are those that show the most concern for their students by encouraging reporting. More frequent reporting reflects more care, more concern, and more professional responsibility on the part of the school staff. It is not indicative of a higher rate of abuse or of an "immoral" school. Administrators should take pride in leading the fight against this problem.

The third type of barrier to reporting suspected child abuse is a fear of personal involvement. This may be a fear of parental reaction or a fear of legal liability if a case is reported in error. Contributing to this fear is a misunderstanding or lack of knowledge about the consequences of reporting (upon the child involved, upon the parent and upon the person reporting). It is often felt that nothing will be done and that reporting is just a waste of time. On the other hand, some people may believe that the consequences of reporting will be too harsh on the parent and that the child will be cast into some faceless institution. These misconceptions arise from the fact that such cases are subject to the privacy provisions of the various statutes.

The purpose of provincial child abuse legislation is therapeutic, in that treatment and rehabilitation of the offender and the protection of the child are the ultimate goals. Although there are criminal sanctions provided by the *Criminal Code* and "quasi-criminal" penalties in all provincial legislation, charges are usually not laid where it is felt that the ends of rehabilitation and protection can be effectively met through other means. There is a sharp difference in philosophy between the criminal law and child welfare law on this matter. The former seeks to punish, deter, and to some extent rehabilitate the offender. The latter seeks to protect and counsel the victim as well as to rehabilitate and counsel the offender. Children may be temporarily removed from the home for their protection but the ultimate goal is to reunite the family in a healthy beneficial environment.

Unfortunately, cases in which these goals are achieved fail to receive a substantial share of the publicity. It is more sensational news to report a case where a child has been returned to the home only to be abused again than to report those where the family has been successfully reunited in a healthy safe environment. Cases at the other extreme also receive undue publicity. These involve instances where a child has been "spanked" by a parent in circumstances which may seem reasonable to many people, but the parent is then subjected to criminal charges and lengthy protective custody hearings. These cases are extremes and only serve to polarize feeling on one side or the other of the issue. Reporting should be seen as the first step towards establishing a positive response to the problem. Most cases are resolved satisfactorily and do not result in either of the extreme situations so often reported in the popular press.

The fear of personal legal liability for wrongful reporting can be laid to rest. Every provincial statute expressly provides immunity from any civil action or disciplinary proceedings where the report is made in good faith and on reasonable grounds. A typical provision in this regard is that found in the Alberta *Child Welfare Act* which states:

> No action lies against a person reporting pursuant to this section unless the reporting is done maliciously or without reasonable and probable grounds for the belief.

Even if it turns out that the suspected abuse did not in fact occur, the teacher is immune from legal action for reporting unless the report was prompted by malice without any belief in its truth. The law will presume good faith in making the report and the onus will be cast upon the person alleging malice to prove his claim to the satisfaction of the court. As a practical matter it is unlikely that the person reported will ever know who made the report since that information is confidential. A typical provision of provincial legislation can be found in *The Family and Child Services Act* of Prince Edward Island which states:

> No person shall reveal or be compelled to reveal the identity of a person who has acted in accordance with subsection (1) [the mandatory reporting requirement.]

A group known as VOCAL, Victims of Child Abuse Legislation, has arisen in the United States and has spawned some Canadian chapters and similar organizations. Their purpose is to aid parents who have been wrongfully accused of child abuse. Their usual targets for legal action are the government agents involved in specific cases although it would appear that they would like to be able to get at the anonymous informants in these cases as well. This group and others like it manage to generate considerable publicity over a few isolated cases. Again it is a case of the extreme example being deemed newsworthy. There is no doubt that some false reports are made and that parents and children involved in such cases suffer severely. There is also no doubt that such false reports made maliciously and without any basis for belief should be dealt with by criminal and civil penalties.

In appropriate cases, action will be initiated against those who make false accusations. The Yukon Territory has enacted the following provision to deal with such cases:

> Any person who maliciously and falsely reports to a peace officer, the Director, or agent of the Director, or to any other person facts from which the inference that a child may be in need of protection may reasonably be

drawn commits an offence and is liable upon summary conviction to a fine of up to $5,000 or imprisonment for as long as six months, or both.

Occasionally, reports which turn out to be false in substance are made based on a bona fide belief that abuse has occurred. Usually these cases are resolved quickly when the facts become apparent. The person reporting in such instances has demonstrated a high degree of concern for the child and should not be castigated by anyone for this honest attempt at responsible citizenship. Legitimate concerns and suspicions should not be deterred by fear of retribution. Courts will, therefore, protect anyone honestly making a report of suspected abuse. Teachers need have no fear of any personal legal liability for reporting their honest beliefs.

In the case of *Re Infant* (1981) 32 B.C.L.R. 20, the parents of a small boy who were wrongly accused of child abuse sought to compel the disclosure of the name of the informant for the purpose of pursuing an action against that person. Section 22 of the British Columbia *Family and Child Service Act* makes it an offence for any person to disclose information obtained under the Act. The Supreme Court of British Columbia held:

> The refusal is not a matter of discretion. It does not require an administrative decision at all. The refusal results from compliance with s. 22 of the Family and Child Service Act.
>
> It follows that I could have no authority under the Judicial Review Procedure Act to grant any of the relief sought.
>
> Had I not come to this conclusion I would have followed the decision of the House of Lords in D. v. Nat. Society for the Prevention of Cruelty to Children, [1978] A.C. 171, [1977] 1 All E.R. 589, which establishes that a common law rule will protect from disclosure the identity of persons who make complaints of child abuse to the equivalent authority in England. I refer in particular to the words of Lord Diplock (at p. 596):
>
> 'I would extend to those who give information about neglect or ill-treatment of children to a local authority or the N.S.P.C.C. a similar immunity from disclosure of their identity in legal proceedings to that which the law accords to police informers. The public interests served by preserving the anonymity of both classes of informants are analogous' ...
>
> Here the common law rule seems to me to be declared in statutory form in s. 22 of the Family and Child Service Act.

A particularly thorny problem is confronted by teachers when faced with the possibility that a fellow teacher is engaging in some form of child abuse. There are professional ethics to be followed as well as legal obligations. There is no doubt that the teaching profession does attract certain people inclined towards child abuse, especially sexual abuse, and that we must rid the profession of such people. The problem arises in making sure that the career of an innocent teacher is not ruined by false allegations. Each teachers' association has adopted a procedure for making complaints against a fellow teacher and it is suggested that these be followed in order to avoid any problems of professional misconduct on the reporting teacher's part. If, however, the reporting teacher also foresees harm to the child if the matter is not reported to the appropriate protection agency, the teacher should also file a report with that agency as well, even if such action appears to violate association procedures. Teacher's associations do not consider themselves to be above the law and, thus would not presume to impose their own standards over the requirements mandated by the legislature.

The increasing number of cases reported in the media involving teachers who have abused children has resulted in teachers changing their treatment of children. Physical demonstrations of love and concern for the child are, unfortunately, becoming a thing of the past. Many teachers are simply afraid to hug a small child with a scraped knee or cut lip out of fear that allegations of misconduct will be made against them. We must regain the confidence of the public in this matter by becoming actively involved in the fight against child abuse and demonstrating our profession's concern and involvement in combatting the problem.

Two recent cases from New Brunswick, reported in School Law Commentary as Cases 1-10-2 and 1-10-3, demonstrate some of the issues that become involved when teachers are charged with sexual abuse of their students. In these cases two teachers were dismissed after an investigation into allegations of sexual misconduct towards students. Both teachers appealed their dismissals and in one case the teacher was reinstated, but in the other the dismissal was upheld.

The allegations were similar in each case and the issue became the credibility of the witnesses. Both teachers denied the allegations which were made in testimony by certain students. In one instance the adjudicator found the teacher's testimony credible and doubted the allegations made by the students. In the other case he did not accept the teacher's evidence and believed the students. In both decisions, the adjudicator commented that it is the responsibility of the board to ensure public confidence in the school system and to see to it that the integrity of teachers employed in the system is above reproach. He declined to award damages for loss of reputation to the teacher who was reinstated since he felt he was restricted to making awards for financial loss only, although he expressed an inclination to want to grant damages for such loss of reputation.

Unfounded allegations against teachers can harm their reputation and career beyond measure. The allegations usually receive wide publicity which is often not matched when they are proven to be unfounded. The attitude that a person must have been guilty or he would not have been charged persists despite the common law presumption of innocence. It is the making of the allegation that can cause the damage irrespective of the eventual outcome of the matter.

In a British Columbia case, reported at [1987] B.C.Dec. 4032-01, a teacher was suspended by the school board on the basis of allegations of abuse of a student. The Superintendent submitted a letter to the Board stating that he found the student's allegations to be credible although the teacher denied them. The Superintendent was present while the Board deliberated the matter. This was held to be a denial of natural justice. The court held that it would not seem fair to the average man to permit a decision to be made affecting a person's career in the presence of someone like the Superintendent who could influence the decision.

In summary, teachers should become thoroughly knowledgeable about the legal and professional aspects of child abuse. As one of the "front line" defences in combatting the problem, they must know what to look for and when and how to report suspected cases of abuse. They should seek clearly defined, legally correct policies and procedures from their administrators. Teachers must also become aware of how to deal with the abused child in the classroom setting.

Teachers are often required to assume a therapeutic role in the treatment of the abused child because of their close contact with the child. Teachers will be required to consult with doctors, psychologists, and social workers in designing and carrying out programs and procedures for abused children in their classroom.

Teachers can also take an active role in prevention and treatment of child abuse by doing what they do best: teaching. They can educate themselves, their students, colleagues, parents and the community about the problem. Parent education is often as important as the education of their children. Parent-teacher meetings can be used to advise parents of the conditions that lead to potential abuse, the effects of abuse on children, and the available help. Self reporting and treatment are the ultimate goals of the program. Students can be educated through family life programs concerning the appropriate treatment of a child, since many abused children do not recognize that the way they are being treated at home is not normal behaviour. They assume that other children are treated in the same fashion and are not aware of how the majority behaves.

Child abuse is everybody's problem and will not be solved only by lawyers, psychiatrists, and social workers. Teachers can play a strong and active role in prevention and resolution of the problem if they are willing to assume their legal, moral, and professional obligations.

Discussion and Review Questions

1. Which legislation imposes legal requirements in child abuse situations upon the shoulders of the classroom teacher?

2. How is child abuse defined? Does your province differ from other provinces, or are there nation-wide definitions?

3. What are the reporting requirements for your province? Is the person who reports protected from legal action?

4. What can you do to help solve the problem of child abuse?

5. What are some of the special behavioral and learning problems that the teacher of the abused child may have to face?

6. What does the code of ethics of your provincial teachers' association say about child abuse?

7. What is the policy of your local school board concerning the child in need of protection?

8. In your opinion, what is the single most important reason why people fail to report suspected cases of child abuse?

9. Compare the reporting requirements of each province. What are the strengths and weaknesses of each? Which do you think addresses the problem best?

You be the Judge

The Case of the Suspicious Substitute

John Smith was a recent graduate from the University of Utopia. Due to provincial budget cuts he was unable to find full-time employment as a teacher and earned a meagre living as a substitute teacher for the Arcadia School Division.

One day he was called upon to substitute for Tom Jones, a grade three teacher at Sunnybrook Elementary School. John was pleased to find a detailed lesson plan for the day and multiple copies of various worksheets and materials that would be required. Such concern for the substitute was a rare occurrence. John decided that Mr. Jones was clearly one of the most competent and caring teachers on the face of the earth.

The morning was going exceptionally well for John. He attributed this to the fine preparation and creative lessons of Mr. Jones (not to mention his own natural talents). He taught a very successful math lesson and had distributed worksheets for the students to complete at their desks. After monitoring their progress for several minutes, he sat at Mr. Jones' desk to review the plan for the next lesson.

John thought that the placement of the desk at the back of the classroom was awkward. His view of the class was cut off by large bookshelves at the side and in front of the desk. He assumed that Jones must never sit at the desk during class and that the odd configuration was to provide privacy during the long hours that the man obviously spent at the school preparing his lesson plans.

John had been sitting for barely a minute when 9-year-old Lolita appeared at his side.

"I'm finished the math sheet, Mr. Smith," she said, placing the paper on the desk.

John swivelled the chair to face Lolita. Before he could say, "Thank you," she climbed into his lap and stared expectantly into John's face.

"What are you doing, Lolita?"

"If we're the first one finished, Mr. Jones lets us sit on his lap and tickles us," she replied.

Horrified, John placed Lolita back on the floor and stood up. "I don't like tickling," he said. "I give stickers instead."

"Oh," said Lolita, "I like it when he tickles my tummy and legs and pats my bum."

"Here's a sticker, Lolita. Please sit down at your desk."

At recess John pondered the morning's events. "That Jones is a pervert," he thought. "No wonder he has his desk hidden from view."

John became convinced that Tom Jones was touching the students in improper places for his own perverse gratification.

What does John do now?

Questions to Guide Discussion

1. What is John Smith required to do under the relevant legislation of your province regharding the reporting of suspected abuse? Is Lolita a child needing protection under the definition contained in your province's legislation?

2. What does your provincial Code of Ethics have to say about making a complaint against a fellow teacher? Is this matter one of those contemplated by such rules?

3. Should Smith report the matter to the police?

4. What reports, if any, should be made to the school administrators?

5. Should the matter be reported to the Teachers' Association?

6. Assuming that all of John's worst suspicions were correct and that Jones was indeed a child molestor, would your answer to any of the above questions change? What degree of proof is required before you act on your suspicions?

References

Aaron, J., "Civil Liability for Teachers' Negligent Failure to Report Suspected Child Abuse," (1981) 28 *Wayne Law Rev.* 182.

Dickens, B. M., "Legal Responses to Child Abuse in Canada" [1978] 1 *Can. Jnl. of Fam. Law* 87.

Manley-Casimir, M. and Newman, B., "Child Abuse and the School" (1976) 52 *Canadian Welfare* 17.

Van Stolk, M., *The Battered Child in Canada* (rev. ed.), Toronto: McClelland & Stewart, 1978.

Van Stolk, M., "Child Abuse and Canadian Law" (1978) 5 *Crime & Justice* 275.

Appendix A

Provincial Legislation Respecting the Reporting of Child Abuse

ALBERTA

Child Welfare Act, S. A. 1984, c. C-81

3. (1) Any person who has reasonable and probable grounds to believe and believes that a child is in need of protective services shall forthwith report the matter to a director.

(2) Subsection (1) applies notwithstanding that the information on which such belief is founded is confidential and its disclosure is prohibited under any other Act.

(3) This section does not apply to information that is privileged as a result of a solicitor-client relationship.

(4) No action lies against a person reporting pursuant to this section unless the reporting is done maliciously or without reasonable and probable grounds for the belief.

(5) Notwithstanding and in addition to any other penalty provided by this Act, if a director has reasonable and probable grounds to believe that a person has not complied with subsection (1) and that person is registered under an Act regulating a profession or occupation prescribed in the regulations, the director shall advise the appropriate governing body of that profession or occupation of the failure to comply.

(6) Any person who fails to comply with subsection (1) is guilty of an offence and liable to a fine of not more than $2,000 and in default of payment to imprisonment for a term of not more than 6 months.

BRITISH COLUMBIA

Family and Child Services Act, S. B. C. 1980, c. 11

7. (1) A person who has reasonable grounds to believe that a child is in need of protection shall forthwith report the circumstances to the superintendent or a person designated by the superintendent to receive such reports.

(2) The duty under subsection (1) overrides a claim of confidentiality or privilege by a person following any occupation or profession, except a claim founded on a solicitor and client relationship.

(3) No action lies against a person making a report under this section unless he makes it maliciously or without reasonable grounds for his belief.

(4) A person who contravenes subsection (1) commits an offence.

MANITOBA

Child Welfare Act, S. M. 1974, c. 30

36. (1) Any person having information of the abandonment, desertion, ill treatment or need for protection of a child shall report the information to the director or to a child caring agency.

(2) Subsection (1) applies notwithstanding that the information is confidential or privileged; and no action lies against the informant for reporting the information unless it is reported maliciously or without reasonable and probable cause.

NEW BRUNSWICK

Child and Family Services and Family Relations Act (renamed as Family Services Act), S. N. B. 1980, c. C-2.1

30. (1) Any person who has information causing him to suspect that a child has been abandoned, deserted, physically or emotionally neglected, physically or sexually ill-treated or otherwise abused shall inform the Minister of the situation without delay.

(2) Subsection (1) applies notwithstanding that the person has acquired the information through the discharge of his duties or within a confidential relationship, but nothing in this subsection abrogates any privilege that may exist because of the relationship between a solicitor and the solicitor's client.

(3) Any professional person who fails to comply with subsection (1) having acquired the information referred to in subsection (1) in the discharge of his professional responsibilities commits an offence.

(4) Where the Minister has reasonable grounds to suspect that any person has failed to comply with subsection (1), the Minister may, in addition to any action he may take with respect to prosecution, require any professional society, association or other organization authorized under the laws of the Province to regulate the professional activities of the person to cause an investigation to be made into the matter.

(5) No action lies, in relation to the giving of information under subsection (1), against a person who in good faith complies therewith.

(6) Except in the course of judicial proceedings, no person shall reveal the identity of a person who has given information under subsection (1) without that person's written consent.

(7) Any person who violates subsection (6) commits an offence.

(10) For the purposes of subsection (3) "professional person" means a physician, nurse, dentist or other health or mental health professional, a hospital administrator, a school principal, school teacher or other teaching professional, a social work administrator, social worker or other social service professional, a child care worker in a day care center or child caring institution, a police or law

enforcement officer, a psychologist, a guidance counsellor, or a recreational services administrator or worker, and includes any other person who by virtue of his employment or occupation has a responsibility to discharge a duty of care towards a child.

NEWFOUNDLAND

Child Welfare Act, S. N. 1972, No. 37, as amended by The Child Welfare (Amendment) Act, S. N. 1981, c. 54

49. (1) Every person having information of the abandonment, desertion, physical ill-treatment or need for protection of a child shall report the information to the Director or a welfare officer.

(2) Subsection (1) applies notwithstanding that the information is confidential or privileged, and no action lies against the informant unless the giving of the information is done maliciously or without reasonable and probable cause.

(3) Any person who fails to comply with or contravenes this section is guilty of an offence and liable on summary conviction to a fine not exceeding one thousand dollars or to imprisonment for a term not exceeding six months or to both such fine and imprisonment.

NORTHWEST TERRITORIES

The Child Welfare Ordinance, O. N. W. T. 1983, c. 2

30.1 (1) For the purposes of this section, "abuse" means a condition of (a) physical harm wherein a child suffers physical injury but does not include reasonable punishment administered by a parent or guardian;

(b) malnutrition or mental ill-health of a degree that if not immediately remedied could seriously impair growth and development or result in permanent injury or death; or

(c) sexual molestation

(2) Every person who has information of the abandonment, desertion or need of protection of a child or the infliction of abuse upon a child shall forthwith report the information to the Superintendent of Child Welfare.

(3) Notwithstanding the provisions of any other Ordinance, every person who has reasonable grounds to suspect in the course of the person's professional or official duties that a child has suffered or is suffering from abuse that may have been caused or permitted by a person who has or has had charge of the child shall forthwith report the suspected abuse to the Superintendent of Child Welfare.

(4) This section applies notwithstanding that the information reported is confidential or privileged.

(5) No action for making the report shall be instituted against any person who reports the information to the Superintendent of Child Welfare in accordance

with this section unless the giving of the information is done maliciously or without reasonable grounds to suspect that the information is true.

(6) Nothing in this section shall abrogate any privilege that may exist between a solicitor and the solicitor's client.

NOVA SCOTIA

Children's Services Act, S. N. S. 1976, c. 8 as amended by S. N. S. 1984, c. 53

77. (1) Every one who has information, whether or not it is confidential or privileged, indicating that a child is in need of protection and who fails to report that information to an agency is guilty of an offence under this Act.

(2) No action lies against a person who gives information under subsection (1) unless the giving of the information is done maliciously or without reasonable and probable cause.

(3) Everyone who causes or contributes to a child being or being likely to become a child in need of protection is guilty of an offence under this Act.

(4) A prosecution for an offence referred to in this Section shall be commenced within one year after the day on which the offence was committed and not thereafter.

ONTARIO

Child and Family Services Act, S. O. 1984, c. 55

68. (1) In this section . . . "to suffer abusem," when used in reference to a child, means to be in need of protection within the meaning of clause 37 (2) (a), (c), (e), (f) or (h).

(2) A person who believes on reasonable grounds that a child is or may be in need of protection shall forthwith report the belief and the information upon which it is based to a society.

(3) Despite the provisions of any other Act, a person referred to in subsection (4) who, in the course of his or her professional or official duties, has reasonable grounds to suspect that a child is or may be suffering or may have suffered abuse shall forthwith report the suspicion and the information on which it is based to a society.

(4) Subsection (3) applies to every person who performs professional or official duties with respect to a child, including,

    (a) a health care professional, including a physician, nurse, dentist, pharmacist and psychologist;

    (b) a teacher, school principal, social worker, family counsellor, priest, rabbi, clergyman, operator or employee of a day nursery and youth and recreation worker;

(c) a peace officer and a coroner;

(d) a solicitor; and

(e) a service provider and an employee of a service provider.

(5) In clause (4) (b), "youth and recreation worker" does not include a volunteer.

(6) A society that obtains information that a child in its care and custody is or may be suffering or may have suffered abuse shall forthwith report the information to a Director.

(7) This section applies although the information reported may be confidential or privileged, and no action for making the report shall be instituted against a person who acts in accordance with subsection (2) or (3) unless the person acts maliciously or without reasonable grounds for the belief or suspicion, as the case may be.

(8) Nothing in this section abrogates any privilege that may exist between a solicitor and his or her client.

PRINCE EDWARD ISLAND

Family and Child Services Act, S. P. E. I. 1981, c. 12

14. (1) Every person who has knowledge or has reasonable and probable cause to believe that a child has been abandoned, deserted or abused must forthwith report or cause to be reported the circumstances to the Director or a peace officer who shall report it to the Director, and shall provide to a child care worker such additional information as is available to him or is known to him.

(3) No person shall reveal or be compelled to reveal the identity of a person who has acted in accordance with subsection (1).

(4) A person who has knowledge or has reasonable and probable grounds to believe that a child has been abandoned, deserted or abused and who makes a report pursuant to subsection (1) is not liable to any civil action in respect of any matter contained in the report.

(5) Nothing in this section affects or abrogates any privilege that may exist because of the relationship between a solicitor and his client.

50. Any person who fails to comply with section 14 is guilty of an offence and is liable to a fine not exceeding three hundred dollars.

QUEBEC

Youth Protection Act, R. S. Q. 1971, c. P-34

24. Every person, even one having privileged information by reason of his office, who has reasonable cause to believe that a child is subject to physical ill-treatment as the result of abuse or neglect is bound to bring the matter to the attention of the committee without delay.

Failure to observe the preceding paragraph is an offence under this act.

25. No civil action may be instituted on the grounds that a person has, in good faith, brought a situation contemplated in section 24 to the attention of the committee.

26. The committee or a person in its service must not reveal the identity of the person who has brought a situation contemplated in section 24 to its attention, without his consent.

SASKATCHEWAN

Family Services Act, R. S. S. 1978, c. F-7

16. (1) Every person having information that a child is in need of protection shall report the information to an officer or peace officer.

(2) A person who makes a report pursuant to subsection (1) is not liable in any action for making the report unless the report is false and is made maliciously.

(3) Every peace officer who is in receipt of information that a child is in need of protection shall forthwith report the information to an officer of the department.

YUKON TERRITORY

Children's Act, S. Y. T. 1984, c. 2

117. (1) A person who has reasonable and probable grounds to believe that a child may be a child in need of protection may report the information upon which he bases his belief to the Director, an agent of the Director, or a peace officer.

(2) No legal action of any kind, including professional disciplinary proceedings, may be taken against a person who reports information under subsection (1) by reason of his so reporting, unless the reporting was done maliciously and falsely.

(3) Any person who maliciously and falsely reports to a peace officer, the Director, an agent of the Director, or to any other person facts from which the inference that a child may be in need of protection may reasonably be drawn commits an offence and is liable on summary conviction to a fine of up to $5,000 or imprisonment for as long as six months, or both.

7

Young Offenders

Learning Objectives

Some of the things the reader will learn from reading this chapter include:

1. The change in philosophy toward the legal rights of young people which resulted from the passage of the *Young Offenders Act.*
2. The procedural safeguards provided to young offenders by the *Young Offenders Act.*
3. The procedural safeguards offered by the *Charter of Rights and Freedoms.*
4. What the right to a "consultant" means within the framework of the *Young Offenders Act.*
5. The dilemma faced by teachers when a crime is committed within the school.
6. The probable legal position of the teacher and principal concerning certain rights and guarantees contained in the Charter.
7. The teacher problems associated with the young offender who is "sentenced to school."

Preview

Teachers owe students a right to legal safety as well as a right to physical safety. This is simply part of the professional responsibility that comes with the job.

Young offenders pose a number of problems, besides their conduct, for the teacher and school administration. To properly handle the situation the teacher must familiarize himself with the provisions of the *Young Offenders Act* and especially the sections which deal with the requirements placed upon the parent since in certain circumstances the teacher may be required to act as parent to the youth.

Questioning young people regarding offenses such as theft must be done in an atmosphere which pays careful attention to the student's legal rights under the *Young Offenders Act* and the Charter. This is especially true when the police are or may become involved later.

Often young people who have been charged with an offense whether committed in the school or not stand in danger of having their *Charter* and *Young Offenders Act* rights violated by the actions of teachers and administrators. Frequently, the problem centres upon efforts to suspend or e the student or with respect to the manner in which school records are handled.

Self-Assessment

1. Can you define what is meant legally by the term young offender?
2. When a young offender is questioned by the police, what rights does he have? When questioned by a teacher or school administrator, what rights does he have?
3. What special role does the parent or guardian have when youth become involved in an alleged illegal activity?
4. What are the implications for the teacher when a young offender is convicted of a crime and sentenced to return to school?

Key Terms

Sentenced to school
de facto
In loco parentis
Person in authority
Privileged communication
Voluntariness
Justified at its inception
Alternative measures

*   *   *   *

The *Young Offenders Act*, S.C. 1980-81-82-83 c. 110, came into force on April 1, 1984, repealing and replacing the *Juvenile Delinquent Act*, R.S.C. 1970 c. J-3. The philosophy of this new act is that youthful offenders should bear responsibility for their criminal conduct and that society must be protected from such offenders. These principles are declared in section 3 of the Act which states:

> 3.(1) It is hereby recognized and declared that
> (a) while young persons should not in all instances be held accountable in the same manner or suffer the same consequences for their behaviour as adults, young persons who commit offences should nonetheless bear responsibility for their contraventions;
> (b) society must, although it has the responsibility to take reasonable measures to prevent criminal conduct by young persons, be afforded the necessary protection from illegal behaviour . . .

This philosophy is in contrast to the rehabilitative philosophy of the former Act which stated in section 38:

> . . . as far as possible every juvenile delinquent shall be treated not as a criminal, but as a misguided and misdirected child and one needing aid, encouragement, help and assistance.

This approach has not been abandoned altogether since elements of it have been retained in the *Young Offenders Act* which states in section 3 (1) (c):

> young persons who commit offences require supervision, discipline and control, but, because of their state of dependency and level of development and maturity, they also have special needs and require guidance and assistance . . .

The *Young Offenders Act* applies to youth who are twelve years of age and over but have not yet reached their eighteenth birthday at the time of commission of a criminal offence. Persons over the age of eighteen at the time of committing an offence are tried as adults and children under the age of twelve cannot be tried or convicted of a criminal offence in any court. The term "criminal offence," as used in the act, means an offence created by the federal government under the *Criminal Code, Narcotic Control Act* or any other federal statute or regulation. It does not include the quasi-criminal offences created by provincial or municipal authorities such as contraventions of traffic or liquor laws. These matters are dealt with under provincial legislation concerning young offenders.

Many of these young offenders are also school pupils and it is, therefore, essential that educators become aware of various laws regarding young offenders. The *Young Offenders Act* and the *Charter of Rights and Freedoms* as it applies to young offenders both have a direct impact on the administration of schools and upon teacher conduct in relation to pupils. Areas of particular importance to the teacher include the legal and constitutional rights of young offenders, youth who are "sentenced to school," school records concerning young offenders, and "publication" of the names of young offenders.

A teacher may, in certain circumstances, be regarded as a "parent" for the purposes of the *Young Offenders Act* and must be prepared to assume the responsibilities imposed upon a parent under the Act. The Act defines a "parent" as:

> parent includes, in respect of another person, any person who is under a legal duty to provide for that other person or any person who has, in law or in fact, the custody or control of that other person . . .

A teacher often has *de facto* custody and control of his students, particularly on extended field trips when the natural parent or guardian may be many miles away. The Act requires that certain notices be given to parents and that parents can be compelled to attend court proceedings. These provisions may apply to teachers in circumstances as described who then are not merely *in loco parentis*, i.e. acting in the place of parents, but are legally considered to be "parents" for purposes of the Act.

Young offenders have, because of their youth, been given broader procedural safeguards and legal rights than are granted to adult offenders. This is part of the philosophy behind the Act and is provided for in section 3 (1) which states:

> (e) young persons have rights and freedoms in their own right, including those stated in the Canadian Charter of Rights and Freedoms or in the Canadian Bill of Rights, and in particular a right to be heard in the course of, and to participate in, the processes that lead to decisions that affect them, and young persons should have special guarantees of their rights and freedoms;
>
> (f) in the application of this Act, the rights and freedoms of young persons include a right to the least possible interference with freedom that is consistent with the protection of society, having regard to the needs of young persons and the interests of their families;
>
> (g) young persons have the right, in every instance where they have rights or freedoms that may be affected by this Act, to be informed as to what those rights and freedoms are . . .

Teachers have an obligation to ensure that the rights of a student are not violated when dealing with matters that may result in criminal charges. In determining what those rights include, teachers must make reference to the *Charter of Rights and Freedoms* as well as to the *Young Offenders Act.* Remember that we are only discussing student rights in the context of criminal proceedings against a student and not in the larger context of student civil rights in the school. Those matters are dealt with in the chapter on student rights.

One of the most fundamental rights granted to any person is the right to obtain legal advice as soon as possible. This right is enshrined in section 10 of the Charter which states:

Everyone has the right on arrest or detention
(a) to be informed promptly of the reasons therefore;
(b) to retain and instruct counsel without delay and to be informed of that right . . .

In addition to this right which applies to everyone, the *Young Offenders Act* (as amended by S.C. 1986 c. 32,s. 9) specifically provides in section 11 (1)

A young person has the right to retain and instruct counsel without delay, and to exercise that right personally, at any stage of proceedings against the young person and prior to and during any consideration of whether, instead of commencing or continuing judicial proceedings against the young person under this Act, to use alternative measures to deal with the young person.

The 1986 amendment added the words "and to exercise that right personally" following a series of cases which held that an infant could not legally retain counsel and that this right had to be exercised by a parent or guardian on behalf of the child. One such case was *R. v. W.W.W.* (1985) 20 C.C.C.(3d) 214 wherein the Manitoba Court of Appeal held that a lawyer can only receive instructions from a legal guardian and not directly from the child. If the parent or guardian is not available to instruct counsel then an application will have to be made to the court to have an interim guardian appointed for this purpose.

That court carried its decision further in the case of *R. v. H.* (1985) 22 C.C.C.(3d) 114, where it was held that because a lawyer could only be retained by a guardian, a young offender could not waive his right to counsel. In that particular case the conviction of a 16 year old youth charged with murder was set aside. He had waived his right to counsel and confessed to the murder but the confessions were held inadmissible since it was held that

~~he could not waive the right to counsel on his own behalf.~~

~~This amendment to the~~ *Young Offenders Act* ~~was made to overrule this line of judicial decisions and also to give full effect to the recognition of rights and responsibilities for young~~ offenders. It was held that if a young person is considered capable of committing crimes, and of participating in the legal process as a consequence, he should be given the right to retain and instruct counsel on his own behalf and also have the right to waive that right. Any waiver of this right can only be made with full knowledge and comprehension of that right as we shall see in other cases dealing with procedural rights regarding statements made by young offenders.

Section 56 of the *Young Offenders Act* sets out the procedure to be followed when taking a statement from a young offender concerning his involvement in an alleged offence. This section provides:

(1) Subject to this section, the law relating to the admissibility of statements made by persons accused of committing offences applies in respect of young persons.

(2) No oral or written statement given by a young person to a peace officer or other person who is, in law, a person in authority is admissible against the young person unless

(a) the statement was voluntary;

(b) the person to whom the statement was given has, before the statement was made, clearly explained to the young person, in language appropriate to his age and understanding, that

(i) the young person is under no obligation to give a statement,

(ii) any statement given by him may be used as evidence in proceedings against him,

(iii) the young person has the right to consult another person in accordance with paragraph (c), and

(iv) any statement made by the young person is required to be made in the presence of the person consulted, unless the young person desires otherwise;

(c) the young person has, before the statement was made, been given a reasonable opportunity to consult with counsel or a parent, or in the absence of a parent, an adult relative, or in the absence of a parent or an adult relative, any other appropriate adult chosen by the young person; and

(d) where the young person consults any person pursuant to paragraph (c), the young person has been given a reasonable opportunity to make the statement in the presence of that person.

(3) The requirements set out in paragraphs (2)(b),(c), and (d) do not apply in respect of oral statements where they were made spontaneously by the young person to a peace officer or other person in authority before that person has had a reasonable opportunity to comply with those

requirements.

(4) A young person may waive his rights under paragraph (2)(c) or
(d) but any such waiver shall be made in writing and shall contain a statement signed by the young person that he has been apprised of the right that he is waiving.

(5) A youth court judge may rule inadmissible in any proceedings under this Act a statement given by the young person in respect of whom proceedings are taken if the young person satisfies the judge that the statement was given under duress imposed by any person who is not, in law, a person in authority.

(6) For the purpose of this section, an adult consulted pursuant to paragraph 56 (2) (c) shall, in the absence of evidence to the contrary, be deemed not to be a person in "authority." (added by S.C. 1986, c.32, s.38)

Because this is recent legislation, there have not been a large number of decisions from the higher courts on the interpretation and full extent of these rights. However, there have already been some cases which have involved teachers and school authorities. These cases and the few that have been decided in other contexts provide some guidance as to how to handle situations where students have been involved in criminal offences. Teachers may be faced with one of two problems in relation to a student who is a young offender. The first would be in relation to an offence committed in the school or in relation to school property. The second would involve situations which occur outside of the school but where the police arrive at school to question or charge a student with the offence.

In the latter situation teachers may believe that they have no responsibility toward the student since it is a police matter unconnected with the school. We suggest, however, that a teacher's duty to protect his students from harm while at school should not be confined only to protection from physical harm, but should also extend to protection from other types of harm as well. When we, as teachers, have become so careful to protect students from physical injury, should we not be equally protective of the students' legal rights, i.e. their right to legal safety? The consequences to the student of a conviction under the *Young Offenders Act* may be far more serious than a broken arm or sprained wrist. We suggest that it may indeed be seen to be unprofessional conduct not to ensure that a student's legal rights are protected while he is in school.

In particular, teachers should make sure that the student's parent or guardian is contacted for consultation pursuant to subsection 2(c). In the absence of legal counsel, a parent or other adult relative, the teacher may find himself being requested to act as "consultant" being an "appropriate adult chosen by the young person." The wording of the section and a subsequent judicial interpretation seem to indicate that another adult may only be consulted in the absence of other persons enumerated in the subsection. In *R. v. G.P.S.* (1985) 24 C.C.C. 61, a judge of the County Court of Ontario held:

> The clause is so phrased that the presence of the accused's mother probably excludes the right to consult an adult relative, or other appropriate adult chosen by the young person . . .

Therefore, teachers should not consent or presume to act in this role unless they are satisfied that a parent or another adult relative is not available. Students may desire, for personal reasons, to consult a teacher rather than a parent but this option does not seem to be open to them unless the parent is not available.

If, however, a parent or adult relative is not available, the teacher may well be requested to act as a consultant for his student and must know what to do and say in such a situation. There is no statutory requirement that the teacher must act in this capacity if requested to do so but it is suggested that for professional reasons the teacher should not refuse. The position of a teacher is to assume the parental role in school and this carries with it a positive legal duty to protect the interests of the child. Morally and professionally, teachers must be concerned with upholding the law including the rights of young offenders. The moral and professional pressures placed upon a teacher in this situation dictate that he assume the role of consultant rather than abandon the child to some unknown fate where the child's rights may not be ensured. It is folly to assume that the police will scrupulously guard a child's rights, as the cases discussed below will clearly show.

The student is entitled to speak to his parent or other adult before the police ask him any questions about the offence. This was made clear by the Manitoba Court of Appeal in *R. v. B.C.W.* (1986) 27 C.C.C.(3d) 481 where it was held:

> A young person is entitled to the advice of a parent before he is even questioned by the police if the opportunity for him to have the benefit of that advice is reasonably available . . . The young person's right to consultation is not a technical one to be recognized in form alone. Not only must the young person be told he has the right to consult an adult, but he must also be given an actual opportunity to do so.

Having assumed the role of consultant, the teacher must be aware of what rights the student does have and what advice should be given. Teachers should not presume to become the child's counsel or lawyer since they are usually not qualified to do so. Probably the best advice to give in this situation is to tell the student to make no statement until the parents are contacted or a lawyer has been retained. Teachers should not discuss the specifics of the child's involvement in the offence since there is a distinct possibility that any statement made to the teacher may be admissible against the student in later proceedings. Your natural curiosity may lead you to want to hear all the details but discretion and concern for the child's rights should compel you to avoid the temptation.

Although the conversation with the student is a private conversation it is not necessarily a "privileged" communication. In *R. v. G.P.S.*, cited above, it was stated:

> The word 'consult' or its equivalent has now been considered by various courts, including the Supreme Court of Canada, with the result that it must be construed to carry with it the right to a private conversation with the person consulted.

What this means is that you and the young offender can, and should, insist that the consultation be done in private without the presence of the police or anyone else. It does not mean that you cannot be called upon to testify as to what that conversation was about at a later date in court proceedings. Communications between a lawyer and a client are called "privileged" and no court can compel a lawyer to divulge what his client has told him. These are the only communications that are in fact privileged despite common misconceptions about doctor/patient, priest/penitent or reporter/source privileges. All of these people can be compelled to testify as to the substance of their conversations or be imprisoned for failure to do so. If the student confesses a crime, a teacher can be compelled to disclose that conversation under oath in court proceedings and the protections of s. 56 would not apply pursuant to subsection (6) which would deem the teacher not to be a person in authority.

As a practical matter, however, a teacher would not be called as a witness unless the prosecution knew that the confession had been made and the evidence would be necessary to prove the case. The Crown will not know what the essence of the conversation was unless the teacher or the student divulges such information. Remember, the teacher is not required to volunteer such information to the police or to the Crown prosecutor but only to the court at the time of trial. So, without prior knowledge of what the teacher's testimony will be it is highly unlikely that he would be called as a witness.

It is a wise course of action to make notes of what occurs in such situations, including what was said by the police, the student, yourself, and anyone else that may have been present. Later, if there is any question as to the procedure followed you will be able to refresh your memory. Trials often occur many months, sometimes a year or more, after the event and it is often difficult to remember what transpired. The notes, although not admissible as evidence, will give you a record of the events as they occurred and they can be referred to in order to refresh your memory.

The requirements of the *Young Offenders Act* have an even greater impact upon the teacher when the offence committed is a school related one. The teacher is placed in a difficult position being, on one hand, the "victim and, on the other hand, *in loco parentis*." Compounding this problem is the need for order and discipline in the school sometimes necessitating actions which are unrelated to the criminal proceedings. All of these factors came together in an Alberta case involving a theft in a school.

R. v. H. (1985) 43 Alta. L. R. 250, was a decision of Judge Russell of the Youth Division of the Provincial Court of Alberta which was affirmed by Justice Dechene of the Court of Queen's Bench on appeal (unreported decision, June 26, 1986). The case involved a 13 year old youth who, together with some other students, stole money from a teacher's purse at school. The teacher reported this matter to the vice-principal. Then, without the knowledge or authority of the vice-principal or the principal, she told the class that if the money was returned nothing further would be done. As a result of this statement the accused and some others came forward and admitted to the theft.

Another teacher reported the names of these boys to the principal who summoned them to his office and interrogated them about the incident. He was apparently unaware of the teacher's promise. The boys again confessed to the theft and the police were called. At no time did the teacher or principal advise the boys of their rights under the *Young Offenders Act* or the *Charter of Rights and Freedoms*.

The only evidence available to the prosecution was the confession and evidence of the accomplices. The defence counsel for H. made application to have the evidence of the principal and accomplices excluded. The court also considered whether the evidence of the teacher should be excluded as well. There were two bases on which such evidence could be excluded. One was the provision in section 24 of the *Charter of Rights and Freedoms* which states:

(1) Anyone whose rights or freedoms, as guaranteed by this Charter, have been infringed or denied may apply to a court of competent jurisdiction to obtain such remedy as the court considers appropriate and just in the circumstances.

(2) Where, in proceedings under subsection (1), a court concludes that

evidence was obtained in a manner that infringed or denied any rights or freedoms guaranteed by this Charter, the evidence shall be excluded if it is established that, having regard to all of the circumstances, the admission of it in the proceedings would bring the administration of justice into disrepute.

The other basis for exclusion of the evidence would be for non-compliance with the provisions of the *Young Offenders Act.*

The first issue that faced the judge was whether the provisions of the Charter applied to the teacher and principal. Many people assume that the Charter applies to everyone and in all situations but this is simply not so. Application of the Charter is detailed in Section 32 which states:

(1) This Charter applies
    (a) to the Parliament and government of Canada in respect of all matters within the authority of Parliament including all matters relating to the Yukon Territory and the Northwest Territories; and
    (b) to the legislature and government of each province in respect of all matters within the authority of the legislature of each province.

The Charter does not apply to actions between private individuals but only to government actions. A parent is free to deny any of the rights contained in the Charter to his child. The issue becomes one of whether a school teacher is acting as part of "the government" or as a delegate of the parent when dealing with a student in school.

After considering the constitutional authority for establishment of school boards and provisions of the provincial School Act, Judge Russell held:

I am of the view that Parliament intended to extend the application of the Charter to include bodies such as school boards exercising a delegated legislative function. I am satisfied that teachers and principals who are employees of school boards are governed by the provisions of the Charter.

Judge Russell then turned her attention to the issue of whether the detention of the students in the principal's office was a "detention" within the meaning of s. 10 of the Charter requiring that the boys be informed of their right to obtain legal counsel. She stated:

To the average young person and indeed perhaps to the average adult who is a graduate of a public school system, the word 'detention' conjures up one meaning: the restraint imposed by a teacher or a principal as a disciplinary measure in relation to a student's behaviour at school.

However, I think it is unlikely that Parliament intended that the rights prescribed by s. 10 of the Charter would extend to the type of detention imposed as a normal disciplinary measure upon a school student. An ordinary school detention usually does not involve any legal consequences . . .

The manner of obtaining the evidence of the principal and the accomplices in this case was that, as a result of a previous admission of the boys, the principal held the boys in detention, interrogated them and obtained further evidence concerning their participation in this offence. This evidence was turned over to the police without the boys having been given the opportunity to consult with their parents or a lawyer. In this process their rights under s. 10 of the Charter were denied. It was not only the rights of the accused that were violated; the rights of the accomplices were violated as well. Moreover, the evidence of the accomplices only became available as a result of this violation. . . .

This was no ordinary disciplinary measure being undertaken by the principal; it was not a typical school detention; the purpose of his interrogation of these students was to determine whether or not to report the matter to the police. The nature of this detention was comparable to that which occurs when a person is being interrogated by the police themselves; the objective of the detention was not to discipline these students in relation to a school matter but to investigate a criminal offence; this accused was aware of that; the psychological compulsion he was under was all the more compelling because of that. I am satisfied that the accused was under detention within the meaning of s. 10 of the Charter and that his rights as prescribed in that section were infringed because he was not informed of his right to retain and instruct counsel.

In determining whether to exclude the evidence of the principal and accomplices the judge then had to decide whether the admission of their evidence would bring the administration of justice into disrepute. In concluding that it would she stated:

But the problem is, that in handing the evidence over to the police the principal became inextricably involved in the administration of justice by doing the work of the police themselves. The evidence he provided the police became the evidence in this case; there was no need for the police to attempt to obtain a statement from the accused; the principal had done their work for them. And, in providing this information to the police, the principal had, whether knowingly or not, broken a teacher's promise which the boys had reason to believe would be honoured.

Another compelling factor in this case is that the principal had been able to obtain that information without taking any steps to comply either with s. 56 of the *Young Offenders Act*, which requires that young persons be advised of their rights to counsel and have a parent present and that their statements must be voluntary. Had the police been interrogating these boys they would have been required by their own policies to take steps to secure a voluntary statement and to advise the accused of his rights both under the Charter and the *Young Offenders Act*. To allow the admission of the evidence obtained by the school principal, who would no doubt have been unaware of these legal requirements, would allow the state to avoid the need to respect the rights of this young person where its own agents are ignorant of the law. I am of the view that such a result would bring the administration of justice into disrepute and, accordingly, the evidence of the principal and the accomplices must be excluded under s. 24 of the Charter.

Judge Russell then considered the issue of whether to exclude the teacher's evidence. There was no suggestion that any Charter violations occurred with respect to the admissions made to her so the issue was whether the provisions of s. 56 of the *Young Offenders Act* were violated. These provisions only would apply if the teacher was considered, in law, to be a "person in authority." She held:

I am satisfied that the accused in this case would regard the teacher as a person in authority . . . the test is whether the accused believed that the person he dealt with had some degree of power over him and whether he thought that person could make good his promise or carry out his threats. It is reasonable to presume that a 13-year-old boy would believe that his teacher would exercise power over him and could make good her promises.

Having determined that the section did therefore apply the judge then had to decide if the requirements of that section had been met by the the teacher. Her judgment states:

. . . s. 56(1) provides that the common law regarding admissibility would apply in considering the voluntariness of any statement. A basic rule governing the voluntariness of statements is that the statement must not have been induced by any fear or hope of favour. Here the statement had been induced by the promise of the teacher that there would be no further consequences. This accused and the other boys believed that they would not be prosecuted if they confessed; but for that promise they would not have confessed. I am satisfied that the admission to the teacher was not voluntary. As well it is admitted that the teacher did not advise the accused of his right to consult either a lawyer or his parents before accepting his statement and as a result the provisions of s. 56(2) of the *Young Offenders Act* have been violated. The evidence of the teacher as it relates to the admission of the accused must be excluded.

The same reasoning could have been used to exclude the principal's evidence had the Charter argument not been accepted. The judge stated:

I am satisfied that the principal's evidence is a statement to which that section applies and, for the reasons following, that he is a person in authority; the statement he obtained was involuntary because the promise of the teacher continued to act on the mind of the accused whether or not the principal was aware of it and he did not comply with the statutory requirements of that section in obtaining the statement and thus his evidence would be inadmissible under that section.

The Crown appealed this decision to the Court of Queen's Bench where Justice Dechene confined his decision to the issues raised by the *Young Offenders Act* and declined to make a ruling regarding Charter violations. He confirmed that the teacher was indeed a person in authority and that the evidence of the teacher and principal should be excluded for violations of the provisions of s. 56 of the *Young Offenders Act*. He avoided any specific ruling on the Charter but indicated by way of *obiter dicta* that he would have found it inapplicable to teachers and principals on the facts of this particular case.

Subsequent to this decision Parliament enacted subsection (6) which deems that a person being consulted by a young person is not deemed to be a person in authority. It is suggested that this addition will not affect the reasoning of the above case because neither the teacher nor the principal were acting as the child's chosen consultant. Another court decision from the Ontario Court of Appeal may have an effect on whether teachers and principals will be considered as persons in authority under this section.

R. v. A.B., (1986) 26 C.C.C.(3d) 17, was a case where a young offender made certain admissions to his mother and subsequently to a physician and psychiatrist. Although the events transpired before the *Young Offenders Act* became law, and its requirements therefore did not have to be met, the appeal still depended upon whether the mother was a person in authority to decide the common law issue of voluntariness.

At trial the judge excluded the statements made to the mother and subsequently to the doctors on the basis that they were not voluntary in that the mother was a person in authority and offered inducements to make the confession. The Ontario Court of Appeal set aside this decision and ordered a new trial. This court held that in certain circumstances the complainant in a criminal prosecution may be a person in authority as may be a parent of that complainant. Here the victims of the offences were the stepsisters of the accused and the mother was therefore not only the parent of the accused but also of the victims. However, the court went on to hold:

In my view, at the time the statement was made, A.B.'s mother was not, in law, a person in authority. Neither she nor her husband had any intention of calling the police or of instituting court proceedings. Rather, she wished to learn the true situation in order to help and obtain assistance for her son. It follows that she could not in any way have affected the course of a prosecution if such a step was not even contemplated. There must be some realistic connection between the decision to call in the authorities and the offered inducement to a child to make a statement before a parent could be considered, in law, a person in authority. . . . It follows that even if the *Young Offenders Act* had been in force in February, 1984, A.B.'s mother would not have come in the purview of s. 56(2). To hold otherwise would be detrimental to young persons, to society and to the fabric of family life. . . .

Thus family discussions leading to the identification of problems and the provision of assistance without judicial intervention are encouraged by the Act. Only the most serious continued and flagrant misconduct could ever be expected to lead parents to call the authorities about their own child. Until that time, parents would not, in law, be persons in authority.

Thus, where a teacher or principal is questioning a student about some matter, without any intention of involving the authorities, and the matter subsequently comes to the attention of the police through some other means, then the statements made to the teacher and principal would be admissible without compliance with s. 56 of the *Young Offenders Act*. It is only where you intend to involve the authorities that you must comply with the provisions of the Act. Those clearly were the circumstances in *R. v. H.* and it is suggested that it remains unaffected by this subsequent decision.

It is strongly suggested that teachers should not become involved in questioning students about criminal offences and should leave this matter entirely to the police in order that the teacher may avoid any problems. If, for any reason, a teacher or principal chooses to proceed with questioning of a pupil about an offence, he must be prepared to follow the requirements of s. 56 to the letter of the law. As we have seen, court interpretations of this or any other statute often go beyond that which may appear on the face of the statute.

A person in authority, before taking any statement, must first clearly advise the young offender about his rights and must do so "in language appropriate to his age and understanding." There have been several cases which have discussed the meaning of this provision and which have, not surprisingly, reached several different conclusions. Fortunately, some higher court decisions have overruled the earlier provincial court cases which imposed what may be considered to be unreasonable requirements.

An early decision dealing specifically with the issue of how one advises a young offender of his rights was *R. v. P.B.* (1984) 44 C.R.(3d) 24, a decision of Judge Campbell of the British Columbia Provincial Court. In this case the police had read a written standard form to the accused accompanied by verbal explanations. The trial judge held that, at the very minimum, the exact words of the statute must be used for a sophisticated youth and similar precision in more common language is required for a youth of less competence. He went on to hold that the Crown had to produce evidence of age and understanding of the accused and prove these elements to a civil standard of proof. This means providing evidence as to the level of intelligence, education, general personality and ability of the youth to take in and assimilate information to such a degree that the judge would be satisfied that the accused probably understood the explanation given to him.

If this decision were to stand it could mean that teachers and psychologists would be spending more time in court giving such evidence (assuming you can give evidence of ability to assimilate information) than they would in the classroom. This case was adopted, however, by another Provincial Court Judge in *R. v. A.F.G.* [1985] B.C.W.L.D. 997. It was criticized by Judge O'Hearn of the Ontario County Court in *R. v. G.P.S.*, cited above, as follows:

> In *R. v. P.B.* (unreported), cited in the appellant's factum, the suggestion was made that it would be compliance with the requirement that the explanation be given to the young person in language appropriate to his age and understanding to use the words of the statute. With respect, this seems to me to be a dangerous counsel. It would not always be the case that a young person as defined in the Act would understand the word 'obligation' or the phrase 'in proceedings against him' and it is quite possible that the word 'consult' would cause difficulties. I do not think that is fatal in this case, because the evidence indicates that the accused understood the statement and had some familiarity with police proceedings.

In *R. v. G.* (1985) 20 C.C.C. 289 the British Columbia Court of Appeal specifically overruled R. v. P.B. The court again was faced with a youth familiar with police procedures and held:

> In the course of his reasons for judgment the trial judge found that the juvenile with whom we are concerned was both mature and street wise. From the evidence I would conclude that the officer complied with the requirements of s. 56(2)(a) and (b) ...
>
> Looking at the circumstances of this case in relation to the form, in my opinion, it is clear that the language employed by the police constable in explaining the rights under s. 56 to this juvenile employed language that was meaningful to him so that he understood his rights and that when he

signed the form he was waiving the right to consult with counsel or a parent or an adult relative and to have such person present. But, further, that he understood that if he did make a statement, that statement would be admissible in evidence against him at his trial . . .

Referring to *R. v. P.B.* the justices held "that case was wrongly decided and ought not to be followed."

A justice of the Manitoba Supreme Court also considered these requirements in *R. v. C.J.M.* (1986) 29 C.C.C.(3d) 569. The decision in this case states:

At the time of the statement in question, the police knew the accused was one month short of 16 years of age . . . He had a grade 8 education.

There is no suggestion that he had ever before been involved with the police or the criminal justice system. I am not satisfied, therefore, that he could in any way be described as sophisticated or 'street-wise' or that he had any prior knowledge of his legal rights as a young person or what might happen to him as a result of being arrested by the police for a serious offence.

In this particular case, I am not satisfied that the accused fully understood what he was waiving, nor am I satisfied that he fully understood the consequences of doing so in the sense that he was giving up the opportunity of hearing whatever advice a lawyer, parent or other adult might wish to give him. . .

I want to make it clear that I am restricting my reasons to the particular circumstances of this case. The explanation to be given to a young person and whether the police need to go further than to ask the young person if he understands must clearly depend on the facts of each case.

This case introduces an element not apparent on a literal reading of the statute. Not only must an accused young person understand what his rights are, he must also understand the consequences of a waiver of those rights, and these consequences must be explained as clearly as are the right. It is a question of fact to be determined by the circumstances of each case whether any particular young offender did understand both his rights and the consequences of waiving those rights. There are no general guidelines that can be followed. Each case will be a judgment call as to whether these matters have been adequately explained.

It is not only a young offender's rights under section 56 that must be maintained but also those found in the *Charter of Rights and Freedoms*. The legal rights enumerated therein are equally applicable to young offenders and adults in the criminal context. Two of the provisions of the Charter have been considered in the school context by the Ontario Court of Appeal.

R. v. J.M.G. (1986) 33 D.L.R. (4th) 277 involved a youth charged with possession of marijuana. The principal had received information that the youth had been seen placing drugs in his sock outside the school. He called the student to his office and requested him to remove his shoes and socks. The student delayed and the principal undertook a search which uncovered the drugs.

The arguments on appeal were that the young offender's constitutional rights under sections 8 and 10(b) of the Charter were violated. These sections provide

8. Everyone has the right to be secure against unreasonable search or seizure.

10. Everyone has the right on arrest or detention (b) to retain and instruct counsel without delay and to be informed of that right.

The court noted that there were no Canadian precedents on point and referred to a decision of the United States Supreme Court in *New Jersey v. T.L.O.* 105 S. Ct. 733, a case involving a similar fact situation. The American court held:

Under ordinary circumstances, a search of a student by a teacher or other school official will be "justified at its inception" when there are reasonable grounds for suspecting that the search will turn up evidence that the student has violated or is violating either the law or the rules of the school. Such a search will be permissible in its scope when the measures adopted are reasonably related to the objectives of the search and not excessively intrusive in light of the age and sex of the student and the nature of the infraction.

Following this reasoning the Ontario court stated:

In light of the duty imposed on the principal (to maintain order and discipline), it is not unreasonable that the student should be required to remove his socks in order to prove or disprove the allegation. In other words, the search here was reasonably related to the desirable objective of maintaining proper order and discipline. Moreover, the search was not excessively intrusive.

. . .

In my view, calling in the police initially would have been quite unnecessary and might even have amounted to a dereliction of duty. The offence was a very serious breach of discipline but in an absolute sense, as the small fine would indicate, it was not a crime of great magnitude. A principal has a discretion in many minor offences whether to deal with the matter himself, whether to consult the child's parents and whether to call in the law enforcement authorities. He cannot exercise that discretion until he knows the nature and extent of the offence. One thing is, however, certain; he cannot in the face of the allegations here made do nothing. What he did in my opinion was eminently reasonable.

...

Although, as I have said, I am prepared to presume that the Charter applies to the relationship between principal and student, that relationship is not remotely like that of a policeman and a citizen. First, the principal has a substantial interest not only in the welfare of the other students but in the accused student as well. Secondly, society as a whole has an interest in the maintenance of a proper educational environment, which clearly involves being able to enforce school discipline efficiently and effectively. It is often neither feasible nor desirable that the principal should require prior authorization before searching his or her student and seizing contraband.

The court then directed its attention to the issue of section 10 and the failure to inform the student of his right to counsel:

First of all this is not in my opinion a "detention" within the meaning of s.10(b). The accused was already under detention of a kind throughout his school attendance. He was subject to the discipline of the school and required by the nature of his attendance to undergo any reasonable disciplinary or investigative procedure. The search here was but an extension of normal discipline such as, for example, the requirement to stay after school or to do extra assignments or the denial of privileges. I have already found the search to be eminently reasonable.

The only distinction between this search and other disciplinary action is that it carried with it possible 'significant legal consequences'. I concede there may come a time when such consequences are inevitable and the principal becomes the agent of the police in detecting crime. But this is not so here; nor was such a position argued. I have read the evidence carefully and there is no suggestion that the principal was doing anything other then performing his duty to maintain proper order and discipline as required by the *Education Act*. It was only after the extraordinary action of the accused in swallowing a cigarette and his attempt to conceal the tin foil containing the three butts that the principal decided to call in the police.

The court referred to another case which held that the Charter right to retain and instruct counsel must be construed in light of its purpose: to allow an accused to obtain advice regarding the circumstances in which he finds himself. This does not extend to physical searches for narcotics to which he is obliged to submit and which no amount of legal advice would deter. Applying this case, the court held that no legal advice could possibly have precluded the search in question and therefore the youth was not required to be informed of the right to retain counsel.

The court also expressed an opinion as to whether the *Education Act* would constitute a reasonable limitation on the Charter rights of a youth.

The court said:

> It is at least arguable that s. 8(a) of the *Education Act* (the duty to maintain order and discipline) necessarily implies the right to search and seize in the circumstances of the case at bar. If that be so s.1 would apply and to quote the words of the section I would have no hesitation in finding the right so "prescribed by law" to be "demonstrably justified in a free and democratic society."

This decision was applied in the case of *R. v. Sweet* (unreported decision of the Ontario District Court, November 7, 1986), involving a 19-year-old student who was detained in the hall on suspicion of smoking marijuana. He denied any involvement and insisted on his right to leave which culminated in an assault on one of the teachers. Judge Vannini noted the inevitable limitations on a student's rights in the school context. It is, therefore, not only minors who have limited rights in the school context but also those over the age of 18.

Another area of potential concern to educators regarding the *Young Offenders Act* is the provision in section 38 which prohibits the publishing by any means the report of an offence committed or alleged to have been committed by a young person whereby the young person's name is disclosed or information is given to identify such a young person. At first glance this would appear to be a ban on the publication of a young offender's name by the media. A recent case has, however, given it a much broader application.

The Peel Board of Education v. W.B (unreported judgment of the Supreme Court of Ontario, April 3, 1987) saw the board ordered not to proceed with a proposed expulsion hearing involving several young people since the hearing would "almost inevitably result" in a violation of section 38.

The students in this case had been charged with kidnapping, unlawful confinement, and sexual assault on a 14-year-old girl. The alleged offences did not occur on school property. The principal handed out a ten day suspension immediately upon hearing of the charges and recommended expulsion. The board upheld the suspension and imposed a further suspension pending the holding of an expulsion hearing.

Justice Reid ordered the board not to proceed with such a hearing since it would constitute a publication of a report in violation of section 38. The word "publish," in his view, means any form of communication between two people, while "report" can include such things as "gossip" or "rumour." The consequences of an expulsion would be to spread rumours and would tend to identify the students as being those charged. Despite the fact that the board would hold the hearings in camera and make no references to names in its proceedings, the judge felt that the names could not be concealed.

This broad interpretation of the Act may have serious consequences for educators when dealing with school records concerning young offenders. Schools may not be able to make any reference to a student name in any report involving an offence, nor indicate on a student record any matter pertaining to the commission of an offence. This decision is currently under appeal and may be modified or overruled to avoid such consequences.

The keeping of school records may also be affected by certain provisions of the *Young Offenders Act*. The Act provides that any records pertaining to the commission of an offence by a young offender are to be destroyed in certain circumstances. The relevant sections of the Act read as follows:

43. (1) A department or agency of any government in Canada may keep records containing information obtained by the department or agency
(a) for the purposes of an investigation of an offence alleged to have been committed by a young person;
(b) for use in proceedings against a young person under this Act;
(c) for the purpose of administering a disposition;
(d) for the purpose of considering whether, instead of commencing or continuing judicial proceedings under this Act against a young person, to use alternative measures to deal with the young person; or
(e) as a result of the use of alternative measures to deal with the young person.
(2) Any person or organization may keep records containing information obtained by the person or organization
(a) as a result of the use of alternative measures to deal with a young person alleged to have committed an offence; or
(b) for the purpose of administering or participating in the administration of a disposition.
45. (1) Where a young person is charged with an offence and
(a) is acquitted, or
(b) the charge is dismissed for any reason other than acquittal, withdrawn or stayed and no proceedings are taken against him for a period of three months,
(c) all records kept pursuant to sections 40 to 43 and records taken pursuant to section 44 that relate to the young person in respect of the alleged offence and all copies, prints or negatives of such records shall be destroyed.
(3) Where a young person
(a) has not been charged with or found guilty of an offence under this or any other Act of Parliament or any regulation made thereunder, whether as a young person or an adult,
(i) for a period of two years after all dispositions made in respect of the young person have been completed, where the young person has

at any time been found guilty of an offence punishable on summary conviction but has never been convicted of an indictable offence, or

(ii) for a period of five years after all dispositions made in respect of the young person have been completed, where the young person has at any time been convicted of one or more indictable offences, or

(b) has, after becoming an adult, been granted a pardon under the *Criminal Records Act,*

all records kept pursuant to sections 40 to 43 and records taken pursuant to section 44 that relate to the young person and all copies, prints or negatives of such records shall be destroyed. ...

(4) Any record that is not destroyed under this section because the young person to whom it relates was charged with an offence during a period referred to in that subsection shall be destroyed forthwith

(a) where the young person is acquitted, on the expiration of the time allowed for the taking of an appeal or, where an appeal is taken, when all proceedings in respect of that appeal have been completed;

(b) where no proceedings are taken against him for a period of six months, on the expiration of the six months; or

(c) where the charge against the young person is dismissed for any reason other than acquittal, withdrawn or stayed and no proceedings are taken against him for a period of six months, on the expiration of the six months. ... (7) Any person who has under his control or in his possession any record that is required under this section to be destroyed and who refuses or fails, on a request made by or on behalf of the young person to whom the record relates, to destroy the record commits an offence.

Schools are an agency of the government and are probably caught by these provisions. If the school record in respect of a student contains a reference to the commission of an offence, or that the student is attending the school under a disposition, the school is required to destroy the record under the circumstances outlined in s. 45. If such records are permanently recorded on a student file, their destruction can pose problems.

It is probably the best course of action to make no reference in a student record to the fact that a student is attending school under a court disposition. This avoids the problem of having to destroy the records at a later date. If the student is alleged to have committed an offence in respect of school property, records will no doubt be kept for the investigation of the matter. It is suggested that a separate record be kept for each incident which can easily be destroyed if any of the circumstances enumerated in s. 43 arise.

If the young person requests that the records be destroyed in accordance with the Act, it is an offence not to destroy every copy of such record.

A final potential concern of teachers and administrators is the management of a student who has been "sentenced to school" as a result of a probation order or alternative disposition under the Act. The authority to order a student to attend school is found in the following provision of the Act:

> 23. (2) A probation order . . . may include such of the following conditions as the youth court considers appropriate in the circumstances of the case:
>
> (d) that the young person attend school or such other place of learning, training or recreation as is appropriate, if the court is satisfied that a suitable program is available for the young person at such place;

Teachers and administrators may well have some concerns over their authority to suspend or expel a student who has been ordered to attend their school. There should be no such concerns since the order does not compel the school to keep the student in attendance if his behaviour warrants suspension or expulsion. Students attending school under a court order are subject to the same disciplinary measures as other students. If such action is taken, the youth worker assigned to the case should be informed and he may initiate a review of the disposition. Upon review, the judge may make any other disposition that he could have made at the time of sentencing. A suspension or expulsion will not put the young person in jeopardy of an additional charge for breach of probation, although his reviewed probation may not be as lenient.

Young offenders can pose a variety of concerns for school personnel. Familiarity with the provisions of the *Young Offenders Act*, the *Charter of Rights and Freedoms*, and the criminal process will provide teachers with a method for dealing with any situations that may arise and may help to avoid any incidents whereby young offenders may be deprived of their legal rights.

Discussion and Review Questions

1. Describe the change in philosophy toward young offenders which has occurred as a result of the repeal of the *Juvenile Delinquents Act* and the passage of the *Young Offenders Act.*

2. Does the *Charter of Rights and Freedoms* apply to schools and school boards since it specifies that it applies only to the federal and provincial levels of government.

3. Recite Section 56 sections (2) of the *Young Offenders Act* in your own words.

4. If you were called upon to caution a 12-year-old boy of his rights under Section 56, what words would you use? If the boy was 16 years of age, what words would you use?

5. Explain the circumstances wherein the teacher could be regarded as the "parent" under the *Young Offenders Act.*

6. Explain the difference between keeping a student "in" for purposes of punishment and the intent of the unlawful detention section of the Charter.

7. Do teachers have to insure that the legal test of "voluntariness" has been met when they question their students? Why?

8. Some courts use the phrase "justified at its inception" to describe a situation with respect to, for example, the searching of students. What legal idea is being expressed?

9. What is the essential distinction between the relationship of policeman to young citizens, and teacher to student?

10. Describe a situation in which the "publication" restrictions contained in the *Young Offenders Act* could result in a teacher committing a crime.

You be the Judge

The Case of the Pilfering Pupil

Pat Peters was the principal at Pleasantville Junior High School. Shortly after school opened one morning he received information from one of his teachers that a student, Paul, had been seen by another student taking a wallet from a teacher's purse and placing it down the front of his pants. Paul was 13 years old and in grade seven.

Paul was summoned to the office and, in the presence of the vice-principal, was told that he was suspected of having stolen the wallet and they believed he had it in his possession. Paul was asked to produce the wallet but made no reply. Paul was searched but no wallet was found. Paul did have $53 in his pocket. Peters detained Paul in the office while the vice-principal searched Paul's locker. Still no wallet.

The vice-principal then searched the garbage container in the boy's washroom and recovered the stolen wallet. There was no cash in the wallet although the teacher who owned it had indicated that it contained approximately $50.

The principal confronted Paul with the evidence and said that if he did not confess the police would be called in to "fingerprint" the wallet and the student. Paul was told that it would be better for him to confess right now rather than being interrogated by the police.

Paul asked if he was going to be arrested. Peters replied, "That depends on how cooperative you are."

Paul still refused to make any admission concerning the theft. Peters said, "Perhaps I should phone your mother to see where you got the money." Paul did not want his mother to know of the matter.

As Peters picked up the telephone, Paul said, "All right. I'll confess. Just don't call my Mom or the police."

Peters asked, "You did take the wallet then?"

"Yes," replied Paul.

Peters then telephoned the police and reported the matter including Paul's confession. When the police arrived, they informed Paul of his rights under the *Charter* and *Young Offenders Act*. Paul said he wanted to talk to a lawyer and made no further statements.

At trial, Paul's lawyer argued that his client's constitutional rights had been violated. He stated that the "confession" was not voluntary within the meaning of s. 56 of the *Young Offenders Act*. Further, Paul had not been advised of his right to obtain counsel as guaranteed by the *Charter*. He asked that the evidence of the principal and vice-principal be excluded. The Crown had no other evidence to present but argued that the teachers were not "persons in authority" nor was Paul "detained."

You be the judge. Should the evidence be excluded? Support your decision by reference to the precedents discussed in this chapter.

Point/Counterpoint

There continues to much debate concerning the best approach to take in dealing with young offenders. Should the juvenile justice system have a predominantly "rehabilitative" philosophy or should it opt for "responsibility" of the young offender? Is it possible to find a combination of both approaches that will work?

> The juvenile court, in its rhetoric and frequently in its practice, has been a center for the application of a rehabilitative philosophy. Mankind's nobler motivations were captured by this court's concern for those who had tripped along the way. The aim was to help, to restore, to guide, and to forget. For long years the court prioritized its two mandated concerns, the best interests of the child and the best interests of the public, by placing the

former prominently in first place. The medical model was dominant. There was an effort to diagnose the psychological and social factors which contribute to children's delinquency and to erect a variety of treatment models to facilitate the reclamation of youth. (H. Ted Rubin in *Juvenile Justice: Policy, Practice and Law*, Goodyear Publishing, 1979)

Perhaps it is not surprising that after many years of relying on the informal procedures and rehabilitative goals of the juvenile court, there was a reaction against the patent failure of the system to protect society or to help the children subject to its jurisdiction. It also was becoming impossible to ignore the fact that the broad discretionary powers the court officials had been granted were resulting in flagrant discrimination . . . In most localities the juvenile court had become the place to prevent or punish crime from the ghetto as severely as possible and to enforce standards of social morality as informally as possible . . . (Barbara Danziger Flicker in *Standards for Juvenile Justice: A Summary and Analysis*, Ballinger Publishing, 1977)

. . . attempts to pursue rehabilitative and punishment goals simultaneously often beccme self-defeating. (Vinter, Downs and Hall, National Assessment of Juvenile Corrections study, 1975)

. . . (there is an) inherent incompatibility between the social control objective and the social rehabilitation objective that juvenile courts are required to pursue. (Hasenfeld and Sarri, National Assessment of Juvenile Corrections study, 1976)

References

Bala, N. and Lilles, H., The *Young Offenders Act Annotated*. Ottawa: Solicitor General Canada, 1982.

MacKay, A. W., "Students as Second Class Citizens Under the Charter" (1986) 54 C.R. (3d) 390.

Robinson, L.R., "Dealing With Young Offenders," *The Canadian School Executive*, October 1984 p. 3 and November, 1984 p.3.

8

The Effect
of a Criminal Conviction

Learning Objectives

Some of the things the reader will learn from this chapter include the following:

1. That for teachers convicted of a crime, the most serious consequence may not be the sentence handed down by the court.
2. That in a number of instances of teacher dismissal, the courts consider the nature of the conduct rather than the conviction.
3. The consequences of failure to disclose a criminal conviction to an employer.

Preview

The public tends to take a harsh approach toward school teachers who are convicted of criminal offences. The nature of the offence will of course make a difference. Offences against children will certainly bring a harsh sentence, termination of employment, and perhaps decertification.

Following the original trial, the matter of a teacher being convicted of a criminal offense tends to return to court in the form of an appeal against a termination of employment. It is at this point that the general direction of the courts toward considering the conduct itself rather than the nature of the sentence becomes obvious. We believe that through this action the courts are sending a clear message to teachers. The message being that teachers should act in an exemplary fashion.

Failure to disclose a criminal conviction when asked at time of employment is grounds for dismissal. This is based upon the belief that the act of failing to disclose is teacher misconduct. All provinces list teacher misconduct as grounds for teacher suspension and possible termination. Teachers are expected to be models of acceptable and lawful behavior.

Self-Assessment

1. Is being convicted of a crime *prima facie* grounds for termination?
2. How serious must the crime be before a conviction will preclude future employment as a teacher?
3. If you as a teacher fail to disclose a previous criminal conviction when asked, what are the probable consequences?

Key Terms

Board of Reference/Board of Appeal
Conditional discharge
Just cause
Prima facie

*   *   *   *

If a teacher is convicted of a criminal offence there may arise serious problems beyond any sentence imposed by the criminal court. The teacher faces dismissal from his job as well as decertification as a teacher and thus loses his capacity to earn a livelihood in his chosen profession. Many School Acts specifically provide that a conviction for a criminal offence is a valid ground for dismissal. Other School Acts are not as specific and provide for dismissal on grounds of misconduct (which can include the actions leading to the criminal charge). Criminal conduct on the part of a teacher will be held to be "just cause" for dismissal under the terms of a collective agreement.

There have been several court decisions dealing with the effect of a criminal conviction upon the teacher involved. It is interesting to note that similar conduct occasionally produces different results, depending upon the jurisdiction involved.

In *Beckwith and Allen v. Colchester-East Hants Amalgamated School Board* (1977) 23 N.S.R.2d 268, two teachers employed under permanent contracts were convicted of possession of marijuana and fined $200.00 each.

The School Board, after conducting a hearing, dismissed both teachers. The applicants appealed and a judge was appointed to sit as a Board of Appeal under the *Education Act*. He confirmed the dismissals and the teachers appealed that decision to the Nova Scotia Supreme Court which also upheld the action taken. The essence of the various decisions is that conviction for this offence is just cause for dismissal under the *Education Act*. Judge Gunn sitting as the Board of Appeal stated:

> I have come to the conclusion and hold that although an individual is entitled to do what he wants in his own time away from his place of employment, nevertheless in the case at bar, the members of the School Board examined all facets regarding the convictions of the Appellants and properly concluded as I do, that the criminal convictions would bring dishonour to them and to their profession.

On the other coast, a teacher pleaded guilty to a possession of marijuana charge and received a conditional discharge from the criminal courts. The effect of such a discharge is that the person is deemed not to have been convicted of the offence. In *Board of School Trustees of School District No. 37 (Delta) v. Vaselenak* (1977) 82 D.L.R.3d 509, the school board dismissed the teacher under the relevant section of the British Columbia *School Act* which empowered boards to dismiss for conviction on a criminal charge. The B.C. Supreme Court, however, held that the teacher was dismissed improperly because there had not been a conviction. At the time of passing the B.C. Act, the possibility of a discharge did not exist under the *Criminal Code* and the board argued that "conviction" should be given its meaning as of the date of the act which included a guilty plea. The court held that it was up to the *Criminal Code* to define conviction and a person who has been given a discharge is not deemed to have been convicted.

Thus, we see that in separate instances, in the same year, the same behaviour resulted in different consequences for the teachers involved. However, the mere fact that a conditional discharge has been granted may not be sufficient to escape dismissal, as happened in the B.C. case.

In *Glass v. Warner* (1979) 17 A.R. 315, a teacher was convicted of possession of stolen goods and was given a conditional discharge. He appealed his dismissal. The judge sitting as a Board of Reference held:

> It is my conclusion from considering the facts as brought out in evidence that the Board of Education did act reasonably in the circumstances. I make this finding on the basis of the criminal offence alone. And, notwithstanding that the possession of stolen property arose out of the appellant's medical problem, the Board had as its primary duty the responsibility for the operation of the local school system. Whether the students were justified or not, knowledge of the thefts and related conviction precluded

the appellant from reasonably carrying out his normal teaching duties in the Warner area. This consideration overrides any suggestion of a leave of absence for medical reasons or the relatively minor nature of the crime, and the fact that the Court saw fit to give the appellant a conditional discharge.

This Court focused on the conduct itself (not on the disposition of the criminal charges) as a basis for dismissal. This reasoning has been upheld in other circumstances where teachers have been dismissed for misconduct even though the teacher received a conditional discharge for the offence.

A British Columbia Board of Reference upheld a dismissal for misconduct where the criminal offence, involving gross indecency in a public washroom, resulted in a conditional discharge. The teacher's conduct was deemed to be such that it would weaken public confidence in the school system and would impair his usefulness to the school and the board (*Board of School Trustees, School District No. 39 (Vancouver) v. John Doe*, B.C. Board of Reference decision August 28, 1979).

Again, the conduct itself and not the result of the criminal charges was the determining factor. Teachers should not feel immune from dismissal if they receive a discharge on the criminal charges. The boards are still going to look at the behaviour involved to determine if it is appropriate behaviour for a teacher. If it is any type of criminal conduct, it is almost certain that the result will be dismissal.

An Ontario Board of Arbitration considered the issue on a grievance filed by a dismissed teacher under a collective agreement. In *Re Etobicoke Board of Education and Ontario Secondary School Teachers' Federation, District 12* (1981) 2 L.A.C. 265, the teacher had been convicted of conspiracy to possess stolen property and was fined $2,000. Despite his previous exemplary record, he was dismissed. The board had to determine if this dismissal was for "just cause." They held:

> The legislation . . . does not require teachers to be saints; it does, however, indicate the need for a higher standard of conduct than that required by other employees. Such high standards are not uncommon in the professions, nor is it uncommon that a failure to achieve them results in the loss of professional status or employment.
>
> Prima facie, a conviction for an indictable offence strikes directly at the exemplary aspect of a teacher's duty.
>
> The education of children to respect the law . . . is central to what school boards do and hire teachers to do. It is fundamental to the educational process, as we see it, that teachers are seen not only to teach students, but to practise, within reasonable limits, that which they teach.
>
> It is vitally important that the result of the relationship and influence not be

to suggest to students that a respected and influential teacher thinks participation in crime is excusable. In our view, the nature of this particular breach of duty is such as to make discharge a reasonable response . . . We can only conclude, with regret, that his long record of exemplary service was, in effect, abandoned when he became involved in the offence of which he was ultimately convicted.

A teacher or prospective teacher should not attempt to hide the fact of a criminal record or criminal activity resulting in a discharge from his employer. A B.C. Board of Reference held that a teacher who failed to inform the school board of a criminal offence involving indecent assault, to which he had pleaded guilty and was given a discharge, even though it occurred prior to his employment, was justifiably dismissed by the board when they learned of the event. The board held that he intended to mislead the school board on his application and he was rightfully fired for misconduct (*Board of School Trustees, School District No. 13 (Kettle Valley) v. John Doe*, B.C. Board of Reference decision, May, 1980).

Because a teacher has been dismissed as a result of criminal conduct, it does not necessarily follow that such a teacher may never teach again. The board in the Etobicoke case cited above considered this possibility and concluded:

> While we support the notion of rehabilitation and do not doubt that the grievor ought to be considered for further employment as a teacher, we do not think that it is properly the function of an arbitration board to enter into an inquiry . . . into the subtle factors which must be weighed before giving the grievor another chance.

An American judge echoed similar sentiments when he stated:

> The teacher who committed an indiscretion, paid the penalty, and now seeks to discourage his students from committing similar acts, may well be a more effective supporter of legal and moral standards than the one who has never been found to violate those standards.

Each case for reinstatement will be judged on its own merits and the factors to be considered will include the nature of the offence, the circumstances surrounding the commission of the offence, the degree of rehabilitation of the offender, previous exemplary conduct, as well as the possible reaction of the community towards the offender. A shoplifter would be more easily tolerated than a person convicted of indecent assault on young children.

Teachers will be held to very high moral standards both on and off the job. Any type of abnormal behaviour, especially criminal behaviour, will not be tolerated. Boards will look at the conduct itself and not whether there has been a criminal conviction in determining their actions. You are expected to be, and should be, a model of acceptable and lawful behaviour.

Discussion and Review

1. Why is being convicted of committing a criminal offense just cause for dismissal? Or is it?
2. What is the meaning of the legal term conditional discharge, and how may it be used to the teacher's advantage?
3. What arguments would you use if you were required to defend a colleague who was threatened with termination because he had been convicted of a criminal offense?

You be the Judge

The Game

John Black was a fifth year teacher at Central High School and was considered to be an excellent teacher, popular with both staff and students. He devoted many hours to extra-curricular activities such as the science fair, the volleyball team and the track meet.

John's passion, however, was hockey. He was a local celebrity as the hard checking right winger of the Central Flyers Senior "A" hockey club. John did not let his hockey interfere with his job, until one cold winter night . . .

The score was deadlocked at 3-3 against the mighty Big City Stars. John had been battling a rugged left winger named Bill Jones all game.

Late in the third period, John was carrying the puck and caught a glimpse of Jones coming at him from the side. He was prepared for the body check but not the vicious elbow that caught him in the jaw. John looked to the referee but to his surprise no penalty was called. John raced to catch up to Jones. As he caught up to him John delivered a slash to the back of Jones' leg.

The gloves were dropped and the game stopped as the two players slugged it out. Jones went down and John continued to rain punches on his face until the officials restrained him.

Jones, who bleeding profusely from his nose, lips and right eye, required several stitches. John was out with a game misconduct penalty.

Later that week John was called to the office where he was met by the principal and a policeman. The officer informed John that he was under arrest for the assault of William Jones at the Central Arena.

John was suspended without pay immediately pending the determination of the criminal charges. John was convicted of the assault, fined $500 and placed on probation for a year.

The Central School Board then terminated John's employment because of the criminal conviction and proceedings were instituted to have his certification as a teacher revoked.

Issues for Decision

1. Would you uphold the Board's decision to terminate John's employment?
2. Should John be decertified as a result of this conviction?

Questions for Discussion

1. To what extent should the circumstances leading to a criminal conviction be considered in termination and decertification hearings?
2. If the assault had happened in a barroom brawl should a different conclusion be reached?
3. Are there certain criminal offences (such as impaired driving) that should not be dealt with as seriously as others? Where do you draw the line?
4. Should this conviction preclude John from teaching again? What types of convictions should preclude a teacher from returning to the classroom?

Part Three

Tort Law Problems

9

Introduction to Tort Law

Learning Objectives

Some of the things that the reader will learn from reading this chapter include:

1. The purpose of the law of torts.
2. The two broad categories of torts.
3. The main kinds of intentional torts.
4. The importance to the teacher of the tort of negligence.
5. A description of the "careful parent" test and what it means to the work of the classroom teacher.
6. The circumstances under which the teacher may be the plaintiff rather than the defendant in a negligence case.

Preview

Tort law covers a broad general category of civil actions where the purpose is to enforce some personal rights rather than to punish an offender. The emphasis is upon obtaining compensation for injury. The word tort is generally used as a synonym for the word wrong. A tort is thus a specific type of civil wrong which results in a suit for damages as compensation for the wrongful act against the interest of the plaintiff.

The law of torts can be divided into two broad categories. Intentional torts are those actions wherein the wrongdoer intended to do the wrongful act: for example, to strike a person, to enter illegally onto another person's property, or to speak or write damaging words about another person. Negligent torts arise from lack of care or foresight on the part of the defendant.

The action is not intentional. This latter topic will be more fully developed in the chapter which follows.

The improper use of corporal punishment may result in the launching of a civil action as well as a criminal action under the *Criminal Code*. In this type of civil action the plaintiff will be seeking damages for injuries inflicted upon the child by the teacher.

Improperly detaining students may result in charges of false imprisonment being launched, although the number of such charges that proceed through the courts are few in number when compared to the number of times that teachers detain pupils at recess or after school.

If a teacher is constantly and continually belittling and harassing a student for no apparent educational purpose, the courts may conclude that the teacher is doing so to cause mental anguish. Further, there are some grounds for believing that Canadian courts will begin to pay more attention to the mental suffering inflicted upon students by the educational malpractice of their teachers.

Teachers must be careful about their intentional actions toward students because they could result in criminal, civil, as well as professional charges against them.

There is very little court precedent concerning medical treatment of students by teachers, but as schools accept responsibility to educate the handicapped and medically fragile students in the regular school setting, there will arise an implied statutory duty to provide adequate medical treatment. Teachers, in general, are not accustomed to this additional responsibility but the direction seems clear enough: failure to provide or obtain medical treatment has become a part of the "careful parent" test.

Self-Assessment

1. Do you know what a tort is? Are you able to define the term?
2. Do you understand the difference between an intentional and an unintentional tort?
3. Can you list two or three examples of intentional torts?
4. Can you define the tort of negligence and explain in general terms why it is of such great importance to the teacher?
5. What are the legal sources of the teacher's duty toward a student?

Key Terms

Tort	Slander
Conversion	Negligence
Assault	Vicarious liability
Chattel	Occupier's liability
Battery	Invitee
Defamation	Licensee
Libel	*Volenti non fit injuria*

*   *   *   *

Tort law is a broad general category covering a multitude of civil, as opposed to criminal, wrongs. It includes such diverse actions as assault, trespass, nuisance, defamation, and negligence. Because of the broad nature of this area of law, legal scholars generally define the category by exclusion rather than inclusion of all possible causes of action that may arise under this heading.

Two eminent legal authorities have defined "tort" as follows:

> We may accordingly define a tort as a civil wrong for which the remedy is a common law action for unliquidated damages, and which is not exclusively the breach of a contract or the breach of a trust or other merely equitable obligation. (R. F. Heuston & R. S. Chambers, *Salmond & Heuston on Torts*, 18th ed., London:Sweet & Maxwell, 1981, at p. 11)

> Broadly speaking, a tort is a civil wrong, other than a breach of contract, for which the court will provide a remedy in the form of an action for damages. (W. L. Prosser, *Law of Torts*, 4th ed., St. Paul: West Publishing Co., 1971, at p. 2)

The word "tort" derives from the Latin *tortus* meaning "twisted" or "crooked" and is generally used as a synonym for the word "wrong." A tort, therefore, is a species of civil injury or wrong that gives rise to civil proceedings for damages. It may be distinguished from a criminal injury or wrong by the nature of the remedy provided, namely damages, rather than the punishment of the wrongdoer.

Just as legal scholars have struggled with a suitable definition of the word "tort," they have struggled to determine exactly what the purpose of such laws should be. Prosser has called the law of torts "a battleground of social theory." Generally, the purpose of the law of torts is thought to be a means to provide compensation for injuries sustained by one person through the actions of another. If this was its sole purpose, however, it could be accomplished more efficiently and effectively by a system of national insurance.

This emphasis on compensation is used to distinguish tort law from criminal law, which has as its purposes punishment of the offender (retribution), deterrence of others, and reformation of the wrongdoer (an educational purpose). However, tort law and criminal law have common historical roots and so the underlying purposes of criminal law also have a place in tort law. Tort law adds the element of compensation, which is absent in criminal law, and retains the elements of retribution, deterrence, and reformation. The damages paid to the injured party are compensation but are also a form of punishment. To this extent, tort law functions as a deterrent to other wrongdoers, as punishment of the wrongdoer, as well as an appeasement to the person wronged.

Many acts which are subject to criminal prosecution are also subject to a civil action for damages. These are concurrent remedies, each independent of the other. Criminal proceedings for an assault may be instituted, whether or not any civil action for damages is undertaken. Likewise, a civil suit for damages may be instituted independently of any criminal proceedings. Criminal charges are not a prerequisite for maintaining a civil action. Neither does the outcome of one action depend on the outcome of the other. A person may be held liable for civil damages for an assault even though he was acquitted of criminal charges stemming from the same incident.

Civil proceedings may often be held in abeyance pending the determination of any criminal charges involving the same event. This is not because the outcome of those proceedings has any bearing on the civil liability, but rather to ensure a fair criminal trial. Defendants in criminal proceedings are entitled to certain procedural safeguards such as the right to remain silent and not be compelled to testify. These rights are not available in civil proceedings where the wrongdoer can be compelled to testify under oath at an examination for discovery. To guarantee the person's rights in a criminal proceeding, civil actions may be commenced but held in abeyance until the criminal trial is over if an application to do so is made by the defendant.

For our purposes, we will view the law of torts as being not only a means of compensating a victim but also as a method of deterring the wrongful action of others and as an educational tool that prescribes which actions are subject to claims for damages and which are not. We will point out instances where teachers have been held civilly liable for certain actions in the hope that their example will deter similar conduct by other teachers. These cases are included to educate teachers about acceptable parameters of conduct in the hope that schools will implement all possible safety precautions against future injury to students.

The law of torts may be divided into two broad categories - intentional torts and negligent torts. Intentional torts are those where the wrongdoer intends to do the wrongful act. Examples of such intentional torts include: an assault, where the wrongdoer intends to strike the victim; trespass, where the wrongdoer intends to go on another's property; or defamation, where the wrongdoer intentionally speaks or writes words that may be damaging to another. Although the particular damage may not be intended, the act causing such damage is a willful one and therefore intentional.

Negligent torts, on the other hand, are those where the wrongful act arises from carelessness or lack of foresight on the part of the perpetrator. A common example of such negligence is an automobile accident where the driver at fault is careless or inattentive in his action. He does not deliberately drive his car into another but rather causes the accident through a careless act such as speeding or failing to stop for a red light.

This distinction between intentional and negligent torts is important for several reasons. Different defences are available to the defendant in each type of action; different things are required to be proved by the plaintiff; and the possibility of the employer being required to pay damages for the acts of an employee varies with each category. These two broad categories do not encompass all torts but are merely provided as a useful dividing point between certain types of injuries. A broader term such as "fault-based torts" could be substituted for negligent torts to include such things as nuisance which is neither a negligent nor an intentional tort. We shall deal with nuisance in our discussion of negligence because both are fault-based and have similar defences to the action. Similarly, the tort of defamation shall be dealt with under the category of intentional torts although it is generally treated as a unique category.

Intentional Torts

Intentional torts can involve intentional interference with persons, land or personal property. All of these may affect the teacher in some way; however, certain specific torts occur more frequently in the school setting and we will concentrate on these.

There are many different torts that may be classified as an intentional interference with a person. These include assault, battery, false arrest, false imprisonment, and intentional infliction of mental suffering. This list is not exhaustive; however, it includes those situations most likely to be encountered by the teacher.

There is only one intentional tort involving interference with land and that is the tort of trespass. This is important from a teacher's perspective since the school building itself, although a quasi-public place, is privately owned land and may be trespassed upon by a wide variety of people. It is essential to know (from a liability point of view) whether a person is lawfully on the premises or if he is a trespasser.

Intentional interference with personal property may involve either damage to the property or the taking of the property from the lawful owner. Such wrongful taking of property is called "theft" in criminal law but is called "conversion" in tort law. All schools have large quantities of personal property or "chattels" (ranging from pencils to computers) which are capable of being damaged or converted. The criminal law does not provide a means of compensation for a wrongful interference with personal property, but an action in tort could provide this remedy.

As we look at specific cases involving these various intentional torts we will see the close connection between tort and criminal law. These cases are illustrative only of types of situations where teachers and schools have become involved in the legal process and are not to be considered as exhaustive of all cases or types of action that may be encountered.

Assault and Battery

These are two distinct torts which may be usefully discussed together since they frequently occur simultaneously and the term "assault" is commonly used as a synonym for what may be a "battery." An assault involves causing someone to believe that you will touch them in a harmful or offensive way. This belief is the essence of an assault action. There need be no actual touching for the tort to be complete. There need not even be the ability to carry out the threat. For example, pointing an empty gun at a person who believes it is loaded is an assault even though you do not have the present ability to carry out the threat. The person's belief must however be a reasonable one. If a small child threatened to beat up his teacher, the teacher's belief that there is actual physical danger would not be a reasonable one.

A "battery" occurs when you do actually hit someone or touch them in an offensive way. It need not be a violent action; kissing someone against his or her wish to the contrary would be a battery. Battery includes the intention to hit or touch someone, so an accidental striking of another would not be a battery although it may be actionable as negligence. Assault and battery often occur at the same time. If you cause a person to believe he is going to be hit and then you actually hit him you have committed both torts.

However, a person may commit a battery without an assault in cases where the victim is struck from behind and therefore was not apprehensive about being hit.

The issue of corporal punishment has been dealt with elsewhere in this book, as it relates to the criminal law. There have been numerous civil actions arising from such conduct, as well. Although the two causes of action are distinct and independent, the same general principles are often applied to both the civil and criminal actions. Thus, if the teacher is found to have acted properly in administering the corporal punishment in a criminal court, a civil court will probably come to the same conclusion. Both civil and criminal cases are used as authorities in either type of court action and little, if any, distinction is drawn between them as far as civil and criminal liability is concerned.

Just as the *Criminal Code* provides teachers with a defence to criminal assault charges, the civil courts have held that teachers are justified in using corporal punishment and are not subject to civil actions, with the provision that they act within certain boundaries. This principle was stated over one hundred years ago as follows:

> Schoolmasters have the right of moderate chastisement against disobedient and refractory scholars, but it is a right which can only be exercised in cases necessitated for the maintenance of school discipline, the interest of education and to a degree proportioned to offences committed, and any chastisement exceeding this limit, and springing from motives of caprice, anger, or bad temper, constitutes an offence punishable like ordinary delicts. (*Brisson v. Lafontaine* (1864) L.C.J. 173)

In the province of Quebec, where the common law does not prevail, the *Civil Code* has long provided that:

> The father and, in his default, the mother of an unemancipated minor have over him a right of reasonable and moderate correction, which may be delegated to and exercised by those to whom his education has been intrusted. (Article 245, *Civil Code*, 1890).

In the exercise of this right, however, no punishment is justifiable which may result in serious or permanent injury to the pupil. In a case where a teacher dragged a child of seven years by the ear to compel him to kneel down, the school authorities were held liable for damages for the injuries sustained (which required medical attention for several weeks). It was not a defence to the action that the boy had been disobedient, since discipline must be so enforced as to avoid bodily injury. (*Lefebvre v. La Congregation des Petits Freres De Ste-Marie* [1890] M.L.R. 6 S.C. 430)

The common law position derived from case law yields similar results. In *Andrews v. Hopkins* [1932] 3 D.L.R. 459, a seven year old child was misbehaving and had received the strap on each hand five times. In so doing, the teacher was negligent in the manner of strapping with the result that the child was struck on the breast causing a chronic condition of mastitis. In this instance, the original punishment itself may not have been considered excessive, but the negligent manner in the administration of such punishment gave rise to the awarding of damages.

Punishment may be excessive and unreasonable even if no serious or permanent injury results. However, any damages that may be recovered in the absence of permanent injury make such a lawsuit unlikely. The courts will only compensate for actual injuries sustained. If the student resists a reasonable punishment and, as a result of such resistance, is injured, the teacher will not be found liable for the injuries. In a case where a girl was pulled from her desk and propelled along the aisle, due to her reluctance to leave the room for corporal punishment, an action was dismissed for the accidental striking of the pupil's head against a desk or a door, partly because there were no serious injuries but also because the teacher was justified in overcoming the resistance. Many school acts specifically require students to submit to punishment. (*Murdock v. Richards* [1954] 1 D.L.R. 766).

If school regulations forbid the administration of corporal punishment, a teacher is still not likely to be liable in civil damages for assault. Corporal punishment is one of those actions that legitimately falls within the legislative sphere of the federal, provincial, and municipal authorities. Each is justified in making whatever laws it desires in relation to its own legislative sphere. School authorities may forbid or restrict corporal punishment but this does not affect a teacher's rights under the *Criminal Code* or the common law.

In a case where a teacher administered corporal punishment in violation of school regulations which allowed only the principal to administer such punishment, it was held that the teacher's right to inflict corporal punishment is not derived solely from delegation of parental authority but also from the need to preserve discipline in the classroom. Thus, even if the teacher is not authorized by the school to strap a pupil, the teacher may still be justified from a legal standpoint in administering such punishment as long as she is able to say, "The punishment which I administered was moderate; it was not dictated by any bad motive, and it was such as is usual in the school and such as a parent of the child might expect that the child would receive if it did wrong." (*Mansell v. Griffin* [1908] 1 K.B. 168)

However, where the teacher does act in contravention of such regulations, the school authority is entitled to be indemnified by the teacher for any amounts it may have to pay by way of damages if it is found that such punishment was excessive and actionable. It will also have its own statutory or contractual remedies to pursue against the teacher, including dismissal for willful breach of regulations. (*Ryan v. Fildes* [1938] 3 All E.R. 517)

In summary, a teacher should be prepared to face not only possible criminal charges for assault, but also civil proceedings and internal disciplinary action, including dismissal, if corporal punishment is carried beyond reasonable limits or is undertaken for bad motives. If school regulations prohibit any form of corporal punishment, the teacher is best advised to adhere to those rules. Even if criminal or civil liability is escaped, the teacher will probably be dismissed for breach of regulations, a far more serious consequence than a criminal or civil penalty in many cases.

False Arrest and False Imprisonment

Again these are two distinct torts but they are so similar that they are best dealt with together. A false arrest is intentionally arresting a person without proper legal excuse or authority. A lawful arrest may be made by any person (not just a peace officer) who actually finds a person committing an offence. False imprisonment is the intentional confinement of a person without a lawful excuse. The person does not have to be physically locked up or restrained; he must only be in a position where he does not feel free to leave of his own will.

It is a fairly common practice for teachers to detain certain pupils at recess time or after school by way of punishment. The student generally feels that he cannot leave the school until dismissed by the teacher. Can this constitute a false imprisonment?

> It is, I suppose, false imprisonment to keep a child locked up in a classroom, or even to order it to stop, under penalties, in a room for a longer period than the ordinary school time without lawful authority. (*Mansell v. Griffin* [1908] 1 K.B. 160 at 167)

There have been several instances where civil actions for false imprisonment have been instituted against teachers and school authorities.

In one case the student was being expelled from the school and was confined to his room for a four hour period to prevent communication with other pupils. The court stated that such confinement was justified as long as the expulsion itself was justified. In this instance, however, a jury found that the expulsion was not justifiable in the circumstances and therefore the confinement constituted a false imprisonment. The judge in this case stated that the – "locking up" may have been unjustified even if the expulsion was lawful if there were other means to separate this student from the others. (*Fitzgerald v. Northcote* (1865) 176 E.R. 734)

In another boarding school case, the action was dismissed because the student was not cognizant of any restraint being put upon him. The schoolmaster refused to allow the mother to take the student home because tuition was owing and had not been paid. The mother made frequent demands for the return of her son, which were refused. The boy was apparently unaware of these happenings or that any restraint was being put upon him. Because he did not feel that he could not leave, the action was dismissed. (*Herring v. Boyle* (1834) 149 E.R. 1126)

Another case took the opposite view, however. There the father requested to take his son from the school overnight during a period when such removals were not allowed. He was refused permission for the overnight visit but was allowed to take his son for the day providing he was returned in the evening. The father did not return the boy until the next day and the school refused to take him back. The school sued the father for the balance of fees for the term. During the course of the judgment it was observed:

> The plaintiff (schoolmaster) when he received the defendant's (father) letter of the 15th of Feb., could not withhold the son from the father. The parental authority in case of conflict must of course prevail, and the father might, no doubt, have had a habeas corpus if the master detained his son against his wish. (*Price v. Wilkins* (1888) 58 L.T.R. 680)

Perhaps the most interesting case involved the detention of a pupil for failure to do homework, in a publically supported school (rather than in a private boarding school). It was common practice for teachers at this school to assign "home lessons." The mother forbade her child to do such lessons and gave notice of this to the school. The child was kept in for a forty-five minute period and made to learn the homework lesson. It was contended that such a detention was an unlawful imprisonment, for it was a restraint on the liberty of the child, and further that the *Education Act* did not authorize such "home lessons." As the order to do the lessons was unauthorized, the child could not lawfully be punished for a breach of it. The court held as follows:

I thought at first that it might be possible to treat this as a matter of school discipline, and within the powers generally exercised by persons in charge of the education of children. Ordinarily an important part of a child's education is the study at home, but here the child has been punished for disobedience of an order which the schoolmaster had no power to make. (*Hunter v. Johnson* (1884) 13 Q.B. 225 at 227)

Like corporal punishment, detentions may be used as punishment providing they are used properly. Their use as punishment would constitute the lawful excuse or authority needed to escape a civil action for false imprisonment. The teacher must be certain, however, that the child is being properly punished with justification. Does your *Education Act* or *School Act* authorize schools to prescribe "home lessons"?

Intentional Infliction of Mental Suffering

Ask almost any student and he would readily agree that everything that goes on in school is "intentional infliction of mental suffering." To be actionable in tort, however, it must go beyond mere dislike for what is being said or taught. A deliberate course of conduct calculated to cause extreme mental anguish or suffering and resulting in substantial physical (or psychological) harm must be proved.

As with all intentional torts, it is impossible to prove "intent" unless you can see into the person's mind. Intent will be inferred by the court as a result of the person's conduct, and in extreme situations it is easily inferred. If a teacher is constantly and continually belittling and harassing a student for no apparent educational purpose, the court can infer that the teacher is doing so to cause mental anguish to the student. Further, if false statements are knowingly made, which would normally cause mental suffering, the courts will infer intent.

Since lawsuits for "educational malpractice" (alleging negligence on the part of educators resulting in mental suffering) have not met with success, it is likely that such suits may be brought under this cause of action instead. One American court has upheld this as a legitimate claim for a student to pursue even though denying him the right to sue for negligence.

In *Hunter v. Board of Education of Montgomery County* (1982) 439 A.2d 582, the student claimed "educational malpractice" as well as intentional injury as a result of his evaluation and placement in a school. While rejecting his negligence claim, the Court of Appeals of Maryland held:

Research reveals that none of the prior cases discussing educational malpractice have squarely confronted the question of whether public educators may be held responsible for their intentional torts arising in the educational context. In declining to entertain the educational negligence and breach of contract actions, we in no way intend to shield individual educators from liability for their intentional torts. It is our view that where an individual engaged in the educational process is shown to have willfully and maliciously injured a child entrusted to his educational care, such outrageous conduct greatly outweighs any public policy considerations which would otherwise preclude liability so as to authorize recovery. It may well be true that a claimant will usually face a formidable burden in attempting to produce adequate evidence to establish the intent requirement of the tort, but that factor alone cannot prevent a plaintiff from instituting the action.

The court went on to state that where individual educators have willfully and maliciously acted to injure a student enrolled in a public school, such actions will not be considered to have been done in the furtherance of the beneficent purposes of the educational system. These actions are an abandonment of employment and as a consequence the Board is absolved of liability for such acts. The result is that the individual teachers in such actions will face the prospect of paying damages from their own pockets. This may well discourage such claims, since the plaintiff would have little likelihood of recovering a large damage award from most teachers.

In one Quebec case a father was awarded damages where the Board refused to promote his child, with the intention of injuring the father. The board refused to promote the child to the level warranted by his abilities. The court held that this was done intentionally to injure the father and he was therefore entitled to remove his son from the school and was awarded damages for the expenses involved in placing the child in a different school. The plaintiff in this case was able to prove deliberate malicious conduct on the part of the Board but such instances are rare and are difficult to prove. (*Brault v. Commissaires D'Ecoles De Ste. Bridge* [1951] R.L. 479)

Damages have been awarded for the negligent infliction of mental suffering by school administrators. It is only the difficulty of proving the intent that has precluded an award for intentional infliction of mental suffering. In *Hollands v. Canterbury County Council* (1966), Kentish Gazette, September 30 and October 28, damages for nervous shock were awarded to a student who was told that she had passed her exams and then abruptly told several months later that she had failed them all. Her nervous shock was caused through the negligent actions of the administration, but what of the cases where students are intentionally promoted when they should not be, only to suffer mental anguish when they find that they do not have the skills normally associated with their grade level?

In one American case, *Johnson v. Sampson* 208 N.W. 814 (1926), a false accusation of unchastity was made against a 15-year-old school girl in her presence and the presence of another. The girl suffered mental distress as a result and this was held to be an actionable claim quite apart from an action for slander.

Teachers should be extremely cautious of their "intentional" actions towards students that might cause the students mental suffering or nervous shock. Building false hopes, which may be shattered, can be actionable.

Nuisance

While it is often said that children can be a nuisance and some students regard school as a nuisance, can either be said to constitute a nuisance within the legal definition of that term.? The issue has confronted at least one court in Canada.

In the law of torts, "nuisance" is the unlawful interference with the use and enjoyment of land (usually involving noise or some form of pollution). The person affected can sue for damages and an "injunction," which is a court order to cease committing the nuisance. The courts have held that, to be actionable, a nuisance must cause some serious interference with the comfort and enjoyment of life of the property owner. What happens, then, if a school is erected next door to someone's property, creating noise and unwanted objects flying into the yard?

Such a situation arose in *Loney v. Toronto Board of Education* (1926) 30 O.W.N. 75. The school board had purchased property adjacent to the plaintiff's and had torn down the houses that had been situated there. The playgrounds were expanded to the edge of the plaintiff's property. He brought an action for damages and an injunction as a result of the incessant noise made by the children and the "bombardment of balls" upon the windows and roof of his house.

The report of the judgment reads as follows:

A large school such as this cannot be carried on without causing considerable inconvenience and annoyance to the residents in the vicinity; but that is not of itself a sufficient ground for complaint. What becomes of importance is, whether, in the exercise of their right and duty to maintain this school, the defendants had used the school premises in a reasonable manner, having regard to the rights of others.

As the situation presented itself to the learned Judge, the one and only ground on which the plaintiff was entitled to any relief was that arising from the manner in which the property had been used for playing baseball – in the layout of the grounds for that purpose, the "home-plate" was placed in close proximity to the plaintiff's house. That might well have been avoided; and the injury was sufficient to justify some objection, though the extent of the injury was not, in all the circumstances, serious. It was not necessary that the playing of baseball be prohibited; but the grounds should be so arranged as to remove to a different place the home-plate, around which a material part of the noise seems to have prevailed. While not unduly curtailing the legitimate use of the grounds, this would remove any substantial reason for complaint.

On the defendants undertaking to arrange the grounds as indicated, the injunction sought should be refused. There was no depreciation in the value of the plaintiff's property from any improper or unauthorized use of the schoolgrounds – the liability of the defendants being limited to what had resulted from the "lay-out", which could be fully compensated for in damages and by the undertaking mentioned.

The damages should be fixed at $50; and, as the plaintiff has failed to establish his claim on the other grounds alleged, there should be no costs.

A similar situation confronted an American court with the same result. In *Ness v. Independent School District of Sioux City* 298 N.W. 855, the plaintiff recovered damages where the playground use constituted a nuisance. Baseballs were constantly pelting his house, resulting in broken windows, damaged slate roofing, and destroyed gardens and flower beds.

Teachers must, therefore, insure that their lawful and legitimate use of the school grounds does not constitute a nuisance for neighbouring property owners. Not only is there the potential for legal action through misuse of the grounds, but it creates bad public relations for the school when adjacent property owners are subjected to unreasonable intrusions on their property.

Defamation

The law of defamation is a very complex and technical body of law. Defamation is the publication, either orally or in a more permanent form, of any matter that may bring a person into the hatred, ridicule, or contempt of reasonable members of society, or may cause him to be shunned by such people. It includes both libel and slander, which are, respectively, written and spoken defamation. The essence of the action is that a person's reputation has been damaged as a result of words written or spoken about him by someone else. The words may, in their ordinary meaning, be defamatory or may be defamatory by innuendo.

There are various technical defences to a defamation suit. No action for defamation will succeed when the complaining party has consented to the publication. The truth of the statement is a defence to defamation provided that the statement is completely truthful. Another defence is that of "fair comment" on a matter of public interest. Perhaps the most usual defence in cases involving teachers is that of "privilege."

It is not the intent to make the reader an expert on defamation but only to point out certain instances where teachers have become involved in defamation actions.

The law of defamation can affect teachers in two ways. Defamatory remarks may be made about a teacher by parents, by administrators or even by another teacher. At times teachers may be called upon to make comments on the work or character of others. Sometimes these reports must be adverse and the issue of defamation may arise. As long as such reports are made in the execution of the teacher's duty, without malice, they will be protected by qualified privilege and will not be actionable against the teacher.

Often it is the teacher who is the plaintiff in such actions, seeking damages against an employer or parent for alleged defamatory remarks. Teachers can just as easily find themselves as defendants in such actions if they are not extremely judicious in what they say about administrators, school board members, fellow teachers, parents or pupils.

LaCarte v. Board of Education of Toronto [1959] S.C.R. 465, saw a dismissed high school teacher suing the board for damages for libel allegedly contained in her letter of dismissal. The Supreme Court of Canada in a 3-2 split decision held that since the letter was written in pursuance of the board's statutory duty to give reasons in writing for dismissal, it was what is termed an "occasion of qualified privilege" and there must be actual malice proved before it can be actionable. There was no evidence that the board was motivated by anything other than the due discharge of its duties. The minority of the Court held that where the person providing the information to the board acts out of malice, that will be treated as malice of the board even though individual members of the board are free from malice on their own part.

The defence of qualified privilege was raised in another action where the teacher sued a parent for damages. In *Goslett v. Garment* [1897] 13 T.L.R. 391, the defendant parent told the headmaster that he had seen the plaintiff intoxicated in a public place and was therefore not sending his sons to school. At the time the words were spoken the plaintiff teacher had ceased to be employed at the school. The defendant alleged an occasion of privilege because there was a common interest in the matter being discussed. The court however upheld the plaintiff's assertion that because he was no longer employed at the school, there was no reason to speak of him at all.

There are occasions when it is necessary to be able to speak and write freely about another and the law recognizes these as privileged and not actionable for defamation. Absolute privilege extends to a limited class of communications such as speeches in Parliament, statements made during court proceedings, and communications between officers of state in carrying out their duties. Qualified privilege extends to reports made in the execution of a public or private duty, as long as they are made without malice.

A privileged occasion is one where the person who makes the communication has an interest or duty, either legal, social, or moral, to make it, and the person receiving the communication has a corresponding interest or duty to receive it. There must be this reciprocity of interest before the defence can succeed. The interest being protected by the communication may be a private interest, a public interest, or a common interest of two people. This privilege is lost, however, by proof of the existence of malice on the part of the person making the communication. Proof that the statements made were false to the knowledge of the person making them constitutes sufficient proof of malice. The person making the statement must honestly believe (at the time of making it) that what he says is true.

In *Mallett v. Clarke* (1968) 70 D.L.R. (2d) 67, a student in a vocational school was expelled and complained to a local newspaper about the alleged injustice of this action. The reporter phoned the principal who stated that the student was "terminated permanently for conduct detrimental to his class" and further that "he lacked the tact and adaptability for his chosen profession." The student sued for defamation.

The court found that the words used were defamatory in nature but that this was an occasion of qualified privilege. The principal was replying to an attack upon him and was defending his personal reputation.

In *McIntyre v. McBean* (1856) 13 U.C.Q.B. 534 a group of citizens complained about the "intemperant and immoral" behaviour of the local teacher. Again this was an occasion of privilege since the statements were made to protect a public interest, namely: the education of children.

Hulme v. Marshall [1887] J.P. 136 provides an example of privilege where there is a duty on the part of the person making a statement to report. Here a teacher reported to the headmaster concerning drunkenness on the part of a colleague. In the circumstances, there was a duty to report on the part of the informant and a corresponding duty to receive the information on the part of the recipient.

Thus, when a teacher complains to his association about the conduct of a fellow teacher, such a statement would be privileged. There is a common interest in the welfare of the teaching profession and a mutual interest in both making and receiving the report.

Even in instances of qualified privilege, certain statements may be actionable. In *Raison v. Board of School Trustees, School District No. 45*, an unreported decision of the British Columbia Court of Appeal, it was held that administrative reports to school boards are privileged only insofar as statements pertaining to the learning situation in the classroom. There is no protection afforded to statements that do not concern the learning situation.

A jury in *Haight v. Robb*, another unreported B.C. case from 1975, awarded a teacher substantial damages against four principals for defamatory statements made in reports. The jury found the statements to be false and motivated by malice, thereby negating any defence of privilege. In commenting on this decision, the provincial Department of Education, the B.C. School Trustees Association, and the B.C. Teacher's Federation issued the following joint statement:

> The prescriptions of the Public Schools Act must be followed, and the authors of reports must be scrupulously introspective to ensure that their comments are valid and fair and free from any taint of animus toward the recipient of the report. The efficient and effective operation of the public school system demands some form of reporting system. This isolated and unusual decision of a court of law should be viewed for its positive contribution in stressing the obligation for fairness in the system. (quoted in Alan C. Nicholls, *An Introduction to School Case Law*, p.93)

Another defence often raised in defamation actions is that of "fair comment" on a matter of public concern. For such a defence to succeed, the defendant must be totally accurate in his facts. The statements made must be true or this will not afford a defence. In an unreported Alberta case, this defence failed because the defendant had made an error in certain facts regarding the length of time a proposed contract of hiring was to run (4 months rather than 5) and the percentage of salary that would be paid (a little less than 170% rather than 170% as alleged). Thus even minor errors in computation can defeat this defence.

Teachers may often be the victims of perceived defamatory remarks and should be vigilant in protecting their reputations. They should also be equally vigilant in protecting the reputations of others with whom they come in contact in their professional capacity.

Trespass

Trespass is the intentional entering onto another's land without his consent or legal cause. There need not be any damage to the land in order for the tort to be actionable; however, only minimal compensation will be awarded in the absence of any damage to the land. Failure to leave someone's property when permission to remain there is taken away or expires is also trespass, even though the original entry onto the land was lawful.

Trespass is important in the school context only for the purpose of categorizing those found on school property at various times. The category into which a person falls often determines the duty of care owed to that person by the owner in an action for negligence. A lower duty of care is owed to a trespasser than is owed to other classes of visitors.

School buildings and land are privately owned property and are not public places to which the public has an unlimited right of access, although they are often treated that way. During school hours, teachers, students and others are permitted on the premises (indeed are required to be there) to conduct the educational function of the school. After hours, however, presence on the school grounds and buildings may be forbidden or restricted, and the student who was lawfully there one minute may be a trespasser the next.

It is also important for teachers to know the law of trespass on occasions when they are required to deal with strangers found on the premises. In addition to being a tort, trespass is also a quasi-criminal act in provinces with a *Petty Trespass Act* in force. Such statutes make it an offence to trespass and grant the owner or occupier of land the right to apprehend, without warrant, anyone found trespassing.

Presumably a civil action could be launched against a trespasser but in reality such action is unlikely, since the nominal damages recoverable would not cover the expense of the litigation. Legal cases involving negligence claims are filled with references to trespass and we shall deal with the subject again when we discuss the duty of care owed by a landowner in the negligence section.

Chattels

The final intentional tort to be considered is trespass or conversion of personal property or chattels. These are the civil equivalents to the criminal concepts of damage to property and theft.

Anyone wrongfully damaging or converting (taking) the personal property of another may be sued civilly for damages or for return of the property. In the school context we are concerned with such actions by both teachers and students.

It is a common law principle that a parent cannot be compelled to pay damages for the torts committed by his children unless the parent was actively negligent in permitting such a tort to occur. For example, if a parent gives a child a loaded gun to play with the parent would be responsible for any damages occasioned by the use of the gun. However, where a child, of his own volition, picks up a rock and launches it through a neighbor's window, the parent cannot be compelled to pay damages. Many provincial school acts circumvent this common law rule by legislating a positive legal obligation on the parent to pay for any damages to school property caused by his child. Schools where such legislation has been enacted can, therefore, sue the parent of the offending child to recover the cost of repairing damaged or stolen property.

Teachers should also be careful in their treatment of school property. It is an all too common practice for employees in all occupations to treat the office supplies as a source for replenishing home supplies. Any removal of school property for personal use or consumption is theft and is actionable in a civil suit as well. Teachers are in a position of trust and are charged with the obligation of protecting the property under their control. Breaches of this trust are viewed very seriously by the courts. As a practical matter, if the amount involved is small, no civil action will be taken. The more serious consequences of such behaviour would be criminal charges and loss of the teacher's job.

Negligence

Negligence is the omission to do something that a reasonable man would do or the commission of an act that a reasonable man would not do. In a word, it is carelessness. The tort of negligence involves three basic elements, each of which must exist before damages will be awarded. These are:

1. There must be a legal duty of care owed to the person who is injured.
2. There must be a breach of this duty of care by failing to conform to the standard of care required.
3. This breach must have caused some injury or damage.

Each of these elements has been considered in the school context in a large number of cases. We will look at these elements to discover general principles of law applicable in all school situations and then deal with specific cases in different settings.

Another important concept that will be discussed is that of vicarious liability, whereby school boards and principals may be held responsible for the negligent actions of their teachers. Plaintiffs will look to the defendant who is best able to pay a judgment: the school board. Teachers must be aware of what negligent actions will involve their school board and when they will have to face the prospect of a large lawsuit on their own.

A legal duty of care is owed to anyone who may reasonably be anticipated to be harmed by the negligent conduct of another. This is an objective test of whether a reasonable person would realize the danger involved, not whether the defendant actually foresaw the danger of his actions. If the dangerous action is being conducted at a place where no one should be present then there is no duty owed to a person who wanders into the area. You may owe a duty to one injured party and not to another where you can foresee that one person may be injured but not another.

In general there is no duty to take specific actions to prevent injuries to someone in peril; there is only a duty not to create risks for him. For example, if you see someone drowning, you are not obligated to take action to save him. This general rule does not apply to teachers in relation to their students for two reasons. Firstly, their jobs involve the protection of students, creating a duty to do so at all times. Anyone in an occupation where the job itself requires the protection of others creates this duty of positive action. Secondly, the governments have legislated that school boards, and their employees, shall protect their students. Governments can create a duty of care by legislative action where one may not exist in common law.

The duty of care owed to students at school is called "the duty of supervision" and is owed by teachers, principals and the school board itself. The standard which has been developed to determine the extent of this duty is known as the "careful parent" test. This test was first formulated in 1893 in an English case, *Williams v. Eady* (1893) 10 T.L.R. 41 when Lord Esher stated:

> ... the school master was bound to take care of his boys as a careful father would take care of his boys, and there could not be a better definition of the duty of a schoolmaster.

Although this statement has been generally accepted by courts in Canada and other common law jurisdictions ever since, it is recognized that the definition poses problems. It has been described as "not enlightening," "not particularly helpful" and presenting "much difficulty in application." One judge commented that "it is doubtful if this concept adds anything to the ordinary requirement of reasonable care in the circumstances." Another said that he was "not satisfied that this definition is of universal application."

The test evolved from the concept that a teacher was acting *in loco parentis* and therefore owed the same duty of care that a parent would owe. However, the courts have retreated from this doctrine and it is generally recognized that schools derive their authority from the state through education legislation and not from parental delegation of authority. The authority and responsibilities of the school are therefore independent from that of the parent.

Courts have recognized that, in the school context, there must be some variation of what a careful parent would do. The large number of children involved has resulted in the test becoming one of a "careful parent of a very large family." In certain areas, teachers are expected to possess skills beyond those that an ordinary parent would have and an elevated standard of care, that of the competent instructor, has been applied in such situations. Where children suffer from some handicap, the standard has also been raised. The school environment has been recognized as differing from a home environment and the test has been adjusted to take that factor into account.

The question of whether this duty and standard has been breached will depend on the facts and circumstances of each case. In the following chapter we will look at various cases to see the circumstances under which school authorities have been held liable or absolved from liability. It will be seen that the test can be very flexible in application and this creates uncertainty on the part of teachers as to the full extent of their duties. Perhaps a new standard, that of a "careful teacher" or "competent instructor," might be more helpful, since it may be easier to determine what a skilled teacher would do in certain circumstances as opposed to what the mythical "careful parent" would do.

In determining whether the standard of care has been met, the judge tries to determine whether the consequences could reasonably be foreseen in the circumstances. Teachers, as "careful parents," are generally expected to foresee and guard against even slight possibilities of danger that an ordinary person would not be expected to foresee. Many cases are concerned with reasonableness and foreseeability.

The breach of the duty must have a reasonably close connection to the injuries sustained in order to find liability for damages. A breach of the duty without any injury is, of course, not actionable. Thus, if the school is not providing proper supervision on the playground and no one is injured, there will be no action for the breach of duty. If the duty is breached, it must be that breach that leads to the injury or contributes to it in some way. If there is not adequate playground supervision and an injury occurs as the result of the actions of another student, which could not have been prevented with any amount of supervision, then the school will escape liability. Some accidents just cannot be prevented whether or not the proper standard of care is exercised. If, however, the accident could have been avoided by proper supervision, the school will be held accountable.

The liability of school boards for damages incurred as a result of a teacher's breach of the duty of supervision is based on the concept of vicarious liability. This concept of law holds one person responsible for the misconduct of another even though he, himself, is free from fault in the matter. It is most commonly found in employment situations where an employer is held responsible for wrongs committed by an employee provided he was acting in the course and scope of his employment. Thus, where an employee sustains a tort liability on the job, the employer will be held accountable as well. If, however, the employee's actions were done on his own time or "on a lark of his own" outside of the employment relationship, the employer will not be called to account for the actions.

Therefore, whenever a teacher breaches the duty of supervision, the school board will become a party to the action. From the injured student's perspective, this creates the opportunity for adequate compensation for injuries. School boards carry insurance and are able to satisfy large damage awards which individual teachers could not possibly hope to pay.

In addition to this indirect liability, school boards may be found to be at fault directly under the law concerning "occupier's liability." This branch of tort law holds that owners and occupiers of land owe a duty to people entering on that land and to protect them from dangers located on the land. The standard of care to be taken and the duty owed depends on the category into which the entrant onto the land falls.

Persons who enter onto land as a matter of contractual right are owed the highest duty of care. They are entitled to be protected from all dangers as is reasonably possible. Into this category fall people such as ticketholders to sporting events. They have paid to be on the property and are therefore, entitled to have their safety assured.

A lower duty is owed to "invitees" and "licensees" who are people who enter onto the land with permission of the owner. "Invitees" are those who are there to confirm some advantage to the owner while "licensees" do not confer any benefit to the owner by their presence on the land. These people must be protected from damage by any unusual danger or trap which the owner knew (or ought to have known) existed. The owner must use reasonable care to bring the danger to their notice or to guard against it. An example of such unusual danger might be a large hole or excavation on the property. The owner must warn each person about it or put up a guard to prevent anyone from falling into it.

The last category of user is a trespasser. These are people who are on the property without permission. The only duty owed to this class of person by the owner is not to do any deliberate injury to him. If a trespasser falls into an excavation the owner will not be liable. If the owner deliberately injures the trespasser in some manner, such as setting land mines on the property, then he will be liable for the injuries sustained.

Students are generally regarded as being "invitees" and the duty owed by the board is to protect them from any concealed or unusual dangers on the property or any inherently dangerous materials that might be found on the property. Schools do not have to protect against obvious dangers or those that should be obvious. Because of the age of the students this has been modified in some cases and an even higher duty of care has been held to exist.

In the chapter on occupier's liability we will look at instances where schools have been held liable under this duty of care. The types of dangers to be protected against will vary according to the circumstances of each case and we will see that what has been regarded as an unusual danger in a particular case has not been so regarded in others.

A common defence to negligence actions is voluntary assumption of the risk as expressed in the Latin motto *volenti non fit injuria.* What this means is that if the injured party knew of the danger involved and willingly underwent the risk with this knowledge then he has consented to the consequences and cannot hold the injuring party liable.

Thus, even if there has been a breach of duty, no liability will attach if the plaintiff knew of the risk involved and was willing to overlook that risk. This defence has been successful in a number of school accident cases. Where the student does not fully appreciate the risks it will not be a valid defence. Nor will it be successful where the student is ordered to do the particular task leading to injury. He is not willingly assuming the risk in that situation but rather is being compelled to undertake the task.

In summary, teachers will be found to be negligent if they do not exercise the degree of supervision that a careful parent would in the circumstances. School boards will be held vicariously liable for these actions. Boards will also be found negligent if the school premises create some unusual danger for the students.

The Teacher as Plaintiff

There have been a number of cases where teachers have been plaintiffs in various tort actions. Teachers have the same rights as others and we would not want to leave the impression that they are only involved in defending themselves from lawsuits launched by others.

In *Emerson v. Melancthon School Trustees* [1904] O.W.N. 12 a teacher sued her board for injuries caused to her by their neglect to employ a person to attend to the heating of the school. She had become seriously ill and alleged that it was as a result of the cold and dampness of the school room. The Act and regulations imposed upon the board a duty to appoint someone to look after the lighting of a fire at the school at least one hour before opening.

The court found no causal connection between her illness and the failure of the board to adhere to their statutory duty. The judge pointed out other factors which could just as easily have led to her condition and dismissed the action. However, he stated in closing;

> The defendants, however, had disregarded their statutory duty to employ a caretaker and to have fires lighted an hour before the opening of school – a duty owed to the teacher, the pupils, and their parents – and have probably narrowly escaped being made liable to heavy damages by neglecting it.

In *Carriere et al. v. Board of Gravelbourg School District No. 2244 of Saskatchewan* [1977] 5 W.W.R. 517, a teacher was injured in a fall on a snow bank while supervising a noon hour recess. The Saskatchewan Court of Appeal held:

> Here the respondent required supervision of the pupils at noon hour by its teachers as a condition of employment. Pursuant to this directive the principal and the teachers formulated the rules to be followed, and in carrying out their duties of supervision both the principal and the teachers, in their professional judgment, considered it necessary, on occasion, to climb the snowbanks surrounding the rink for the purpose of effective supervision. There was, therefore, a duty resting upon the respondent to take reasonable care that the duty of supervision which it imposed upon its teachers could be carried out with safety. That duty could have been discharged by

providing some safe means of ingress and egress to the skating surface, but none was provided. The respondent, having failed in this duty to take reasonable care for the safety of its teachers, is accordingly liable to the appellant for the injuries which she sustained in carrying out her assigned duties of supervision.

Teachers, as well as students, are entitled to expect safe premises. The board must ensure that it fulfills its statutory duty in maintaining the premises and if any teacher should sustain injury as a result of any neglect of duty, that teacher is entitled to take action. Suing your school board does not generally make for harmonious relations; however, teachers need not be overly concerned about dismissal for such action. The mere bringing of a valid cause of action is not grounds for dismissal.

In *Sirois et al. v. L'Association des Enseignants Francophones du Nouveau-Brunswick (AEFNB) et al,* (1984) 8 O.L.R. (4th) 279, teacher's association for economic losses suffered by the negligent misrepresentations of the association concerning entitlement to unemployment benefits. Because they relied on information contained in a news bulletin published by the association, the teachers did not apply for benefits as soon as they could and thus sustained a loss of benefits.

The plaintiffs were successful and recovered 75% of their lost benefits. The court held that the association had a duty of care towards its members and that it breached that duty by publishing inaccurate information. The plaintiffs had reasonable grounds to rely on the information and were injured as a result of that reliance. The teachers were found to be contributorily negligent to the extent of 25% of the loss because they failed to make any other inquiries, which the news bulletin suggested and their own experience should have dictated.

Teachers, therefore, may sue anyone who tortiously injures them whether it be their employer, association or anyone else. If there is a job related injury, it may not be actionable due to Workers' Compensation legislation which provides that job related accidents will be compensated through a fund established for that purpose. Such legislation takes away the right to sue an employer or fellow employee for the injury, however, recent cases have indicated that such provisions may not be applicable. Teachers should consult a lawyer if they are injured on the job in circumstances where there may be negligence.

Discussion and Review Questions

1. What are the sources of a teacher's duty toward the student?
2. What is a tort? What is an intentional tort? Give four or five examples of intentional torts. Describe one.
3. What is an unintentional tort?
4. What are the three basic elements which must be present before the court will award damages for negligence?
5. Explain how the absence of each one of these elements noted above could destroy the plaintiff's case.
6. Explain what is meant by the term "careful parent test." What are some of the limitations to its application?
7. What are the criteria upon which the teacher will be judged to be competent?
8. Will a careless teacher automatically be held liable for damages? If not, what are some of the intervening factors?
9. Explain why the actions of a teacher can cause the school board to be held liable for damages when perhaps they were not even aware of the accident or directly involved in any way.
10. What are the teacher's best legal defenses against liability suits?
11. Define the terms "invitee," "licensee" and "trespasser" and explain the relevance of these terms to the school teacher.

You be the Judge

"And the Chapel Bell was Ringing"

"Hello Mr. Brown, this is Mr. New calling from Guy Weadick Elementary, I am so sorry that Jimmie could not be saved . . . ."

Mr. New had recently graduated with a specialization in Elementary Education. At the staff organization meeting, Mrs. Fair, principal of Guy Weadick (a new school which was to open its doors for the first time August 27th) reviewed the capabilities of the staff and the needs of the children as she understood them. She asked Mr. New if he would accept as part of his assignment the teaching of a grade six boys' class in physical education. Mr. New agreed.

As Mr. New reviewed the student records of his physical education class, he noted that Jimmie Brown had a medical history of severe asthmatic attacks, caused in part by excessive excitement.

Mr. New spoke to Mr. and Mrs. Brown about this. The Browns asked that Jimmie not be excluded from physical education classes since he was now able to handle the situation. They noted that Jimmie was able to sense when an attack was coming on and that he would grab the equipment supplied by the doctor to assist his breathing. They assured the teacher that all would be well with Jimmie in a few minutes. Mr. New disguised the alarm which he felt, but after the meeting with the Browns he began doing some research.

The principal confirmed to Mr. New that two previous schools were aware of the situation and had permitted Jimmie to take part in physical education and other sports activities. There had been previous attacks at school, but Jimmie was able to use the equipment to assist his breathing. All had been well.

Mr. New, although inexperienced, was a cautious soul. He met again with the Browns, reviewed his concerns, got confirmation of the previous instances, and had them provide him with a letter stating that they were aware of the medical problems suffered by Jimmie, but requesting that Jimmie be involved in the normal school activities available to other boys. All went well . . . until midwinter, when, during a tumbling exercise, Mr. New noticed that Jimmie was having problems breathing. Jimmie ran to his locker. Mr. New followed, after cautioning the remainder of the class to sit quietly for a few minutes.

Mr. New found Jimmie in front of his locker, eyes rolling, and unable to breathe. Jimmie was only able to gasp, "It's empty!"

The Fire Department, which was nearby, responded within 2 to 3 minutes. An ambulance arrived shortly thereafter and took Jimmie to the hospital. He was pronounced dead on arrival.

The Coroner's report noted the facts of the situation, including the quick response and noted that Jimmie had died by suffocating in his own vomit.

Questions for Discussion

1. Did Mr. New act as a careful parent would have acted?
2. Is Mrs. Fair liable? Why?
3. Suppose the Browns take Mr. New and his employer to court,
   a. What will be Mr. New's defense?

b. What will be the defense of the School Board?

4. Who will win?

5. How, or could, the school or the teacher have prevented this tragic event?

References

The following references are in addition to those given in Chapter One. General materials concerning School Law contain extensive sections on tort liability.

Alexander, E. R., "Tort Responsibility of Parents and Teachers for Damages Caused by Children," (1965) 16 *University of Toronto Law Journal* 165.

Barnes, J., *Sports and the Law in Canada*. Toronto: Butterworths, 1983.

Barnes, J. "Myers: Annotation," (1978) 5 C.C.L.T. 272.

Carson, B., "Negligence: Standard of Care: Reasonably Careful Parent or Competent Instructor in Field," (1968) 3 *Ottawa Law Review* 359.

Fleming, J. G., *The Law of Torts*. Toronto: Carswell, 1983.

Hoyano, L. C. H., "The Prudent Parent: The Elusive Standard of Care," (1984) 18 *U.B.C. Law Review* 1.

Klar, L. (ed.), *Studies in Canadian Tort Law*. Toronto: Butterworths, 1977.

Lamb, R. L., *Legal Liability of School Boards and Teachers for Accidents*. Ottawa: Canadian Teachers' Federation, 1959.

Sibley, C. E., "Negligence in the Science Laboratory," *Alberta Science Education Journal*, Sept. 1978, p. 70.

Thomas, A. M., *Accidents Will Happen: An Inquiry into the Legal Liability of Teachers and School Boards*. Toronto: OISE Press, 1976.

Wright, C. A. and Linden, A. M., *Canadian Tort Law*. Toronto: Butterworths, 1975.

10

The Duty of Supervision

Learning Objectives

Some of the things that the reader will learn from this chapter include:

1. A definition of the "duty to supervise" imposed upon the teacher.
2. The parts of the school program in which the teacher is most vulnerable to charges of negligence, the reasons for the vulnerability, and some examples of current judgements against and in favour of the teacher and his employer.
3. The criteria upon which the teacher's competency will be judged.
4. The measure of care needed.
5. The factors which mitigate the teacher's duty.
6. The legal requirements respecting the nature and condition of school equipment.
7. The degree of responsibility which students have for their own safety.
8. The degree to which the duty to supervise extends beyond the school premises and school hours.
9. The school's responsibility for injuries inflicted on one student by another.
10. The problems associated with providing medical treatment to students.

Preview

Because of the central importance of the duty to supervise in the legal life of the teacher, an entire chapter has been devoted to the topic.

If the duty to supervise students is not a statutory duty in the province where you work, it is still a common law duty. There is a long history of "court-made law" to confirm this fact. Through trial after trial, educators have come to appreciate this duty and to understand the tests which will be applied by the courts in order rendering a judgement.

The curriculum areas of vocational education, science, home economics, and physical education have been selected to illustrate the extent of a teacher's duty to supervise in high-risk activities. Field trips, playground supervision, and student transportation have been selected as illustrating the supervisory requirements for out-of-building parts of the school program.

When students leave the school without permission, a number of additional legal considerations come into play. The teacher should be aware of the unique burden imposed in these situations.

Self-Assessment

1. Under what circumstances will a teacher be required to pay damages for a student's injury?

2. Under what circumstances will a teacher be found negligent? How careful must the teacher be? How closely must the teacher supervise the students? When must the teacher warn students of potential dangers, and what happens if the students do not heed the warning?

3. Why are school boards most often named as defendants in negligence cases rather than individual teachers?

4. What is vicarious liability?

Key Terms

Volenti non fit injuria   Careful parent test
Volens   Occupier's liability
Duty of Care   Gratuitous passenger
Causa causans

*   *   *   *

In this chapter we shall look at various cases dealing with the duty of teachers to supervise the activities of students in the way that a careful parent would. As we shall see, the degree of supervision required will vary according to factors such as the nature of the activity, the number and ages of the children involved, and the person who is doing the supervising.

Sometimes there will be found to be no duty to supervise, due to factors such as the time that the accident occurred, the place at which the accident occurred, or the nature of the activity. The duty does not extend to all times, places or activities that may be encountered in the school.

There are many different ways in which these cases could be approached or categorized. We have chosen to present them according to curriculum subjects and other school related activities such as field trips and recess. The reason for this is to bring home the need for safety precautions in particular areas of the school and to warn teachers of potential dangers involved in their own subject area. We have included cases which are illustrative of potential claims and those that are considered significant in establishing an important precedent. Not all possible cases have been included but those presented should give you a feel for the types of issues involved and, may create an awareness of the types of dangers that should be guarded against.

Vocational Education

The industrial arts room (or "shop") provides an ideal setting for potential negligence claims. The mechanical contrivances found therein are as adept at severing limbs as they are at sawing lumber. Surely only the bravest or most foolhardy of teachers would dare to enter there. Surprisingly, however, there are relatively few reported cases involving shop accidents.

It is suggested that this may be due to several factors. First, the inherent dangers of the machines are recognized and extraordinary safety precautions are taken in this setting. Warning signs and safety posters abound. Various safety devices and guards are affixed to the machines. Second, shop teachers are possibly more attentive to the students while working on the machines because of the potential danger. Safety lessons are given before students are allowed to run the machines. Unlike other disciplines, "discovery learning" is not encouraged. Third, the students in these classes are generally mature. The courses are offered at junior and senior high school levels where students have the manual dexterity and intellectual skills that are necessary to avoid the dangers. Finally, there are fewer students taking such optional courses compared to other potentially dangerous ones such as physical education, which is often compulsory.

Despite the precautions taken, a few students do manage to get injured in the shop. We will look at some of these situations and see what precautions are necessary to avoid such occurrences.

One of the earliest cases involving student injury by a machine was *Smerkinich v. Newport Corporation* (1912) 76 J.P. 454. This case involved a 19-year-old student who severed his thumb on the blade of a small circular saw. The evidence indicated that the saw was not fitted with a guard and that the plaintiff knew of this situation. He was aware that it would be safer with a guard but never suggested to the instructor that it be fitted with one. His claim was successful at trial but was appealed. On appeal the King's Bench Division considered two issues. Were the defendants obligated to provide a guard such that failure to do so would constitute negligence on their part? Secondly, did the doctrine of *volenti non fit injuria* apply in this situation?

The court's decision, in part, was as follows:

> The question is whether it was reasonable and proper, according to the experience of persons accustomed to saws, that such shields should be provided, and the evidence, so far as we can understand it, is that with such a saw there is no such protection usually provided. It does not follow from the fact that the accident could have been prevented by the use of a guard that therefore it was the duty of the corporation to provide such a guard. The other point is as to whether the doctrine *volenti non fit injuria* applies. That of course is not a new question. In this case the man knew that there was a danger in using this machine and that if he brought his hand in contact with the saw he would be injured. He asked the instructor to allow him to use the saw without his assistance . . . If he clearly foresaw the likelihood of such a result and, notwithstanding, continued to work, I think that, according to the authorities, he ought to be regarded as *volens*.

An unusual accident in Ontario led to the amputation of a leg on a 16-year-old boy. *Ramsden v. Hamilton Board of Education* [1942] 1 D.L.R. 770 came before the courts after the plaintiff "flicked" the blade of a chisel against a revolving sanding wheel at the desk of another student. The wheel violently threw the chisel into the plaintiff's thigh severing the femoral artery. Blood clotting led to gangrene and eventually a portion of the leg was amputated. The Ontario High Court found the plaintiff solely to blame for the accident. The judge stated:

> I further find that Ramsden did not voluntarily force the blade against the perimeter, nor was it a purely accidental coming together of the blade and perimeter – but I find, as a fact, that it was as the result of Ramsden voluntarily and knowingly assuming the risk . . . of imprudently and negligently "flicking" the blade in too close proximity to the moving perimeter of the

sander . . . the "flicking" of the blade, in the manner and under the circumstances above described, constituted negligence, and that the said negligence was the direct cause or *causa causans* of this sad affair.

The plaintiff alleged various acts of negligence on the part of the instructor and further that the machine was a dangerous one which should have been provided with a guard. In answer to these allegations the court said:

> . . . I do find that the presence or absence of Mr. Scott (the instructor), in or from the room, had nothing to do with the accident.
>
> I do find, as a fact, that it was not negligence on Scott's part in not having seen Ramsden return in this round-about way, nor was it negligence, on Scott's part, in not having prevented Ramsden from having so gone around.
>
> . . . I have no hesitation in finding from the evidence that the sanding machine in question, when in operation, was not a dangerous machine. . . . I must find that, not only did the sanding machine (not being dangerous) not require a guard, but, as a fact, that a guard could not be placed on a sanding machine while in operation – the only "dangerous" part of the machine being in fact the sanding surface, and the sanding surface could not be used if it were covered up with a guard!

The plaintiff further alleged that the teacher should have foreseen the possibility of such an accident occurring and should have taken precautions to avoid it. The court said:

> Human prudence would be taxed beyond reason, were it to endeavour to foresee every possibility of human ingenuity, or boyish mischievousness, in its search for opportunities to get into trouble, in even the remotest and most unlikely corners, nooks, or crannies.

The Supreme Court of Canada has had the opportunity to consider a shop accident in the case of *Dziwenka et al. v. The Queen in Right of Alberta et al.* (1971) 25 D.L.R. (3d) 12. This case provided another unusual element in that the plaintiff had a physical handicap. The plaintiff was an 18-year-old student at the Alberta School for the Deaf at the time of the accident. He suffered a severe injury to his hand when it came into contact with the unguarded blade of a circular power table saw which he was operating. He was performing an operation that required the guard to be removed. His attention drifted momentarily and his hand struck the saw. The instructor was at another work bench taking occasional glances to the power saw operation.

The trial judge assessed the relative negligence of the instructor at 60% and the plaintiff at 40%. The Appellate Division of the Alberta Supreme

Court dismissed the action finding that the plaintiff was solely to blame for the accident. The plaintiff pursued the matter to the Supreme Court which rendered a split 3-2 decision.

Justice Laskin delivered the majority opinion stating;

> The finding of want of sufficiently close supervision must also be judged in the light of evidence that the plaintiff was the only student working with power equipment at the time of the accident. There were six students, in addition to the plaintiff and Turner, who were then in the woodworking shop, and they were engaged on projects for which they used hand tools.
>
> The question of the negligence of Mapplebeck (the instructor) in this case is not foreclosed by the proof given of the plaintiff's awareness of the danger in the operations to which he was assigned. Nor can his momentary inattention provide complete exoneration of the defendants if there was a breach by Mapplebeck of his duty of care to the plaintiff. . . I do not agree with the view of the Appellate Division that Mapplebeck was free from negligence in following allegedly approved general practice in the way he handled the assignment to the plaintiff.
>
> The duty of care owing to a student, especially a handicapped one as in this case, in respect of his personal safety while operating dangerous machinery, is a stricter one than that owed by an employer to an employee working with dangerous machinery.
>
> I do not find it improbable that the accident would not have happened if the instructor had directly supervised the operations until they were finished.

Justice Ritchie delivered a dissenting opinion taking the view that the accident was the fault of the plaintiff and could not have been avoided by the instructor. He said:

> . . . I am of the opinion that the proper inference to be drawn from the evidence as a whole is that the accident was caused by momentary inattention on the part of the appellant.
>
> This accident appears to me to be of the kind described by Denning, L.J., in *Clark v. Monmouthshire County Council* . . . "The incident would take place in the fraction of a second which the presence of . . . a master would not have done anything to prevent at all."

Accordingly, the judgment at trial was restored and the negligence split between the parties. In these circumstances the plaintiff only recovers that portion of the damages which are attributed to the defendant's negligence. For example, if the damages are calculated to be $20,000 in total and the defendant is 60% at fault, the plaintiff will recover only $12,000 from the defendant.

This principle was also applied in a more recent case in British

Columbia. *Hoar v. Board of School Trustees, District 68 (Nanaimo) and Haynes* [1984] 6 W.W.R. 143 involved a 17-year-old student who lost part of three fingers while using a jointer. The British Columbia Court of Appeal upheld the trial judge's equal apportionment of liability in the circumstances of the case.

The judgment reveals that the instructor, Haynes, stressed the importance of safety in using the various machines. He gave each student a 15-page set of safety instructions and a textbook containing safety instructions for each machine. He also gave demonstrations on the use of each machine and tested the students concerning safety on two occasions. The plaintiff missed the demonstration on the use of the jointer but had used the machine without incident on approximately 15 previous occasions. Where, then, was the negligence on the part of the instructor?

The trial judge described the negligence as follows:

> The question to be answered here is: Was there a particular precaution which Mr. Haynes might reasonably have taken which he did not take? I answer the question affirmatively and say that the precaution was to inform himself of absence from demonstration so that without fail he could give a make-up demonstration after the student returned. If he was 'bound to take notice of the ordinary nature of young boys' he could anticipate that at least some of his students would not bother to ask for make-up demonstrations and would be willing to take their chances without them.

> In all other aspects I find Mr. Haynes conduct to have been exemplary. He struck me as intelligent, skilled, articulate, reasonable and well-informed. He can only be faulted in one particular but that is a vital particular. Since he thought it essential to give demonstrations it follows that it was essential that the demonstrations be received by each student and I hold that he bore responsibility to check to make sure that the demonstrations were received by absent students.

The Court of Appeal upheld the decision and added the following comments about safety in the woodworking shop:

> The machines being operated by the students in the woodworking shop are unquestionably dangerous, some more so than others. Instruction in their use is of critical importance to the safety of the students.

The court also looked at the issue of the standard of care owed by a teacher to his students. Various cases were noted and the court said that the standard being imposed upon the teacher here was no higher than the "careful parent" test enumerated in other cases. The board also alleged that the plaintiff had not shown a connection between this negligence and the loss that occurred. The court held:

But in the circumstances of this case, where safe operation of dangerous machines is one of the principle objects of instruction given by teachers, I think it cannot be said the respondent has failed to advance evidence linking the act of negligence of Mr. Haynes with the loss which the respondent sustained.

Liability was apportioned equally because it was not possible to establish different degrees of fault between the plaintiff and the instructor.

As these cases have made clear, safety is of prime importance in the shop. Teachers must make sure that proper instruction in safety is given to each student and that potentially dangerous activities are closely supervised. Where students willfully disregard safety procedures known to them, the teacher will not be liable unless there was also some degree of contributory negligence on his part causing the loss sustained. The cases further demonstrate our opening proposition that industrial arts teachers tend to take extraordinary measures to ensure the safety of students in light of the inherently dangerous nature of the machines. In none of the cases has the teacher been held solely to blame for the accident. The concern for safety demonstrated in these classes should be an example for all teachers.

The Science Laboratory

The science laboratory is also fertile ground for potential negligence claims. Dangerous chemicals can cause severe injuries if they are used improperly. Considerations in this area should be directed towards questions of both occupier's liability, in storing dangerous objects, and the duty of supervision. Indeed, the case that has become the cornerstone for much of our school law involved chemicals.

Williams v. Eady (1893) 10 T.L.R. 41 involved some phosphorous that had been left in the school conservatory. A student opened a bottle of the substance and inserted a lighted match. The resulting explosion injured the plaintiff who was standing nearby. The court held that leaving a dangerous substance such as phosphorous in a place accessible to children was negligence. It was this case that led to the often quoted phrase of Lord Esher describing the duty owed by a teacher:

> The school master was bound to take such care of his boys as a careful father would take of his boys, and there could not be a better definition of the duty of a school master. Then he was bound to take notice of the ordinary nature of young boys, their tendency to do mischievous acts, and their propensity to meddle with anything that came in their way.

A similar situation happened in a Canadian case. In *Duncan v. Ladysmith School Trustees* [1930] 3 W.W.R. 175 a student was injured as a result of an explosion created by other students playing with chemicals which had not been safely locked away at lunchtime. The judgment indicates that the teacher would be negligent in these circumstances but unfortunately the issue was never decided since the plaintiff had commenced the action beyond the time limited by statute. The case was dismissed because the province had passed legislation stating that actions against school boards for negligence must be started within a certain period. If the action is commenced too late, then the right of action is lost. This limit is 6 months in many jurisdictions. However, because students are minors and cannot commence actions on their own, this limitation period has been held to commence on the attainment of the age of majority as opposed to the date of the accident.

The case of *O'Brien v. Procureur General de Quebec* [1961] S.C.R. 184 involved another explosion. In this case a high school pupil deliberately caused an explosion that injured another pupil. The teacher was absent from the room at the time. The Supreme Court of Canada held, however, that this was an unforeseen possibility for which the teacher could not be held responsible. The age of the students involved was a compelling factor in reaching such a decision.

In *James v. River East School Division No. 9* (1976) 64 D.L.R. (3d) 338 there was another type of explosion causing eye damage and facial scarring to an 18-year-old student. In this case the plaintiff and another pupil were carrying out an experiment in accordance with instructions found in a lab manual and verbal and written instructions from their teacher. While heating a mixture it bubbled up and exploded in the face of the plaintiff. She was not wearing protective goggles.

The trial judge found negligence on the part of the instructor for failure to order the plaintiff to wear goggles and also held:

> I find here a failure to instruct properly, a failure to caution and to supervise properly and that an unfortunate and foreseeable accident occurred, and that it could have been avoided if the defendants had not been negligent and if Mr. Peniuk (the teacher) had not omitted to do what he should have done in the circumstances.

The defendants appealed but the Manitoba Court of Appeal upheld the trial judge. The school board argued that the experiment was conducted in accordance with standard practice and that the duty of care owed was similar to that in medical malpractice suits, namely: to follow standard practice. The Court of Appeal held:

No one would deny that students, in order to learn, must perform experiments by themselves. But this does eliminate the need for careful supervision, where dangerous acids are in use. This is especially so where there has been inadequate prior instruction.

In the case at bar, there was a failure to instruct properly; the students were not advised of the possible danger to the person from spattering, the apparent contradictions in ex. 4, in giving instruction as to heating, were not cleared up, the hazard in underheating the mixture of tin and acid was not brought to the attention of the class, and students were not cautioned adequately about the danger in working with heated concentrated acid. All of these factors constituted negligence within the classic meaning of that term.

Quoting from a legal textbook, *Canadian Negligence Law* by Linden, the court pointed out:

All the same, even a common practice may itself be condemned as negligent if pregnant with obvious risks. "Neglect of duty does not cease by repetition to be neglect of duty," for in the last analysis the standard of reasonable care is measured by what ought ordinarily to be done rather than what is ordinarily done.

Applying this statement the court went on to say:

The question here is not whether other schools carry out this experiment in the same way. There is expert evidence . . . which shows the methodology used in this experiment was inadequate for a high school class. It was a reasonable inference by the learned trial Judge from this evidence, which he accepted, that those inadequacies constituted negligence, notwithstanding a continued use of the method without previous accidents.

As in the industrial arts shop, safety in the science lab must be stressed at all times. Science teachers must ensure that each student receives proper instruction on the procedure to be followed and is made aware of all possible dangers that may be encountered. Students should specifically be instructed in the handling of dangerous and corrosive materials. The teacher must be thoroughly knowledgeable about the subject and acquaint himself with the potential hazards to be encountered in the lab. To ensure familiarity with potential hazards it is suggested that the teacher perform each experiment himself following the instructions given. Finally, the teacher must ensure that any available safety equipment (such as eye protection) is worn at all times. If the accident cannot be prevented, then the seriousness of the injury can be reduced.

Science teachers must realize that the environment of the laboratory contains more potential for accidents than an ordinary classroom.

Dangerous materials must be locked safely away and only used under proper supervision with adequate safety precautions.

Home Economics

Although a stove has never severed a leg nor has a mixture of cookie batter ever exploded, there are some dangers lurking in the home economics room as well. The reported cases generally involve unfortunate fires caused by gas stoves. Natural gas can be a very dangerous substance and teachers should ensure that it is handled properly.

It has been held that a building owner should be able to rely on the gas company to make a safe installation and no duty rests on the school to inspect such installations to ensure that they are safe (*School Division of Assiniboine South No.3 v. Hoffer et al.* 1972 (1972) 21 D.L.R. 608). This is fine if your only concern is legal liability. If you are concerned for the safety of your students it would be prudent to carry out periodic safety inspections of the premises to ensure that the gas installations are indeed safely installed and operating properly.

A British case points out the potential danger of a faulty stove. In *Fryer v. Salford Corporation* [1937] 1 All E.R. 617, an 11-year-old girl was receiving instruction in cooking when her apron caught fire from a gas-cooker. There was no guard around the cooking apparatus. The court held that this danger was one which ought reasonably to have been anticipated and one which the school authorities should have taken precautions to prevent by provision of a guard around the stove.

The fact that such an accident had never happened before did not sway the judge from finding fault. He stated:

> In the present case, I do not think that it can be said that what here happened was that which no reasonable person could anticipate, merely because such an accident had not happened before, or because there was no reason to suppose that it would happen. In my view, the very nature of the case is such as to render reasonably apparent the possibility of danger emerging.

A similar situation confronted Canadian courts in *McGonegal v. Gray* [1952] S.C.R. 274. There a 12-year-old boy was instructed to light a gas stove so that the teacher could make some soup. While attempting to do so the boy was severely burned. It was held that the injury was as a result of the negligence of the school board in not seeing that the gasoline stove was kept in proper working order.

Therefore, home economics teachers should ensure that their equipment is kept in proper working order and that students are supervised when using equipment which may cause harm.

Field Trips

The duty of supervision does not end at the school door if the students are being taken outside the school for educational purposes. Teachers often believe that they are protected from liability on field trips because they have "permission slips" or "releases" signed by the parent. As we shall see there is a need to be as vigilant on field trips as in the classroom.

In *Beauparlant et al. v. The Appleby Separate School Trustees et al.* [1955] O.W.N. 286 the teachers of two grades decided to give their pupils a half-holiday for the purpose of attending a concert in a neighbouring town. They arranged for the students to be transported in the back of a privately owned truck. During the journey, one side of the truck gave way and a number of pupils, including the plaintiff, were thrown out.

The trial judge stated:

I have no hesitation whatever in holding that there was negligence on the part of the teachers responsible for seeing that the children were on the truck. It was heavily overloaded, no examination was made of the sides of the truck to see if they were reasonably strong for the purpose, and during the course of the journey there was some singing and swaying by the pupils, and Gilles Lefebre, the teacher who went along on the truck, presumably to supervise it, was apprehensive.

Despite this clear statement as to the negligence of the teachers involved, the school board managed to escape liability for the injuries sustained by the student. The judgment continued:

There is no doubt that a school board is liable in law for an accident due to a teacher's negligence if it is in a matter which may reasonably be regarded as falling within the scope of his employment.

The chairman of the school board and the secretary-treasurer, both of whom gave evidence, say that no request of any kind was made to the school board by any of the teachers, nor was any permission given.

After much careful thought and anxious consideration of this matter, I have come to the conclusion that the teachers, in organizing this trip and in allowing the children their freedom from their regular studies, were exceeding their authority and were not acting within the scope of their authority, express or implied.

It does not seem to me that this expedition can even be brought within the broad and comprehensive general subject of "social studies."

It is imperative, therefore, that teachers organizing field trips obtain permission from the board to do so and that the trips have a solid educational objective. If this is not done, the board may well escape liability and any damages awarded will come directly from the teacher's pocket.

A tragic drowning accident occurred on a field trip in the case of *Moodejonge et al. v. Huron County Board of Education et al.* (1972) 25 D.L.R. (3d) 661. The board had sponsored a field trip to a reservoir under the supervision of a teacher. Some of the students persuaded the teacher to take them swimming in a conservation area. The teacher could not swim nor were any life-saving devices available The teacher was familiar with the area and instructed the students as to the limits of the shallow water. A breeze developed, creating a surface current, which carried a 14-year-old girl (who could not swim) and another child into the deeper water. Another 14-year-old girl swam to their assistance and was able to save the other child before she and the non-swimmer both drowned.

The judge applied the careful parent test and found the teacher negligent for allowing a girl who could not swim to play in such a dangerous area. This negligence was compounded by the fact that there was no means of rescue should an accident occur and the fact that he had moved away from the children when they were close to the danger area.

The judge also held the teacher responsible for the death of the girl who drowned while attempting the rescue. He reasoned that when a person by his negligence exposes another to danger it is a foreseeable consequence that a third person will attempt to rescue the one in danger, and the attempted rescue is part of the chain of causation started by the negligent act. Because the trip was sponsored by the board and the teacher was acting in the scope of his employment, the board was also held liable.

Most schools require parents to sign "permission slips" before allowing children to participate in such activities. Often these slips purport to release the board from any claims as a result of injuries sustained on the trip. These forms are of no legal effect and will not protect the board or the teacher from liability where there is negligence on their part. The forms may have some psychological effect in discouraging the parents from initiating action in the event of any injury but will not pose a bar to recovery in the event that action is taken.

The reason for this is quite simple. The law will not allow someone to sign away another's right of action even if that person is the parent. Contracts made on behalf of a minor will be enforced only if they are for his benefit. The law will protect a minor from anything purported to be done on his behalf that is not in his best interests. In other cases involving similar waivers the courts have stated:

> Holding as I do that the defendant's negligence caused the accident, it follows that the infant can recover irrespective of the agreement signed by his parents. (*DeKoning et al. v. Boychuk* (1951) 2 W.W.R. (N.S.) 251)

> If the document is allowed to stand then it could be argued that the infant's cause of action has been effectively destroyed. In most cases, the parent is the next friend. There is always the possibility that, facing the threat of indemnification, the parent will not initiate the action, thereby precluding the infant from securing recovery for his injuries. Settlements of this type are, in my opinion, so contrary to the procedures set up in our courts for the protection of infants that the documents should be held to be unenforceable. (*Stevens v. Howlitt* (1969) 4 D.L.R. (3d) 50)

Teachers should be ever vigilant when taking students on field trips. The very fact that such trips are not in the confines of the classroom make the possibility of injury even higher. Most claims against teachers and school boards result from extra-curricular activities as we shall see.

Playground Supervision

Teachers routinely provide supervision of playgrounds during recess, lunchtime, and before school hours. This may be a matter of contract with the board or as a result of legislation. The issue has even come before the Supreme Court of Canada in the case *Winnipeg Teachers' Association No. 1 v. Winnipeg School Division No. 1* [1976] 1 W.W.R. 403. In that case it was held that "school teachers are under a duty arising from an implied contractual obligation to provide noon-hour supervision."

For many students, recess and lunch are regarded as the best parts of the day. For teachers they are welcome breaks, unless they are on supervision. The risk of injury to a student appears to be extremely high during recess and lunch periods, judging from the number of cases reported. The reasons are obvious. Students are free to run around and hurt themselves in a variety of interesting ways. Certain pieces of playground equipment have a dangerous element to them. Teachers who have only 30 students to watch out for in class may now have to try to watch 300 students or more. Many of the cases involving playground accidents revolve directly on the question of whether there was adequate supervision in all of the circumstances of the case.

In *Scoffield et al. v. Public School Board of Section No. 20, North York* [1942] O.W.N. 458 a student was injured at 8:45 in the morning when she fell from a makeshift toboggan on school property. The Regulations provided that:

> For the purpose of preventing accidents and improper conduct when the pupils are not in the classrooms, the accommodations should be under suitable supervision.

The Regulations also provided that teachers must be in their classrooms 15 minutes before the start of classes, which in this case started at 9:00 a.m. The opinion of the court stated:

> It has been held that it cannot be said that there is an absolute duty never to leave children without supervision.
>
> In the case at bar, would supervision have prevented the accident? The teachers were in their classrooms at that hour as they were required to be by the rules and regulations. I cannot see any breach here.
>
> I therefore conclude that in the circumstances the defendant board is not liable. I think it fully discharged all the duties imposed upon it under the Act. It appointed teachers whom it believed to be competent and capable, whose duty it was to see that the rules and regulations were properly and efficiently carried out . . . I have also found that, so far as supervision is concerned, there was supervision, and further that no amount of supervision would have prevented this accident. The duty of the teachers, as provided by the rules and regulations, was to be in their classrooms by 8:45.

Thus the judge held that no supervision on the playground is required if the teachers are supervising in a place where they are supposed to be, albeit that the children are somewhere else.

In *Koch v. Stone Farm School District* [1940] 2 D.L.R. 602, a 12-year-old boy was injured while jumping from the roof of woodshed just after the teacher had rung the bell to open school for the day. The court found no negligence since the teacher was properly attending to her duties of opening the school and looking after younger children.

These cases make sense in the context of their time and the fact that a teacher cannot be in two places at the same time. However, in our present society, with both parents often working, children are being left at the schoolgrounds well before the start of classes. Some schools provide organized activities before school and teachers involved in such programs must conform to the same standard of care as at all other times. Schools should ensure that the children are safe at all times, not just during regular school hours.

The duty to supervise playgrounds is somewhat more clear during recess. Schools must ensure that there is an adequate system of supervision in place for recess and teachers must undertake this duty as a "careful parent."

In *Ellis v. Board of Trustees for Moose Jaw Public School District* [1946] 2 D.L.R. 697 a student was injured during recess while playing with a pulley that had been attached to the school by a contractor doing repair work. The court decided the issue on the duty of supervision rather than on occupier's liability.

The court held that the principal was under a duty of supervision with respect to the students and this involved a higher standard of care than that required under principles of law relating to occupier's liability. It was stated:

> In this case it seems to me that in view of the duty of supervision which the law imposes upon school authorities more specific care is demanded of them than that which is ordinarily required from premises in respect of invitees thereon.

Since the principal had only given oral warnings to stay away from the construction and did not send anyone to supervise the area to ensure that the warnings were heeded, he was held liable. The judge described the supervision as being "wholly inadequate" to save children from the possible dangers.

Many of the recess injury cases involve the unregulated activities of other pupils. The courts have attempted to define what degree of supervision is necessary to prevent such accidents.

In *Adams v. Board of School Commissioners for the City of Halifax* [1951] 2 D.L.R. 816 the plaintiff student lost an eye as a result of a stone-throwing fight which broke out during recess. Only one teacher was on supervision duty and she was involved elsewhere breaking up another fight. There had been previous stone-throwing incidents but none this serious. A jury awarded damages and the case was appealed on the issue that the jury had been improperly instructed by the judge on the standard of care to be applied. The verdict was overturned and a new trial was ordered. The majority of the court stated that the "careful parent" test was to be applied but did not indicate if they felt there was adequate supervision in this case.

In a similar case from the same jurisdiction, *Dyer v. Board of School Commissioners for the City of Halifax* (1956) 2 D.L.R. (2d) 394, a pupil was injured by students throwing acorns at noon-hour recess. There were four teachers on duty to supervise five hundred students and this was held to be adequate supervision. The court felt that such an accident could not have been avoided regardless of the amount of supervision that had been provided.

The Supreme Court of Canada had the opportunity to consider the question of an adequate system of supervision during recess in the case of

The Board of Education for the City of Toronto v. Higgs [1960] S.C.R. 174. Here a student was injured by being dropped onto some ice by another pupil. None of the four teachers on duty saw the incident. At trial a jury found a failure to supervise; they felt that this was an insufficient number of teachers in view of the numbers of children, their ages and the size of the schoolyard. The Ontario Court of Appeal affirmed this judgment and the board appealed to the Supreme Court.

This court could find no negligence on the part of any individual teacher and so looked at the supervisory system in place to see if it was adequate. The headnote summarizes the decision:

> The finding of the jury raised the question of the adequacy of the system for supervising the break period used by the school principal, who alone had the authority to control the matter. That system had been employed satisfactorily by the principal for several years, and, in the absence of proof to the contrary, he had no reason to believe that it did not constitute a reasonable safe system having regard to the number and ages of the children, and there were not any unusual circumstances that day which made it reasonably foreseeable that a greater number of teachers would be required. The winter conditions specified by the jury did not constitute such an unusual circumstance. Even if the "failure" as found by the jury had constituted a breach of duty, it had not been shown to be probable that any of the ingredients of that "failure" caused or contributed to the injury. The particulars of the failure found by the jury were such as to negative the other grounds of negligence suggested. Even on the view that the jury's answers included a finding of "inadequate supervision," it is not the duty of school authorities to keep pupils under supervision every moment while they are in attendance at school.

The English case of *Beaumont v. Surrey County Council* (1968) L.G.R. 580 seemed to raise the standard of care required in playground supervision. In this case, a 15-year-old boy was struck in the eye with a piece of elastic during a morning break. The elastic had been taken from a waste bin by another student and as a result of some horseplay was flicked in the plaintiff's eye. The judge held:

> The duty of a headmaster towards his pupils is said to be to take such care of them as a reasonably careful and prudent father would take of his own children. That standard is a helpful one when considering, for example, individual instructions to individual children in a school. It would be very unwise to allow a six-year old child to carry a kettle of boiling water – that type of instruction. But that standard when applied to an incident of horseplay in a school of 900 pupils is somewhat unrealistic, if not unhelpful.

> In the context of the present action it appears to me to be easier and preferable to use the ordinary language of the law of negligence. That is, it is a

headmaster's duty, bearing in mind the known propensities of boys and indeed girls between the ages of eleven and seventeen or eighteen, to take all reasonable and proper steps to prevent any of the pupils under his care from suffering injury from inanimate objects, from the actions of their fellow students, or from a combination of the two. That is a high standard.

Applying this standard, the judge held that the elastic should not have been placed in a waste bin near the playground. It was as much a menace there as if it had been left on the playground itself. In addition, the judge found that the system of supervision was not working properly on that day, since the teacher responsible was not on the playground where he should have been. The judge felt that if he were present, the horseplay would not have happened or would have been stopped before an injury occurred. The judge stated:

> It is, as I say, a high standard of care, and in ordinary circumstances had it been an ordinary day at the school (the teacher) having been able to get out on the playground, would have seen these things and the accident would never have happened.

Physical Education

Physical education classes and extra-curricular sporting events have produced the majority of school negligence cases. Many of the activities are inherently dangerous and require careful supervision. It is often not possible to supervise 30 or more students at the same time in a large area such as a gymnasium or playing field. As a result, there are often injuries, many of them severe. One of the largest damage awards ever made in Canada involved a gymnastics accident. Physical educators must take all possible precautions to avoid future accidents of the nature that we shall encounter in this chapter.

"Piggy-Back"

Students have been injured while playing games that seem as harmless as piggy-back. The courts have regarded this activity as one that is not inherently dangerous and one that a careful parent would allow his children to participate in with a minimum of supervision.

In *Jones et al. v. London County Council* (1932) 48 T.L.R. 577 a 17-year-old boy was injured while playing a game of "Riders and Horses." The instructor was described as having "great experience." The English Court of Appeal found that there was no evidence that the game was particularly dangerous. The judgment stated:

> Even if it were assumed that the game was one in which one or more of the competitors was likely to fall, that would not be sufficient to establish a case of negligence; otherwise it might be said that no instruction in physical exercises or games could ever be given in a school without the authorities' being liable if a boy fell and happened to hurt himself.

A similar situation occurred in Canada in *Eaton et al. v. Lasuta et al.* (1977) 2 C.C.L.T. 38. The plaintiff in this case was a 12-year-old girl, described by the judge as "a tall girl, uncoordinated, gangling, awkward and not athletically inclined." The court held that these physical characteristics did not classify her as "handicapped," an allegation made by the plaintiff in an attempt to increase the standard of care required. The court applied the careful parent test, which it said must be modified to take into account the large size of the class and the "supraparental expertise" required for a physical education instructor.

The Jones precedent was applied and it was held that a piggy-back race was not an unsuitable activity for the plaintiff. It was not a dangerous activity or one likely to cause injury. The judge remarked that a "careful and reasonable parent would not hesitate to allow his 12-year-old daughter to engage in a piggy-back race on a grass-hockey field on a sunny afternoon in May."

These cases indicate that teachers must exercise reasonable supervision and guard against reasonably foreseeable risks, taking into account the students' ages and need to develop self-reliance. The mere occurrence of an injury will not result in liability nor will the remote possibility of an accident make the injury foreseeable.

Wrestling

The standard of care required for supervision of wrestling matches depends on how competitive the matches are. In *Hall et al. v. Thompson et al.* [1952] O.W.N. 133, a 9-year-old boy was injured while engaged in an organized wrestling match on the playground. He was a boy of average size and strength. No instruction had been given regarding holds or technique. The purpose of the match was to gain a fall in one minute. The plaintiff was thrown and fractured his elbow. The judge applied the careful parent test and considered whether wrestling was a dangerous activity which a reasonable parent would prohibit. He stated:

No evidence of any kind was submitted to support the claim that wrestling is inherently dangerous and no authorities were submitted to me, nor can I find any, to support the proposition. It may, of course, be true that in all games or contests of skill involving the testing and development of physical strength accidents will happen, but it does not follow, in my opinion, that they should therefore be classed as inherently dangerous.

Piszel v. Board of Education for Etobicoke et al. (1977) 77 D.L.R. (3d) 52 involved a 16-year-old who fractured his elbow during a "take-down" from a standing position which had previously been demonstrated by the instructor. There were mats on the floor but they had become separated immediately before the fall. Students who were not participating were required to sit on the floor and hold the mats in place by pressing their feet to the edges of the outside mat.

The trial judge found that this "perimeter system" for keeping mats in place was a dangerous one when the wrestling reached a competitive stage. He found that the board had not discharged its duty since it did not adopt the best safety precautions reasonably possible. The Ontario Court of Appeal upheld this decision and said:

> In our view, having found that the system used was unsafe and unsatisfactory, it was not necessary to attempt to define the minimum safety requirements in high school wrestling or in that particular school, whether in teaching or competitive situations. We are all satisfied that the trial Judge did not intend to make it a minimum requirement that Boards of Education provide a separate wrestling room with a permanent mat covering the entire floor space. The expert's evidence accepted by the trial Judge leaves other alternatives which are equally safe and less costly . . . It was sufficient to find that, in the circumstances, the "perimeter system" of guarding against a known risk with foreseeable consequences did not meet the standard of care imposed on school authorities for the protection of students taking part in physical education courses.

Thus, where an activity has reached a competitive stage (as opposed to being done for exercise or "fun") greater safety precautions are required since the risk of injury becomes greater and is consequently more foreseeable.

Gymnastics

Gymnastic exercises appear to be the most dangerous activity in the physical education curriculum, if the number of reported cases is any indication. The injuries sustained are also of a more severe nature, which may account for the number of cases being litigated. The cases presented here will demonstrate some of the areas of potential danger in gymnastic classes and, hopefully, provide useful suggestions to avoid such accidents.

In *Murray et al. v. The Board of Education of the City of Belleville* [1943] 1 D.L.R. 494, a teenage boy broke his wrist when a "human pyramid" which the class was making collapsed. The judge in this case outlined the factors which led him to conclude there was no negligence:

1. That the defendant's instructor properly and adequately instructed the infant plaintiff as to his proper conduct both in forming and in breaking the "pyramid."
2. That the instructor had also taken all care, in the conduct and supervision of this demonstration of skill, necessary to ensure the safety of the participants.
3. That the physical exercise, of which this had been a feature, were prescribed by the curriculum, but that this did not have the effect of compelling students who were not mentally or physically fit to take part in such exercises.
4. That the infant plaintiff was not in any way, directly or indirectly, coerced or forced into taking part in the exercise, but did so of his own free will.
5. That the exercise was not of an unreasonable nature.
6. That it was one suitable to the age, mental alertness and physical condition of the infant plaintiff.
7. That the infant plaintiff was mentally alert and physically fit to take part in the exercise.

The judge felt that the element of danger in all sports could be reduced to a minimum where the students had been progressively trained and coached as these ones had. The judge did not consider any previous school negligence cases since he felt that this case was unique in that it did not involve issues of supervision or occupier's liability. He addressed the issues from the standpoint of whether there was competent instruction.

There have been a number of cases dealing with injuries incurred while vaulting over a boxhorse. In *Gibbs v. Barking Corporation* [1936] 1 All E.R. 115, a boy was injured when he landed "in a stumble" after vaulting over a horse. The instructor did nothing to assist him in completing the vault. It was held that it is the duty of an instructor to "spot" students and see that they do not fall. In the circumstances, the instructor had not taken reasonable care which could have prevented the accident and was, therefore, liable.

The first Canadian case involving this type of accident was *Butterworth et al. v. Collegiate Institute Board of Ottawa* [1940] 3 D.L.R. 466. There a 14-year-old boy injured his elbow in the course of vaulting. He had received one previous lesson in vaulting and, on the day in question, the instructor was absent having delegated senior boys to supervise the activity. The boy knew there was a danger in vaulting and that he was clumsy at it.

In this situation the boy did not recover damages. The judge found that any alleged lack of supervision was not the effective cause of the accident and stated:

> I am of the opinion that boys of 14 years of age are capable of and indeed should be held to exercise reasonable intelligence and care for their own safety. With great respect, I am further of the opinion that paternalism in respect of boys of teen age in collegiate institutes should not be extended to a degree which would virtually deprive them of that exercise of intelligence demanded of young people of that age in other walks of life.

This trend towards a less stringent requirement for a teacher's presence during vaulting exercises was carried forward in *Wright v. Cheshire County Council* [1952] 2 All E.R. 789. In this case a group of boys were vaulting with each "spotting" the vaulter behind him. As the 12-year-old plaintiff was taking his turn, the bell rang and his spotter ran off. The instructor was supervising another activity at the time. Evidence was given that student spotting was a common practice.

The English Court of Appeal held that the test of what was reasonable care might be answered by experience arising from years of generally successful practice. Having regard to the nature of the activity this was not a negligent practice and there was no liability. The duty of a careful parent, in the words of the court:

> does not involve that the adopted system would have to be such that in no foreseeable circumstance or situation could there be any possible or conceivable contingency of some slight mishap. If that were so, the activities of the young would be unduly circumscribed and only inactivity and inanition could be planned.

Thus, even where the activity is somewhat dangerous, the teacher need not be present to supervise as long as some form of spotting is in place which may involve the students themselves. When the activity becomes more dangerous, the presence of the instructor is most certainly required. This was made clear in the case of *Thornton, Tanner et al. v. Board of School Trustees of School District No. 57 (Prince George) et al.* [1976] 5 W.W.R. 240.

This case involved a 15-year-old boy who was rendered a quadraplegic as a result of a gym accident. The plaintiff and others were performing somersaults while jumping from a boxhorse onto a springboard and landing in a bundle of foam chunks. The boys were not experienced gymnasts nor were they given any warnings or instruction in the exercise. The instructor was sitting at a desk marking report cards at the time of the accident. One boy had injured his wrist just prior to the plaintiff's mishap and additional mats were placed about the perimeter but no warnings were given. The plaintiff landed on his head on one of these mats sustaining a severe spinal injury.

At trial the plaintiff was awarded over $1,500,000. The trial judge found that the apparatus was inherently dangerous. This made close supervision necessary and the lack thereof constituted negligence. Although the individual pieces of equipment may not have been dangerous, the way in which they were used made them so. The judge stated:

> If it is used in the unusual fashion previously described it seems to me that the risk inherent in such use is greater. Accordingly, in my opinion, the "configuration" should have been recognized by any reasonable physical education instructor as one fraught with danger.

The judge discussed the instructor's specific duty, considering his qualifications, as well as his duty as a careful parent. He quoted from *Halsbury,* a legal encyclopedia, regarding the former duty:

> The practice of a profession, art, or calling which, from its nature, demands some special skill, ability or experience, carries with it a duty to exercise, to a reasonable extent, the amount of skill, ability, and experience which it demands.

> What then is the standard of care required of him? He knew these boys were doing, or attempting to do, somersaults. That was the purpose for which the configuration was used. There was conflicting evidence concerning this particular manoeuvre. All the witnesses agreed, however, that some degree of "progression" is required before this stunt is tried . . .

> The whole of the evidence leads me to find that these boys, possessing such limited expertise in gymnastics, had undoubtably not progressed to the point where they could be trusted to somersault from this unpredictable, dangerous configuration . . .

> He should have given them some advice, some instruction, a word of caution, and at least imposed some limits on what they could or could not do in the circumstances. His attention to them was, in my opinion, casual.

The judge then went on to discuss the standard to be applied under the careful parent test. He found:

Quite apart from the breach of duty as an experienced physical education instructor as I discussed it earlier, there is at least a duty on him to act as the "careful parent of a large family" – a concept adopted almost universally since *Williams v. Eady* . . . Once one youngster had become hurt would not a prudent father want to know how and why his child had become hurt in order to avoid the same kind of risk to another child? I think he would have. I think any reasonable interpretation of that evidence must surely include the fact that Edamura "qua teacher or surrogate parent" should have foreseen further trouble. That is the least amount of care at that time in those circumstances that Edamura should have taken.

The judge found that the teacher had breached both his duty as a qualified physical education instructor and his "lesser duty of a careful parent." Regarding a claim of contributory negligence it was held:

> Should he be taken to possess the same familiarity and knowledge of the equipment as his instructor? The answer is clearly No. He had neither the experience or the qualifications. In view of his lack of familiarity and knowledge he ought not to be taken to know that what he was attempting to perform involved any threat or harm. It necessarily follows that there was no need for him to go to Edamura for guidance or assistance. In the circumstances I find the defendants have failed to establish contributory negligence.

The defendants appealed this decision to the British Columbia Court of Appeal which reduced the damage award to $650,000 but sustained the findings of negligence. Justice Carrothers had this to say about the standard of care to be applied:

> Inherently and readily foreseeable there is an element of risk or danger in gymnastics, and in performing aerial front somersaults off a springboard in particular, of which risk the evidence discloses both the school authorities and Thornton were aware. This was an exercise scheduled in the syllabus for Grade X boys and Thornton participated in the gymnastics group and in this particular exercise of his own free will. This is not to say that Thornton exclusively assumed the risk of the exercise to the absolution of the school authorities or that the school authorities were relieved of their common law duty to take care of this pupil during this activity in the manner of a reasonable and careful parent, taking into account the judicial modification of the reasonable-and-careful-parent test to allow for the larger-than-family size of the physical education class and the supraparental expertise commanded of a gymnastics instructor. Nor does it mean that the school authorities would be strictly or absolutely liable for any consequential injury however occurring to any pupil in respect of whom the school authorities had accepted the responsibility of care and control, and hence ought to have prohibited the performance of this exercise. In my view of the factually relevant cases, what it does mean is that it is not

negligence or breach of the duty of care on the part of the school authorities to permit a pupil to undertake to perform an aerial somersault off a springboard: (a) if it is suitable to his age and condition (mental and physical); (b) if he is progressively trained and coached to do it properly and avoid the danger; (c) if the equipment is adequate and suitably arranged; and (d) if the performance, having regard to its inherently dangerous nature, is properly supervised. These are the component criteria constituting the appropriate duty or standard of care which is saddled upon the school authorities in a case of this kind and upon which we are to judge whether there has been observance sufficient for the school authorities to avoid a finding of negligence and its consequential liability ...

Considering each of the criteria, the court held that: (a) the exercise was suitable for the plaintiff's age and condition; (b) there was some progressive training such that he could attempt this exercise with proper instruction and supervision; (c) the "configuration" used was dangerous; and (d) there was a lack of proper supervision. With respect to this last point the court stated:

> But apart from consenting to what the boys were about, on the day in question, the instructor was busy doing paper work at a nearby desk and gave no instructions or cautions, no training, no demonstration and no immediate supervision. The emphasis on individual responsibility and initiative seems to have displaced instruction and supervision.

> Some witnesses indicated that the instructor or someone arranged by him ought to have "spotted" the exercise, despite the difficulties presented by a deep landing pit, to ensure rotation as each performer jumped. The trial Judge stated that the evidence which he accepted convinced him that any gymnastic exercise such as this should not be attempted by amateurs without the assistance of what are called spotters, but in Thornton's case, as he overflew the landing pit altogether, the trial Judge did not find the lack of a spotter causative of Thornton's injury.

The defendants appealed the issue of damages to the Supreme Court of Canada. The final award of damages in the case was $860,000. This is one of the largest damage awards ever granted in Canada and indicates how expensive the lack of proper supervision can be.

The Supreme Court of Canada has recently had the opportunity to pronounce judgment on the standard of care required in gymnastic exercises in the case of *Myers et al. v. Peel County Board of Education et al.* (1981) 123 D.L.R. (3d) 1.

In this case a 15-year-old boy was injured in attempting to dismount from the rings in a gym class. The accident occurred in an exercise room which could not be seen by the instructor who was in the gymnasium at the time. The plaintiff had permission to use the room and had taken a friend to act as spotter. The friend had moved away from the rings thinking that Myers had completed his exercise. Myers, however, attempted a straddle dismount, fell onto the crash mats and broke his neck. He, too, was rendered a quadriplegic. Myers was successful at trial but that decision was overturned by the Ontario Court of Appeal. The Supreme Court of Canada restored the trial judge's decision.

The highest court recognized that the four tests used in the Thornton case were appropriate and stated that the standard of care required is that of the "careful or prudent parent" and will vary according to circumstances:

> It is not, however, a standard which can be applied in the same manner and to the same extent in every case. Its application will vary from case to case and will depend on the number of students being supervised at any given time, the nature of the exercise or activity in progress, the age and degree of skill and training which the students may have received in connection with such activity, the nature and condition of the equipment in use at the time, the competency and capacity of the students involved, and a host of other matters which may be widely varied but which, in a given case, may affect the application of the prudent parent standard to the conduct of the school authority in the circumstances.

By applying this standard, the court concluded that there was negligence, particulars of which were cited in the headnote to the case as follows:

> This standard of care was not met. Training in gymnastics and, particularly, gymnastic exercises on rings carries with it a potential for danger. The danger, as far as the rings are concerned, is that the student may fall to the floor and, because of the nature of the exercise he is performing and the position of his body during such performance, may fall in such a manner that the possibility of serious injury will be increased. Injury was foreseeable and was foreseen. All the witnesses gave evidence of the necessity for steps and precautions to be taken to guard against injury and it was accepted that students would from time to time fall from the rings. Against this background, a prudent parent would not be content to provide as protective matting only the two and one-half inch compressed slab mats when other and more protective mats could be obtained. Nor, considering the nature of the activity which was contemplated in the gymnastics course, would a prudent parent have been content to have his son permitted to depart from the gymnasium into a room where there would be no adult supervision to practice gymnastic manoeuvres on the rings which could involve the straddle dismount with its potential dangers. It cannot be said that the trial Judge was wrong in finding that the absence of adequate mats contributed to the injury. The appellant fell with some force from a height in the neighbourhood of eight feet. All gymnastic experts called recognized that mats were a necessary protective feature. The expert evidence indicated that when the danger of falling was greatest, i.e., in the early

stages of training, crash mats rather than slab mats should be used. It is not incumbent upon the plaintiff to prove positively that the presence of the crash mats would have prevented the injury. The plaintiff is bound to prove, according to a balance of probabilities, that the failure of the school authorities to provide the adequate matting and insist upon its use contributed to the accident. As to the absence of supervision, again it is not incumbent upon the plaintiff to prove that the presence of a teacher would have prevented the accident. It was the opinion of the trial Judge that, on the balance of probabilities, which the evidence supported, the absence of supervision contributed to the cause of the accident.

The Supreme Court of Canada had previously applied the careful parent test in another gymnastics case involving a fall from parallel bars but had expressed doubt as to whether it would be applicable in all cases. In *McKay et al. v. The Board of the Govan School Unit No. 29 of Saskatchewan et al.* [1968] S.C.R. 589, Mr Justice Ritchie said:

> While I am not satisfied that this definition is of universal application, particularly in cases where a schoolmaster is required to instruct or supervise the activities of a great number of pupils at one time, I am nevertheless of the opinion that a small group, such as that which Molesky had in his charge in the improvised gymnasium, is one to which Lord Esher's words do apply.
>
> I take the view that a reasonably careful parent would have been unlikely to permit his boy, almost totally inexperienced in gymnastics, to execute the manoeuvre which young McKay performed without exercising a great deal more care for his safety or ensuring that someone else did on his behalf.

In that case, the teacher's supervisory duties required him to guard against foreseeable risks to which the inexperienced plaintiff was exposed. It was held that falling from the bars was a real risk and there was a concomitant duty to guard against that risk eventuating. The teacher in this case was held not to be "a qualified instructor in gymnastic work on the parallel bars." However, in view of the application of the careful parent test, this is irrelevant. If a higher standard, that of the reasonably competent instructor, had been adopted, then the teacher's qualifications would be an issue.

Extra-curricular Activities

The same duty and standard of care will be applied to extra-curricular sporting activities which are sponsored by the school. One of the earliest cases to establish this principle was *Walton v. Vancouver Board of School Trustees* [1924] 2 D.L.R. 387. In that case the school had arranged for a rifle competition as part of its Empire Day celebration. The 12-year-old plaintiff lost an eye when the rifle he was using exploded. The principal, who had taken charge of the competition, was not present at the time nor had he inspected the rifles being used. In the words of the court, "He practically left the young boys to their own devices."

The matter was tried by a jury, which dismissed the claim against the principal, yet found the board guilty of negligence. On appeal the jury's decision was sustained. In upholding this finding it was stated:

> The negligence of the trustees as found by the jury was of another kind than that attributed in the statement of claim to Thomas (the principal). It was negligent in not providing safeguards ... It cannot, I think, be doubted that school boards have a duty to see that school premises are not used in a manner dangerous to the children under their jurisdiction. The jury have found that the competition in question was a dangerous one if not properly supervised, therefore, when the trustees authorized the holding of the school sports including this competition, it was clearly enough their duty to take the precautions suggested by the jury ... the duty to supervise it properly must be held to rest upon them and a breach of that duty will subject them to damages.

Another judge reviewed all of the authorities before reaching a similar conclusion. He noted:

> There was, as the evidence well shows, no proper system of control that would ensure reasonable safety to the boys at the rifle practice and competition carried on in the shooting gallery and it may well be that the jury not only believed that there was no proper system but that the principal was incompetent.

> In the present case a dangerous rifle was put into the hands of this young boy. The defective nature was not "familiar nor obvious." Further the boy was too young in any case to comprehend possible danger. There is nothing to the point strenuously argued that the jury having absolved Thomas from liability, that it must mean the board is absolved. That in no way follows – the jury were at perfect liberty to do this.

In *Gard v. Board of School Trustees of Duncan* [1946] 2 D.L.R. 441 the plaintiff was injured in an after-school grass hockey game. There was no teacher present and the injury occurred as the result of being struck in the eye by another pupil's stick which constituted a breach of the rules of the game. The British Columbia Court of Appeal held:

> While, as I have said, danger may eventuate in any game, and in that sense injury to one of the players might be foreseen, yet that danger is one of the risks of the game, which every parent knows goes with the game, and I would think the chances of any risk eventuating in a game of grass hockey

played by children would be very slight. The possibility of danger emerging was only a mere possibility which would never occur to the mind of a reasonable man; and therefore there was no negligence.

Transportation of Pupils

Teachers, especially in rural areas, are often called upon to provide transportation for students, either to or from school or on field trips. The advent of compulsory automobile insurance has provided a compensation fund for persons injured in highway traffic accidents. Recovery for damages is not as easy for a passenger, injured through the negligence of his driver, as it is for injured passengers in another vehicle. The ability of a passenger to recover from his own driver is dependent upon the status of the passenger. A "gratuitous passenger," one who is not providing any compensation for the ride, can only sue his driver for "gross negligence." Students would normally fall into this category of passenger but for the statutory duty of the board to provide conveyance in certain circumstances and the duty of supervision. We shall see that students are owed a high duty of care indeed when they are being transported.

One of the earliest cases involving a transportation accident was *Shrimpton v.Hertfordshire County Council* (1911) 104 L.T. 145, a decision of the House of Lords from England. The conveyance used in this case was a horse-drawn tram. The plaintiff was injured in a fall when attempting to get off the vehicle. A jury found negligence on the part of the driver coupled with the fact that there was no conductor or adult person to accompany the children. The vehicle itself was not in very good condition. Because the plaintiff lived less than a mile from school, there was no statutory duty to provide conveyance to her. The school attendance officer did, however, authorize her to be on the vehicle. The House of Lords held as follows:

> I agree with the learned counsel for the respondents that here there was no duty or obligation whatever on the county council to provide for the carriage of this child, but if they did agree to do so, and did provide a vehicle, then it is clear to my mind that their duty was also to provide a reasonably safe mode of conveyance. This was not done according to the findings of the jury. They have found that it was not a reasonable and proper way for the county council to convey children to school in this vehicle without a conductor or some adult person to take care of them.

A similar situation arose in Canada in the case of *Tyler et al. v. Bd. Trustees Ardath School District* [1935] 2 D.L.R. 814. The brief reported judgment reads as follows:

The plaintiff herein was injured in an accident to the van used in carrying the children to and from school. The driver lost control of the horses when one of the reins got loose from the bit. The Court found negligence on the part of the driver and the School Board sought to avoid liability on the grounds that the only duty laid upon the Board by the relevant sections of the School Act, R.S.S. 1930, c. 131, was to pay the expenses of the conveyance of the pupils and that the driver was an "independent contractor." The Court held that the board controlled the route and were empowered to discontinue the use of the van at any time without notice to the contractor and that the contract could not be assigned by the driver without consent and the performance of the contract was subject to departmental rule. It was quite clear that the Board of Trustees had power to provide for the conveyance of the scholars and when they exercised that power, whether they had authority to do so or not, they were under a duty to see that the pupils would be carried with reasonable safety and hence they were responsible for any neglect by the person or persons employed by them to effect the purpose. Judgment was accordingly given against the board.

Thus, school boards and those engaged in the transportation of the students will be held responsible for even slight negligence. Teachers using their own vehicles should ensure that they have adequate insurance coverage and must exercise constant vigilence in their driving. Even when the teacher is not driving, but is on the vehicle, the duty of supervision continues. As we saw in the Beauparlant case, the teachers were found by the court to be negligent in failing to ensure that the method of transportation was safe. This was so even though the court held that they were acting outside the scope of their employment in undertaking the excursion.

The duty of supervision extends to making sure that children get on and off the bus in safety. In *George et al. v. Board of School Trustees, School District 70 (Port Alberni)* [1987] 3 A.C.W.S. (3d) 361 an 8-year-old child was struck by a school bus in the parking lot. No supervision had been provided and the school board had been told that there was no supervision. The driver did not ensure that it was safe to move the bus before putting it in motion. The driver was found to be negligent. It was held that he had a high standard of care and did not act as a reasonably careful driver in the circumstances. The board was also negligent for failing to provide supervision when it was aware of the lack of supervision. The accident that occurred was foreseeable and the board was therefore negligent.

Generally, once a child has been safely and properly discharged from the bus, the duty towards that child ends. If, however, the child gets off the bus elsewhere than the place designated, the duty of care extends until the child gets home safely.

In *Mattinson et al. v. Wonnacott et al.* (1975) 59 D.L.R. (3d) 18 a kindergarten child got off the bus before his designated stop and ran into the path of an oncoming car. The driver of that car was found to be negligent as were the bus driver and the board. Liability was apportioned 75% to the school authorities and 25% to the driver of the car that struck the plaintiff. The court held:

> In my opinion, Rose Cook (the bus driver) was negligent in her duty to Richard. She was aware that he lived on the south side of a busy, heavily-travelled highway, and had agreed to see that he was dropped off on the south side of the highway at the end of his lane. She has conceded that she did not intend to let Richard off the bus at Green River School. She was aware of the risk to Richard should he attempt to cross the highway unsupervised. When the 10 transferring children left her bus, there would not be more than eight or nine kindergarten children remaining with her. It does not seem to be a standard of perfection to require kindergarten children to be in specific, designated seats behind her when the older children got on the bus. The intermingling of the children getting on and off must have been an apparent danger, and yet it could have been prevented easily. If necessary, the assistance of the teacher on duty at the school yard could have been obtained. . . Mrs. Cook was entrusted with the carriage of the youngest school children. They required the greatest degree of supervision and care.
>
> The board did not instruct the bus company with regard to that type of loading and unloading of children, nor did it provide a teacher to specifically supervise such an operation.
>
> It has often been held that the duty owed by a teacher or supervisor is that he ought to take the same care of children in his charge as a prudent father would of his own children . . . It would seem reasonable for a prudent father to take particular care of a five-year-old in the vicinity of a heavily-travelled highway.
>
> I would not think it reasonable that the school board's duty to Richard would terminate the minute he left Brougham School and climbed on the bus. The transportation was specifically provided by the school board and the board retained a substantial degree of control over the bus company and certainly of discipline of the pupils while they were on the bus.

Schools must therefore ensure that students are supervised in the bus loading area, that they are transported in safety; and that they get off the bus only at the designated point. The cases indicate that the standard of care required may be stricter than that required of a careful parent. Even the slightest negligence will be a breach of the statutory duty and render those involved liable to pay damages.

Escaping Students

The Mattinson case is one example of the dangers that may befall the escaping student. Teachers are required to make sure that students are in school during the designated hours and may face a host of potential lawsuits if a student "escapes" their custody during this time.

In *Carmarthenshire County Council v. Lewis* [1955] A.C. 549, a 4-year-old boy wandered away from nursery school and onto a highway. The teacher had gone to the washroom, expecting to return in a few minutes, but found another injured child there and attended to a cut. She was gone about ten minutes during which time the boy wandered off and went onto the road through an unlocked gate. A driver swerved to miss the boy, struck a telephone pole and was killed. The widow of the driver sued the teacher and the school authority claiming that their negligence caused her husband's death. The House of Lords found no negligence on the part of the teacher involved but did find negligence on the part of the school authority. It was held:

> Her duty was that of a careful parent. I cannot think it would be considered negligent in a mother to leave a child dressed ready to go out with her for a few moments and then, if she found another of her children hurt and in need of immediate attention, she could be blamed for giving it, without thinking that the child who was waiting to go out with her might wander off into the street. It is very easy to be wise after the event and argue that she might have done this or that; but it seems to me that she acted just as one would expect her to, that is to attend to the injured child first, never thinking that the one waiting for her would go off on his own. . . I cannot bring myself to lay the blame for this tragic accident on Miss Morgan (the teacher).

> However careful the mistresses might be, minor emergencies and distractions were almost certain to occur from time to time so that some child or other would be left alone without supervision for an appreciable time. The actions of a child this age are unpredictable and I think it ought to have been anticipated by the appellants, or their responsible officers, that, in such a case a child might well try to get out on the street and that, if it did, a traffic accident was far from improbable.

A similar situation led to the injury of the pupil in *Barnes v. Hampshire County Council* [1969] 3 All E.R. 746. A 5-year-old was let out five minutes early, and, not finding her mother at the school gate, proceeded home by herself. She was injured while crossing a busy street. The decision of the House of Lords held:

It was the duty of the school authorities not to release the children before the closing time. Although a premature release would very seldom cause an accident, it foreseeably could, and in this case it did cause the accident to the appellant.

Injuries by Other Pupils

Often it is the action of another pupil that leads to a student injury. The duty of care involves not just protection from unsafe premises and equipment but also a duty to prevent injury from foreseeable dangers posed by other students. There have been many playground cases where injury resulted from the acts of other pupils. If a proper system of playground supervision is in place, the school will usually not be held liable. Such accidents are often described as "unavoidable" and no amount of supervision could prevent them. In the confines of the classroom, however, the number of students to supervise and the area under control of the teacher are greatly reduced.

The liability of the classroom teacher will depend on the "foreseeability" of the event. If a particular student is known to be likely to cause injury to others, then there must be closer supervision of that pupil to prevent such an occurrence. Teachers are also required to take notice of the "mischievous" tendencies of children according to the rule laid down in *Williams v. Eady.* Are we then to assume that every time a teacher's back is turned that some child might be injured? Can the teacher leave children unsupervised in the classroom, even for a few minutes? Must teachers prevent every such occurrence?

In *Chilvers v. London County Council et al.* (1916) 80 J.P. 246, a small child lost an eye when he fell on a toy soldier which had been brought to school by another child. The teacher was reading at the time of the accident allowing the children to play freely. The "unavoidable accident" defence was successful. The court held:

> The accident no doubt was deplorable; but it was for the plaintiff to show that the teacher was negligent. No such negligence has been proved. The accident might have happened in a nursery where there were several nurses looking after the children.

Wray v. Essex County Council [1936] 3 All E.R. 97 saw a student, carrying an oil can, collide with another striking him in the eye. The student carrying the can had been instructed to take it to the handicraft room. The students were moving between classes at the time. Neither boy was found to be negligent in any way. The court then considered whether the oil can was a dangerous object and had this to say:

> It may not be possible precisely to say what article is inherently dangerous and what is not by any general definition, yet when you come to particular articles there is, I think, no difficulty in drawing the line you take as the standard in the one case. Things like a naked sword or a hatchet or a loaded gun or an explosive are clearly inherently dangerous – that is to say, they cannot be handled without a serious risk. On the other hand, you have things in ordinary use which are only what is called "potentially dangerous"; that is to say, if there is negligence or if there is some mischance or misadventure then the thing may be a source of danger; but that source of danger is something which is not essential to their ordinary character; it merely depends on the concurrence of certain circumstances – in particular, generally, negligence on the part of someone. I feel, I am bound to say with no doubt at all, that this can does not come within the category of inherently dangerous articles.

We saw in the O'Brien case that the teacher was not responsible for injuries resulting in a science lab explosion during the teacher's absence. In *McCue et al. v. The Board of Education for the Borough of Etobicoke et al.* (reported in *The Canadian School Executive,* October, 1983 p. 30) a student lost an eye when another student shot a paperclip from an elastic band. The class had not yet commenced and the teacher was not in the room. The court dismissed the claim against the board of education, the teacher, and the principal. Damages were awarded against the student causing the injury and the plaintiff was held to be contributorily negligent to the extent of 20%.

It was held that there was no previous conduct on the part of the boys to lead the school authorities to anticipate that they might cause injury to each other or other students. The court found an adequate system of supervision to be in place and no breach of that system.

The implication of this case is that if there is any indication of a potentially dangerous activity being undertaken by pupils, then some action must be taken to deal with that problem. If paper clip shooting incidents were common among these boys, and known to be so by the teacher or principal, then liability may well have attached to them if they failed to take measures to prevent such happenings.

Medical Treatment

Both the careful parent duty and a stated or implied statutory duty will mandate the provision of adequate medical treatment to students when required. Two cases clearly illustrate that even if the school is not found liable for the original injury, there will be liability for any additional injury incurred as a result of failure to provide or obtain medical treatment.

In *Board of Education for the City of Toronto et al. v. Higgs et al.* [1960] S.C.R. 174, the board was absolved of blame for the injury to a student during recess. However, a teacher ordered him into line and into class even though he was limping and complaining. The initial injury to his hip was found to have been aggravated when he was required to walk. *The Public Schools Act* imposed a duty on teachers to "give assiduous attention to the health and comfort of the pupils." The Supreme Court of Canada affirmed the jury's finding of negligence on the part of the teachers in requiring the student to walk to class and not obtaining medical assistance immediately.

In *Poulton et al v. Notre Dame College et al* (1975) 60 D.L.R. (3d) 501, a 17-year-old student at a boarding school cut his big toe on ill-fitting hockey skates. A few days later he was hit on the hip with a hockey puck and the injury became worse due to the infection from the toe. The student asked to see a doctor but the teacher refused and forced the student to participate in further hockey games. Eventually some fellow students took him to the hospital.

The court found that the school was not at fault with respect to either the cut on the toe or the hip injury. Nor did the plaintiff establish that the subsequent infection was caused by any fault on their part. However, applying the careful parent test, it was held that a careful father would arrange for medical attention for his son when so requested. Earlier treatment of the injury would have been more beneficial to the plaintiff. Accordingly damages were awarded for the aggravation of the injury that occurred. The judge stated:

> The plaintiff was, however, entitled to treatment at the earliest reasonable time when the potential severity of the illness was or ought to have been known and he was entitled to have treatment for relief of his pain at an earlier time, and the opportunity that such earlier treatment might have prevented the serious later development of the infection.

Damage to Student's Belongings

The Poulton case had another interesting twist to it. While he was absent from school in the hospital some of his clothing was stolen from the school. He sued to recover damages for its value as part of his claim. What is the extent of teacher responsibility for the safety of student possessions in the school?

This issue was addressed by the Appellate Division of the Ontario Supreme Court in the case of *Stevenson v. Toronto Board of Education* (1919) 46 O.L.R. 146. There a student's coat went missing from a cloak-room at her school. The court stated:

> Boards of Education are not insurers of school children's clothing: they are responsible for its loss or injury only when the loss or injury is caused by their negligence; that is, their want of reasonable care, the care which is ordinarily taken under similar circumstances.

> The case would be different if experience had proved the cloak-room in question an unsafe place. To the contrary it was said that only one similar loss had occurred in 15 years, and that very few thefts had been committed in all Toronto's public schools at any time.

In the Poulton case, it was held that the school owed a duty to give reasonable care to the student's belongings during his absence in hospital which was known to them. The loss of clothing was attributable to the absence of such care and damages were awarded. The fact that the school was a boarding school probably affected the outcome in that case. The school would have a duty to ensure that the students' belongings are protected at all hours of the day when the students are absent and unable to look after them. Such circumstances are not usually found in public schools. A situation could arise, however, where a student has to leave school due to an injury and is unable to look after his own belongings. In such a case, the school should ensure that his possessions are put in a safe place pending his return.

Discussion and Review Questions

Teacher Liability For Accidents

1. Under what circumstances will a teacher be required to pay damages for a student's injury?

2. When may a teacher be found negligent? How careful must the teacher be? How closely must the teacher supervise the students? Under what circumstances must the teacher warn students of dangers, and what happens if the students do not heed the warning?

3. Define contributory negligence. How does this concept influence the school system's defense?

4. Does the student's negligence prevent recovery of damages?

5. Under what circumstances do students assume the risk of being injured, and how does the legal notion of *voluntary assumption* influence the school system's defense?

6 Does the presence of a parental *release form* prevent the injured student from suing the school or the teacher?

7. How does the school board use the notion of territorial limitations when it formulates its defense in cases of alleged negligence?

8. What factors seem to determine the level of damages awarded by the courts to successful plaintiffs?

At What Point Does Responsibility Begin?

1. When does a teacher become accountable as an employee of a school jurisdiction?

2. Is a teacher obligated to break up fights between students on the school grounds; on the way to and from school; and at extra-curricular events?

3. If a teacher observes a student committing an act of vandalism to non-school property, what is his obligation?

4. How should a teacher handle the matter of letting students into the classroom before the first bell?

5. Can a teacher adequately supervise students in a classroom while preparing for the day's activities?

6. Who has responsibility for supervising students who are loitering in the hall-ways before classes commence?

7. What should a teacher do about classroom supervision when he is assigned playground supervision duties?

8. To what extent is a teacher required to inspect, maintain, or repair school equipment?

9. Can a teacher be held responsible when other staff members forget or fail to perform their supervisory duties?

10. What are a teacher's responsibilities for supervising student parking lots, and bicycle rack areas?

11. Must the extremes of student misconduct be foreseen?

12. What must the teacher do if called from the classroom during class time?

13. What circumstances would justify the teacher in leaving a class unattended?

14. What are the teacher's responsibilities in guarding against mischievous conduct, criminal conduct, or pathological behavior by the students?

15. Is the teacher responsible for providing preventative safety instructions for apparently common-place dangers?

16. Is the teacher in an "open classroom" school responsible for the safety of the 25 children in his class, the 50 children in the team, or the 100 children in the pod?

17. Can a teacher be required to answer for the negligent acts of his team teacher, his teacher aide, his student teacher, his students' assistant, or his parent helper?

18. What responsibility does the teacher have for the personal safety of the girl who is assaulted in the back of the bus on the way home from a basketball tournament, or the boy who refuses to board the activities bus at the assigned time?

19. What are the necessary steps to be taken before a teacher takes a sick child to a doctor or hospital emergency ward?

20. What are the teacher's responsibilities in permitting a sick child to return home during school hours?

School Board Liability:

1. Why are school boards most often named as defendants in negligence cases rather than individual teachers?

2. What is vicarious liability and what is the *master and servant* relationship?

3. If a school board is ordered to pay damages as a result of the doctrine of vicarious liability, may it recover this amount from the teacher or school principal?

4. How do the courts determine when a teacher is acting outside his "course of employment"?

Student And Parent Liability:

1. When do children become liable for their own tortious acts, or do they?
2. How does the standard of care expected of a child compare to that expected of an adult, and of a teacher?
3. To what extent can parents be held responsible for the negligent acts of their children?

You be the Judge

Case #1

Murphy and Ignatz were two students in Mr. Conway's Senior Chemistry class. Both boys were reputed to be class clowns. One day Murphy and Ignatz were in the chemistry laboratory to perform an experiment. Mr. Conway explained the procedure and provided a step-by-step instruction sheet before he left the room. Most of the students went to work using micro test tubes according to instructions, but not Murphy and Ignatz. They began rooting around in the drawers of the lab and came up with a giant-sized test tube. The decided to do the experiment in king-sized proportions. *Bigger is better* was their motto.

During the course of their experiment, something blew! The contents of the test tube were spread around the lab. The sulfuric acid in the mixture burned the ceiling tiles, the counter top, a couple of stools and Murphy's eye. Fortunately, none of the nearby students were harmed.

Ignatz was a fast thinker. He rushed Murphy to the eye flushing station and flushed his eyes with copious amount of water. Then the two boys set about cleaning up the mess. Both had visions of this being their last day in this school! The mop-up operation was barely completed when Mr. Conway returned. Although it was not difficult for him to see that something had gone on, to Murphy's and Ignatz's surprise, nothing was said. The two boys wondered about this because they felt sure they were *dead in the water.*

That night at the dinner table, Murphy's mother noticed some red spots on her son's face. Prompted by numerous questions, the story slowly unfolded. That night Murphy couldn't sleep. His eye hurt. Early next morning, his father took him to the emergency department at the local hospital. He was examined by an opthalmologist who removed a tiny piece of glass from Murphy's eye. The doctor than placed a patch over the eye and informed Murphy how fortunate he had been. The glass had scratched the cornea but there probably would be no permanent damage.

Murphy's father accompanied his son to school that day and demanded of the principal to know what had been going on in Mr. Conway's chemistry class. The principal, however, knew nothing of the incident. Mr. Conway was called to the office. He stated that he really couldn't say what had gone on the day before. "Fine," said Mr. Murphy, "you'll be hearing from my lawyer."

Discussion Questions

1. If Mr. Murphy proceeds with a suit for negligence, will he be successful? Please support your answer.
2. Are all of the elements of negligence present in this case?
3. What will be Conway's defense?
4. Is Mr. Conway covered by the board's liability insurance in this case?

Case #2

The Introduction

Shawn Able is a 15-year-old grade 10 student at Scholastic High School. He is an extremely agile and talented athlete and for this reason he was entered in the city-wide track meet as a contestant in the decathalon. Despite his innate athletic ability, Shawn is a bit of a hypochondriac. In an effort to be the focus of attention at all times, Shawn frequently uses crutches, and often complains of various aches and pains. Not wanting to contradict himself in his apparent injuries, Shawn frequently waits until he is publicly 'encouraged' to participate in athletic events. This has been especiallly true for the coming track and field meet.

Mr. Rambo is a member of the physical education team at Scholastic High. He is now in his tenth year of teaching and this will be his ninth year as coach of the track and field teams. Scholastic High, under Mr. Rambo's coaching, has won virtually every trophy presented at the city-wide track meet, including the decathalon trophy. Last year, however, a student from Vocational High won the decathalon and therefore took the trophy. In every practice Mr. Rambo would tell his team, "I simply have to have that trophy back . . . for the school's sake, of course."

The Scenario

Monday morning at 7 a.m. the pole-vaulting team met Mr. Rambo in the gymnasium. Shawn Able was in attendance, ready for practice, along with six other team mates. Without an adequate warm-up session, vaulting began. Given that the track meet was only two days away, and that the team had been practicing all term, the height of the vaults was routine to all and so the students were simply refining their respective styles. In an effort to maximize the students' potentials, Mr. Rambo was extremely boisterous in his encouragement of the pole-vaulting team.

Shawn set himself up for his second vault. Realizing that the height of the bar was below Shawn's potential, Mr. Rambo suggested to Shawn that he raise the bar. After the necessary amount of encouragement, Shawn agreed and the bar was raised. Shawn began his approach but didn't quite make it up to full speed. He failed to clear the bar knocking it off its rungs. When Shawn hit the porta-pit the bar was caught between him and the foam pit. Shawn expressed his discomfort in a loud voice and everyone ran to his aid. His injury was dismissed as minor. Mr. Rambo suggested that Shawn's tailbone was only slightly bruised. Shawn spent the rest of the practice walking it off and felt only minor discomfort by the time classes began. Mr. Rambo told Shawn that he was glad that he was all right and that he would see him at javelin practice after school. Shawn said, "Okay, see you after school."

At the start of javelin practice Shawn felt a little discomfort in the area of his tailbone but after the adrenalin began to flow the pain was quick to dissipate. Practice went on as usual. At the end Mr. Rambo announced that Tuesday would be a day of rest and that he would see his team on Wednesday, the day of the track meet.

The Track Day was upon them for another year. Mr. Rambo gave a pep talk to his team on the way to the meet. "I am very proud of the way you have all practiced so very hard. I want you know I speak for the teachers and student body of Scholastic High when I say let's get out there and win those trophies." After he supervised the bus loading Mr. Rambo took Shawn Able aside and said, "especially you, Shawn, you just have to get the decathalon trophy back, you just have to." "O.K. Coach, I'll give it all I've got." Mr. Rambo said, "I don't really care what you give it as long as you win that trophy!"

Pole vaulting was the first even at the meet. Shawn was performing fairly well but he did appear to be hesitating on his approach runs. He was running fast enough, but gingerly, and Mr. Rambo knew Shawn's speed was not going to be sufficient to achieve the heights necessary to win. He told Shawn firmly that he was going to have to get his act together. Shawn told his coach that his tailbone was sore and that he didn't feel he could finish the event. Mr. Rambo said, "I am sick and tired of playing your 'little boy who cried wolf' game. Now you get out on that track and win this event. If your tailbone is really sore take a couple of aspirins!" Shawn took the aspirins, once again his adrenalin began to flow, but unlike in javelin practice, he was not free of pain. He knew that if he could clear the bar this time he would win. Shawn's tailbone continued to ache however and he thought it best to withdrew from the event. He informed Mr. Rambo of his decision. Mr. Rambo's reply was "I thought we cleared all of this up, you must have bruised you tailbone on Monday, it's no big deal, now stop being such a cry baby and go and clear that bar." But Shawn could not generate the speed he needed, he hit the bar and again it landed under him when he hit the porta-pit. It was evident that he was in considerable pain.

Shawn was admitted to the hospital and after examination the physician informed Mr. and Mrs. Able that their son's tailbone had broken, and splinters of the bone had lodged in the base of Shawn's spine. With great difficulty, the physician informed Mr. and Mrs. Able that their son would never be able to walk again. Shawn was a paraplegic.

Two days later, after being informed of the sequence of events on the days prior to and including the day of the track and field meet, Mr. and Mrs. Able informed the principal of Scholastic High of their intention to sue. Your decisions should be based on answers to the following questions:

Discussion Questions

1. Based upon the rules of evidence (balance of probabilities in tort actions) was Mr. Rambo negligent and therefore liable?

2. What evidence taken from the description would you use to argue your decision? Is this evidence direct or circumstantial?

3. Will you award the Able's compensatory damages or punitive damage? Will you award both? What factors will you consider?

4. Is the School Board liable?

5. Can the Board terminate Mr. Rambo? If so, on what basis?

6. Was Mr. Rambo so adamant in his instructions to Shawn Able that he is guilty of assault?

11

Occupier's Liability

Learning Objectives

Some of the things that the reader will learn from reading this chapter include the following:

1. The nature of the school system's responsibility to maintain a safe place.
2. The nature of the teacher's responsibilities as occupier of school property.
3. The degree to which the liability of the occupier can be extended beyond the school premises.
4. The responsibility of the teacher to warn students about the dangers inherent in non-district owned equipment and machinery.

Preview

In many instances a statute may impose a duty of care upon the owner and occupier of a facility, but even in the absence of a statutory duty, a common law principle referred to as occupier's liability extends the schools system's responsibility by requiring it to keep a safe place. This common law requirement expands both the teacher's and the school board's responsibilities to a substantial degree.

There are strong suggestions that the obligation to keep a safe place may be extended beyond the physical boundaries of the school in certain instances.

The class of person entering the premises, whether an invitee, a licensee or a trespasser will determine the amount of care owed. School children attending school during regular school hours are referred to as invitees. They are owed the highest standard of care. Even those children and others who trespass upon school property are owed a certain but limited degree of care. The legal distinction as to the class of person on the premises is of extreme importance to the classroom teacher.

Self-Assessment

1. What is the common law principle of occupier's liability?
2. The common law recognizes three broad classes of persons who could be on the premises. They are, invitees, licencees, and trespassers. Are you able, in a general sense, to describe and give an example of each class of person and perhaps explain the degree of care owed to each by the occupier of the school buildings and grounds.

Key Terms

Potentially dangerous
Inherently dangerous
Invitee
Licencee
Trespasser

*   *   *   *

In this chapter we shall look at cases involving the safety of school premises and situations wherein school boards have been sued in negligence for an apparent breach of duty to maintain the safety of their premises or equipment. Although it is not necessarily the teacher's direct responsibility to ensure the safety of the premises themselves, we suggest that teachers should assume this duty to make sure that their students are not injured. By watching for (and reporting) potentially unsafe areas and equipment, teachers are serving both their employer and their students.

Often these cases also involve the issue of breach of duty to supervise as well as claims of occupier's liability. The duty of supervision has been held to be higher when there are unusual dangers present. It is often difficult to distinguish under which category of liability a particular case has been decided. Where they also provide insight into issues of safety of school premises, cases which apparently turn on breach of duty to supervise have therefore been included in this chapter. A recent case has argued against drawing any distinction between the two sources of liability.

In *Lapensee et al. v. Ottawa Day Nursery Inc. et al.*(1986) C.C.L.T. 129, a toddler received severe head injuries after falling down an unguarded stairwell at a private home approved as a day care facility. The operator of the home was not feeling well at the time and was in the bathroom. She had left the child and two others in a bedroom.

The court stated that the applicable standard of care was that of a careful parent. The case headnote reveals that the judge also reasoned that the question of occupier's liability should not enter the matter:

> The question should be viewed as one of negligence simpliciter, unembarrassed by concepts of "unusual dangers," "allurements," or any other of the discarded paraphernalia of the old common law as to occupier's liability. The obligation was to take such care as a prudent parent would take, to guard against risks which a reasonable person would regard as significant and not to be discounted. The standard did not, upon a proper reading of the authorities, vary with the locality, the neighbourhood, or the socio-economic status of the defendant.

> Applying this standard, Mrs. C. (the home operator) failed in the circumstances to discharge her duty of care. Knowing that the staircase was unguarded, she could have adopted various courses to keep these very small children secure (e.g. with a playpen) or at least in sight. The risk was foreseeable and the danger significant.

The first issue to be addressed is the extent of the duty to maintain safe premises relative to time and space. That is, during what hours and over what area does this liability extend?

In *Pearson v. Vancouver Board of School Trustees et al.* [1941] 3 W.W.R. 874 it was stated:

> There is not around school grounds a zone over which the school authorities exercise supervision as, for example, do the authorities of a state over its territorial waters. School supervision does not extend beyond the school premises.

In reaching this conclusion that the duty of supervision did not extend beyond the school boundaries, the court relied on a former case, *Patterson v. Vancouver Board of School Trustees* [1929] 3 D.L.R. 33. In that case a student was injured, while standing on a highway adjoining the school, when a tree from another property fell on him. This case held that the duty of supervision ended at the school boundaries and also that an occupier of land is not responsible for injuries sustained by a person on the adjoining highway.

The Saskatchewan Court of Appeal addressed the issue in *Magnusson et al. v. Board of the Nipawin School Unit No. 61 of Saskatchewan* (1975) 60 D.L.R. (3d) 572. In that case, a 14-year-old boy was injured by broken glass when he left the schoolground at recess and went onto adjoining fair grounds, which had been used by the school on the previous day for a track meet. The court stated:

> ... the respondent was not in actual possession of the premises and did not have the immediate supervision and control and the power of permitting or prohibiting the entry of other persons .. therefore ... the respondent was not the occupier of the premises ...

> The appellant submits that if the respondent is not found to be the occupier of the fair grounds, it is still liable on the alternative ground that it failed to provide proper supervision of the students during the recess period. It is contended that the respondent could reasonably expect that broken glass may be laying around in the fair ground and that being so should have erected a fence or stationed a teacher or supervisor on the boundary to prevent students from entering the fair grounds.

> In the instant case the respondent assigned two teachers to supervise the students during the recess period. The trial Judge stated that it was not established to his satisfaction that there was a lack of supervision during the recess period. In other words he found that the supervision provided was adequate under the circumstances.

> I am prepared to concede to the appellant that if there was on the adjoining fair grounds something which was essentially dangerous in itself, the finding that there was adequate supervision could be seriously questioned. What is really involved here is a consideration of the danger presented by the presence of odd bits of glass.

The court held that the glass must be categorized as something "potentially" dangerous and not as something "inherently" dangerous. As such it is not reasonable to expect a careful parent from forbidding a child to go on the fair grounds just because there might be some broken glass there.

Assuming that the liability extends only to actual school premises, we must then consider the status of the student in relation to the premises. As we shall see, this may vary from time to time.

In *Pook et al. v. Ernesttown Public School Trustees* [1944] 4 D.L.R. 268 a pupil was injured by some rubble littering the school grounds during a recess scuffle with another student. The court pointed out that the accident occurred "during the regular school sessions" and the plaintiff was therefore "lawfully and properly playing in the school grounds." The court recited the various statutes and regulations that required the board to maintain the premises in good repair and noted that not one witness could cite a single act done by the board in the way of clearing the grounds of the particular school.

In reaching his decision, the judge referred to an English case, *Ching v. Surrey County Council* [1910] 1 K.B. 736 which stated :

> They are not merely permitted or invited to come to the school, but directed to do so, and I think that, as members of the public, if they are injured by neglect of a statutory duty with regard to a place where they are expected to play, they are entitled to make those upon whom the statute has imposed the duty responsible for injuries sustained by them through breach of such duty.

Using this authority the trial judge found:

> It is clear from the evidence that there was an accumulation of refuse, stones, brick-bats, etc., on the playgrounds. Section 89 clearly imposes a duty on the Board to refrain from piling rubbish or debris in the school-yard. I cannot see how this difffers from the breach of any other statute. The school board has no more right to flout the *Public Schools Act* or any other Act than an individual would have to disregard a provision of the *Highway Traffic Act*. The statute is mandatory, and being commanded by the statute is being commanded by His Majesty, the King, and cannot be disregarded anymore than the children can disregard the statute which compels them to go to school, no matter what the school is like or how it is kept up.
>
> In the case at bar we are dealing with a hidden danger having regard to the mental developments and capacity of children of tender years.

The judge went beyond the principles of occupier's liability and found a breach of a specific statutory duty. He did so because the students, as invitees, were only to be protected from hidden or unusual dangers rather than from those dangers that were readily apparent. Debris on the schoolgrounds is usually apparent and, therefore, there is no duty to warn or guard against it. The judge went on to add that he held the debris to be a hidden danger due to the mental capacities of a child. What is not a hidden danger to an adult may be so for a child.

A statutory duty to maintain safe premises can be found in the provisions of all provincial school or education acts and this duty is often delegated to school personnel.

A 10-year-old boy was injured by a piece of wire which he found in the schoolyard and stuck in his eye in the case of *Durham v. North Oxford Public School Board* [1960] O.R. 320. The court held that the wire was potentially dangerous and not inherently dangerous. The board was, therefore, not liable under the invitor-invitee standard of care. Because the accident happened after school hours there was no issue of supervision involved.

In *Portelance et al. v. Board of Trustees of R. C. Separate School. S.S. No. 5* (1962) 32 D.L.R. (2d) 337 some students were injured at noon hour by running into some bushes and being cut by thorns. Because they knew of the presence of the bushes it was not an unusual danger nor was it hidden from them.

The duty to maintain safe premises extends to the walkways providing entrance to the school. Many local by-laws require property owners to remove ice and snow from the public walkways adjacent to their property. In such cases the school will be responsible for maintaining these public areas as well as its own sidewalks on school property.

In *Phillips v. Regina Public School District No. 4 Board of Education et al.* (1976) 1 C.C.L.T. 197 a student fell on an icy sidewalk leading to the school. The court held that the relationship was that of occupier and invitee and that the ice was an unusual danger of which the board knew or ought to have known. The danger was unusual because of the kind of premises (a school) and the type of individuals being invited thereon (children). The plaintiff knew of the danger and failed to use reasonable care for her own safety. As a result she was found to be 25% negligent.

In *Cropp v. Potashville School Unit No. 25* (1977) 4 C.C.L.T. 12 a student was injured in a fall caused by the poor condition of a gravel walkway. He was successful at trial where the judge held that he was not an ordinary invitee and was owed a higher duty of care. He held further that schools have a duty to supervise students' use of walkways and to warn of dangers.

The changing nature of a student's status on the school grounds is illustrated by the case of *Storms v. School District of Winnipeg No. 1* (1963) 41 D.L.R. (2d) 216. In this case an 11-year-old boy was injured during the summer vacation while playing on the schoolgrounds. He was struck on the head by a fire escape on which two companions were playing. He and his companions had been warned not to play on the fire escapes. No attempt was made during the summer months to keep children off the playground and no supervision was provided during this period.

The court found a tacit permission to use the schoolgrounds during the summer and as such the boys were "licensees." This license, however, did not extend to the use of the school building or any part thereof. Accordingly, they were trespassers insofar as the fire escape was concerned. This distinction is important because an occupier is liable for traps and allurements with respect to young children who are licensees. The fire escape could be considered an allurement to a child of tender years although the judge held that an 11-year-old boy was not such a child. The judge stated:

The accident was not caused by reason of any inherent danger in the escape. It was caused by the unauthorized use made of it . . to the plaintiff's knowledge, combined with his own separate negligence and deliberate act.

. . . I hold that the infant plaintiff did not exercise the care to be expected of a child of his age, intelligence and experience, and that he had full knowledge of the nature and extent of the risk which he ran when he deliberately went underneath the fire escape at the point he did and at the time when his companion was bouncing it up and down somewhat in the nature of a teeter-totter, and, therefore, was the author of his own misfortune. He could, by the exercise of ordinary care, have avoided the accident, and his negligence was the real direct and effective cause of the misfortune.

Many occupier's liability cases involve the presence of construction equipment on the schoolyard. Schools must take special precautions to warn students of the inherent dangers posed by construction areas and equipment. The amount of supervision required also increases when such dangers are present.

In *Schade et al. v. Winnipeg School District No. 1 et al.* (1959) 28 W.W.R. 577 a student was injured during the noon recess while playing baseball. He tripped on a marking stake placed by construction workers. The stake was clearly visible and students had been warned to keep away from that area. The Manitoba Court of Appeal concluded:

While it must be recognized that there is a duty on teachers to supervise certain school activities, a duty that of necessity bears some relation to the age of the pupils, the special circumstances of each case and, in particular, the type of activity engaged in, nevertheless it must also be recognized that one of the most important aims of education is to develop a sense of responsibility on the part of pupils, personal responsibility for their individual actions, and a realization of the personal consequences of such actions.

In the instant case the accident was caused by the infant plaintiff's own negligence under circumstances which placed a responsibility on him to have regard to his safety. Bearing in mind his age, his intelligence and his knowledge of the circumstances, he failed to take the necessary care. This is the decisive fact which determines the result of this case and makes it impossible for the plaintiffs to succeed against either of the defendants. Having reached that conclusion it is unnecessary for me to decide whether or not the infant plaintiff was a trespasser. . . .

Boryszko et al v. Board of Education of the City of Toronto et al. (1963) 35 D.L.R. (2d) 529 also involved a construction site accident. An 8-year-old boy was struck by a building block which was dislodged from a pile of blocks by another boy. The accident occurred after school hours and the pupils had been warned to stay away from the area. The court held that the pile of blocks could not be regarded as a trap nor could the school authorities reasonably foresee that someone might dislodge some of the bricks. Further, the injured boy could see what the other one was doing and the danger was therefore an open and obvious one.

There have been several cases involving students crashing through glass panels at schools. In *Ralph v. London County Council* (1947) 111 J.P. 246 a student put his hand through a glass partition during a tag game in physical education period. The decision was based on the careful parent test and the court held:

> The view that I take without hesitation is that in a room of this size, one side of which is almost entirely of glass, any reasonable and prudent person, having regard to the wild nature of the game while it lasted, must (or should) have contemplated that this kind of accident might happen. In these circumstances I find that there was negligence so far as the council are concerned.

Sombach et al. v. Board of Trustees of Regina R. C. Separate High School District of Saskatchewan (1969) 9 D.L.R. (3d) 707 aff'd (1970) 18 D.L.R. (3d) 207 saw a 14-year-old schoolgirl walk through a glass panel beside a door. She thought she was stepping through an open door. The accident occurred after school and although a teacher was present it was held there was no duty of supervision. The case was resolved on the basis of occupier's liability. The court held:

> The defendant's duty toward Karen in respect to the school building is that of an invitor to an invitee.
>
> ... where there is a duty to supervise there is a higher duty owing than that of an invitor to an invitee. This would not apply to the fact herein as there was no supervision involved at the time of the accident.
>
> The unusual danger has been held to mean unusual from the point of view of the particular invitee.
>
> It would seem to me to be clear that a school building which is used by some 1,200 pupils each day must be designed differently than a building generally used by adults. The defendant had knowledge of one incident of a pupil "walking through" the same panel in September, 1967 . . . The defendant would thus be aware of the danger inherent in the entrance. . . .
>
> I find that the glass doors and panels in the front entrance of Miller constituted an unusual danger to the infant plaintiff and that the defendant knew of the danger or ought to have known of it. In view of the physical facts and the fact that Karen thought the panel was an open door (although mistakenly) I do not find any contributory negligence an her part.

In *Boivin v. Glenavon School District* [1937] 2 W.W.R. 170 a pupil was injured when she fell from a horizontal ladder in a playroom. There were no mats on the floor. The court found that there was a duty to keep both the premises and equipment reasonably safe for their intended use. However, the absence of the mats did not cause the injury and it was just as likely to have happened if mats were present. The plaintiff's action therefore failed.

A student was struck in the eye by a bamboo cross-pole used for high jumping in *Edmondson v. Board of Trustees for the Moose Jaw School District No. 1* (1920) 55 D.L.R. 563. The end of the pole was splintered and jagged. The plaintiff was watching others use the equipment after school hours. The Saskatchewan Court of Appeal held:

> There was nothing unusual or out of the common in the apparatus in question, and it was being used in the ordinary way. That the pole should be knocked down is an ordinary incident of any jumping competition, and under ordinary circumstances there is no resulting danger. The accident which unfortunately happened might equally well have happened whether the end of the pole was broken or not.

Other playground equipment has been held to be dangerous under certain circumstances. In *Lamarche v. L'Orignal Separate School Trustees* [1956] O.W.N. 686 a child was injured playing on an unsafe swing. It was installed on sloping ground and had been upset on previous occasions. The plaintiff was 11 years old and was in Grade 5, a grade that was not allowed to use the swings. The swings in this case were knocked over by other students. A supervisor was present. The judge held:

> It should be remembered that school children are not merely permitted, or invited, to come to school, but are required to do so, and, as members of the public, if they are injured by neglect of a statutory duty with regard to a place where they are expected to play, they are entitled to make those upon whom the statute has imposed the duty, responsible for injuries sustained by them through breach of such duty.
>
> The duty of the board of trustees, under the circumstances, is to see that the premises provided for the accommodation of the school-children are as safe as reasonable care and skill can make them.

Liability was imposed in a similar incident in *Brost v. Board of School Trustees of Eastern Irrigation School Division No. 44* [1955] 3 D.L.R. 159. There a 6-year-old was injured in a fall from a swing caused by another pupil "pumping" the swings. There was no teacher present and the board was found not to have proven adequate supervision. There was a foreseeable danger of injury on the apparatus and in the absence of supervision, liability was imposed.

Therefore, when considering the issue of safety of the school premises, there are three different categories of liability that will be considered by the courts. First, was there a duty to supervise? If so, the careful parent test will be applied and a higher standard of care than is owed by an invitor to an invitee will be imposed. Second, was there a breach of a statutory duty to maintain the premises? If so, then liability will be imposed if the breach was a cause of the injury. Finally, was there a breach of the general common law principles of occupier's liability? Teachers must ensure that their obligations in all three areas are met.

You be the Judge

Harry F. Stop was a first year junior high school language arts teacher who had developed a keen interest in photography. His personal interest in this hobby blossomed into a desire to offer a photography course to some of his students, so he proposed the idea of a photography option to his school principal. Within no time at all, school board approval had been granted and funds were provided so that a dark room could be improvised out of a basement storage area. Harry was disappointed with some of the aspects of the modifications but he had convinced himself that with a little care the crowded quarters and the open shelving would not present an insurmountable problem. Besides, the children would enjoy the course and so he put these matters to the back of his mind.

The darkroom was situated next to a lunchroom which contained tables and chairs. It was Harry's plan to utilize both rooms by having a small group of students working in the darkroom while the remainder of the class worked on other assignments in the lunchroom. He was confident that he could control both groups because of the proximity of the two instructional spaces.

As part of his preliminary instruction, Harry had carefully outlined to his students some of the dangers involved in the chemicals necessary to the photographic processes. He cautioned his students about the potential dangers inherrent in working with caustic chemicals in the subdued light of the darkroom. "We must be careful," he stated.

During one class period while Harry was working in the darkroom with a group of Grade Nine students, he became concerned with noises coming from the lunchroom. He instructed the darkroom students to continue processing their photographic prints while he excused himself in order to check on the rest of the class. The twenty-six students left in the lunchroom were supposed to be working on a short story about the development of photography. Harry settled down the story writers, but trouble was brewing in the darkroom.

Frank, one of the aspiring photographers left to work in the darkroom had momentarily lost interest in the art of photography, and instead had begun to focus his attention on the "art" of attending to his young female classmates. While trying to initiate a game of "blindman's bluff" in the pale light of the darkroom, an erratic elbow knocked over a bottle of stop bath fluid, which contains glacial acetic acid. The fluid splashed across the floor and onto innocent Suzy. In a threatening voice young Frank warned Suzy not to breathe a word to Mr. Stop. In spite of a stinging sensation on her face and in her eyes, Suzy said nothing when the teacher returned. The spilled fluid was explained as a simple accident. When Mr. Stop inquired as to whether anyone had been sprayed, there was a stoney silence in the small, dimly lit room. In the lurid glow of the safe light, Suzy suffered in silence. At that very moment the buzzer sounded, and the students filed on to their next class.

That evening Suzy discovered that the acid had damaged her best school dress, and had left burn marks on her cheeks and forehead. More importantly, Suzy's eyes were "tearing." When questioned, Suzy explained that a bottle had spilled in the darkroom and splashed her with fluid. Her parents were to discover that the teacher had been out of the lab at the time, and that he had done nothing about the situation when he returned to the darkroom. The parents rushed Suzy to the hospital. The doctor on duty flushed out both eyes, placed patches over them, instructed Suzy to rest them for twenty-four hours before returning for a further examination. The burns on her face were treated, however, the doctor described them as being extremely superficial. Although Suzy's eyes caused her some discomfort during the next few days her doctor declared that no permanent damage would result. Suzy was very relieved and firmly in favour of forgetting the entire incident but her parents viewed the situation somewhat differently. They were determined to launch a negligence suit against the school for allowing dangerous chemicals to be stored on inadequate and open shelving in a classroom. They also wanted the school to reprimand Harry Stop for insufficient supervision. The parents also insisted on a termination of the photography program.

Questions for Discussion

1. Was the school negligent? In what way?
2. Was Harry negligent in his supervision of the photography class?
3. What will be the nature of Harry's defense, if the matter goes to court?
4. What defenses will the School Board employ?
5. How would you, if placed in a similar situation, have conducted yourself?

12
Educational Malpractice

We hear sometimes of an action for damages against the unqualified
medical practitioner, who has deformed a broken limb in pretending to
heal it. But, what of the hundreds of thousands of minds that have been
deformed for ever by the incapable pettifoggers who have pretended to
form them?

Charles Dickens,
Nicholas Nickleby, Preface

Learning Objectives

Some of the things you will learn from reading this chapter include:

1. That failure to educate may be an actionable tort.
2. The two broad categories of educational malpractice.
3. The similarities between educational malpractice and other forms of
   professional malpractice such as medical or legal malpractice.
4. How the movement towards professionalism of teachers has
   increased public expectations concerning the level of education to be
   provided to their children.
5. How recent legislation has produced situations whereby there has
   been an increase in the number of educational malpractice suits.
6. The level of care owned by all professional practitioners.
7. What standard of educational care is owed by the teacher
   practitioner.
8. The direction which educational malpractice litigation is taking both
   the United States and Canada.

Preview

Educational malpractice is a claim for mental or emotional damages resulting from the failure to teach competently, the failure to correctly assess and place the student in an appropriate educational environment, the failure to correctly inform the student and parent, or the failure to provide a program appropriate to the student. Failure to education and failure to diagnose accurately account for most of the current litigation.

There are legal disagreements concerning the issue, however, on balance, educational malpractice is considered to be an actionable tort. The existence of a duty to educate can be established, a standard can be determined, and when a sufficient relationship can be determined between the lack of action or the imperfect action of the school employee and a resulting damage to the student a monetary award can be granted to the plaintiff.

Although there has not been a flood of litigation to this point, there are very clear signs which point toward increased educational malpractice suits. Teachers and other educational professionals such as psychologists should regard the necessity to keep their students safe from educational harm as deligently as they view the necessity to keep their charges safe from physical harm.

The movement toward a professional status by teachers and educational psychologists, a generally increased expectation for education on the point of the public, and the increased legislative action guaranteering educational rights have all combined to produce a situation whereby a number of suits charging educational malpractice have been considered by the courts. Sufficient precedent has been established to point toward future directions.

Questions are frequently raised as to the standard of care owed by all professionals. The general answer is that the standard will be that of the average competent practitioner. For teachers then, the standard of educational service required to be provided is not the level provided by the perfect teacher but that of the average competent teacher. For each specific case the courts will determine what constitutes the level of competency. In several Canadian cases in which the plaintiff demanded compensation for physical injury, the courts have made specific reference to the presence or absence of competent instruction, so it seems evident that judges consider themselves able to define what constitutes competent instruction.

If the United States provides a pattern for us then Canadian teachers can anticipate increased litigation. Since, even when the plaintiff fails at the superior courts of the United States, there has always been a clearly enunciated minority position in support of the child against the educational establishment. Often a one vote swing would have changed the outcome. Minority arguments often provide guidance as clearly as do majority judgments.

Self-Assessment

1. Do Canadian school teachers owe their students a legal duty to teach in a competent manner?
2. How would you define teaching a student in a competent manner?
3. What are the bases upon which a high school diploma, for example, is granted? What are the criteria by which student success is measured?
4. Can a school system be held responsible when a student fails to learn or does the responsibility rest upon the shoulders of the individual teacher?
5. Are school systems responsible for the negligent misrepresentation of student acheivements or again is it the responsibility of the individual teacher?
6. Should psychologists be held to a different standard of conduct than teachers when performing student diagnoses?
7. Can teachers be held liable for failing to detect learning- related medical problems?
8. Can money be used as a proper substitute for a good education and, if so, on what bases would the amount be determined?

Key Terms

Misfeasence
Nonfeasance
Tort
Careful parent test
Prima facie

*   *   *   *

Educational malpractice is a claim for damages for mental or emotional damage. This damage is allegedly caused by poor or negligent teaching, which may include poor pedagogy, inaccurate or inadequate diagnosis, inappropriate class placement, and inaccurate advice as to a student's progress.

Such suits can be divided into two general categories of action: failure to educate, and improper diagnosis and placement. The "failure to educate" cases involve individuals who are of normal ability but do not possess the basic skills required after attending school for a number of years. The "improper diagnosis and placement" cases involve people who were improperly diagnosed as either handicapped or normal and placed in a class according to such diagnoses when in fact they should have been placed in an alternate class. Educational malpractice is a form of professional negligence based on principles similar to those found in other malpractice claims such as those against lawyers or doctors. The essence of the action is that a teacher has a duty to educate and undertakes to conduct that duty with a reasonable degree of care and skill. If the duty is not carried out with the requisite skill it is negligence and the teacher is liable for any injuries that may be caused as a result of this negligence.

Despite Dickens' plea for the necessity of such actions a century ago, malpractice suits against teachers are a recent phenomenon. Very few have been filed and fewer still have met with any degree of success. Many courts refuse to entertain such actions and have expressed doubts as to whether such a tort can even exist. However, the classes of negligence are never closed and there have been a few successful educational malpractice suits in the United States which will provide precedent for others.

The movement towards "professional" status for teachers is bound to carry with it the increased obligations of such status. There is a growing social trend toward more litigation, especially against the largely impersonal institutions of government. People are demanding more from their educational systems and are prepared to go to court to satisfy their demands. Legislators are passing more and more laws guaranteeing educational rights which will soon be tested in Canadian courts as they have been in the United States.

An example of recent legislation imposing a positive duty to provide competent instruction is Bill 59 of the 1987 Legislative Assembly of Alberta, a proposed new *School Act*, which states:

> 13. Subject to this Act and the regulations, a teacher while providing instruction or supervision has a duty to:
> (a) provide instruction competently to students;
> (b) teach the courses of study and education programs that are prescribed or approved pursuant to this Act;
> (c) encourage and foster learning in students;
> (d) promote the goals of basic education;
> (e) regularly evaluate students and periodically report the results of the evaluation to the students, the students' parents and the board . . .

This duty is more stringent than the usual duty to "teach diligently and faithfully" that is found in most provincial legislation.

The Saskatchewan legislature also appears to implicitly recognize an action for educational malpractice. The *Education Act* c. E-0.1 1978 R.S.S. (Supp.) states:

> 228. (2) No teacher engaged, under the supervision of the principal, in innovative or experimental projects related to teaching methodology or curriculum content that are approved by the board of education shall be liable for damages for alleged malpractice as a teacher or for any other claim based on the results of such innovation or experimentation.

By providing this exclusion of liability under certain circumstances, it is suggested that the legislature recognizes that malpractice claims can be made and that it wishes to protect certain teachers from them. It is not a blanket immunity from all malpractice claims but only in the circumstances stated in the Act. Thus a teacher engaging in such practices without supervision or approval would be liable to an action for malpractice.

The concept of educational malpractice has gained root in several court opinions and it will not be long before those roots grow and bear fruit. The purpose of this chapter is to provide a warning that such claims can be successful in appropriate circumstances and that teachers and administrators should conduct themselves accordingly.

In this chapter we shall look at the general principles of professional malpractice, various court decisions pertaining to educational malpractice, and outline possible types of actions that may be successful. The reader should also bear in mind the general principles of negligence law since they are applicable in such actions as well.

Professional Malpractice

Actions for professional negligence or malpractice are common, especially in the medical profession. Indeed, they have become so rampant in certain jurisdictions that insurance coverage for such claims has become prohibitive. A large body of law has therefore developed, giving us general principles that may be applied in all such actions. In general, a person practicing a profession that requires skill or knowledge superior to that possessed by others will be liable for damages when a person in his care is injured due to lack of care or competence on the part of the professional.

As in all negligence actions, there must be a duty of care owed to a person before a negligent act becomes actionable. In the medical profession this duty is owed to the patient. In the legal profession it is owed to the client. Teachers, as we have seen, owe a duty of care to their students which extends to protection from physical injury and may also extend to protection from emotional or mental damage. Teachers have been held responsible for their actions and their omissions. By analogy to other negligence and intentional tort actions, and by reference to various statutes, an argument can be made that this duty of care includes a duty to educate in a competent manner.

The standard of care required by a professional in fulfilling his duty has been established for many years. An English case from 1838 stated the basic requirements to be expected from any professional:

> Every person who enters into a learned profession undertakes to bring to the exercise of it a reasonable degree of care and skill . . . There may be persons who have higher education and greater advantages than he has, but he undertakes to bring a fair, reasonable and competent degree of skill. (*Lamphier v. Phipos* (1838) 8 C. & P. 475)

This concept has been approved by the Supreme Court of Canada which adopted the following standards for a professional:

> He is bound to exercise the degree of care and skill which reasonably could be expected of a normal, prudent practitioner of the same experience and standing. (*Crits v. Sylveser* [1956] O.R. 132 at 143 affirmed by the Supreme Court of Canada [1956] S.C.R. 991)

The degree of care and skill required is that of an average competent practitioner of the profession. Professionals are not expected to be "perfect" or to guarantee success. They are merely expected to be as competent as the average practitioner and to use their skills reasonably. Each licensing body sets down certain qualifications for licensing and each practitioner will therefore be expected to have these minimum qualifications. Each profession will establish its own standards of conduct for the performance of various duties. The medical profession will establish standard procedures for setting bones that should be known and followed by all doctors. The legal profession will establish standard procedures for real estate conveyancing to be followed by all lawyers. In all professions there may be situations where the normal practice is not applicable for sound professional reasons. The professional must exercise his skills and training in making such a departure and be able to justify his decision. He will not be liable for a mere error of judgment as long as it was a reasonable judgment that was made after consideration of the relevant factors.

If these standards are breached, and the client is injured in either a physical or a monetary way, the professional will be held responsible for the damage caused by his failure to do what any competent practitioner would have done. These standards are required to be proven in court at the trial of such an action and may be difficult to determine where there are conflicting views honestly held by different practitioners. Should a doctor prescribe a certain medication or another? Should he operate or try a treatment with drugs? These are matters on which there may not be any set standard but there will be guidelines to determine whether the decision was appropriate. Was the doctor aware of the contra-indications for each medicine? Did he test for any possible allergies to the one chosen? Was he aware of professional literature on the dangers of this medicine? The practitioner must make reasoned judgments using his skill and knowledge before determining his course of conduct.

Once a breach of the duty is established, it must then be proven that the breach was the causal factor for the injury sustained. Even if the doctor prescribed the wrong medicine, that may not have been the cause of the patient's complaint. The symptoms experienced by the patient may be totally unrelated to the wrong prescription and be caused by some intervening factor. The patient may have wrongfully assumed that the medication caused the subsequent symptoms. Similarly a lawyer may have given bad advice on a real estate matter but it was not that advice that led to the damages. The real estate agent may have drawn an unenforceable contract and even if the lawyer had acted correctly the result would have been the same.

A final element is that of foreseeability or remoteness of the damages. The damage incurred must be of a sort that it is reasonably foreseeable by the wrongdoer that such damage would ensue from his conduct. We have probably all seen or heard of a Rube Goldberg machine where a simple task is accomplished by a complicated series of machines. The end result is not one that would be anticipated from the initial action that set the machine in motion. Similarly, damages must not be so remote from the act as to be unforeseeable. An example of remoteness of damages could be the mental anguish suffered by the owner of a new car which is demolished by the negligence of another driver. The owner was not in the car nor was he aware of the accident until later and he suffered great emotional distress over his loss upon hearing the facts. The driver responsible for the accident will, of course, have to pay for the damaged car and any injuries sustained by the occupants but the owner's claim is too remote as to be reasonably foreseeable.

As should be apparent by now, it will be exceedingly difficult to establish these types of matters in an educational malpractice suit. What is the standard way of teaching language arts? Was it the teaching method used that led to Johnny's inability to read? How many and what types of tests should be given to determine "intelligence"? Even if it is accepted that there is a duty of care to teach, diagnose, and effect placements in a competent manner, it is exceedingly difficult to establish the requisite standard of care, proof of injury, and a causal connection between the alleged breach and the resulting injury.

Before considering whether these standards can be established for a teacher, we will first look at the leading court decisions in the area of educational malpractice.

Educational Malpractice Cases

There are a few American cases that are considered to be "leading" or precedent-setting cases in this field. Some of these have received great notoriety in the popular press and have been thoroughly scrutinized in educational and legal journals.

Perhaps the first case to receive popular attention was *Peter W. v. San Francisco Unified School District*, 131 Cal. Rptr. 854 (1976). This was a classic "failure to educate" lawsuit. The plaintiff was a high school graduate who had only a fifth grade reading and writing ability. He sued for damages for his reduced ability to earn a living. He claimed that the school had failed to diagnose his reading disability, had promoted him beyond his ability into courses in which he could not progress, and had graduated him when his abilities did not warrant it. He had spent twelve years in the defendant school district.

The California Court of Appeals stated in its judgment dismissing his claim that "classroom methodology affords no readily acceptable standards of care, or cause, or injury." Thus the plaintiff could not establish the basic elements of a negligence suit. The Court went on to state:

> The science of pedagogy itself is fraught with different and conflicting theories of how and what a child should be taught, and any layman might - and commonly does – have his own emphatic views on the subject. The "injury" claimed here is plaintiff's inability to read and write. Substantial professional authority attests that the achievement of literacy in the schools, or its failure, are influenced by a host of factors which affect the pupil subjectively, from outside the formal teaching process, and beyond the control of its ministers. They may be physical, neurological, emotional, cultural, environmental; they may be present but not perceived, recognized but not identified. We find in this situation no conceivable 'workability of a rule of care' against which the defendant's alleged conduct may be

measured . . . to 'reasonable degree of certainty that . . . the plaintiff suffered injury' within the meaning of the law of negligence . . . and no such perceptible 'connection between the defendant's conduct and the injury suffered,' as alleged, which would establish a causal link between them within the same meaning.

The essence of this decision was stated by the court in the opening lines of the majority opinion as:

The . . . question on this appeal is whether a person who claims to have been inadequately educated, while a student in a public school system, may state a cause of action in tort against the public authorities who operate and administer the system. We hold that he may not.

This case was cited with approval in *Donohue v. Copiague Union Free School District*, 391 N.E. 2d 1352 (1979) by the New York Court of Appeals faced with a similar fact situation. The plaintiff was a high school graduate who could not read or complete an employment application. The New York court held, as a matter of public policy, that claims of this sort would not be entertained at all. The result has been that failure to educate is not considered an actionable tort in many jurisdictions of the United States. The opinion of the court delivered by Judge Jasen stated:

This appeal poses the question whether a complaint seeking monetary damages for 'educational malpractice' states a cause of action cognizable in the courts.

Even a terse reading of this provision (of the state Constitution) reveals that the Constitution places the obligation of maintaining and supporting a system of public schools upon the Legislature. To be sure, this general directive was never intended to impose a duty flowing directly from a local school district to individual pupils to ensure that each pupil receives a minimum level of education, the breach of which duty would entitle a pupil to compensatory damages.

The fact that a complaint alleging 'educational malpractice' might on the pleadings state a cause of action within traditional notions of tort law does not, however, require that it be sustained. The heart of the matter is whether, assuming that such a cause of action may be stated, the courts should, as a matter of public policy entertain such claims. We believe they should not.

To entertain a cause of action for 'educational malpractice' would require the courts not merely to make judgments as to the validity of broad educational policies – a course we have unalteringly eschewed in the past – but, more importantly, to sit in review of the day-to-day implementation of these policies. Recognition in the courts of this cause of action would constitute blatant interference with the responsibility for the administration of the public school system lodged by Constitution and statute in school administrative agencies.

In a concurring opinion Judge Wachtler expressed his opinion on such claims as follows:

> I agree that complaints of 'educational malpractice' are for school administrative agencies, rather than the courts, to resolve.
>
> The practical problems raised by a cause of action sounding in educational malpractice are so formidable that I would conclude that such a legal theory should not be cognizable in our courts. These problems . . . include the practical impossibility of proving that the alleged malpractice of the teacher proximately caused the learning deficiency of the plaintiff student. Factors such as the student's attitude, motivation, temperament, past experience and home environment may all play an essential and immeasurable role in learning. Indeed as the majority observes proximate cause might 'be difficult, if not impossible, to prove.'

The New York Court of Appeals extended this immunity from action beyond "failure to educate" cases when it considered the case of *Hoffman v. Board of Education*, 400 N.E. 2d 317 (1979) which involved a child who was tested as "retarded" but was actually of normal intelligence. The school was sued for negligence in its original assessment and for its failure to follow the psychologist's recommendation to retest in two years. Here the court was presented with a case of actual misfeasance, a positive wrongdoing, rather than passive nonfeasance, doing nothing, as in Donohue.

Daniel Hoffman developed a severe speech impediment as a young child but was otherwise of normal intelligence. Four months after entering kindergarten he was assessed by a psychologist (employed by the school board) as having an I.Q. of 74. The test used was primarily verbal and the psychologist had trouble discerning Daniel's answers. His determination was, at best, an estimate of Daniel's I.Q. and he recommended a re-evaluation within two years. This was never done and Daniel remained in classes for retarded children for eleven years and was treated as a retarded child. At a manual training centre, he was tested and found to have a normal level of intelligence. He was told to go out and make it on his own without further support from the state. He suffered from depression, poor self-image, and feelings of inadequacy as a result of this treatment.

At trial, a jury awarded Daniel $750,000. The judgment was affirmed at the intermediate appeal level where the court said that "any other result would be a reproach to justice" but damages were reduced to $500,000. This court had no trouble distinguishing Peter W. and Donohue as cases of nonfeasance which were not applicable to these facts of misfeasance.

Defendant, in effect, suggests that to avoid such horrors, educational enti-ties must be insulated from the legal responsibilities and obligations com-mon to all other governmental entities no matter how seriously a particular student may have been injured and, ironically, even though such injuries were caused by their own affirmative acts in failing to follow their own rules. I see no reason for such a trade-off, on alleged policy grounds, which would warrant a denial of fair dealing to one who is injured by exempting a governmental agency from its responsibility for affirmative torts. . . If the door to 'educational torts' for nonfeasance is to be opened, it will not be by this case which involves misfeasance in failing to follow the indivi-dualized and specific prescription of the defendant's own certified psychol-ogist, whose very decision it was in the first place, to place plaintiff in a class for retarded children.

In a dissenting opinion, Justice Damiani felt that this distinction was immaterial and there was no duty owed to be breached whether it be an active or passive breach. The New York Court of Appeals, in a 4-3 decision, reversed the trial and appeal court findings. Again the Court cited public policy as prohibiting such actions:

> The policy considerations which prompted our decision in Donohue apply with equal force to allegations of educational misfeasance and nonfea-sance. In order to affirm a finding of liability in these circumstances, this court would be required to allow the finder of fact to substitute its judg-ment for the professional judgment of the board of education as to the type of psychometric devices to be used and the frequency with which such tests are to be given. Such a decision would also allow a court or jury to second-guess the determinations of each of plaintiff's teachers. To do so would open the door to an examination of the propriety of each of the pro-cedures used in the education of every student in our school system.
>
> In our view, any dispute concerning the proper placement of a child in a particular educational program can best be resolved by seeking review of such professional educational judgment through the administrative processes provided by statute.

Similar judgments have been handed down by courts throughout the United States in various circumstances. The California Court of Appeals followed its previous decision when faced with a case involving a student wrongly placed in remedial training, as opposed to being wrongfully denied the benefits of such training. In *Smith v. Alameda City Social Services Agency,* 153 Cal. Rptr. 712 (1979) this court stated:

> Appellant next seeks to set out a cause of action against the school district for negligently placing him in classes for the mentally retarded under cir-cumstances where the district allegedly knew or should have known that he was not retarded. Our decision in Peter W. is completely dispositive of

this issue.

In [Peter W.] it was alleged that the plaintiff did not receive an adequate education because he was not given proper remedial training; herein the plaintiff alleges that he did not receive an adequate education because he was improperly given remedial training. In each case, the 'duty of care' assertedly breached was that of providing appropriate educational training.

In *Hunter v. Board of Education of Montgomery County* 439 A.2d 582 (1982),the Court of Appeals of Maryland allowed a suit to proceed on the basis of an alleged intentional tort but rejected any claims for educational malpractice based on negligence. They said:

> We find ourselves in substantial agreement with the reasoning employed by the courts in Peter W. and Donohue, for an award of money damages, in our view, represents a singularly inappropriate remedy for asserted errors in the educational process. . . . Moreover, to allow petitioners' asserted negligence claims to proceed would in effect position the courts of this State as overseers of both the day-to-day operation of our educational process as well as the formulation of its governing policies. This responsibility we are loathe to impose on our courts . . . it is preferable . . . to settle disputes concerning classification and placement of students and the like by resorting to . . . informal measures than through the post hoc remedy of civil action.

The same court was faced with a similar claim against the same school board later that year in *Doe v. Board of Education of Montgomery County,* 453 A.2d 814 (1982). Obviously tired of these claims, the court's judgment begins:

> Once again we shall reject an attempt to obtain money damages as a result of alleged negligence or 'educational malpractice' in the Montgomery County school system.

The claimants in this case tried to pursue a claim of medical, as opposed to educational, malpractice since the diagnosis and testing were conducted by a psychologist employed by the Health Department. In rejecting the claim the court stated:

> . . . what we have here is not a claim for malpractice in the treatment of young Doe, but a claim that public employees improperly evaluated him for the school system and that the Board improperly placed him within the school system as a result of such evaluation.

> The Does see this case as different from Hoffman since here there are individual defendants who are alleged to have improperly evaluated young Doe. We view that as a difference without a distinction, however. . . it is for error in evaluation for purposes of educational placement, regardless of the manner in which others may see fit to characterize it, for which

plaintiffs here seek to recover.

In *D.S.W. v. Fairbanks North Star Borough School District,* 628 P.2d 554 (1981), the Supreme Court of Alaska rejected actions claiming damages for negligent classification, placement, and teaching of students suffering from dyslexia. The court reviewed other cases and agreed with the results:

> In particular we think that the remedy of money damages is inappropriate as a remedy for one who has been a victim of errors made during his or her education. The level of success which might have been achieved had the mistakes not been made will, we believe, be necessarily incapable of assessment, rendering legal cause an imponderable which is beyond the ability of courts to deal with in a reasoned way.

The plaintiffs here relied on a claim under the Alaska statute concerning the education of exceptional children but the court held that the statute provided a remedy of appeal of a placement and did not authorize a damage claim.

> The same considerations which preclude a damage claim at common law for educational malpractice preclude inferring one from the Act.

Therefore a statutory duty of care will not be construed from legislation requiring special education programs for exceptional children. A similar decision was reached in the case of *Pierce v. Board of Education of the City of Chicago,* 370 N.E.2d 535 (1977), where a student with a learning disability was not placed in special education classes despite recommendations from several physicians. The student alleged a breach of a statutory duty to place him in such a class. The decision of the Supreme Court of Illinois is summarized as:

> Statute directing school boards to establish and maintain such special education facilities as may be needed for handicapped children does not impose upon school boards a duty to place students in special education classes; ultimate responsibility for determining whether a pupil is eligible for special education rests with the State Board of Education and not with the board of education in the local district.

> Complaint which did not allege that parents of student had complied with administrative procedures established for review of school board's failure or refusal to admit the student to special education classes did not show exhaustion of administrative remedies and thus did not state cause of action against the school district for the alleged severe and permanent emotional injury suffered by the student when he was forced to compete in normal classes with students not suffering the learning disabilities he suffered.

The case of *Loughran v. Flanders* 470 F. Supp. 110 (1979) involved a boy with a learning disability seeking damages for failure to implement a special education program for him earlier in his school career; federal legislation was used as a basis for the cause of action. The United States District Court determined:

> Federal legislation in the field of special education is designed to serve two functions:
> (1) to assist the states in providing an appropriate educational opportunity for each handicapped child and
> (2) to serve as a catalyst by encouraging innovation and research in the field of special education.
> Allowing the provisions of (the statute) to serve as a basis for a private cause of action for damages would prevent the statute from ever fulfilling its catalytic function.

This immunity from action has also been extended to private, as opposed to public, schools. The Supreme Court of New York held in *Helm v. Professional Children's School* 431 N.Y.S.2d 247 (1980):

> As a matter of public policy, the courts should not entertain a cause of action in educational negligence or, as it is sometimes referred to, educational malpractice, against either public or private schools.

Another case involving a private school sought relief in the form of an action for breach of contract rather than tort. *Paladino v. Adelphi University* 454 N.Y.S.2d 868 (1982) held:

> In our view, the soundness of this policy of noninterference is equally applicable when the action is brought against a private educational institution and is formulated in contract. Professional educators – not judges – are charged with the responsibility for determining the method of learning that should be pursued for their students. When the intended results are not obtained, it is the educational community – and not the judiciary – that must resolve the problem. For, in reality, the soundness of educational methodology is always subject to question and a court ought not in hindsight, substitute its notions as to what would have been a better course of instruction to follow for a particular pupil. These are determinations that are to be made by educators and, though they are capable of error, their integrity ought not be subject to judicial inquiry. In this regard, we cannot perceive how the professional judgment of educators concerning the course of teaching a particular student in a private school, as opposed to a public school, becomes more amenable to attack in the courts. Public policy should similarly prevent a court from interfering with private schools when the controversy requires the examination of the efficacy of the course of instruction.

A recent case has summarized all of these decisions and others in arriving at a similar conclusion. An Iowa court in *Moore v. Vanderloo* 386 N.W.2d 108 (1986) set out the law as follows:

The first justification for not recognizing an educational malpractice cause of action is the lack of a satisfactory standard of care by which to measure an educator's conduct.

The second reason for refusing to recognize a claim of educational malpractice is the inherent uncertainty in determining the cause and nature of any damage.

A third justification offered for failure to recognize an educational malpractice cause of action is the resulting burden that would be placed on schools in what reasonably may be predicted to be an ensuing flood of litigation.

A fourth reason related by the courts in denying educational malpractice claims that is applicable here is that that recognizing a cause of action would force the courts to blatantly interfere with the internal operations and daily workings of an educational institution.

Finally, we refuse to interfere with legislatively defined standards of competency.

Despite this apparent unanimity in rejecting such claims, there have been a few cases which have broken through this judicial barrier. These cases are not significantly different factual situations from those discussed already but the courts have taken a different approach. Most significant, perhaps, is a decision of the New York Supreme Court, Appellate Division, where Hoffman, Donohue and others were unsuccessful.

Snow v. State of New York 469 N.Y.S.2d 959 (1983) involved a claim in which a three year old was tested to have an I.Q. of 24 and placed in a state school for nine years thereafter. It turned out that he in fact had a hearing problem and several teachers had commented that he was bright and could learn quickly. He was not re-evaluated despite these observations. The plaintiff's claim was phrased in terms of medical malpractice and the court awarded damages of $1,500,00 on this basis. The court was careful to state that this was not a case of educational malpractice:

It is clear to the Court that the malpractice, which was committed was not one of educational malpractice, but rather medical malpractice. This finding is substantiated by the very nature of the Willowbrook State School. The patients are under continuous treatment. They receive continuous medical, as well as, psychological treatment.

The allegations in Donohue v. Copiague Union Free School Dist. are pale in comparison to the reality of Donald Snow's situation. That case [Hoffman] is readily distinguishable from the instant situation in several important respects. Initially we note that there was no evidence that the original evaluation of Daniel Hoffman was conducted improperly. Secondly, the failure to have re-evaluated Daniel Hoffman's intelligence constituted a justifiable exercise of judgment in view of his teacher's daily observations regarding his lack of progress. In marked contrast, the recorded observations of Donald Snow's teachers were sufficient to have impugned the accuracy of the original diagnosis. Moreover, upon discovery of Donald's deafness, the State, having based the initial I.Q. classification upon a test designed for persons who could hear, was required to re-assess the results of that test. The failure to so act constituted a discernible act of medical malpractice on the part of the State rather than a mere error in judgment vis-a-vis claimant's educational progress. Consequently, this appeal does not involve a noncognizable claim for educational malpractice, and the Hoffman line of cases is not controlling.

A majority of the Supreme Court of Montana simply ignored the many cases cited above in the case of *B.M. v. State of Montana* 649 P.2d 425 (1982). This was an action on behalf of a 6-year-old whose I.Q. had been tested at 76 by a psychologist employed by a state mental health centre. The testing was carried out upon the recommendation of the superintendent of schools. The child was placed with other pupils who had I.Q.'s below 75 in a mainstreamed class. This was changed to a "resource room" program without the parents' consent. She was in this program for nine weeks during which a change for the worse in her behaviour was noticed. The state was sued for misplacement of the child in a program for the mentally retarded when she should not have been placed there. On appeal from a lower court it was held:

> We reverse the trial court and hold that the State is not protected by immunity and that the State has a duty to use due care in placing students in special education programs. The question of whether the State breached that duty of care and whether the breach was the cause of any injury raise material questions of fact for which a trial is necessary.
>
> The school authorities owed the child a duty of reasonable care in testing her and placing her in an appropriate special education program.

In a concurring opinion, the Chief Justice felt obliged to distinguish this from the other cases of educational malpractice which the majority had ignored in coming to their decision. He said:

> This is not a case of educational malpractice in the genre of Peter W. or Donohue, involving negligent failure to adequately educate a child in basic academic skills . . . Here the claim involves violation of mandatory statutes alleged to constitute negligence and denial of procedural due process.

Three dissenting justices could not make such a distinction and felt that the facts of this case were governed by those precedents. It is important to note that in almost every one of these educational malpractice cases there have been split decisions with strong dissenting judgments. It only requires a shift of one vote to turn around many of these cases. Often such dissenting opinions become majority opinions as times change and judicial attitudes are broadened.

The victory in B.M. was a hollow one, however, for the plaintiff ultimately lost her claim because there was no real injury suffered as a result of her placement in this program for nine weeks at the age of six. She was unable to provide expert testimony to prove causation and damages. Her case may however become a leading one in establishing the right to sue for this type of tort.

Although these American cases have no direct bearing on Canadian law and decisions, they do focus on the problems and indicate possible judicial responses should such a claim be advanced in Canada. There is one relatively obscure British decision which involved something akin to educational malpractice although it dealt with administrative negligence resulting in emotional distress. It is not a great leap in legal reasoning to apply this decision to situations like Peter W. and Donohue.

Hollands v. Canterbury City Council and Hooke (1966) Kentish Gazette, September 30 and October 28, involved an 18-year-old student who was advised by letter that she had passed all four of her final examinations and her certificate would be sent in due course. She told her friends and employer of her success only to be informed several months later that her certificate was not sent because she had failed every subject. The trial judge found in her favour on a claim for nervous shock. He said:

> I am quite satisfied on the evidence as a whole she did get into an acute nervous state of shock in the medical sense . . . Anyone who has children knows how they get worked up over their examination results. In this case she thought she had passed, and a few months later she was told she had not . . . I do think, however, that she suffered nervous shock, and on this claim I award her 50 in damages.

There appears to be no great distinction between this situation and one where the student is told he has graduated from high school and then finds out he can't read. The shock must be just as great to the student involved. The difference lies in that one is a negligent administrative error and the other involves negligent teaching. If there is to be responsibility for small clerical errors, should there not be responsibility for even greater errors in graduating students who have not attained the requisite level of skill?

There is one reported Canadian decision dealing with a situation akin to educational malpractice. In *Bales v. Board of School Trustees, School District 23 (Central Okanagan)* [1984] 8 Admin. L. R. 202, the British Columbia Supreme Court was asked to award damages for negligence as a result of the school board placing a child in a special school for the handicapped rather than in a mainstreamed classroom. The parents contended that such action deprived their son of certain benefits associated with mainstreaming in a regular classroom. The relevant portions of the judgment dealing with the negligence claim are as follows:

> Mr. and Mrs. Bales contend that the board has no authority to operate a 'segregated' school for handicapped children such as Arron. They also maintain that his assignment to such a school was without legal force and that the denial to him of an education with non-handicapped peers in the ordinary school environment constitutes a breach of the board's common law duty of care.

> In addition to a declaration of his rights and an order that the board re-enroll Arron in an ordinary primary school with a pre- determined individual educational program, Mr. and Mrs. Bales seek judgment against the board for damages in the amount of Arron's tutoring fees. The plaintiffs rely in the first instance on the duty imposed on the school board of each district by (the School Act), to 'provide sufficient school accommodation and tuition, free of charge, to all children of school age resident in that school district'. That the duty is one enforceable at law was established by our Court of Appeal in *McLeod v. Salmon Arm Bd. of Sch. Trustees.* . . . Since eligible children thus have a legal right to an education, it seems to follow that they must be entitled to one which meets some basic educational standard. If it were not so, the right would seem, for practical purposes, meaningless.

> With respect to the claim in negligence, the evidence falls short of establishing that education in a segregated environment, such as Glenn Avenue, causes harm to handicapped children, or that the program there would cause harm to Arron. It is unnecessary to discuss further the standard of care owed by school boards in the education of handicapped children. This is because the law of negligence enforces only the duty to take care to avoid causing foreseeable harm. It does not impose a duty to provide such care as will confer the greatest benefit. In the circumstances as I have found them the question whether Arron ought to receive the benefits which integration is thought to provide in the education of the handicapped is not a question which a Court may decide.

This case is noteworthy in that it recognizes a duty of care in the education of children. That duty of care is to avoid causing foreseeable harm through the education program provided. The burden of proving that actual harm has been done is on the plaintiff and in this case, the plaintiffs were unable to meet that burden. The case also establishes the principle that students are entitled to an education which meets some basic educational standard. The court did not, however, define that standard. In any event, the claim was not summarily dismissed, as has been done in most United States decisions.

A strong case can be argued that such educational malpractice suits should be recognized. There are, no doubt, serious problems in proving such a case but there are just as certainly some cases that cry out for this type of remedy.

Can Educational Malpractice be Established as a Tort?

To determine whether a case of educational malpractice can be established we will look at each of the elements of negligence and see how they relate to the school situation. We will turn our attention firstly to the concept of a legal duty of care.

Do teachers and school boards owe students a duty of care to protect them from intellectual harm or damage as a result of their actions? The judge in the Bales case indicated that there was such a duty and an analysis of this concept seems to indicate that this is the correct response. The question of "to whom" a duty is owed has been discussed in many cases over many centuries and has resulted in the following recent statement as to the present status of the common law: ". . . the position has now been reached that in order to establish that a duty of care arises in a particular situation, it is not necessary to bring the facts of that situation within those of previous situations in which a duty of care has been held to exist. Rather the question has to be approached in two stages. First one has to ask whether, as between the alleged wrongdoer and the person who has suffered damage there is a sufficient relationship of proximity or neighbourhood such that, in the reasonable contemplation of the former, carelessness on his part may be likely to cause damage to the latter – in which case a prima facie duty of care arises. Secondly, if the first question is answered affirmatively, it is necessary to consider whether there are any considerations which ought to negative, or to reduce or limit the scope of the duty or the class of persons to whom it is owed or the damage to which a breach of it may give rise. . . . (Lord Wilberforce of the House of Lords in *Anns v. Merton London Borough Council* [1977] 2 W.L.R. 1024)"

The present approach to determining whether a duty exists is to start with the assumption that it does and then leave it to the defendant to establish that that he is entitled to some exception from the general rule. In order for the assumption of a duty to arise all the plaintiff has to show is a "sufficient relationship" and some damage.

The proximity of the relationship between a teacher and student is obvious. Who else would suffer harm if the teacher does not teach in a competent manner or carry out assessments in a professional way? Any reasonable person can see that if the teacher is inadequate, incompetent or negligent, the student is the one who will suffer harm. Even courts which have dismissed such claims on public policy grounds have recognized this duty. In Peter W. the court observed:

> Of course, no reasonable observer would be heard to say that these facts did not impose upon defendants a 'duty of care' within any common meaning of the term; given the commanding importance of public education in society, we state a truism in remarking that the public authorities who are dutybound to educate are also bound to do it with 'care'. . . .

The existence of such a duty was forcefully argued in a dissenting judgment in the Hunter case:

> In my view, public educators are professionals. They have special training and state certification is a prerequisite to their employment. They hold themselves out as possessing certain skills and knowledge not shared by non-educators. As a result, people who utilize their services have a right to expect them to use that skill and knowledge with some minimum degree of competence. In addition, like other professionals, they must often make educated judgments in applying their knowledge to specific individual needs. As professionals, they owe a professional duty of care to children who receive their services and a standard of care based upon customary conduct is appropriate. There can be no question that negligent conduct on the part of a public educator may damage a child by inflicting psychological damage and emotional distress. Moreover, from the fact that public educators purport to teach it follows that some causal relationship may exist between the conduct of a teacher and the failure of a child to learn. Thus, it should be possible to maintain a viable tort action against such professionals for educational malpractice . . . In recognizing a cause of action for educational malpractice, this Court would do nothing more than what courts have traditionally done from time immemorial – namely provide a remedy to a person harmed by the negligent act of another. Our children deserve nothing less.

Further support in favour of the existence of such a duty can be found in cases involving physical injuries to students. Most of these cases centre around the duty to supervise or maintain safe premises but there have been some cases that deal with the issue of a duty to teach.

McKay v. Board of Govan School Unit No. 29 (1967) 62 D.L.R.2d 503 rev'd (1968) 68 D.L.R.2d 519 involved a student who was seriously injured in a gymnasium accident. At trial the jury found a failure in duty of care due to "Lack of competent instruction" and "Instructor not sufficiently qualified" among others. The Saskatchewan Court of Appeal found a positive duty to provide instruction:

> The work Molesky was doing as each pupil mounted the bars was more than just supervisory in a general sense. It involved the direction and instruction of this one pupil in a special individual exercise. The question posed then is as to what standard of conduct is to be expected where a teacher is giving individual supervision and instruction as here . . . A physical training instructor in directing or supervising an evolution or exercise is bound to exercise the skill and competence of an ordinarily competent instructor in the field.

On appeal to the Supreme Court of Canada this decision was reversed but that Court expressed doubts as to whether the "careful parent" test was the only measure of duty:

> . . . I am not satisfied that this definition (the careful parent test) is of universal application, particularly in cases where a schoolmaster is required to instruct or supervise the activities of a great number of pupils at one time. . .

In *James v. River East School Division No. 9* (1976) 64 D.L.R.3d 338 the trial judge found liability in part for failure to teach properly:

> I find here a failure to instruct properly, a failure to caution and to supervise properly and that an unfortunate and foreseeable accident occurred, and that it could have been avoided if the defendants had not been negligent and if Mr. Peniuk had not omitted to do what he should have done in the circumstances.

On appeal this failure to instruct properly was upheld as the basis for a negligence claim:

> In the case at bar, there was a failure to instruct properly; the students were not advised of possible danger . . . , the apparent contradictions . . . were not cleared up, the hazard . . . was not brought to the attention of the class, and students were not cautioned adequately about the danger . . . All these factors constituted negligence within the classic meaning of that term. . . .

Thornton v. Board of School Trustees of School District No. 57 (Prince George) [1976] 5 W.W.R. 240 var'd [1978] 2 S.C.R. 267 dealt with the issue of proper instruction and treated it as being just as important as supervision and proper equipment in imposing liability:

In my view of the factually relevant cases, what it does mean is that it is not negligence or breach of the duty of care on the part of the school authorities to permit a pupil to undertake to perform an aerial front somersault off a springboard: (a) if it is suitable to his age and condition (mental and physical); (b) if he is progressively trained and coached to do it properly and avoid the danger; (c) if the equipment is adequate and suitably arranged; and (d) if the performance, having regard to its inherently dangerous nature, is properly supervised. These are the component criteria constituting the appropriate duty or standard of care which is saddled upon the school authorities . . . the instructor was busy doing paper work at a nearby desk and gave no instructions or cautions, no training, no demonstration and no immediate supervision. The emphasis on individual responsibility and initiative seems to have displaced instruction and supervision.

Smith v. Horizon Aero Sports Ltd. (1981) 130 D.L.R.3d 97 involved a parachute accident to an adult student in a privately run class. The British Columbia Supreme Court found that the same teacher-student relationship existed in this case as exists in a public school setting. The teacher's duty in such relationships was held to be:

The defendants knew that they had an obligation both to teach and to ensure that the plaintiff had learned the techniques. That obligation is owed not simply to the class as a whole but individually to each member . . . . Applying the tests proposed (in Thornton) I have reached the conclusion that the defendant Kinsey (the instructor) . . . failed to use reasonable care to teach the plaintiff . . . There was insufficient testing and questioning to ensure that she grasped the essentials of the jump thoroughly enough to perform it safely.

By analogy to the school system this case would seem to imply that teachers must not only teach competently but must also ensure that the student is learning what is being taught. This is done by adequate testing of the student to determine if he understands the basics of what has been taught.

Hoar v. Board of School Trustees, District 68 (Nanaimo) and Haynes [1984] 6 W.W.R. 143, an accident involving a student in a school shop class, held a teacher liable for failing to instruct an individual student in the proper use of a particular machine. The trial judge stated:

He can be faulted in only one particular but that is a vital particular. Since he thought it essential to give demonstrations it follows that it was essential that the demonstrations be received by each student and I hold that he bore responsibility to check to make sure that the demonstrations were received by absent students.

The Court of Appeal upheld this decision with several justices expressing their opinions:

> Instruction in their use is of critical importance to the safety of the students.

> I consider that it was his obligation to see to it that this 17-year-old plaintiff did not operate any of those machines without instruction in their use.

All of these cases show that there is a duty imposed on teachers to instruct in a competent way so as to avoid the risk of physical injury. It is only a short step in legal reasoning to extend this duty to other types of damage. Given that the whole raison d'etre of the schools is to provide an education, it is difficult to comprehend why educators would owe a duty of care in respect to physical safety and well-being of the student but would not owe a duty to safeguard his intellectual and emotional well-being. If the teacher's duty is merely to protect the children from physical injury, the school is relegated to a role of "super babysitter."

Additional support in finding such a duty of care in educational malpractice claims may be found in legislation such as Alberta's Bill 59 or the Saskatchewan *Education Act* discussed previously, as well as in the codes of professional conduct. Teachers are subject to dismissal and decertification for incompetence; therefore they have some sort of duty to be competent and perform their teaching assignments in a competent manner.

An argument often advanced against finding such a duty of care in malpractice cases is that the educational system confers a benefit on the student and there is no duty to ensure that such a benefit is received and no liability for failure to confer that benefit. This was expressed in the Bales case discussed above as:

> . . .the law of negligence enforces only the duty to take care to avoid causing foreseeable harm. It does not impose a duty to provide such care as will confer the greatest benefits.

An answer to this can be derived from an analogy to the duty owed in cases of a rescue. A person who is drowning, like a student entering school, is in peril from the outset and will receive a benefit if his rescue is undertaken. The common law imposes no duty to undertake this rescue except in certain circumstances. However, once a person decides to undertake this rescue, there is a duty of care imposed to act reasonably in the circumstances. Similarly a teacher (in undertaking to confer the benefit of an education) has no duty to succeed in overcoming the many obstacles but must act reasonably along the way and use whatever resources and alternatives available to him in accomplishing the task.

Assuming, therefore, that the first part of the test proposed by Lord Wilberforce can be met, we must look at the second part to determine if there are any considerations which should limit or negate this prima facie duty. The most relevant area for this inquiry is public policy. Even though a prima facie duty can be said to exist, should this duty be negated because of reasons of public policy? This has been the attitude adopted in many of the American decisions.

We will explore the rationale behind these decisions and see what counter arguments can be advanced.

Should Educational Malpractice be Actionable?

The failure to recognize this tort action raises the question of whether the courts have failed to fulfill their social role of redressing wrongfully inflicted injuries and deterring socially harmful conduct. We recognize that teachers have an obligation to educate their pupils but what use is this duty when we fail to provide a remedy for its breach?

It would appear obvious that a student will suffer harm if he is knowingly or negligently taught false information, has his self-confidence shattered by insult or ridicule, or is taught in an incomprehensible manner (or not at all). There is also a broader societal loss when a student is improperly educated. There is wide-spread dissatisfaction by parents and students with our schools and a growing trend towards accountability in education. Once the courts are convinced that the consequences of miseducation are important, then the logic of legal reasoning should dictate that the same common law principles that apply to medical malpractice or negligence in the gymnasium should be applied to the classroom learning situation.

The reluctance to entertain such suits is primarily based on grounds of "public policy." The "flood of litigation" argument that has been raised in many of these cases assumes that students will sue their competent and caring teachers with willful abandon should such cases be allowed. This is based on a type of "devil" theory about child nature (that is not supported by research) and on misconceptions about the ease of utilizing the legal process. Infants may not commence proceedings on their own but must have a guardian or "next friend" commence proceedings on their behalf. Litigation is expensive and time-consuming; these facts will inhibit most frivolous and speculative lawsuits. Any action being seriously pursued in the courts would be based on a deeply felt wrong, supported by substantial evidence.

Even a flood of spurious lawsuits would not justify denying a remedy to those with legitimate claims. The rash of medical malpractice claims has caused some doctors to request a ban on all such actions, but this notion is not seriously entertained by the courts or legislators. A court decision refusing to exempt doctors from negligence claims has equal applicability to teachers:

> Why should the medical profession be deemed to have placed upon it 'an unreasonable burden' anymore than any other profession where malpractice may be charged? What statute or theory of law grants preferential treatment or immunity to the medical profession? The court is the guardian of the rights of all the citizenry, not only of a chosen few . . . To use the worn-out, rejected cliche of "public policy" is to single out and grant preferential treatment to the medical profession over all other professions and enterprises where malpractice could result in payment of ensuing resultant damages. This was never truly contemplated by either the general public, the Legislature or the Court. This Court further believes that contrary to the fear . . . as to 'fraudulent claims' or a 'sensible stopping point', that the Judiciary can intelligently sift the wheat from the chaff and that it has the ability to succinctly deal with any fraudulent scheme or claim and make short shrift thereof. (*Park v. Chessin* (1976)387 N.Y.S.2d 204)

This argument about opening the doors to numerous lawsuits was also considered by a Canadian court in a case involving an action by a university student claiming he had not been taught in accordance with the advertised description of a course. In *Chicoine v. Ryerson Polytechnical Institute* (1985) 15 Admin L. R. 261 (Ontario Prov. Ct.) it was held:

> The Court has not been swayed by the arguments of the defendant that allowing this action to proceed will "open the floodgates" to unhappy students.

The courts have opted to leave questions of teacher negligence to be dealt with by administrative procedures. Schools often do not provide parents and students with formal administrative procedures for solving their grievances. There may be certain procedures established for placement of handicapped children in some provinces but there is often no way that a parent can complain about the competence of the instruction (as opposed to the program of instruction). Professional bodies and provincial departments usually deal with questions of competency and licensing but not in a way that provides any redress for harm already done.

The failure to provide a judicial remedy removes pressure on the school systems to provide internal procedures for resolution of conflicts. Internal administrative actions may be attacked on procedural grounds, thus bringing the issue into court to determine if proper procedures have been followed. It is easier then, not to have any internal grievance procedures. The deterrent effect of tort law becomes ineffective in regard to negligent teaching practices. Transgressors know that there is no redress in the courts and therefore do not have an incentive to improve.

By granting students who are educationally harmed the same right of action that exists for students who are physically harmed or patients psychologically harmed by an incompetent psychiatrist, teachers will be reminded that the educational process requires a degree of care, competence, and effort on their part.

Point/Counterpoint

There have been numerous articles written in both legal and educational periodicals concerning educational malpractice. Some authors see the recognition of such a cause of action resulting in improved education. Others see the potential cost of such actions as weakening the educational system. We present a brief selection of different views and invite you to debate the merits of the recognition of "educational malpractice" as a legal cause of action.

Opposed

Reflection upon the governmental nature of public education should reveal the detriment of creating a tort of educational malpractice. To create such a tort implies that the law should also create torts to compensate persons who claim some loss because of inefficient police patrol, tardy court administration, or inflationary management of the money supply. Despite the sympathy felt for injured crime victims, frustrated plaintiffs, and poor persons with fixed incomes, they are not allowed to sue constables, magistrates, or central bankers. Some important reasons not to permit such suits are the risk of error which derives from the multiplicity of causes of loss and the problematic nature of proof of cause in fact, the unforeseeability of many losses, and judicial incompetence to formulate, articulate, and promulgate measures of adequate governmental conduct when little consensus exists as to what are good or bad practices, and when many factions propose very different standards about which there is heated ethical, technical, and political controversy. The common theme underlying these reasons is the inappropriateness of courts to determine such issues. But more importantly, to allow educational malpractice suits contradicts the bases of representative government. (Patrick D. Halligan, "The Function of Schools, The Status of Teachers, and the Claims of the Handicapped: An Inquiry into Special Education Malpractice," (1980) 45 Missouri Law Review 667 at 669)

This article will examine the present case law on educational malpractice.

It will then analyze each of the principal theoretical bases that have been advanced to support an educational malpractice cause of action: contract, misrepresentation, constitutional right, and negligence. It is the article's thesis that, for one reason or another, each of these theories is logically unsound and inadequate to support the desired cause of action. In each case, the theory advanced either proceeds from an inapposite analogy or requires an unjustified extension or distortion of present doctrine. Moreover, even if a legally sufficient justification for recognizing a cause of action for educational malpractice could be found, compelling considerations of public policy argue against such recognition. (Richard Funston, "Educational Malpractice: A Cause of Action in Search of a Theory" (1981) 18 San Diego Law Review 743 at 748)

In Favour

Nevertheless, judges cannot be expected to remain indifferent to the suffering caused by poor teaching or careless placement, or to ignore shallow and half-hearted attempts by the profession to prevent such malfeasance. The legal arguments supporting educational malpractice, particularly those grounded on justice for the individual, are sound, and advocacy to recognize educational malpractice as a legal solution for injured children will therefore continue. (B. Glen Epley, "Educational Malpractice: The Threat and Challenge," (1985) 50 The Educational Forum 57 at 63)

There is little doubt that educational malpractice will continue as a subject for judicial consideration. A frustrated public continues to seek the ultimate solution to the problem of declining effectiveness of schools, and the courtroom provides an avenue for redress to dissatisfied parents and students. Situations such as those in *Peter W.* and *Donohue* should not exist. Schools must be held responsible to students who, like the plaintiffs in these cases, attended and progressed through twelve years of schooling, earned a diploma, and then were unable to secure and sustain employment because of their poor academic backgrounds.

A trend towards holding schools responsible for their students' learning can be seen in accountability and CBE (Competency Based Education) movements. No court has yet addressed the educational malpractice issue in a jurisdiction with accountability or CBE statutes. Arguments that can be made in support of holding school districts liable will be substantially strengthened if a statute of this type applies to the defendant school district.

The time is right for judicial intervention in upgrading educational standards. Malpractice by school districts cannot be allowed to continue. The courts are proper arbiters, and dismissal of such actions only perpetuates the status quo. If schools are to continue to be responsible for the general education of children, they must be held to this duty and must be liable for its breach. (Nancy L. Woods, "Educational Malfeasance: A New Cause of Action for Failure to Educate?" (1978) 14 Tulsa Law Journal 383 at 409)

The policy considerations articulated in *Hunter* and *Doe* do not justify a complete bar against all educational malpractice claims. By recognizing the distinction between inadequate education claims and negligent evaluation claims and by limiting the recovery to remedial tutoring, the court could resolve the policy and practical problems associated with allowing this new tort. In addition to examining the practical difficulties in recognizing such claims, the court also should consider that its traditional role is to provide a forum for aggrieved litigants and not to protect the state school system completely from liability for negligent conduct. (Comment, *Hunter v. Board of Education & Doe v. Board of Education* – No Cause of Action for Educational Malpractice Against Public School Teachers and Psychologists. (1983) 42 Maryland Law Review 582 at 595)

Discussion and Review Questions

1. What are the two major categories of educational malpractice suits?
2. What are the basic elements of a successful suit for educational malpractice?
3. How has the continuing professionalization of the Canadian teacher influenced the outcomes of educational malpractice suits?
4. In your judgement, what criteria would be used to determine the level of service required from a competent teacher?
5. Should Canadian school systems be shielded by legislation from charges of educational malpractice which could be brough forward in many instances by unscrupulous parents who are seeking an easy income?

You be the Judge

The Pitiful Case of Peter W.

Peter attended schools in the same district for 13 years and received a high school diploma. He has an above average I.Q., attended school regularly and presented no discipline problems. His grades throughout school were average and he did not fail or repeat any courses.

His parents made inquiries on several occasions but were assured that Peter was doing well and that he required no remedial instruction in any subjects.

Following his graduation, Peter found that he could not complete a simple job application form and so he went for an independent assessment of his abilities. It was found that he was "functionally illiterate" and could only read at a grade 5 level. There is no indication of any type of learning disability.

Questions for Discussion

1. Did the school system owe Peter a duty to teach him in a competent manner?

2. Did the school system owe Peter a duty to diagnose the level of his reading ability?

3. Can the courts determine appropriate standards for instruction?

4. Should Peter have been given a high school diploma when his achievement did not warrant it?

5. Should school systems, as a matter of public policy, be exposed to lawsuits from students such as Peter who have "failed to learn"?

The Gruesome Case of the Non-Graduate

Grace was an 18-year-old student who completed high school and wrote departmental examinations. She despaired of passing and being able to go on to college. Imagine her relief when she received a letter informing her that she had passed all subjects and would be receiving her certificate in the mail.

Armed with this letter she enrolled in a junior college course. The registrar kept inquiring as to the whereabouts of her certificate. Grace finally called the school authorities to see where it was and was abruptly informed that she would not be getting a certificate since she had failed every examination.

Grace went into a state of nervous shock and was unable to continue her college course. She sued for damages for her emotional distress.

Questions for Discussion

1. Are school authorities liable for negligent misrepresentations that they may make to their students?

2. Was there any reason for Grace to get so upset, after all she didn't think she would pass in the first place?

3. Should schools be liable for intentionally telling students things that they know are false?

The Delinquent Diagnosis of Daniel H.

Daniel developed a severe speech impediment as a young child but was otherwise of normal intelligence. Four months after entering kindergarten he was assessed by a psychologist employed by the school board as having an I.Q. of 74. The test used was primarily a verbal one and the psychologist had trouble discerning Daniel's answers. His determination was at best an estimate of Daniel's I.Q. and therefore he recommended that further testing be done within two years.

This was never done and thus Daniel remained in classes for retarded children for a period of eleven years and was treated as a retarded child. At a manual training centre he was finally re-tested and found to have a normal level of intelligence. Since he was now 18 years of age and no longer "retarded" he was told to go out and make it on his own.

Daniel suffered from depression, poor self-image, and feelings of inadequacy as a result of this treatment. He would require extensive remedial instruction and speech therapy.

Questions for Discussion

1. Was the board negligent in not re-testing Daniel despite their own psychologist's recommendation that this be done within two years?

2. Should the courts impose standards on school boards for evaluating students?

3. How should disputes regarding classification and placement of students be resolved?

4. Should psychologists be held to a different standard of conduct than teachers in performing learning ability related diagnoses?

The Entangling Case of the Erroneous Evaluation

At the age of three Donald was tested by a psychologist employed by the local health authorities and found to have an I.Q. of 24. As a result of this testing he was placed in a school for the retarded and remained there for nine years thereafter.

Teachers in the school commented on how bright Donald appeared to be and how quickly he could learn the routine tasks that were taught to the children. Despite these observations no further testing was done.

Donald's parents finally arranged for independent testing which revealed that Donald in fact had a severe hearing impairment and was of above average intelligence.

Questions for Discussion

1. Is this case in any way substantially different from that of Daniel H.?
2. Does the diagnosis involved herein raise a question of medical malpractice or educational malpractice?
3. Were the teachers negligent in not requesting further testing?
4. Were the teachers negligent in not detecting the fact that Donald had a hearing impairment?

The Traumatic Case of the Terminated Teaching

Sam and Dave were two students suffering from dyslexia. Both attended the same school.

Sam was in his second year of grade 6 before his disability was detected. He was given special courses for about a year before the courses were terminated despite the board's awareness that the problem had not been overcome.

Dave was diagnosed as dyslexic in the first grade but did not receive special training until the fifth grade. This continued for just under two years when it too was terminated with full knowledge that he had not been adequately trained to overcome the disability.

The board was in a jurisdiction that had passed legislation requiring special needs students to be given an appropriate education suitable to their needs. The legislation provided for an internal appeal procedure to be followed if parents were not satisfied with the placement.

Both boys sued for their loss of an education, loss of future opportunities of employment, and loss of future income and earning ability.

Questions for Discussion

1. Can monetary damages compensate these boys for their loss?
2. Can the dollar amount of compensation that is required or justified be ascertained?
3. Is an internal appeal procedure rather than legal action a more suitable method of resolving these types of disputes than legal action? Explain your answer?
4. Is money a proper substitute for a good education?

References

Canadian Articles (Legal Periodicals)

Foster, W.F., "Educational Malpractice: A Tort for the Untaught?" (1985) 19 *U.B.C. Law Rev.* 161.

Janisch, H., "Educational Malpractice: Legal Liability for Failure to Educate" (1980) 38 *The Advocate* 491.

MacKay, A.W., "Case Comment: Bales v. Bd. of Sch. Trustees: Parents, School Boards and Reasonable Special Education" (1984) 8 *Admin. L.R.* 225.

Canadian Articles (Educational Periodicals)

Covert, J.R., "The Profession of Teaching: A Reply to Professor Foster." (1987) *Canadian Journal of Education,* 12(1), 214-217.

Foster, W.F., "Educational Malpractice: Educate or Litigate," (1986) *Canadian Journal of Education,* 11(2), 122-151.

Foster, W.F., "Educational Malpractice: A Rejoinder," (1987) *Canadian Journal of Education,* 12(1), 218-227.

Kimmins, R., Hunter, W.J., & MacKay A.W., "Educational Legislation and Litigation Pertaining to the Practice of School Psychology in Canada," (1985) *Canadian Journal of School Psychology,* 1, 1-10.

Martin, Y.M., & Nicholls, A.C., "Teacher Competence – emerging legal criteria," *The Canadian School Executive,* December, 1983, 20-21.

O'Reilly, R.O., "Still No Malpractice Suits in Special Education in Canada or the United States," (1985) *Canadian Journal for Exceptional Children,* 2(1), 22-24.

Struthers, Steve, "Law Wars: The Right to an Adequate Education," *Resource News,* October, 1984.

American Articles (Legal Periodicals)

Elson, J., "A Common Law Remedy for the Educational Harms Caused by Incompetent or Careless Teaching" (1978) 73 *Northwestern Univ. L. Rev.* 641.

Engh, C., "Implications of Minimum Competency Legislation: A Legal Duty of Care?" (1979) 10 *Pacific Law Journal* 947.

Funston, R., "Educational Malpractice: A Cause of Action in Search of a Theory" (1981) 18 *San Diego L. Rev.* 743.

Halligan, P.D., "The Function of Schools, The Status of Teachers, and the Claims of the Handicapped: An Inquiry into Special Education Malpractice" (1980) 45 *Missouri Law Rev.* 667.

Tracy, D.S., "Educational Negligence: A Student's Cause of Action for

Incompetent Academic Instruction" (1980) 58 *N. Carolina Law Rev.* 561.

Wallison, E.J., "Nonliability for Negligence in Public Schools – 'Educational Malpractice' from Peter W. to Hoffman" (1980) 55 *Notre Dame Lawyer* 814.

White, C.M., "Educational Malpractice and Handicapped Students" (1985) *Brigham Young Univ. L. Rev.* 297.

Woods, N.L., "Educational Malfeasance: A New Cause of Action for Failure to Educate?" (1978) 14 *Tulsa Law Journal* 383.

"Hunter v. Board of Education & Doe v. Board of Education – No Cause of Action for Educational Malpractice Against Public School Teachers and Psychologists" (1983) 42 *Maryland Law Rev.* 582.

"Educational Malpractice" (1976) 124 *Univ. Pennsylvania Law Rev.* 755.

"Is There a Case for Failure to Educate?" *TRIAL*, February, 1987, 81-84.

American Articles (Educational Periodicals)

Epley, B. Glen, "Educational Malpractice: The Threat and the Challenge," *The Educational Forum,* Vol. 50, No. 1, Fall 1985, 57.

Flygare, Thomas J., "Another State Rejects 'Educational Malpractice' Suit," *Phi Delta Kappan,* May 1983, 631.

Leary, James L., ". . . But these six factors have reduced the threat of education malpractice suits," *The American School Board Journal,* March 1987, 33.

Reitz, Donald J., "Malpractice in the schools," *Momentum*, February 1984, 50.

Part Four

Civil Rights Problems

13

Civil Rights
from the Student's Perspective

Learning Objectives

Some of the things that you will learn from reading this chapter include the following:

1. The relationship between the common-law principle that the teacher acts *in loco parentis* and the teacher's authority with respect to the presence or absence of students rights.

2. The encompasing legal consequence of such words as "everyone" when used in the Charter respecting the rights of Canadians, especially school children.

3. That the Charter addresses the relationship among governments and between governments and individual citizens, and perhaps does not fully address the relationship between teacher and student.

4. The possible education management consequences of the Charter words, "such reasonable limits prescribed by law as can be demonstrably justified in a free and democratic society."

5. The possible consequences for student rights of the Charter section which states that provincial legislation can be enacted which is declared to not be subject to the provisions of the Charter.

6. The current legal interpretations of the Charter as they relate to student rights.

7. What Canadian courts consider to be reasonable standards of discipline and conduct in the school.

8. That the teacher's role *in loco parentis* may be fading.
9. That the fundamental freedoms of conscience and religion appear to cause the most conflict between home and Canadian schools.
10. The possible implications of the Charter on student searches and detentions.

Preview

The *Charter of Rights and Freedoms* has brought into focus the question of the degree to which the basic freedoms enunciated in the Charter and enjoyed by the citizenry at large, can be enforced and enjoyed by children in the school setting.

To date the number of Canadian cases involving student rights are few in number, but as legal interpretations of the *Charter of Rights and Freedoms* begin to define the impact of the legislation upon the teacher and school administrator, school systems should anticipate new and increased numbers of challenges to their authority to manage their schools. The role of teacher when acting *in loco parentis*, that is, in the place of the parent or guardian, may be fading, but Canadian courts still appear to be sensitive to the need for reasonable standards of discipline and conduct within the school setting.

In any case, question concerning the fundamental freedoms of conscience and religion seem to create the most litigation. Although the freedom of religion does not as yet appear to be an absolute one, the problem of reaching some kind of conclusion is difficult since the religion referred to in the recorded cases is the religion of the parent involved, and not that of the child. For teachers, the problem continues.

Freedom of expression rights have generally been tested through challenges to school board initiated dress regulations. It seems clear that school boards have established their right to pass reasonable regulations concerning habits of order, obedience, courtesy, grooming and other matters which courts seem to feel are necessary for the proper administration and management of school affairs.

In challenges under the freedom of assembly, freedom of association, and liberty sections of the Charter, the courts once again tend to favour the schools if these rights appear to be interfered with for the purposes of sound administration and management of educational affairs.

Self-Assessment

1. Upon what bases may children be excluded from participation in patriotic or religious exercises?
2. Is the practice of Transcendental Meditation allowed in schools?
3. Does the freedom of conscience and religion extend to the student's right to wear religious symbols which may be potentially dangerous to other children?
4. May students distribute religious materials in schools?
5. Can a school board enforce a set of student dress regulations? If so, what kind of clothing regulations would probably be upheld?
6. Can the school principal limit student movement within school for the purpose of restricting which students will meet with which other students?
7. What does the *Charter of Rights and Freedoms* say about the right to privacy?
8. Can underground newspapers be banned in schools?
9. Do students have the right to remain silent?
10. Why do parents have a right to infringe upon the Charter rights of their children? Does not the Charter refer to everyone?

Key Terms

In loco parentis
Dicta

*   *   *   *

There have been very few Canadian cases involving issues of student rights in comparison to the situation in the United States. The *Charter of Rights and Freedoms* would seem to provide new rights to students and therefore its passage could result in a new round of court challenges to the school authorities. The emphasis of this chapter will be on the rights and freedoms enumerated in the *Charter* and how they have and may be interpreted within the school context. Provincial human rights legislation also provides certain rights to students and provides another source of challenge to the schools. We will therefore look at some decisions involving provincial legislation as well.

The format of this chapter will be to identify potential student rights using the outline of the *Charter* as a guide with the addition of other potential rights that are not specifically enumerated therein. The *Charter of Rights and Freedoms* is included as Appendix A to this chapter. Some reference will be made to American case law to see how an issue has been decided in that jurisdiction. Present indications are that Canadian courts will not go as far as their United States counterparts in extending rights to students.

Before pursuing this topic further, we must first consider whether students have, or are entitled to, the basic rights and freedoms guaranteed by the *Charter* and provincial legislation. Historically children have been regarded as the property of their parents and as dependants. Accordingly they were not accorded independent rights of their own. School authorities have been regarded as acting *in loco parentis* and not as agents of the government in their dealings with pupils.

The status of children's rights in relation to the school is far from clear even at this point. There has been a movement away from the total denial of any independent rights to students but full adult rights have not yet been accorded to minors in many situations.

The wording used in the *Charter* seems to imply that the rights and freedoms guaranteed therein reside with children as well as with adults. The terms used are "everyone," "every individual," and "anyone." There is no specific reference to age or exclusion of minors in this wording. Indeed, s. 15 of the *Charter* specifically prohibits discrimination on the basis of age; therefore, it is logical to conclude that it was intended to apply (and should apply) with equal protection to both adults and children.

In the United States, students have been recognized as possessing full constitutional rights. In the case of *Tinker v. Des Moines* 393 U.S. 503 (1969) it was stated:

> Students in school as well as out of school are "persons" under our Constitution. They are possessed of fundamental rights which the state must respect.

In Canada, children have been confirmed as being persons within the terms of the *Charter* for purposes of criminal proceedings and they are entitled to all the adult legal rights when charged with a criminal offence. The issue of whether they have additional rights has yet to be addressed by our courts. Until some student asserts through the courts that he is possessed of a certain right which has been denied by the school, we will not have a definitive answer to this question.

We can also approach the issue of whether students are entitled to

Charter rights by referring to section 32 of the *Charter* which defines what bodies are bound by the provisions of the document. Only governments are subject to the provisions of the *Charter* and not private individuals. Parents, for example, do not have to accord any of the rights and freedoms of the *Charter* to their children. If schools are considered to be acting *in loco parentis*, then they too would be exempt from the provisions of the *Charter*.

If, on the other hand, schools are engaged in administering governmental functions then they would be subject to the *Charter* provisions and would be required to respect the rights and freedoms guaranteed to students by the *Charter*. Students would receive the full benefit of *Charter* protection in all dealings with the school. This could have very broad implications, especially in matters of student discipline.

The issue of whether schools are bound by the *Charter* has been considered in a few Canadian cases although the answer is far from conclusive. In *R. v. H.* (1985) 43 Alta. L. R. (2d) 250, a decision from the Alberta Provincial Court, Judge Russell stated:

> I am of the view that Parliament intended to extend the application of the *Charter* to include bodies such as school boards exercising a delegated legislative authority. I am satisfied that teachers and principals who are employees of school boards are governed by the provisions of the *Charter*.

On appeal, Justice Dechene did not specifically rule on the application of the *Charter* to teachers and principals but indicated as *dicta* that he would have found it not to apply.

The Ontario Court of Appeal was confronted with the issue in *R. v. J.M.G.* (1986) 33 D.L.R. (4th) 277, but declined to deal with it directly. Justice Grange stated:

> I do not find it necessary to decide this difficult issue. I am prepared for the purposes of this appeal to assume that the school board directing the affairs of the school and the school itself, including the principal and the other teachers, are subject to the *Charter* in their actions and dealings with the students under their care.

Despite the lack of judicial authority directly on point it is reasonable to assume that students will be provided some protection under the *Charter*. The extent of the protection has yet to be determined, but in the final analysis it will always be modified by the provision of section 1 of the *Charter* which provides that any of the enumerated rights and freedoms are subject to "such reasonable limits prescribed by law as can be demonstrably justified in a free and democratic society." For example, limitations on students rights can be imposed due to their age and the need for discipline in the school. The burden will be on the government to justify the imposition of such limits and prove that they are reasonable.

The *Charter* contains another section which may severely limit student rights should any government seek to avail itself of the provision. Section 33 of the *Charter* provides that Parliament or a provincial legislature may declare that any legislation shall not be subject to the provisions of section 2 and sections 7 to 15 of the *Charter*. Although it is unlikely that this provision will be used to any great extent, it could become a tool with which to remove the administration of schools from the protection of the *Charter* if the government feels that interpretations concerning the extent of student rights have gone too far. Thus, a province could declare that its *School Act* is to operate notwithstanding the provisions of the *Charter* and effectively remove any student rights.

Freedom of Conscience and Religion

Of all the fundamental freedoms enumerated in the *Charter*, those of conscience and religion seem to have provoked the most conflict between schools and homes over the years. Even before the *Charter* was enacted there were confrontations between parents seeking "freedom of religion" and school boards imposing mandatory religious exercises.

During World War II there was a strong mood of nationalism and patriotism throughout Canada, which contributed to a pair of interesting "flag salute" cases involving children of Jehovah's Witnesses. At the time there was, of course, no guarantee of religious freedom as found in our new *Charter*.

The first of these cases occurred in Alberta when two children were dismissed from school for their refusal to salute the flag. In *Ruman v. Board of Trustees of Lethbridge School District* [1943] 3 W.W.R. 340 (S.C. of Alberta), the relevant provincial legislation provided that boards could require patriotic exercises in such manner as they may direct. Pursuant to this legislation the Lethbridge board passed regulations requiring the patriotic exercise of saluting the flag. The children involved refused to participate in the exercise because it conflicted with their religious beliefs as members of the Jehovah's Witnesses.

In a brief opinion, the dismissals of the children were upheld as being a legitimate exercise of the board's powers. Since freedom of religion was not guaranteed, the plaintiffs sought to challenge the board decision on the basis that it had not followed the requirements of the School Act (rather then on the basis of a violation of a right.) The case is illustrative of the conflicts that have been raging through the years.

A similar situation arose in Ontario in the case of *Donald v. Hamilton Board of Education* [1944] 4 D.L.R. 227; [1945] 3 D.L.R. 424. Here the parents sought to justify their children's refusal to participate in the flag salute on the basis that it was a religious exercise and they could legitimately exempt their children from it pursuant to provincial Regulations which provided:

> No pupil in a public school shall be required to read or study in or from any religious book, or to join in any exercise of devotion or religion, objected to by his parent or guardian.

The trial judge held that such an exemption did not apply to patriotic exercises and that such exercises could not be construed as being religious in nature "at the whim of any particular pupil." On appeal, this finding was reversed. The Ontario Court of Appeal stated:

> That certain acts, exercise and symbols at certain times, or to certain people, connote a significance or meaning which, at other times or to other people, is completely absent is a fact so obvious from history, and from observation, that it needs no elaboration.
>
> The fact that the appellants conscientiously believe the views which they assert is not here in question. A considerable number of cases in other jurisdictions, in which a similar attitude to the flag has been taken, indicates that at least the same view has been conscientiously held by others. The statute, while it absolves pupils from joining in exercises of devotion or religion to which they, or their parents, object, does not further define or specify what such exercises are or include or exclude. Had it done so, other considerations would apply. For the Court to take to itself the right to say that the exercises here in question had no religious or devotional significance might well be for the Court to deny that very religious freedom which the statute is intended to provide.

Before the enactment of the *Charter* religious freedom was recognized to some extent by provincial legislatures and school boards through such exclusionary clauses. Conflicts were avoided and religion was imposed only on those willing to receive it. With the enactment of the *Charter*, however, the issue has been renewed despite the generally non-compulsory nature of religious exercises in schools.

Our first glimpse of how such cases will be treated under the new *Charter* provisions was provided by the Ontario Divisional Court in *Re Zylberberg et al. and Director of Education of Sudbury Board of Education* (1986) 25 C.R.R. 193.

This case was an application by parents of various children for a declaration that the Ontario Regulations requiring prayer in school were in contravention of the provision of section 2(a) of the *Charter*. While participation in such exercises was not mandatory, the applicants argued that the process of exempting their children pressured students into participation and that the use of Christian prayers in Sudbury discriminated against non-Christians.

The split decision in this case shows the range of judicial interpretations that may be brought to bear on similar cases in the future. It should be noted that the decision is under appeal to the Supreme Court of Canada at the time of publication and so we will soon have a definitive ruling on how such cases will be treated.

In the Zylberberg case, Justices O'Leary and Anderson dismissed the application while Justice Reid provided a strong dissenting opinion that would have allowed the challenge. Each provided detailed reasons for his decision.

Justice O'Leary first considered the preamble to the *Charter* which recognizes "the supremacy of God" and section 27 which seeks to preserve and enhance our multicultural heritage. He then stated:

> The recognition in the Constitution of the existence of God and that our society is multicultural in nature cannot, of course, excuse a violation of s.2(a) or s.15(1) of the *Charter* but must be kept in mind when such violations are alleged. . . .

> I accept that there is or may be pressure on all who are culturally or religiously different to conform to the ways of the majority. In particular, I accept that the holding of religious exercises in the school may constitute some pressure on students to participate rather than disclose to teachers and fellow-students that their conscience or religious beliefs dictate they should not participate. . . .

> The type of coercion complained of is pressure to conform rather than face the embarrassment of disclosing that a different belief is held. If such coercion infringes the guarantee of freedom of conscience and religion then such freedom is likewise infringed whenever prayer is said at functions provided for by statute. For example, a religious exercise or prayer in Parliament or the Legislature would infringe the right to freedom of conscience and religion.

> In my view the pressure to conform complained about here does not constitute coercion to such an extent as to infringe the right of freedom of conscience and religion.

> If contrary to the view I have just expressed it can be said that the pressure to participate in religious exercises . . . is an infringement of freedom of conscience and religion, then, in my view, it is such an infringement as can be demonstrably justified in a free and democratic society and so

constitutes a reasonable limit on such freedom under s.1 of the *Charter*.

. . .

> That some pupils may feel pressure to participate in religious exercises to avoid the embarrassment of disclosing a different belief is, in my view, at most, a minor infringement of their freedom of conscience and religion and must not be allowed to stand in the way of the obligation of schools to teach morality in the most effective and least offensive way they know how, namely by holding religious exercises.

> In a country whose constitution is founded on the supremacy of God, but where regular church attendance is the exception rather than the rule, care must be taken not to put unnecessary obstacles in the way of the schools bringing our children into touch with God by prayer, reflection and meditation as a a means of instilling in them the morality required for social order and individual happiness.

Regarding the argument that the provisions were discriminatory against non-Christians he went on to hold:

> Non-believers, on the other hand, may argue that the mere holding of religious exercises gives believers an opportunity to reinforce their beliefs that is not afforded non-believers. If this is religious discrimination then it constitutes a reasonable limit or infringement under s.1 of the *Charter* right given by s.15(1).

> Where a country is founded on the principle of the supremacy of God there is no obligation on the schools to spend the same effort in reinforcing the belief of non-believers that God does not exist as in teaching believers about the nature of God.

. . .

> It is clear that the religious exercises directed by the Sudbury Board has generally a Christian orientation. But no parent or student has suggested the inclusion of other readings or prayers. The Board has indicated its willingness to co-operate with the parents to that end and until an effort has been made by the applicants to work out with the Board the content of religious exercises that would be acceptable to them, it would be improper for the court to rule on whether the Board is discriminating against the applicants.

Justice Anderson did not disagree with these reasons but chose to dispose of the case on narrower grounds. He felt that the Regulation under attack did not, either in purpose or effect, coerce or constrain anyone in his religious freedom. He said:

> It contains . . . a complete and unconditional provision that no pupil shall be required to take part in any religious exercise. In the face of such a right to be excused, I am simply not prepared to hold that anyone is compelled, coerced or constrained to religious exercises to which he or she objects. . . .

I can conceive of circumstances in which insensitive practice, asserting or implying that to exercise the right to be excused was in some way discreditable or reprehensible, might produce an element of compulsion, coercion or constraint. The material before us disclosed no suggestion of any such situation. In my view, the mere possibility of abuse should not condemn the regulation.

In a dissenting opinion Justice Reid took a different view of the Regulation and its effect. He felt that the purpose of the disputed provision was to impose religious exercises on public school children and that the regulations were designed in such a way as to make those who did not wish to participate feel different. He concluded that there was coercion to conform to the majority and that such coercion resulted in inequality and discrimination. He stated:

> I cannot accept the view that the objectors must pay a price for their objection, when the willing conformists pay no price. It does not seem to me to be the majority's function, or the government of Ontario's function, to shake a finger at some parents and say, you are too sensitive; you and your children must pay a price for your beliefs; you should expose your children to the embarrassment you fear because it is good for them, and you must learn to wear your difference with pride. If there were no reasonable basis for the feelings expressed by the applicants; if they were being silly, or mischievous, their complaints should be ignored. But to me their reactions are readily understandable. I cannot write them off as merely contentious or fanciful. I accept them as real.
>
> It is my profound conviction that the quality of freedom of any society is measured by the way it treats its minorities. This has always been so, but one need only look at pre-war Germany, or present-day South Africa, where black people are a political minority, to see that it is still so. It is thus simply not acceptable for the majority to say, you minorities cannot expect to enjoy the freedom we do because freedom cannot be perfect when, for us, the majority in this matter, it is. With respect, I consider that to be contrary to ethical principle but, more importantly for this case, contrary to the *Charter*.
>
> I must thus conclude that the effect of (the regulation) is contrary to s.2(a) and s.15 of the *Charter*.
>
> . . .
>
> In my respectful opinion, no governmental concern has been demonstrated so pressing as to justify an interference with the religious freedom of some but not of others. That would make the *Charter* contradict itself. If any interference may be justified by reason of s.1, it seems to me it must be an interference not with the right of some to religious freedom, but with the right of all. In the result, I do not think the regulation can be defended upon s.1.

The Supreme Court of Canada has considered freedom of religion in another school context, that of compulsory education legislation. We may gain some insight into judicial attitudes on this topic by looking at how this court dealt with the case of *Jones v. R.*(1987) 73 A.R. 133. The Court was unanimous in rejecting Pastor Jones' contention that Alberta compulsory education laws violated his freedom of religion although there was some difference among members of the Court as to their reasoning.

The majority opinion was delivered by Mr. Justice Laforest who stated:

> Assuming the sincerity of his convictions, I would agree that the effect of the School Act does constitute some interference with the appellant's freedom of religion. For a court is in no position to question the validity of a religious belief, notwithstanding that few share that belief. But a court is not precluded from examining into the sincerity of a religious belief when a person claims exemption from the operation of a valid law on that basis. Indeed it has a duty to do so. The trial judge went into the question in this case and concluded . . . that "The accused has failed to establish a factual basis for his claim that the requirement of certification or approval offends his religious beliefs." . . . It would require strong grounds to justify this court in reversing the finding of a trial judge, which was moreover not questioned by the Court of Appeal, on a factual question like this one.
>
> . . .
>
> If the applicant has an interest in, and a religious conviction that he must himself provide for the education of his children, it should not be forgotten that the state, too, has an interest in the education of its citizens. Whether one views it from an economic, social, cultural, or civic point of view, the education of the young is critically important in our society. From an early period, the provinces have responded to this interest by developing schemes for compulsory education. Education is today a matter of prime concern to government everywhere. . . .
>
> The interest of the province in the education of the young is thus compelling. It should require no further demonstration that it may, in advancing this interest, place reasonable limits on the freedom of those who, like the appellant, believe that they should themselves attend to the education of their children and to do so in conformity with their religious convictions. Section 1 of the *Charter* allows for this.

Justice Wilson adopted a different approach by holding that there was no violation of section 2(a) and, therefore, no need to "save" the legislation by resorting to section 1. Indeed, she felt that such an infringement could not be saved by section 1. She stated:

> In my view, the School Act does not offend religious freedom; it accommodates it.
>
> . . . It does not, in my view, offend the appellant's freedom of religion that

he is required under the statute to recognize a secular role for the school authorities.

. . .

. There are many institutions in our society which have both a civil and a religious aspect e.g. marriage. A person's belief in the religious aspect does not free him of his obligation to comply with the civil aspect.

. . .

. . . not every effect of legislation on religious beliefs or practices is offensive to the constitutional guarantee of freedom of religion. Section 2(a) does not require the legislature to refrain from imposing any burdens on the practice of religion. Legislative or administrative action whose effect on religion is trivial or insubstantial is not, in my view, a breach of freedom of religion.

. . .

If I am correct in my conclusion, then it is not necessary for me to consider the application of s. 1. However, I would like to say a brief word about it because, unlike my colleague, I do not believe that the School Act can be saved by s. 1 if it does in fact violate s. 2(a). While there can be no doubt that the province has a compelling interest in education, more than this is required under s. 1. There has to be a form of proportionality between the means employed and the end sought to be achieved. In particular, the means employed must impair as little as possible the right or freedom in issue.

In summary, freedom of religion is not an absolute freedom and may be infringed upon by schools under certain circumstances. In Canada, we do not have the tradition of separation of church and state (especially in relation to schools) that exists in the United States; this tradition resulted in the total absence of religion in American public schools. Canadian teachers must take care, however, not to engage in "insensitive practices" or abuse whatever legislation may exist lest they find themselves the target of a lawsuit claiming violation of a student's religious freedom.

It is interesting to note that the religious freedom being decided in these cases is that of the parents involved and not that of the children, directly. To a large extent, children are regarded as being subject to parental control in the matter of religious belief. An autonomous freedom of religion independent of that of the parent has not been addressed by Canadian courts in the school context.

In other contexts, however, the courts will intervene to protect the child from the consequences of parental beliefs. The usual case involves the matter of blood transfusions where the parents object to the practice on religious grounds. The state will intervene and ask the courts to appoint a guardian for the child in order that consent for the medical procedure can be obtained. Almost invariably such requests are granted.

It is likely that there will continue to be conflicts between parents and schools concerning matters of religion and that the *Charter* rights will be invoked by the parents. It is equally likely that children will continue to be excluded from these debates and decisions concerning their religious beliefs. Justice Douglas of the Supreme Court of the United States in *Wisconsin v. Yoder* (1972) 406 U.S. 205 did take the approach of considering the child's beliefs and rights when he stated:

> If the parents in this case are allowed a religious exemption, the inevitable effect is to impose the parents' notion of religious duty on their children. Where the child is mature enough to express potentially conflicting desires, it would be an invasion of the child's rights to permit such an imposition without canvassing his views.

Freedom of Expression

"Freedom of expression" has in general become a school issue with respect to board regulations governing student dress and grooming. Although there have been a number of cases in the United States dealing with such matters as the wearing of black armbands to protest a war, wearing of long hair by males, and wearing of fly-front pants for females, there appear to be only two Canadian decisions dealing with these issues and both were decided before the *Charter* was enacted. In both instances the school board's right to enact and enforce such policies was upheld.

In *Choukalos v. The Board of Trustees of St. Albert Protestant Separate School District No. 6* (unreported decision of Justice Milvain of the Trial Division of the Supreme Court of Alberta, July 31, 1962), the respondent school board passed a resolution that prohibited the wearing of blue jeans and T-shirts in their schools. The plaintiff student attended school wearing blue jeans, a T-shirt, and a pullover sweater which were acknowledged to be "neat and clean." He was suspended and his parents brought an action for an order declaring that the regulation was invalid and that he be accepted in school dressed as he was.

In his decision Justice Milvain stated:

> It seems to me too, that as a further facet of the development of an ethical outlook on life in young people, that it is one of the duties and functions of a school to implant ideas of orderliness, neatness, politeness, and the proper self pride that comes to an individual who is orderly in mind and, therefore, it seems to me that the inherent and deeply embedded in the

common law, which is common sense, which governs the operation of schools, there stands outside of any particular statutory enactment, the inherent power to impose proper discipline on the children that attend the school.

It would be just as senseless to create a school system without the power of disciplining the students, as it would be to build a school house without doors through which to enter it. It could be the finest structure in the world, but useless if there is no means of entering; it could be the finest school system in the world on paper, but utterly useless without the power in those that administer the school, to impose discipline on the children that attend it.

I feel, therefore, that this school board, as does every school board, had at all times the inherent power to pass necessary regulations for the orderly running of the school as a school, and that as an essential part of those inherent powers, has the right, and, moreover, the duty of regulating the field of discipline in that school. . . .

Now then, the question is raised as to whether or not a dress regulation is properly a part of discipline. It seems to me that that question has been fully answered by Lord Goddard in the case of *Spiers v. Warrington Corporation*. It is cited in [1954] 1 Queen's Bench Division at page 61, and he was there dealing with a case in which the headmistress of a school had made certain oral regulations with respect of dress, one of which was to the effect that girl students should not wear slacks in the school. . . .

In dealing with this matter, Lord Goddard . . . goes on to say at page 68:
'The headmistress obviously has the right and the power to prescribe the discipline for the school, and in saying that a girl must come to school not wearing a particular costume unless there is a compelling reason of health, surely she is only acting in a matter of discipline, and a matter which must be within the competence of the headmaster or headmistress of any school, whether it is one of the great public schools or a country secondary or country primary school. There must be somebody to keep discipline, and of course that person is the headmistress.'
Lord Goddard has made it clear, at least in his view, that control of dress is a matter of discipline.

I must say that I agree with him 100%; that had he not so decided in 1954, I would have been perfectly prepared to so decide myself now because one cannot think in logic of anything more connected with discipline in a group of young people, than the manner in which they are dressed, the manner in which they conduct themselves, and the problem of what is considered to be proper or improper dress may well vary from point to point or from time to time and in accordance with changing conditions. At the time these particular regulations were passed by the Board, they did so because there was current in society, a feeling that the blue jeans and the T-shirt were the uniform of the hoodlum. That, of course, does not mean that each person who wears them is necessarily a hoodlum, but where a group, a large group of young children are brought together for the purpose of being educated in a school, I cannot say that any school board is acting unreasonably should they decide that any of the unpleasant elements or those indicia of unacceptable elements are kept away from children in their care. It strikes me as reasonable that they do so, and I am satisfied on the basis of the law, which is set out in many cases . . . that where it appears that a public authority has been acting reasonably without what may be generally termed in the law of bias, and bias is a wide term in the law, that they have acted bona fide, that a court is not going to interfere with their conclusions even though they feel, the particular court may feel, that the public authority exercised its discretion in a slightly different way to what the individual court may have done.

Before the court will interfere, there must be such unreasonableness that it goes to the root of the jurisdiction and destroys it. That cannot be said in this case.

I, therefore, conclude that the dress regulation passed by this Board was valid and one which the teaching staff properly enforced. . . .

I feel further that the Board in passing their resolution, were not infringing in any way the regulation which had been passed by the Department . . . because in my view the Department, in passing regulations dealing with dress, as they did, merely stipulated that there should be neatness and cleanliness, in effect, would be passing that type of regulation which would properly apply to all schools anywhere in the province. The Department quite properly would not reach out and pass regulations of the particular nature that might be made to apply in different areas. That duty is upon the local Board to do what it honestly sees fit to do in the best interests of the children and the community within which they operate, and it seems to me that the Board of the district in question did just that. . . ."

The other Canadian decision in this type of matter came from Justice Tucker of the Saskatchewan Court of Queen's Bench in *Ward v. Board of Blaine Lake School Unit No. 57* [1971] 4 W.W.R. 161. In this case an 11-year-old student was temporarily suspended until he observed a board resolution defining the maximum length of hair for male students. Again it was argued that the board had no power to make such a resolution or to suspend the student for violation of it. In his decision the judge referred to the Spiers case cited by Justice Milvain above as well as some American cases. His decision reads in part:

As to the general power in matters of discipline, Farwell L.J. in *Smith v. Martin et al.*, [1911] 2 K.B. 775 at 784, said:

In my opinion, the Education Acts are intended to provide for education in its truest and widest sense. Such education includes the inculcation of habits of order and obedience and courtesy: such habits are taught by giving orders, and if such orders are reasonable and proper under the circumstances of the case, they are within the scope of the teacher's authority, even although they are not confined to bidding the child to read or write, to sit down or to stand up in school, or the like.

In *Hutt et al. v. Governors of Haileybury College et al.* (1888), 4 T.L.R. 623 at 624, Field, J. said: 'the master must take into consideration the interests, not only of one boy, but those of the whole school.' ...

I am of the opinion that the power of prescribing within reasonable limits the extent of cleanliness required of pupils attending school, the extent of clothing they should wear, their general appearance, including hair grooming, was within the powers of the Board under the heading 'administering and managing the educational affairs of the school district' and 'exercising a general supervision and control over the schools of the unit'. In these days of the so-called 'permissive society' one does not need to indulge in much in the way of flights of the imagination to envisage how difficult it would be to conduct a class of boys and girls where they could wear as little or as unusual clothing as some children or some parents might see fit. This would include not only care, cleanliness and covering of various parts of the body but also prevention of unusual types of dress and hair styling which might be calculated to distract the pupils from their work in the classroom or adversely affect a proper and reasonable air of discipline in the school.

If the resolution was necessary or wise and required more conformity than reasonably necessary, is the remedy to go to the courts or to the electors who elect the legislators and members of the School Board?

On the authorities cited, in my opinion, on all the evidence, the Board was acting bona fide in the exercise of its powers under the sections cited of the School Acts and it was within its jurisdiction in passing this regulation and in so acting it was not performing a judicial act and so its action in passing the regulation is not reviewable on certiorari. ...

It is not for this Court to substitute its opinion, as to whether the resolution should have been enforced by reasonable disciplinary action, for the opinion of the duly elected Unit Board. As stated by the Chief Justice of the Supreme Court of Canada 'it is necessary for good administration, municipal or school, that those who are charged with it ... are not hampered in the exercise of their duty by intervention of the courts of justice except for grave reasons'.

Shortly following this decision, the following criticism appeared in (1972) 36 Saskatchewan Law Review 479:

This case is illustrative of how the State in modern society is, by a series of unauthorized and petty invasions on the individual's and the family's right to make its own decisions on personal matters, gradually but persistently imposing its values and patterns of behaviour on those who are most susceptible to its influence – the young. Gross invasions of individual rights usually do not escape criticism, but petty invasions often go practically unnoticed and are soon accepted as being within the jurisdiction of the

State to legitimately regulate . . . The area of education is particularly vulnerable to this phenomenon. We should be on guard to insure that the State does not stifle our minor eccentricities, on the pretext of educating us. If we are not, we as individuals and as a society will become stagnant and barren of any free thought, or of expression itself.

School boards generally have become more tolerant of such matters, and students are usually permitted the freedom to wear their hair or dress as they or their parents please. However, some school boards are still passing resolutions dealing with certain aspects of student attire as can be seen in a recent case involving the right of a Sikh student to wear his kirpan, a small dagger, to school.

In *Tuli v. The Board of Trustees of the St. Albert Protestant Separate School District No. 6*, (1987) 8 C.H.R.R. D/3906 (decision rendered April 19, 1985), the school board passed a resolution which stated:

> That the Board of Education refuse to grant permission to Suneet Singh Tuli to wear a kirpan (sword) in school.

Tuli applied to the Alberta Court of Queen's Bench for an interim injunction prohibiting the board from acting on the resolution pending the hearing of a complaint by the Human Rights Commission. The injunction was granted and the court stated:

> Surely the fact that this person would be seen to having (sic) fallen from his faith in my view is sufficient to warrant the relief that he seeks, to say nothing of his possible loss of a scholarship and potential loss of a school year. It is my view that within this application that something positive can result. To allow the applicant to wear the requirements of his religion upon baptism, including the kirpan, would provide those who are unfamiliar with the tenet of his faith an opportunity to be introduced to and to develop an understanding of another's culture and heritage. In this case, that being the traditions of a very well established, respected and old religion.
>
> That does not mean that everyone who wishes to wear such an instrument is entitled to do so. The case must be made out, as was made out in this particular application. It is in my view a positive educational tool which can far outweigh the potential danger as analyzed by the respondent, so long as it is recognized, at least at this time, that it is a privilege and still not a right.

By the time the matter was heard by the Board of Inquiry, (1987) 8 C.H.R.R. D/3736, Tuli had graduated and the Board found that there had in fact been no discrimination under the Alberta *Individual Rights Protection Act* since he did attend school wearing his kirpan. In the Board's decision it was stated:

Here, the complainant was not denied permission to use the school services or school facilities. He was denied permission to wear a kirpan to school. He was not, in fact, treated differently . . .

It may well be reasonable and justifiable for a school board to make a general rule prohibiting all non-Khalsa (unbaptized) Sikhs from using school services or facilities while wearing a kirpan. In light of the degree of commitment, involving both spiritual and personal maturity, which must be exhibited by a person accepted for baptism into the Sikh faith, that general rule would likely not be reasonable and justifiable if it also applied to a Khalsa Sikh. That is not to say that a school board would not be entitled lawfully to pass a rule requiring advance notice to be given to it and a hearing to be held before the date when a student intends to become a Khalsa Sikh. An individual Khalsa Sikh might lawfully be prohibited after a hearing from using publicly funded school services and facilities generally or in limited circumstances or on certain conditions while wearing a kirpan. The circumstances for such determination would have to withstand the test of reasonableness and justifiability in each case.

Also included within the freedom of expression is the freedom of the press and media communication. This has implications for schools in the context of school newspapers and radio programs. Again the American courts have had considerable experience in this matter but the issue has yet to come before a Canadian court in a school context. The only case connected to the issue was the pre-*Charter* case of *R. v. Burko* [1968] 3 D.L.R. (3d) 330 in which six university students were charged with trespass when distributing newspapers in a high school.

The students contended that the school was a public place and they had a right to be there. The court held that use of school property is limited to usage in a reasonable manner consistent with the purpose for which the school is maintained. The magistrate hearing the case stated:

I find, as a fact, that the distribution of newspapers is not an ordinary and reasonable usage of the corridor in Eastwood Collegiate. It has nothing to do with the furnishing of an education to the students in accordance with the curriculum as laid down by the state . . . the act of distributing newspapers is not completely harmless.

Freedom of Assembly

The freedom of peaceful assembly guaranteed by the *Charter* may have implications for teachers especially with respect to student protests. The Burko case discussed above shows the tendency of Canadian courts to rule in favour of order in the school. The Magistrate therein stated:

. . . it is contrary to the public good to permit individuals on public or secondary school property without the permission of the proper authorities for the purpose of disseminating information or ideas, particularly when such information or ideas may not be in accordance with the curriculum established by the state for the public good.

Even in the United States cases concerning freedom of assembly tend to be decided in favour of school order and discipline. Although there are no post-*Charter* precedents to test the limits of this freedom, it is reasonable to assume that our courts will allow schools to maintain order in the face of student assemblies for the purpose of protest. The freedom of assembly is closely aligned to the freedom of association where we do have a few precedents which illustrate judicial attitudes that may well be followed in any subsequent cases.

Freedom of Association

Issues involving the s. 2(d) "freedom of association" and the s. 7 "right to liberty" may come into play in the school context when restrictions are placed on student activity and movement within the school. For example, can a board, principal or teacher forbid a student to associate with others? Can the movements of some students within the school be restricted while others are not? These issues have not been addressed in our courts in the context of the *Charter*, although they have been considered in terms of the board's authority to make such rules.

In *G.H. et al v. Board of Education of Shamrock School Division No. 38 of Saskatchewan*, [1987] 3 W.W.R. 270, the applicant students were restricted in their movements within the school following the laying of charges against them relating to sexual assaults on other students. The plaintiff students sought a court order setting aside the restrictions on the grounds that the board had no authority under the *Education Act* to impose such restrictions. Unfortunately, their counsel did not argue that there was an infringement of their rights and freedoms as guaranteed by the *Charter* so that issue was not addressed in the court's decision.

In this case the school board placed three students on "short bounds" and detailed the restrictions that would be placed on their movement in the school. Their reasons for this action were contained in a letter to the parents which stated in part:

I would also like to point out that the purpose of this action is to enforce a separation between the alleged offenders and the alleged victims in the matter of the charges of sexual assault. Such a separation will have benefits to both sides: it will hopefully prevent intimidation and/or retaliation against the alleged victims, and it will hopefully prevent the laying of baseless accusations against the alleged offenders.

The applicant students applied for a court order holding that these restrictions were beyond and in excess of the powers granted to the board under the *Education Act*. The judge's decision held as follows:

In my opinion, the action of the board in restricting the movement of students within the school fell within the power of the board to "administer and manage the educational affairs of the school division" and also came within the duty to "exercise general supervision and control over the schools of the division."

If the board perceived a potential conflict between certain students, for whatever reason, the board most certainly had the power to restrict, in a reasonable manner, the movement of students so as to prevent any possible confrontation. It is not uncommon for the courts, for example, when granting bail to impose a condition upon an accused that he or she refrain from contact with the alleged victim. The action by the board amounts to no more than that.

Students are not free to move throughout a school as they wish. The board must have the power to control their movements. If the board did not possess that power, it would be impossible, for example, to maintain separate washrooms or locker rooms.

On this application the board does not have to justify the necessity of the 'short bounds' placed on the applicants. It is not for me to decide the rightness or wrongness of the decision of the board. I do not sit on appeal from the board. I am only asked to determine whether the board possessed the authority under the Act to impose the restrictions.

There was no suggestion by the applicants, for example, that there had been a denial of natural justice. Nor was their any argument that there had been an infringement of any of the rights and freedoms guaranteed to the applicants under the Canadian *Charter of Rights and Freedoms*.

The reasons that the board gave for its action, as contained in two affidavits filed on its behalf, may or may not be convincing. I make no decision on that point. I am satisfied that the board acted bona fide in a matter within the scope of its powers. As to the wisdom or unwisdom of the board policy, it is for the electors and not the court to decide that issue.

Although on the facts of this particular case it seems clear that such restrictions would fall within the "reasonable limits" clause of s. 1 of the *Charter*, circumstances could arise where such board restrictions may infringe on rights or freedoms in a manner that could not "be demonstrably justified in a free and democratic society." Although a board has the power to restrict the "liberty" and "freedom of association" of a student within the school it must only do so with justification. To single out a particular student or group of students for such restrictions without a justifiable reason is not acceptable.

Schools may seek to place restrictions on certain types of associations operating within the school, for example: student political clubs. Such restrictions would probably be justified since freedom of association would not be allowed to interfere with the daily operation of schools for the purpose of education. If, however, such clubs are permitted on an extra-curricular basis, schools cannot then discriminate among such clubs and must allow all to operate on an equal basis.

Courts will continue to allow schools to place reasonable limits on freedom of association and freedom of assembly when the purported exercise of those rights interferes with the administration of the schools. Students will not lose those rights; they will just not be able to exercise them in such a way that school discipline is adversely affected.

Right to Privacy

Although it is not one of the rights enumerated in the *Charter*, the right to privacy in regard to educational records is a matter of concern to teachers and administrators. The original 1980 draft of the *Charter* contained a clause guaranteeing protection from "arbitrary or unlawful interference with privacy" which was not included in the final draft. Although it has been said that there is no "right to privacy" such statements oversimplify the issue. There is no such right expressed in the Constitution but there is such a right in certain circumstances derived from provincial legislation.

The right to privacy is usually considered to contain the following elements: the right to have documents about oneself kept confidential; the right to inspect documents kept about oneself; and the right to revise any erroneous information contained in such documents. For our purposes we will look at the right of an individual to determine when, how and to what extent information compiled by school authorities is communicated to others. Schools collect and maintain a large body of information concerning students and are constantly faced with requests for some of that information.

To guide them in deciding what must or may be divulged and to whom, educators can look to three sources. These are provincial education acts and regulations, local school board policy, and the code of ethics of their professional organization. As in other matters, these rules vary considerably from province to province and teachers are advised to consult their own provincial and local sources for specific information.

We find that most provinces only prescribe in general terms what records must be kept and leave it to local school jurisdictions to determine how they should be maintained. The question of confidentiality of such records is often not addressed in the legislation or regulations. Saskatchewan, however, has adopted the following general provision in its *Education Act:*

> 146. All records of a school pertaining to a pupil shall be held in confidence, but the pupil with his parent or guardian, duly authorized officers of the department and school officials designated by the board of education shall have access to such records under such conditions as may be prescribed by the board.

Ontario has the most comprehensive provincial legislation dealing with the maintenance of school records and could be regarded as a model for other provinces or local authorities to follow when considering a revision of their existing rules. Section 237 of the Ontario *Education Act* sets out detailed laws regarding pupil records. Portions of that section read as follows:

> (2) A record is privileged for the information and use of supervisory officers and the principal and teachers of the school for the improvement of instruction of the pupil, and such record,
> (a) subject to subsections (3) and (5), is not available to any other person; and
> (b) except for the purposes of subsection (5), is not admissible in evidence for any purpose in any trial, inquest, inquiry, examination, hearing or other proceeding, except to prove the establishment, maintenance, retention or transfer of the record, without the written permission of the parent or guardian of the pupil or, where the pupil is an adult, the written permission of the pupil.
> (3) A pupil, and his parent or guardian where the pupil is a minor, is entitled to examine the record of such pupil.
> (4) Where, in the opinion of a pupil who is an adult, or of the parent or guardian of a pupil who is a minor, information recorded upon the record of the pupil is,
> (a) inaccurately recorded; or
> (b) not conducive to the improvement of instruction of the pupil, such pupil, parent or guardian, as the case may be, may, in writing, request the principal to correct the alleged inaccuracy in, or to remove the impugned information from, such record. . . .
> (8) No action shall be brought against any person in respect of the content of a record.

(9) Except where the record has been introduced in evidence as provided in this section, no person shall be required in any trial or other proceeding to give evidence in respect of the content of a record.

(10) Except as permitted under this section, every person shall preserve secrecy in respect of the content of a record that comes to his knowledge in the course of his duties or employment, and no such person shall communicate any such knowledge to any other person except,

(a) as may be required in the performance of his duties; or

(b) with the written consent of the parent or guardian of the pupil where the pupil is a minor; or

(c) with the written consent of the pupil where the pupil is an adult.

In addition to this detailed section of the Act, Ontario has also established extensive regulations governing the form and content of the records to be kept. These may be found in Regulation 271 of the *Revised Regulations of Ontario 1980* and Regulation 380 of the *Ontario Regulations 1986*. Between the Act and the regulations, Ontario has addressed the major concerns of educators and established a standard practice throughout the province. Teachers working in other provinces should look to their local school rules and professional codes of ethics for guidance.

A proposed *Freedom of Information Act* for Ontario has caused some concerns for parents regarding school records. The effect of this legislation, which is to take effect in 1991, would be to deny parents the right to see the records of any child over the age of 16 without the child's consent. School records are a form of provincial government record and access to such records may also be governed by other statutes pertaining to release of information. The federal *Freedom of Information Act* has no application in so far as provincial records are concerned. Teachers should check their provincial statutes to see what laws, other than the *School Act*, may be in effect governing release of student information

Legal Rights

As we have seen in the chapter discussing young offenders, the legal rights enumerated in sections 7 to 14 of the *Charter* are guaranteed equally to children and adults in the realm of criminal prosecutions. An interesting issue arises as to whether these rights extend to students in the school as opposed to the criminal context. We have seen that in certain circumstances these may overlap when the school becomes involved in the criminal process. But are actions by school authorities in relation to the administration of the school subject to these same guarantees?

Section 7 of the *Charter* provides:

Everyone has the right to life, liberty and security of the person and the right not to be deprived thereof except in accordance with the principles of fundamental justice.

If the *Charter* is held to apply to school administrative procedures then this section may have an impact on various disciplinary actions taken by schools. Many provinces have already legislated the procedures to be followed in cases of suspension and expulsion and often provide students with the opportunity to be heard in response to allegations made against them. Such hearings would also have to meet the constitutional requirement of "fundamental justice." The Supreme Court of the United States has held that their consitutional requirement of "due process" applies to school disciplinary matters. In *Goss v. Lopez* (1975) U.S. 565 it was held that:

. . . the student be given oral or written notice of the charges against him and, if he denies them, an explanation of the evidence the authorities have and an opportunity to present his side of the story.

The Court did recognize that in instances where the student poses an immediate danger to others or where he is a source of disruption to the academic process, he could be removed immediately without going through the requirements of due process. Summary discipline procedures may well be regarded as a reasonable restraint on the rights granted under the *Charter* pursuant to s. 1. It is suggested that school authorities ensure that students who are subject to severe disciplinary action are afforded a fair hearing in accordance with legislative and constitutional requirements.

We have seen in the chapter on young offenders how courts have recently regarded school searches in the case of *R. v. J.M.G.* That case involved a criminal prosecution but many school searches and seizures will be for purely internal reasons unrelated to the criminal process. Section 8 of the *Charter* provides:

Everyone has the right to be secure against unreasonable search or seizure.

Some American cases have held that school searches do not need to meet constitutional requirements because they are conducted by the school while acting *in loco parentis* rather than as an agent of the state. Since a parent need not comply with the constitutional procedures for a reasonable search, neither do schools. Although the issue has not been decided in Canada outside of the criminal context, it is reasonable to assume that principals and teachers will be regarded as having the right to search students and seize contraband under their duty to maintain order and discipline. Recent American decisions have held school authorities to a lower standard of "reasonable" suspicion than is required of police officers conducting a search. What will be regarded as reasonable will depend on the circumstances of each case. The case of *New Jersey v. T.L.O.* cited in the J.M.G. case provides the following test:

> Determining the reasonableness of any search involves a twofold inquiry: first, one must consider "whether the . . . action was justified at its inception" . . . second, one must determine whether the search as actually conducted "was reasonably related in scope to the circumstances which justified the interference in the first place" . . . Under ordinary circumstances, a search of a student by a teacher or other school official will be "justified at its inception" when there are reasonable grounds for suspecting that the student has violated or is violating either the law or the rules of the school. Such a search will be permissible in its scope when the measures adopted are reasonably related to the objectives of the search and not excessively intrusive in light of the age and sex of the student and the nature of the infraction.

Thus, if a teacher reasonably suspects a violation of school rules or breach of the law, he is justified in conducting a search. Reasonable suspicion must involve something concrete to support the suspicion rather than mere conjecture on the part of the teacher. The extent of the search must then be reasonably related to the objective of the search. When confronted with a minor breach of school discipline (chewing gum or passing notes), an intrusive search could hardly be justified. If the search is conducted in relation to a more serious matter, such as a criminal offence involving drugs, then the search can be more intrusive and may even involve a strip search if warranted.

Locker searches in the United States have generally been regarded as justifiable on the view that the lockers are the property of the school. Principals may therefore search the lockers, as custodians of school property, and may also consent to police searches on behalf the school. There are no reported Canadian cases involving locker searches but it is safe to assume that this type of reasoning may well be adopted in Canada.

School detentions may be regarded as being "detained or imprisoned" within the meaning of s. 9 of the *Charter* which states:

> Everyone has the right not to be arbitrarily detained or imprisoned.

As we have seen in the discussion on false imprisonment in the chapter on torts, imprisonment does not only mean confinement in a jail. If a teacher is detaining a student, it must be for a legitimate reason. The practice of keeping a whole class in after school "until I find out who did it" may well be considered an arbitrary detention if the *Charter* is held to apply to school disciplinary actions. It is the equivalent of the police rounding up a number of suspects and refusing to let any of them go until one confesses. Whether this action is held to be unconstitutional or not, it is certainly a denial of fair treatment for the innocent students and should be discouraged.

The s. 10 right to instruct counsel has been discussed at length as it relates to young offenders. It is unreasonable to expect that this section will be applied to the case of the ordinary school detention. Staying 15 minutes after class for violation of a school rule is simply not the type of situation that this section was meant to cover.

The s. 12 prohibition against cruel and unusual punishment has been discussed in the chapter on corporal punishment. It may well apply to school disciplinary measures, but any actions that may be regarded as cruel could be effectively dealt with under the *Criminal Code*. It is unlikely that schools would generally adopt disciplinary measures which could be regarded as cruel or unusual; however, there may be the occassional teacher who might impose some harsh form of discipline. The *Charter* affords some additional protection to students against such measures if the offending teacher cannot be dealt with under the criminal law.

The legal rights enumerated in the *Charter* are mainly directed towards the criminal process and will only occasionally have any significance in other contexts. As we have seen, school officials may become involved in the criminal process, and in such instances must see that a student's legal rights are protected. In the realm of routine disciplinary matters, teachers need not be overly concerned about facing legal action involving the *Charter*. This does not mean that teachers should not respect the rights of their students and try to live up to the spirit of the *Charter* in all dealings with students. School is the student's first experience with a governmental agency and should provide a model of constitutional behaviour for students to emulate.

You be the Judge

The Case of the Loaded Locker

During a physical education skating class, two 15-year-old students were seen smoking cigarettes by their teacher, Mr. Lane. The boys, Sebastian and Joel, appeared to be pouring a liquid on the cigarettes before smoking them. Other students had informed Mr. Lane that the boys were pouring hash oil on their cigarettes. When Mr. Lane approached the boys, they quickly stamped their cigarettes into the snowy ground.

Upon returning to the school, Mr. Lane informed the principal of the events as he had seen them.

The principal obtained the boys' locker combination from the files and proceeded to the locker which the boys shared. He asked Mr. Kent, another teacher, to stay with him while he conducted the search. Kent stood by for a short time but was called away to settle a noisy dispute in his classroom. When Kent returned, the principal had found a large quantity of vials containing the hash oil.

The boys were summoned to the office and confronted with the evidence. The principal informed them that they were suspended for three days immediately and that the matter would be reported to the School Board.

The circumstances were reported in writing to the Board who confirmed the suspension and ordered that the boys be expelled from classes for two months.

When the parents received the expulsion notices they were furious. They maintained that their sons were not drug users nor would they have had enough money to purchase the quantity of drugs alleged to have been in the locker. If the expulsions were to be upheld, both students would miss the end of semester examinations and would lose credits.

Issues for Decision

1. Was the search and seizure of the hash oil done in a proper and legal fashion?
2. Were the students deprived of any constitutional or legal rights?
3. What evidence is there that the substance seized was hash oil and that it belonged to the students?
4. Were there any grounds for suspension or expulsion of the students?
5. How should this matter have been handled by the teacher. Mr. Lane? By the principal? By the School Board?

The Case of the Traumatic Transfusion

One morning, Miss Everly, a grade four teacher, was supervising children on the playground. One of her students, Cathy, was running and playing tag near the slide when she tripped and fell. Her leg was cut severely on a piece of metal protruding from the bottom step of the slide.

Miss Everly ran to Cathy's assistance and saw that the wound would require medical attention. Scooping the child into her arms, she carried her into the office where she and the principal attempted to control the bleeding while the school secretary tried to contact Cathy's mother. The father worked out of town and today her mother was not home. A check of the registration form showed no alternate adult to be contacted in case of an emergency. An ambulance was called to transport the girl to the hospital.

When the ambulance arrived Cathy's leg was still bleeding profusely. A paramedic feared that an artery had been severed. Cathy was very frightened and it was decided that Miss Everly would accompany her to the hospital in the ambulance.

Cathy was rushed to surgery and Miss Everly completed the admitting forms. The operation repaired the damage and everyone was relieved to hear that there would be no permanent damage. The operation had required the transfusion of two pints of blood to replace what had been lost. Cathy remained in hospital for a few days to recuperate.

The following Monday morning, Cathy's parents arrived at the school most upset and angry. They were going to sue the school not only for negligence but for violation of Cathy's freedom of religion. "You are well aware," the father said, "that we are Jehovah's Witnesses and object to the transfusion of blood."

1. Was there a violation of Cathy's constitutional guarantee of "freedom of religion"?

2. How much knowledge of various religious practices should teachers have to ensure that they do not offend the religious tenets of their students?

3. Should damages be awarded in this case? What price should be put on a "loss of salvation"?

Canadian Charter of Rights and Freedoms

Whereas Canada is founded upon principles that recognize the supremacy of God and the rule of law:

Guarantee of Rights and Freedoms

1. The *Canadian Charter of Rights and Freedoms* guarantees the rights and freedoms set out in it subject only to such reasonable limits prescribed by law as can be demonstrably justified in a free and democratic society.

Fundamental Freedoms

2. Everyone has the following fundamental freedoms:
(a) freedom of Conscience and religion;
(b) freedom of thought, belief, opinion and expression, including freedom of the press and other media of communication;
(c) freedom of peaceful assembly; and
(d) freedom of association.

Democratic Rights

3. Every citizen of Canada has the right to vote in an election of members of the House of Commons or of a legislative assembly and to be qualified for membership therein.

4. (1) No House of Commons and no legislative assembly shall continue for longer than five years from the date fixed for the return of the writs at a general election of its members.

(2) In time of real or apprehended war, invasion or insurrection, a House of Commons may be continued by parliament and a legislative assembly may be continued by the legislature beyond five years if such continuation is not opposed by the votes of more than one-third of the members of the House of Commons or the legislative assembly, as the case may be.

5. There shall be a sitting of Parliament and of each legislature at least once every twelve months.

Mobility Rights

6. (1) Every citizen of Canada has the right to enter, remain in and leave Canada.

(2) Every citizen of Canada and every person who has the status of a permanent resident of Canada has the right
(a) to move to and take up residence in any province; and
(b) to pursue the gaining of a livelihood in any province.

(3) The rights specified in subsection (2) are subject to

(a)any laws or practices of general application in force in a province other than those that discriminate among persons primarily on the basis of province of present or previous residence; and

(b) any laws providing for reasonable residency requirements as a qualification for the receipt of publicly provided social services.

(4) Subsections (2) and (3) do not preclude any law, program or activity that has as its object the amelioration in a province of conditions of individuals in that province who are socially or economically disadvantaged if the rate of employment in that province is below the rate of employment in Canada.

Legal Rights

7. Everyone has the right to life, liberty and security of the person and the right not to be deprived thereof except in accordance with the principles of fundamental justice.

8. Everyone has the right to be secure against unreasonable search and seizure.

9. Everyone has the right not to be arbitrarly detained or imprisoned.

10. Everyone has the right on arrest or detention
(a) to be informed promptly of the reasons therefor;
(b) to retain and instruct counsel without delay and to be informed of that right; and
(c) to have the validity of the detention determined by way of *habeas corpus* and to be released if the detention is not lawful.

11. Any person charged with an offence has the right
(a) to be informed without unreasonable delay of the specific offence;
(b) to be tried within a reasonable time;
(c) not to be compelled to be a witness in proceedings against that person in the respect of the offence;
(d) to be presumed innocent until proven guilty according to law in a fair and public hearing by an independent and impartial tribunal;
(e) not to be denied reasonable bail without just cause;
(f)except in the case of an offence under military law tried before a military tribunal, to the benefit of trial by jury where the maximum punishment for the offence is imprisonment for five years or a more severe punishment.
(g) not to be found guilty on account of any act or omission unless, at the time of the act or omission, it constituted an offence under Canadian or international law or was criminal according to the general principles of law recognized by the community of nations;
(h) if finally acquitted of the offence, not to be tried for it again and, if

finally found guilty and punished for the offence, not to be tried or punished for it again; and

(i) if found guilty of the offence and if the punishment for the offence has been varied between the time of commission and the time of sentencing, to the benefit of the lesser punishment.

12. Everybody has the right not to subjected to any cruel and unusual treatment or punishment.

13. A witness who testifies in any proceedings has the right not to have any incriminating evidence so given used to incriminate that witness in any other proceedings, except in a prosecution for perjury or for the giving of contradictory evidence.

14. A party or witness in any proceedings who does not understand or speak the language in which the proceedings are conducted or who is deaf has the right to the assistance of an interpreter.

Equality Rights

15. (1) Every indivdual is equal before and under the law and has the right to the equal protection and equal benefit of the law without discrimination and, in particular, without discrimination based on race, national or ethnic origin, colour, religion, sex, age or mental or physical disability.

(2) Subsection (1) does not preclude any law, program or activity that has as its object the amelioration of conditions of disadvantaged individuals or groups including those that are disadvantaged because of race, national or ethnic origin, colour, religion, sex, age, or mental or physical disability.

Official Languages of Canada

16. (1) English and French are the official languages of Canada and have equality of status and equal rights and privileges as to their use in all institutions of the Parliament and government of Canada.

(2) English and French are the official languages of New Brunswick and have equality and equal rights and privileges as to their use in all institutions of the legislature and government of New Brunswick.

(3) Nothing in this Charter limits the authority of Parliament or a legislature to advance the equality of status or use of English and French.

17. (1)Everyone has the right to use English or French in any debates and other proceedings of Parliament.

(2) Everyone has the right to use English or French in any debates and other proceedings of the legislature of New Brunswick.

18. (1) The statutes, records and journals of Parliament shall be printed and published in English and French and both language versions are equally

authoritive.

(2) The statutes, records and journals of the legislature of New Brunswick shallbe printed and published in English and French and both language versions are equally authoritative.

19. (1) Either English or French may be used by any person in, or in any pleading in or process issuing from, any court established by Parliament.

(2) Either English or French may be used by any person in, or in any pleading in or process issuing from, any court of New Brunswick.

20. (1) Any member of the public in Canada has the right to communicate with, and to receive available services from, any head or central office of an institution of the Parliament or government of Canada in English or French, and has the same right with respect to any other office of any such institution where

(a) there is a significant demand for communications with and services from that office in such language; or

(b) due to the nature of the office, it is reasonable that communications with and services from that office be available in both English and French.

(2) Any member of the public in New Brunswick has the right to communicate with, and to receive available from, any office of an institution of the legislature or government of New Brunswick in English and French.

21. Nothing in sections 16 to 20 abrogates or derogates from any right, privilege or obligation with respect to the English or French languages, or either of them, that exists or is continued by virtue of any other provision of the Constitution of Canada.

22. Nothing in sections 16 to 20 abrogates or derogates from any legal or customary right or privilege acquired or enjoyed either before or after the coming into force of this Charter with respect to any language that is not English or French.

Minority Language Educational Rights

23. (1) Citizens of Canada

(a) whose first language learned and still understood is that of the English or French linguistic minority population of the province in which they reside or

(b) who have received their primary school instruction in Canada in English or French and reside in a province where the language in which they received that instruction is the language of the English or French linguistic minority population of the province, have the right to have their children receive primary and secondary school instruction in that language in that province.

(2) Citizens of Canada of whom any child has received or is receiving primary or secondary school instruction in English or French in Canada, have the right to have all their children receive primary and secondary school instruction in the same language.

(3) The right of citizens of Canada under subsections (1) and (2) to have their children receive primary and secondary school instruction in the language of the English or French linguistic minority population of a province

(a) applies wherever in the province the number of children of citizens who have such a right is sufficient to warrant the provision to them out of public funds of minority language instruction; and

(b) includes, where the number of those children so warrants, the right to have them receive that instruction in minority language educational facilities provided out of public funds.

Enforcement

24. (1) Anyone whose rights or freedoms, as guaranteed by this Charter, have been infringed or denied may apply to a court of competent jurisdiction to obtain such remedy as the court considers appropriate and just in the circumstances.

(2) Where, in proceedings under subsection (1), a court concludes that evidence was obtained in a manner that infringed or denied any rights or freedoms guaranteed by this Charter, the evidence shall be excluded if it is established that, having regard to all the circumstances, the admission of it in the proceedings would bring the administration of justice into disrepute.

General

25. The guarantee in this Charter of certain rights and freedoms shall not be construed so as to abrogate or derogate from any aboriginal, treaty or other rights or freedoms that pertain to the aboriginal people of Canada including

(a) any rights or freedoms that have been recognized by the Royal Proclamation of October 7, 1763; and

(b) any rights or freedoms that may be acquired by the aboriginal peoples of Canada by way of land claims settlement.

26. The guarantee in the Charter of certain rights and freedoms shall not be construed as denying the existence of any other rights or freedoms that exist in Canada.

27. This Charter shall be interpreted in a manner consistent with the preservation and enhancement of the multicultural heritage of Canadians.

28. Notwithstanding anything in this Charter, the rights and freedoms referred to in it are guaranteed equally to male and female persons.

29. Nothing in this Charter abrogates or derogates from any rights or privileges guaranteed by or under the Constitution of Canada in respect of denominational, separate or dissentient schools.

30. A reference in this Charter to a province or to the legislative assembly or legislature of a province shall be deemed to include a reference to the Yukon Territory and the Northwest Territories, or to the appropriate legislative authority.

Application of Charter

32. (1) This Charter applies

(a) to the Parliament and government of Canada in respect of all matters within the authority of Parliament including all matters relating to the Yukon Territory and Northwest Territories; and

(b) to the legilature and government of each province in respect of all matters within the authority of the legislature of each province.

(2) Notwithstanding subsection (1), section 15 shall not have effect until three years after this section comes into force.

33. (1) Parliament or the legislature of a province may expressly declare in an Act of Parliament or of the legislature, as the case may be, that the Act or a provision thereof shall operate notwithstanding a provision included in section 2 or sections 7 to 15 of this Charter.

(2) An Act or a provision of an Act in respect of which a declaration made under this section is in effect shall have such operation as it would have but for the provision of this Charter referred to in the declaration.

(3) A declaration made under subsection (1) shall cease to have effect five years after it comes into force or on such earlier date as may be specified in the declaration.

(4) Parliament or a legislature of a province may re-enact a declaration made under subsection (1).

(5) Subsection (3) applies in respect of a re-enactment made under subsection (4).

Citation

34. This Part may be cited as the *Canadian Charter of Rights and Freedoms*.

References

Bates, F., "Child Law and Religious Extremists: Some Recent Developments," (1978) 10 *Ottawa Law Review* 299.

Humphreys, E. H., *Privacy in Jeopardy: Student Records in Canada,* Toronto: OISE Press, 1980.

Kerr, R. W., "Constitutional Law-Political Rights and High School Political Clubs," (1972) 50 *Canadian Bar Review* 347.

MacKay, A. W., "Students as Second Class Citizens Under the Charter." (1986) 54 C.R. (3d) 390.

MacKay, A. W., "Schools Censorship and Free Expression: Old Issues in a New Context," (1983) 2 *Canadian School Executive* #7, p. 6.

Manley-*Casimir, M. E. and Sussel, T. A., Courts in the Classroom: Education and the Canadian Charter of Rights and Freedoms,* Calgary: Detselig Enterprises Ltd., 1986.

McLachlin, B., "Educational Records and the Right to Privacy," (1981) 15 *U.B.C. Law Review* 175.

Ontario Institute for Studies in Education, *Interchange on Students' Rights,* Toronto: OISE Press, 1978.

14

Civil Rights
from the Teacher's Perspective

Learning Objectives

Some of the things which the reader will learn from reading this chapter include the following:

1. When certain apparent violations of a teacher's rights are permitted with respect to the employment, discipline and termination of a teacher.
2. By virtue of their membership in a professional association, teachers are restrained in their freedom of speech concerning some matters.
3. In the course of his employment a teacher's freedom of conscience, religion, thought and belief may be restricted.
4. The boundaries of "academic freedom" permitted a classroom teacher.
5. How the Charter and provincial legislation control discrimination in respect to employment of teachers.
6. How a teacher's lifestyle may result in disciplinary procedures or termination of employment.

Preview

School teachers are presumed to enjoy the same basic rights and freedoms that are enjoyed by other members of our society. In practice this is not entirely true.

Under certain circumstances, the freedom of conscience and religion section of the *Charter* can be limited in application to the classroom teacher. For example, the conduct of employees of religious schools may be restricted where their personal conduct is considered to be detrimental to the image and well-being of the school. Most frequently, such cases involve marital arrangements which violate the tenets of the faith of the denominational school.

Membership in a professional association brings with it certain controls and restrictions upon a member's freedom of speech and expression.

The courts will usually hold teachers to a very high standard of personal conduct since they are exemplars for their students. These standards may impinge upon a teacher's chosen lifestyle and restrict his behaviour.

Key Terms

Academic freedom	Board of Arbitration
bona fide	Exemplar
Board of Reference	*ultra vires*

*　　*　　*　　*

Just as students have certain basic civil rights, so do teachers. What constitutes a civil right can be a complex question and will involve matters that are not enumerated in the *Charter* or in other legislation. The concept of "academic freedom" may be regarded by some teachers as their most important civil right, yet it does not receive legislative recognition. In this chapter we will look at certain issues that are of importance to teachers. We will not attempt to exhaust all areas of civil rights; that would take many volumes. Teachers have the same basic rights as any other citizen but there are particular issues that may be of greater importance to teachers.

Issues of equality rights will be tested more frequently in the courts now that s.15 of the *Charter* has been proclaimed in force. This section provides:

> Every individual is equal before and under the law and has the right to the equal protection and equal benefit of the law without discrimination and, in particular, without discrimination based on race, national or ethnic origin, colour, religion, sex, age or mental or physical disability.

Courts have considered issues of equality rights in connection with the human rights legislation of various provinces. These decisions will give some idea of how the courts may approach such matters in the constitutional context. We will explore some of the fundamental freedoms and equality issues as they have been considered in Canadian cases. The United States courts have had more experience with such matters but their decisions, particularly in equality rights, will not have much bearing on how our courts will decide a case. Precedent from provincial legislation will give a clearer picture of judicial attitudes in Canada.

Freedom of Conscience and Religion

In Canada we do not have the strict separation of church and school that exists in the United States. In fact, certain types of "religious discrimination" receive constitutional protection in the school context. Both the *Constitution Act, 1867* and the *Canadian Charter of Rights and Freedoms* guarantee the rights and privileges of the separate school systems and, accordingly, also guarantee the right to discriminate in favour of members of their religion regarding employment in the schools. There have been several cases from different provinces that have involved teachers being terminated on religious grounds. Because the constitutional guarantees of each province vary, the results of these cases have been different.

In *Caldwell v. Stuart et al.* [1984] 2 S.C.R. 603, the plaintiff teacher was a Roman Catholic employed in a Catholic school in Vancouver. She married a divorced Methodist in a civil ceremony and as a result her contract was not renewed. She filed a complaint under the British Columbia *Human Rights Code* which provided:

> 8. (1) Every person has the right of equality of opportunity based on *bona fide* qualifications in respect of his occupation or employment, or in respect of an intended occupation, employment, advancement or promotion; and, without limiting the generality of the foregoing,
> (a) no employer shall refuse to employ, or to continue to employ, or to advance or promote that person, or discriminate against that person in respect of employment or condition of employment; and
> (b) no employment agency shall refuse to refer him for employment, unless reasonable cause exists for the refusal or discrimination.
> (2) For the purposes of subsection (1),
> (a) the race, religion, colour, age, marital status, ancestry, place of origin or political belief of any person or class of persons shall not constitute reasonable cause.

The school board alleged that religion and marital status were bona fide occupational requirements for teachers in Catholic schools. Further, the Code provides that religious organizations may provide preference to its members and that Mrs. Caldwell was no longer a member by virtue of her breach of church doctrine. The matter eventually made its way to the Supreme Court of Canada which gave a unanimous opinion. Justice McIntyre's judgment stated:

> Ordinarily, a person who is academically qualified and duly licensed by the proper authority would certainly possess the *bona fide* qualifications for employment as a teacher in a public school. I am in complete agreement with the proposition that, if Mrs. Caldwell had been employed in a secular or public school and had been dismissed because of her marriage, she would have the full protection of s. 8 and be entitled to reinstatement. This result may not always follow and particularly in cases relating to denominational schools.
>
> As has been pointed out, the Catholic school is different from the public school. In addition to the ordinary academic program, a religious element which determines the true nature and character of the institution is present in the Catholic school. To carry out the purposes of the school, full effect must be given to this aspect of its nature and teachers are required to observe and comply with the religious standards and to be examples in the manner of their behaviour in the school so that students see in practice the application of the principles of the Church on a daily basis and thereby receive what is called a Catholic education. Fulfillment of these purposes requires that Catholics observe the Church's rules regarding marriage. It must be celebrated in the Church and the marriage of divorced persons is not recognized. The Board found that Mrs. Caldwell knew this when she was employed, that inquiries were made respecting these matters before she was hired to insure her eligibility for employment in this respect.
>
> It was therefore open to the Board to find that when Mrs. Caldwell in contravention of the Church's requirements married a divorced man in a civil ceremony, she deprived herself of a *bona fide* qualification for the employment. In my view the Board made no error in law in so finding and in concluding that the provisions of s.8 were not operative to protect her. The religious or doctrinal aspect of the school lies at its very heart and colours all its activities and programs. The role of the teacher in this respect is fundamental to the whole effect of the school, as much in its spiritual nature as in the academic. It is my opinion that objectively viewed, having in mind the special nature and objectives of the school, the requirements of religious conformity including the acceptance and observance of the Church's rules regarding marriage is reasonably necessary to assure the achievement of the objects of the school. It is my view that . . . the requirement of conformance constitutes a *bona fide* qualification in respect of the occupation of a Catholic teacher employed in a Catholic school, the absence of which will deprive her of the protection of s. 8 of the *Human Rights Code*. It will only be in rare circumstances that such a factor as religious conformance can pass the test of *bona fide* qualification. In the case at bar, the special nature of the school and the unique role played by the teachers in the attaining of the school's legitimate objects are essential to the finding that religious conformance is a *bona fide* qualification.

A highly publicized situation arose in Alberta in 1987 where an unwed mother was offered a position by a Roman Catholic board which then refused to enter into a contract with her because of her marital status. The board's position was that pre-marital sex was forbidden by the Church and that the child in question was evidence of the teacher's breach of Church teaching in this regard. Because no contract had been signed, the matter was not subject to arbitration.

Another Alberta teacher was dismissed from her position for a similar reason. In *Casagrande v. Hinton Roman Catholic Separate School District No. 155* (1987) 51 Alta L.R. (2d) 349, the Alberta Court of Queen's Bench upheld the termination of an unmarried pregnant teacher who was dismissed for contravening Catholic doctrine by engaging in premarital intercourse. The board policy required teachers to follow a life-style consistent with Catholic teachings and beliefs including abstinence from premarital sexual intercourse. The teacher in this case had been specifically warned to refrain from such conduct after she had previously given birth out of wedlock. The teacher claimed that she could not be dismissed for denominational cause and further that she was the object of sexual discrimination because her dismissal was essentially for pregnancy.

The court referred to the Caldwell case and other decisions and stated:

> By this decision, the Supreme Court of Canada recognized the special position of separate schools and that this unique character and position of separate schools permitted the imposition of rules requiring teachers to adhere to certain religious and moral standards.

> I am satisfied on the basis of these decisions that the right to establish separate schools . . . included all rights and powers necessary to maintain the denominational character of such schools, and more specifically included the right to dismiss teachers for denominational causes.

> It is clear that s. 29 (of the *Charter*) reaffirms and continues the constitutional rights granted in respect of denominational schools, giving these rights precedence over the individual rights protected by other provisions of the *Charter*.

Regarding the argument that the teacher was the victim of sexual discrimination, the court held:

> To succeed in this argument the applicant must establish that the board's rules of conduct applied to the applicant in a discriminatory fashion. This would be based on a finding that she was dismissed because she was pregnant. Here the applicant again asks me to reverse a finding of fact made by the Board of Reference; that being that the respondent school board did not

dismiss the applicant because she was pregnant but that her pregnancy was merely evidence of the fact that she had engaged in premarital sexual conduct. The Board of Reference found that what was prohibited was premarital sexual conduct and that a breach of this prohibition constituted a valid denominational reason for the dismissal. This finding of fact was supported by the evidence which was accepted by the Board of Reference ... While the pregnancies were frequently referred to as such, the superintendent and the board members who were called by the respondent made it clear that pregnancy per se was not the cause for the termination of the contract of employment. The cause for terminating the contract was the life-style which the pregnancy evidenced.

Before a finding of adverse affect discrimination can be made it is necessary that I find that the rule in question affected the applicant differently than it affected other members of the staff of the school. It is clear on the findings made by the Board of Reference that the rule which was breached by the applicant was the prohibition of the Roman Catholic Church against participation in sexual intercourse outside the marriage sacrament. This rule applied equally to all Catholic teachers, both male and female. Although evidence of a breach of the rule was more readily available in the case of a female teacher who was pregnant, the rule did not result in any intentional or unintentional discrimination against the applicant as a female teacher. In light of these findings, the concept of adverse effect discrimination does not apply.

Teachers in other provinces who have been faced with a similar circumstance have not resorted to human rights legislation but rather have looked to Boards of Reference or labour arbitration boards for relief. In *Re Essex County Roman Catholic Separate School Board and Porter et al.* (1978) 89 D.L.R. (3d) 445, two teachers were dismissed by the separate school board for contracting civil marriages. The *Schools Administration Act* gave a Board of Reference the power to direct the continuance of a contract by a board if a teacher was dismissed. The teachers appealed to the Board of Reference which ordered their reinstatement. The board applied for judicial review of this decision on the grounds that the school board had powers reserved to it under s. 93 of the *Constitution Act, 1867* and that these powers could not be taken away by provincial legislation. They contended that the Board of Reference had no jurisdiction to hear the matter.

The Ontario Court of Appeal agreed with the school board and held that if a board can dismiss for cause, a denominational board can dismiss for denominational cause. This power to dismiss for denominational cause is one of the rights and privileges with respect to denominational schools protected under s. 93. To subject this right to review by a Board of Reference would prejudicially affect the right and consequently the Board of Reference had no jurisdiction to deal with teacher dismissals on denominational grounds. The *Schools Administration Act* was *ultra vires* to the extent that it purported to give such a power to the Board of Reference.

A few years later, this same school board dismissed another teacher for the same reason. She filed a grievance under the terms of the collective agreement with an arbitration board. In *Re Essex Roman Catholic Separate School Board and Tremblay-Webster et al.* (1983) 142 D.L.R. (3d) 479, it was held that such a grievance was subject to arbitration. In this case the Ontario High Court held that arbitration of such discharges does not offend s. 93 of the *Constitution Act, 1867* as would a reference of the matter to a Board of Reference. The Porter decision was affirmed in this respect. The court held that arbitration for dismissal on denominational grounds was not compulsory under the provincial legislation but was a matter for agreement under the terms of a collective agreement. Where the collective agreement provides that the parties will submit disputes over discharge to such a grievance procedure, then the board of arbitration may hear the matter.

Whether a board of arbitration would uphold such a dismissal is a matter of fact to be determined in each case. The Essex Board refused to hire a non-Catholic teacher, who had been employed on a contract basis, for a full time position in the case of *Re Essex County Roman Catholic Separate School Board and OECSTA and Kersey* (an unreported 1982 decision of an Ontario Board of Arbitration). The Arbitration Board in that case found that the teacher was entitled to the benefits of the collective agreement and that denominational qualifications had not been shown by the school board to be a basic requirement of the job. It stated:

> Since there is nothing in the Collective Agreement and no relevant past practice . . . indicating that Roman Catholicity is a basic requirement in all recall situations, and since denomination was not included within the list of qualifications specified on the particular job posting in question, there is no basis on which to conclude that being a Roman Catholic is a "required" qualification for the available position.

In Newfoundland a teacher was dismissed by a Catholic school board because he was divorced by his wife on grounds of cruelty. The matter was brought before an arbitration board under the collective agreement and the school board challenged the constitutional right of such a board to determine whether the dismissal was for just cause.

In *Stack v. Roman Catholic School Board for St. John's* (1979) 99 D.L.R. (3d) 278, the Newfoundland Supreme Court held that such matters were subject to arbitration. At the date of Union Newfoundland legislation provided that teachers could be dismissed for "immoral conduct." This provision was repealed in 1974. The school board argued that this repeal affected its denominational rights. The court held, however, that the Newfoundland Legislature could enact laws of general application relating to education providing they do not affect a right or privilege attached to denominational teaching or the integrity of the specified schools. The Act related to terms and conditions of employment of all teachers in all public schools (which in Newfoundland are all denominational schools) and did not affect any denominational privilege. Therefore an arbitration board could determine whether the dismissal was for just cause.

Therefore, the issue of whether a teacher must conform to the practices of the church has become a matter of collective agreement. Provided that the religious requirements are made clear at the time of hiring, and are mutually accepted by the parties, the school board is free to demand compliance and to dismiss for failure to follow church doctrine. Although this may be seen by some as a denial of religious freedom it may equally be regarded as preservation of religious freedom for the denomination involved. If a teacher's beliefs do not correspond to those of the denomination running the school, he should not expect to be treated on the same footing as those willing to adhere to the religious requirements of the board. Where teachers are given preferential treatment in hiring because of their professed religious beliefs, they cannot expect the same preference when they abandon the belief or do not conduct their lives in conformity with that belief.

Another school related case, *Attorney General of British Columbia v. Board of School Trustees of School District 65 (Cowichan)* (1985) 63 B.C.L.R. 130, made an interesting decision regarding the meaning of "freedom of conscience" in s. 2 of the *Charter*. The issue in dispute was the right of the province to direct the type of budget that a local school board could adopt through by-law. The board asked for a declaration that the provincial act was of no force or effect since it impinged upon the board's freedom of conscience and opinion.

The Supreme Court of British Columbia rejected this argument and held that the freedom of conscience safeguarded in the *Charter* relates to freedom of conscience in matters of religion only. Thus, unless governmental action impinges on a religious belief, it may not be subject to court challenges. This limitation of the meaning of the phrase makes sense in that everyone has his own "conscience" and it would be virtually impossible to find any legislation to which someone does not "conscientiously" object.

Freedom of Expression

The right to express oneself freely is subject to a variety of legal constraints including laws relating to defamation and the propagation of hate literature. Teachers, by virtue of belonging to a professional association, are further restrained from certain types of expression except in accordance with rules laid down by their association in its code of ethics. A typical provision is that found in the *Code of Ethics* of the British Columbia Teacher's Federation which states:

> 5. The teacher directs any criticism of the teaching performance and related duties of a colleague to that colleague, and only then, after informing the colleague of the intent to do so, may direct in confidence the criticism to appropriate officials who are in a position to offer advice and assistance.

The issue of whether such a provision infringes upon the *Charter* right to freedom of expression was decided by the Supreme Court of British Columbia in the case of *Dian Cromer v. B. C. Teacher's Federation* [1984] B.C.D. Civ. 4031-01. The applicant teacher in this case was shocked and concerned about a questionnaire on sexual conduct that was provided to her children by a counsellor in their school. She taught at another school and was a member of the Federation. At a meeting of parents concerning the questionnaire she made a number of derogatory remarks regarding the counsellor (in her presence) and in public. The Federation brought disciplinary procedures for violation of clause 5 of the Code.

The teacher asserted that her comments were made in her role as a concerned parent and had nothing to do with the teaching profession. She claimed protection of the *Charter* and stated that the Code contravened her freedom of expression. She sought an order prohibiting the Federation from proceeding with its action.

The report of the decision states:

> Codes of ethics adopted by professional societies "are designed to ensure a proper standard of professional and ethical conduct by each member of the profession. Such standards of conduct and/or ethics are necessary to warrant the continued confidence of the public in the profession. It is a matter of concern to the profession as a whole when a member fails to observe any of the provisions of its Code of Ethics and conduct because the failure to do so reflects adversely upon the profession and, if serious enough, may bring disgrace upon it." A teacher cannot "wear two hats" and therefore must not, acting in his/her capacity as a "concerned parent" criticize another teacher in public, there being within the teachers' Code of Ethics a procedure laid down for the registration of such criticism. Such

proscription cannot be considered to be an infringement of the teacher's right of free expression guaranteed by the Canadian *Charter of Rights and Freedoms*, s. 2.

No professional person acts in his or her professional capacity at all times. But his or her membership in the relevant profession, and the rules which have been adopted by such profession must always be obeyed. Those rules are concerned with the general actions of the person concerned, and not simply with the impropriety in the practice of his/her professional duties.... . Whether or not the remarks made by the petitioner offend the Code is for the pertinent Committee to decide; but the procedure toward such decision cannot be precluded on the grounds presented here.

A similar provision was considered by the Nova Scotia Supreme Court before the *Charter* was enacted. *Re Busche and Nova Scotia Teacher's Union* (1975) 62 D.L.R. (3d) 330 involved a teacher who wrote two letters to the editor of a local newspaper criticising a meeting of the Halifax local of the Union which advocated militant action. The professional committee found her to be in breach of the code and she brought an application to quash their decision. The Court found that the hearing was not conducted properly and quashed the decision on that basis. However, the judge went on to state:

> In my opinion, it is quite clear that art. 11(a) of the Code of Ethics, providing that a teacher should not make defamatory or disparaging remarks concerning another teacher, is restricted to remarks concerning another teacher *qua* teacher. In my opinion, that article does not refer, and was not intended to refer, to remarks concerning another person who happened to be a teacher, if the remarks did not concern the conduct of that other person as a teacher. Many teachers enter the field of politics, at the municipal, provincial and federal level. If one such politician referred to statements and actions of another politician, with regard to public affairs, including matters related to education, it is inconceivable that the first teacher could be charged with a breach of the code of ethics, merely because somebody considered the remarks were defamatory or disparaging with respect to the other politician.
>
> I am also of the opinion that art. V (c), providing that the teacher should not take any individual action in matters which should be dealt with by his local or by the N.S.T.U., cannot properly be construed in such a way as to stifle public discussion of matters of public interest, such as the form of legislation proposed to deal with education.

Another type of restriction on freedom of speech was considered in the pre-*Charter* case of *Jamieson et al. v. Attorney-General of British Columbia* (1971) 21 D.L.R. (3d) 313. This was an application by a group of teachers for a declaration that an Order in Council be declared *ultra vires* as being in relation to freedom of speech and expression. The Order stated that no person teaching in an institution receiving government support shall continue in his employment if he advocates the policies of the Front de Liberation de Quebec or the overthrow of the government by violent means. None of the applicants had advocated the proscribed doctrines nor were they in jeopardy of losing their employment. It was held, therefore, that they lacked status to maintain the action and it was struck out. The headnote reads as follows:

> To be entitled to maintain an action the interest of the plaintiffs must be an actual, present and "concrete interest" not dependent upon hypothetical events which might but have not yet occurred. While the impugned Order in Council may have the effect of limiting academic freedom and imposing constraints in the full and free discussion of certain subjects, an interest in preserving academic freedom in the abstract, in the absence of any attempted enforcement of the Order in Council against the plaintiffs, is not sufficient to give them status to maintain the action.

Academic Freedom

Although not specifically enumerated in the *Charter*, the concept of academic freedom involves the various fundamental freedoms guaranteed therein. To what extent do teachers enjoy the right to freedom of conscience and religion, freedom of thought, freedom of belief, freedom of opinion and freedom of expression within the school? All of these rights are subject to certain constraints imposed by the curriculum. Academic freedom does not mean teaching whatever you feel like teaching. Nor does it mean that teachers can impose their own beliefs upon their students, since students are entitled to the same right.

This issue has recently been addressed by the courts in the nationally publicized case of James Keegstra, an Alberta teacher who advocated some unorthodox views of history. There were several different legal actions involved throughout the matter. Keegstra was charged under s. 281.2 of the *Criminal Code* with unlawfully promoting hatred against an identifiable group, the Jewish people, by communicating statements while teaching students at a high school. He was dismissed and he appealed the dismissal to a Board of Reference. There was also an action to prevent the broadcast of a CBC program in Alberta pending the outcome of various legal actions to ensure a fair hearing for him.

A jury convicted Keegstra of the criminal charge. Prior to the trial, however, there was a constitutional challenge to the validity of the *Criminal Code* section under which he was charged. Keegstra contended that this section of the Code violated his *Charter* right of freedom of expression. The Alberta Court of Queen's Bench rejected that argument and held that not only does this section of the Code not infringe on freedom of speech but rather is a safeguard which promotes it. Even if it were considered an infringement upon the freedom, it would be saved by s. 1 of the *Charter* because it was a very minimal limitation on the right.

The decision of the Board of Reference regarding the dismissal is reported as *Keegstra v. Board of Education of the County of Lacombe # 14* (1983) 45 A.R. 348. The facts as reported were that the board dismissed Keegstra for failure to comply with the prescribed curriculum, failure to modify his teaching approach to reflect the desires of the community and board, and refusal to comply with the directives of the board as contained in a letter to him. The Justice sitting as the Board of Reference held:

> In continuing the teaching practices I outlined earlier the (appellant) refused to comply with the lawful and reasonable direction of his employer. The appellant also refused to comply with the Alberta Social Studies curriculum.
>
> I am satisfied that the Board had before it sufficient evidence to support the conclusion which it reached. The Board has established before me on a balance of probabilities that the reasons given for termination of the contract did in fact exist and that these constitute sufficient cause for summary dismissal at common law.
>
> I further find that in its proceedings, the respondent acted fairly, and without bias. The respondent gave the appellant ample warning of its position, an opportunity to modify his teaching to conform with the curriculum and its directive, and to be heard, before reaching its decision.

It appears from the decision that the question of academic freedom was discussed at some point in the investigation of the matter. The Superintendent had sent Keegstra a letter which stated:

> I am not giving you this directive to muzzle your academic freedom or to limit your intellectual integrity, but simply to insist that all sides of a historical question must be presented in as unbiased a way as possible, so that students can judge contradictory points for themselves.

The lesson for teachers in this case is that they must not promote their own beliefs and opinions to the exclusion of others, particularly when their beliefs do not conform to the approved curriculum. If the department of education and the board prescribe that the theory of evolution be taught in the science curriculum, a teacher cannot refuse to teach the theory because it contravenes his own religious beliefs. Nor can he choose to teach "creation science" in lieu of the prescribed curriculum. Academic freedom is limited by the curriculum and the directives of the employer.

Sex Discrimination

The *Charter* and various provincial Acts prohibit discrimination on the basis of sex. There have been a few cases involving teachers where this was the subject matter of litigation.

In *Re Board of Governors of the University of Saskatchewan et al.* (1976) 66 D.L.R. (3d) 561 the university refused to allow a homosexual sessional lecturer to supervise practice teaching in the public schools. A complaint was filed under the Saskatchewan *Fair Employment Practices Act.* The Saskatchewan Court of Queen's Bench held that the provision in that Act which prohibits discrimination in employment on the basis of sex does not apply in refusing to employ a person in a certain position because of that person's homosexuality and his publicizing of that fact. The word "sex" means a person's gender and not his sexual propensities.

Some provincial legislatures are considering the amendment of their human rights legislation to include sexual preference as well as gender. The *Charter* equality rights provision refers only to "sex" and will be construed as meaning "gender."

There is evidence to indicate that sexual discrimination against female teachers occurs at the administrative level. Considering the number of females teaching, there are relatively few female administrators. Although suspicion may be strong, it is very difficult to prove, in any particular case, that a woman was not appointed to an administrative position because of her gender. One woman who felt that she had been denied a position on the basis of her gender took the matter to a Board of Inquiry under the *Ontario Human Rights Code.*

In *Offierski v. Peterborough Board of Education* (1980) 1 C.H.R.R. D/30, the complainant alleged that she was, on three occasions, refused admission to take a principal's course and that she did not succeed in obtaining the position of vice-principal because she was a female. The Board of Inquiry found that she was not refused the position because of her gender but rather because the man chosen was "well-qualified and liked" and "was considered to be the applicant who was the best qualified." The complainant was not chosen for the course because of her reputation of inability to get along with people, whether it was deserved or not, and not because she was a woman.

Hiring decisions are a subjective matter. Courts and tribunals will not substitute their impression of who is more qualified for a position in place of that of the hiring authority. Unless there is some clear statement or action on the part of the board that indicates their decision was made (totally or partially) on the basis of gender, tribunals will have no evidence upon which to find discrimination. Those who may be practising *de facto* discrimination will rarely make any overt statements to indicate that is their reason for a particular decision.

Because it is difficult to prove gender, racial, or other forms of discrimination, the *Charter* recognizes the need for affirmative action programs to assist disadvantaged groups to achieve their full role in society. Section 15 (2) of the *Charter* provides:

> Subsection (1) does not preclude any law, program or activity that has as its object the amelioration of conditions of disadvantaged individuals or groups including those that are disadvantaged because of race, national or ethnic origin, colour, religion, sex, age or mental or physical disability.

It can be shown statistically that a certain group is underrepresented in a particular industry and an affirmative action program can be implemented to give preference to those "less qualified." The *Charter* does not provide for court mandated affirmative action programs which have occurred in the United States. It is left up to those who have created this situation of *de facto* discrimination to remedy it.

Racial Discrimination

It is as difficult to prove racial discrimination as it is to prove sex discrimination. The issue was raised by at least one teacher in fighting a termination. *Arny Iancu v. Simcoe County Board of Education* (1983) 4 C.H.R.R. D/1203 involved the termination of a probationary teacher by a school principal. The teacher alleged that he was dismissed because he was not a Franco-Ontarien.

The Board of Inquiry found that while there was a considerable controversy in the community regarding French language education, there was no evidence to indicate that Mr. Iancu's dismissal was due to the fact that he was not of Franco-Ontarien extraction. They found that he was dismissed because of unresolved problems in his relationships with students. The Board also noted that if there had been a breach of the *Human Rights Code* because of the principal's decision, then the Board would have been vicariously liable for that decision since the principal was the "directing mind" of the Board.

Therefore, if a particular principal, or other administrator making an employment decision, can be shown to have discriminated, the Board cannot absolve itself of liability for such actions. School boards must ensure that their administrative personnel do not practice any form of discrimination.

Age Discrimination

In *Gadowsky v. The School Committee of the County of Two Hills, No. 21* (1980) 1 C.H.R.R. D/184 a teacher made a complaint of discrimination based on age and was awarded substantial damages. Mary Gadowsky had been teaching grade 1 at the same school for 26 years. She was told that she would no longer be employed in that position because of declining enrollments and was offered other alternatives which were not acceptable to her. She was the only member of the staff who was offered any of the alternate postings and was the oldest and most senior staff member. As a result she felt that she was pressured into resigning and did so.

The matter came before the Court of Queen's Bench which found:

The Board decided to assign Mrs. Gadowsky to junior high school and I am satisfied that the sole reason was because Mrs. Gadowsky was closer to retirement than any other teacher and that such decision is clearly discrimination against Mrs. Gadowsky because of her age.

It is clear that the County did make a distinction between Mrs. Gadowsky and the other members of the staff of the Myrnam School because of her age and she has therefore been discriminated against.

If the consideration of Mrs. Gadowsky's age was present in the mind of the Respondent, however a minor part it may have played in the eventual decision, it was, in my opinion, discrimination.

There is no question in my mind that Mrs. Gadowsky's age was either the main reason for her forced retirement or was incidental to it, and that the actions of the County offended the dignity and equality of Mrs. Gadowsky and these actions were discrimination against Mrs. Gadowsky because of her age.

There have been various challenges to compulsory retirement legislation or policy in many provinces, usually under provincial legislation. The equality rights provision of the *Charter*, section 15, did not come into force until 1985 and consequently has only recently been the subject of litigation regarding such matters in the context of a *Charter* violation although there have been a number of cases dealing with the subject as a breach of provincial legislation. Courts have generally held that compulsory retirement provisions are enforceable only when there is a *bona fide* occupational requirement for them. At the time of writing, doctors in British Columbia had successfully challenged, using the *Charter*, a prohibition placed on doctors over 65 using operating rooms at hospitals. The Supreme Court of Canada will soon be ruling on a number of these discrimination cases and we will have a definitive decision on the extent of the equality provisions of the *Charter*.

The Supreme Court has given us a glimpse of their views on the matter in the case of *Winnipeg School Division No. 1 v. Doreen Maud Craton* (1985) 6 C.H.R.R. D/3014, which addressed the compulsory retirement of teachers in Manitoba. The mandatory retirement provision of the Board was challenged under the Manitoba *Human Rights Act*. The court held that mandatory retirement did contravene the Act. The Board argued that mandatory retirement was provided for in their collective agreement with the teachers but the court stated that:

> The *Human Rights Act* is legislation declaring public policy and may not be avoided by private contract.
>
> Human rights legislation is of a special nature and declares public policy regarding matters of general concern. It is not constitutional in nature in the sense that it may not be altered, amended, or repealed by the Legislature. It is, however, of such nature that it may not be altered, amended, or repealed, nor may exceptions be created to its provisions, save by clear legislative pronouncement.

Lifestyle

A teacher's lifestyle may be the basis for disciplinary proceedings or dismissal. We have seen that a criminal conviction will be grounds for dismissal, but other behaviour, even if not proscribed by the criminal law, can result in dire consequences for the teacher. The teacher's role as exemplar demands that he conform to certain acceptable standards of behaviour. This naturally imposes some limitation on a teacher's "freedom of lifestyle."

Abbotsford School District 34 Board of School Trustees v. Shewan and Shewan (1986) 70 B.C.L.R. 40 provides an example of how the actions of two teachers outside of the classroom may result in disciplinary action and suspension. The teachers involved were a husband and wife who were suspended by the board for misconduct following the publication of a nude photograph of the wife in Gallery Magazine. A Board of Reference overturned the suspensions and the school board appealed to the courts.

Justice Bouck of the Supreme Court of British Columbia made the following observations concerning teacher "morality":

> In my view, the issue in the case before me involves the "moral standards of the community" where the respondents taught and lived and not the Canadian standards of tolerance test applied to obscenity cases. I say this partly because the moral conduct of a teacher amounting to misconduct may have nothing to do with obscenity as defined under the Criminal Code. Lying by a teacher is an example. A lie amounts to a breach of morality and may be misconduct but it is not obscene. Hence, using the "tolerance" test which was designed for obscenity cases is a poor way of testing "moral conduct."
>
> While the test for obscenity is different from the test for misconduct, nonetheless it seems to me the rules as to admissibility and weight given to expert evidence in obscenity cases is helpful in examining the weight and admissibility of expert evidence when determining the misconduct of a teacher. In effect, the cases indicate opinions of experts on the issue of misconduct of a teacher have little probative value and are more or less irrelevant when the facts themselves are before the tribunal. Besides, hearing expert evidence on what amounts to misconduct is much like hearing expert evidence on whether a person is honest or not. Misconduct, like honesty, is tested mostly by other objective testimony which uses fact and not opinion evidence to arrive at the ultimate answer.
>
> Breaches of the Criminal Code or school regulations by a teacher are examples of objective facts indicating improper behaviour. By themselves, they may be sufficient to reach a finding of misconduct. But other types of abnormal behaviour are not so easy to assess. In certain situations, they may appear to be misconduct to the presiding tribunal whereas to the outside world they may not. The opposite may also be true.
>
> In this instance, the Board of Reference had the right to hear evidence about what a teacher does from day to day and his or her position in the community at large. In this way it could assess the conduct of the average teacher. Then it could examine the alleged act of misconduct. From this evidence it was in a position to decide if there was misconduct because it could compare the conduct of the average teacher as shown by the evidence with the evidence presented to show an act of misconduct on the part of the teacher who was charged. It might not be misconduct for a person in some other trade or calling but the same act committed by a teacher might indeed amount to misconduct. . . .
>
> Did the respondents meet the moral standard of the community by the publication of the nude picture in Gallery Magazine and, if not, did that have any effect on their ability to teach. One way of determining the point is to look at the conduct of other teachers. If a good number of teachers in or about Abbotsford are publishing their nude photographs in a magazine such as the one in question, then the conduct of the respondents may be within community standards. If no other teachers are doing this, then it may be misconduct. Evidence of this nature was not heard by the Board of

Reference but I believe I am entitled to draw an inference from the proven facts as to whether a substantial number of teachers in the Abbotsford area do indeed publish their nude pictures in men's magazines. It seems clear they do not.

This is not a conclusive test because the key ingredient is whether the act of misconduct affects the teacher in his or her educational capacity. If it does not, then it is not an offence under the School Act.

In the opinion of the Board of Reference the conduct of a teacher outside of work does not have to comply with "strictest behaviour in the community." That opinion seems correct but in passing I should say that neither is the conduct necessarily proper if it satisfies the lowest standard of behaviour in the community. To objectively determine what is the community standard is difficult. I think some help can come from other cases where tribunals have adjudicated upon the conduct of public sector officials including teachers.

Justice Bouck then considered a number of other cases where conduct was held to amount to misconduct. He quoted briefly from nine cases including the following:

Re Peace River North Sch. Dist. 60 Bd. of Sch. Trustees and Stockman, 25th January 1874 (unreported). A teacher continued his association with a girl contrary to the wishes of the school board. The details of the association are not set out in the ruling. As a result of his actions, he was suspended. He grieved the suspension which was upheld by the majority. In its award the majority commented upon what is or is not misconduct at p. 2:

. . . In the opinion of the majority of the Board of Reference, Mr. Stockman's continuing association with the girl justified the School Board in concluding that it would not be fulfilling its responsibilities to the community and particularly to parents of the School District's school children, if it did not take steps to terminate the association. However, the evidence is clear that although Mr. Stockman was prepared to make certain concessions with regard to his relationship with the girl, such as limiting public appearances, he was not prepared to terminate the relationship.

In the opinion of the majority of the Board of Reference, Mr Stockman's decision to continue the association with the girl was misconduct within the meaning of the Public Schools Act in that the continued association would likely bring the School Board into disrepute in the community and amounted to a refusal to obey a lawful direction by the School Board.

Peace River North Sch. Dist. 60 Bd. of Sch. Trustees v. Olson, 13th June 1983 (not yet reported). Mrs. Olson was suspended from her position as teacher and then later dismissed. She grieved the discharge. Evidence led before the Board of Reference indicated she knew stolen property was being kept in her house but turned a blind eye to its existence. She also condoned the use of hash and marijuana by others while they were guests in her house. The grievance was dismissed. At p. 14 of the award, the Board of Reference commented upon the position of a school teacher in these words:

Taylor is a small community. Mrs. Olson agreed that word of improprieties travels quickly. The sort of conduct which Mrs. Olson has engaged in or condoned in her home is a failure of her duty to her employer, to her broader constituency, the community and to her profession. It is likely to detract from the esteem for education in the community. It is abusive of the trust that reposed in her which Mrs. Olson acknowledged in her evidence. As such this conduct not only undermines her ability to do her job in this community, it also erodes the ability of the schools to deliver the standard of education that the community is entitled to expect.

Having considered the various decisions of other tribunals in such cases, the judge went on to hold:

What do these decisions tell us? They say a teacher is an important member of the community who leads by example. He or she not only owes a duty of good behaviour to the school board as the employer but also to the local community at large and to the teaching profession. An appropriate standard of moral conduct or behaviour must be maintained both inside and outside the classroom. The nature of that standard will, of course, vary from case to case. Moral standards are those of the community where the teacher is employed and lives not those of some other city or municipality. In most instances there will be little difference, but what may be acceptable in an urban setting may occasionally be misconduct in a rural community and vice versa. For example, a small religious community might find it unacceptable for a female teacher to live with a man out of wedlock or a male teacher to live with a woman who is not his wife. On the other hand, these kinds of relationships may be tolerated in an urban setting where the two people are lost in the anonymity of the crowd because they live far away from the school or because the values of the city are different from the values of the country.

There was an act of misconduct in this case since the incident amounts to abnormal behaviour which reflects unfavourably on the respondents. They are supposed to be examples to the students. Their actions lower the esteem in which they were held by the community including the students, because they set a standard that the community found unsuitable. All of this amounts to misconduct.

In determining an appropriate penalty to be imposed upon the teachers in this case, Justice Bouck looked at several more cases involving teacher misconduct to see what penalties had been imposed in those instances. Among those cases he cited were:

North Vancouver Sch. Dist. 44 Bd. of Sch. Trustees v. Machado-Holsti,
Gifford, 20th August 1981 (unreported) – A female teacher with approximately 12 years experience at a senior secondary school was found responsible for condoning and participating in a breach of school regulations regarding the use of alcohol at a school-supervised function; misleading the school principal with respect to the circumstances which took place; and encouraging and setting an example for students of unsatisfactory qualities of personal behaviour. Penalty – dismissal by the school board; reduced to suspension of 4 months and 19 days by the Board of Reference.

Greater Victoria Sch. Dist. 61 Bd. of Sch. Trustees v. Smith, Lightbody, 6th October 1983 (not yet reported) – A male teacher at a senior secondary school with 10 years' experience admitted to a sexual relationship with a 17-year-old female student. She was not a student in any of his classes. Penalty – dismissal by the school board, reduced to six months suspension by the Board of Reference.

Revelstoke Sch. Dist. 19 Bd. of Sch. Trustees v. Malpass, Cumming, 28th August 1979 (unreported) – A female teacher with an unknown number of years of experience who was teaching at a secondary school was involved in a scuffle of a sexual nature with a female student. Penalty – 1 month plus 13 days suspension by the school board; upheld by the Board of Reference.

The end result was that each of the teachers involved was suspended for a one month period. It is interesting to speculate what the result may have been if the wife in such an incident was not a teacher. The fact that both were teachers seemed to play an important part in the decision. If, however, a male teacher submitted his wife's photo to such a magazine, where the wife was not a teacher, would that have been viewed as seriously? The court suggested that the test should be whether other teachers submitted "their" nude photographs to magazines.

From these cases it is evident that a teacher's lifestyle must conform to that of the community in which he or she resides. Any behaviour that may be regarded by the majority of such community as "abnormal" may result in disciplinary action. A "swinging" urban lifestyle might not be tolerated in a small community. Behaviours most likely to offend a community would usually involve sex, drugs, or alcohol. Teachers' rights in this area are subject to the demands of their professional status.

Discussion and Review Questions

Academic Freedom

1. What is academic freedom?
2. In your opinion, should the concept of academic freedom for the teacher protect the teacher regarding:
     - using controversial books and articles?
     - discussing controversial issues?
     - preaching their religious beliefs in school?
     - non-use of approved texts and curriculum?
     - use of non-relevant materials?
     - using instructional materials with obscene or vulgar words?
     - using controversial teaching methods?
     - ethnic or sexual biases?

Freedom of Conscience

1. May teachers be excused from saluting the flag or reciting the Lord's Prayer in class?
2. May teachers refuse to follow the curriculum if they do so on the basis of their personal religious convictions?
3. May teachers take religious holiday leaves which are not specifically approved by statute on the basis of their religious freedoms?
4. May teachers be prohibited from wearing distinctive religious clothing in the classroom?
5. May a teacher be terminated for violations of the religious tenets of the Church which operates a private or separate school in which the teacher is employed?

Freedom of Association

1. Can teachers be prohibited from promoting political parties or specific political candidates in the classroom?
2. Can teachers be prohibited from wearing political buttons, badges, or similar items in their classroom?
3. Can teachers refuse to pay association dues if a portion of such dues is used to support a political candidate or party?
4. Is compulsory membership in a teachers' association a denial of a teacher's freedom of association?

5. Can a teacher be dismissed for belonging to a Neo-Facist or revolutionary organization?

Freedom of Expression

1. Can teachers publically criticize their professional association?
2. Can teachers publically criticize their local union for taking strike action?
3. Can teachers report suspected criminal activity in the classroom by a fellow teacher without first informing the other teacher?
4. Can teachers be required to conform to a specific school code of grooming?

Lifestyle

1. Can a teacher be dismissed for alleged immoral conduct? What is considered to be immoral conduct?
2. Can a teacher be dismissed for homosexuality?
3. Can a teacher be dismissed for being an unwed mother?
4. Can a teacher be dismissed for immoral conduct with students?
5. Can a teacher be dismissed for excessive drinking?
6. Can a teacher be dismissed or transferred because students have a crush on him/her?
7. Can a teacher be dismissed for "conduct unbecoming" to a teacher?
8. What remedies should be available to the improperly dismissed teacher?

You be the Judge

Case #1

Miss Victoria Hogan had taught Math at a large city high school for 14 years. She was the school's representative to the Teachers' Association and also coached the girl's basketball team. She was a dedicated worker.

Seventeen year old Vicky Thomas, one of Miss Hogan's students and a member of the basketball team, began experiencing some "coping" problems with family and friends. She went to her teacher/coach for advice. The two women talked at length on many occasions both during and after school.

Vicky's parents called the school one day after such a session to verify that Vicky had been with her teacher and to inquire whether statements such as, "I'm an adult, I can think for myself" and, "I will choose my own friends," were the thoughts of their daughter or those of her teacher Miss Hogan.

The conversations was overheard by Mr. Ryan, the principal, who later questioned Miss Hogan about her talks with Vicky. He cautioned her about overstepping "the boundary" since the school had extensive counselling services available for students. He suggested that she refer Vicky to a school counsellor.

Feeling that her continued close relationship with Vicky was more beneficial than any services presently available in the school, Miss Hogan continued to meet her often in school and on long walks after school. Eventually visits to the teacher's home became part of the routine.

Following up a call from the father, Mr. Ryan again directed Miss Hogan to stop counselling Vicky and requested that she refer her to social services if there was a need. Miss Hogan responded, "This is a personal matter unrelated to my teaching. I shall continue to meet with Vicky after hours, in my home, as I see fit."

In a further discussion between Mr. Ryan and the parents, Vicky's father said, "If you don't stop this stuff, I'll have the police do it!"

Sure enough, three weeks later, the parents arrived at Miss Hogan's home accompanied by a police officer. Upon entry, evidence pointed toward a homosexual affair between the young student, Vicky, and her teacher, Victoria.

Miss Hogan was suspended from her teaching duties.

Issues for Decision

1. What grounds exist to support a suspension?
2. What would be Miss Hogan's defence to these charges?
3. Would you uphold the suspension? For how long? Would you take any further action such as termination of employment or decertification?
4. What could Principal Ryan have done differently during the course of events as they unfolded?

Case #2

The staff room had a warm and comfortable feeling about it – the aroma of instant coffee, cigarette smoke, duplicating fluid – but most of all the atmosphere of friendship and caring that had always marked the relationships at Catholic Separate High School.

"What a lovely ring."

"Where did you go for your honeymoon?"

"Where does he work?"

The conversation centred on Jenny, a good-natured woman of 38 years who had taught typing at Catholic High for six years. Jenny had just announced her marriage to Ronald over the Christmas vacation. Ronald, a divorced Baptist, worked for the city's traffic control department.

News travels fast. By the last period of the day, the whole school knew of the marriage and Jenny found herself sitting in the outer office waiting to see Sister Principal. She was still basking in the many good wishes that had been extended to her by both staff and students as she entered the inner office.

"Jenny, it hurts me to do this, but you know the rules. God's message, through the Holy Father, is clear. You have wilfully or thoughtlessly defied The Church. You must leave. I am sorry. We will have difficulty replacing you, but it must be done for the good of the school. Good-bye Jenny."

Issues for Decision

1. Was Jenny's termination justified?
2. What are the legal and the moral issues involved in this case?
3. Would your decision be any different whether or not the school received public funding?
4. Would a public school be justified in firing or refusing to hire a teacher who is Catholic?
5. Is there anything Jenny can do to retain her job?

References

Fish, B. L., "Constitutional Aspects of Teacher Dismissal," (1979) 17 *Alberta Law Review* 545.

Manley-Casimir, M. E. and Sussel, T. A., *Courts in the Classroom: Education and the Charter of Rights and Freedoms,* Calgary: Detselig Enterprises Ltd., 1986.

Glossary

AB INITIO: Latin – "from the beginning."

ABSOLUTE DISCHARGE: A judicial disposition of a criminal case wherein the accused is found guilty of the offence but is discharged without any conditions and is deemed in law not to have been convicted of the offence.

ACCUSED: A person charged with a crime – the defendant in a criminal case.

ACQUIT: To set free or release from a criminal charge by verdict or legal process.

ACTION: A legal process or suit.

ACTIONABLE: Furnishing legal grounds for an action. Often used in tort law when speaking of an "actionable tort."

ACTUS REUS: The "guilty act" or the act by which a criminal offence is committed. See MENS REA.

ADMINISTRATIVE LAW: That branch of law dealing with the operation of various governmental agencies and tribunals that administer specific branches of the government.

ADMINISTRATIVE TRIBUNAL: A quasi-judicial body empowered by law to examine or adjudicate certain matters.

APPEAL: An application to a higher court to review the judgment of a lower court and to correct errors of law or injustice. The person initiating the appeal is called the appellant and the opposite party is called the respondent.

APPEARANCE NOTICE: A notice issued by a peace officer to a person not yet formally charged with a criminal offence, requiring him to appear in court at a specific time to answer to a criminal charge. It is given in lieu of the arrest of the person where the charge is not serious and there is little likelihood that the person will not appear to answer the charge.

ARBITRATION: A procedure for settling disputes by referring them to a neutral person or persons, whose decision the parties have agreed to accept.

367

ASSAULT: The intentional application of force to another person, or an attempt or threat to do so by act or gesture with the apparent ability to cause injury. See BATTERY.

ATTRACTIVE NUISANCE: Any machine, apparatus or condition that is potentially dangerous to young children and which may attract them onto the owner's property. If a child is injured by such apparatus or condition, the owner may be held responsible and pay damages.

BATTERY: An unlawful touching, however trifling, of another person without his consent.

BALANCE OF PROBABILITIES: The level of proof required in a civil case. This level is lower than that required in criminal cases. It requires that the matter be proven to the point where it is more probable than not that such a fact is true. See BEYOND A REASONABLE DOUBT.

BENCH WARRANT: An order issued at the direction of a court or a judge for the arrest of an individual.

BEYOND A REASONABLE DOUBT: The level of proof required to convict a person of a crime which is the highest level of proof required in any type of trial. The evidence presented must be such that the judge or jury do not have any reasonable doubt as to the guilt of the accused. This must be a real doubt not speculation or a fanciful or illusory doubt. Compare with BALANCE OF PROBABILITIES, the level of proof in civil cases.

BILL OF RIGHTS: A formal declaration by a government of the fundamental rights and freedoms of an individual. In Canada, the Canadian Bill of Rights was enacted in 1960 and The Charter of Rights and Freedoms in 1982. In the United States the Bill of Rights consists of the first ten amendments to the American Constitution.

BOARD OF ARBITRATION: An administrative tribunal set up to arbitrate a dispute between parties and render a binding decision. Such a Board would often hear a labour grievance between an association and an employer. See ARBITRATION and ADMINISTRATIVE TRIBUNAL.

BOARD OF REFERENCE: An administrative tribunal empowered by statute to hear and determine appeals concerning the dismissal or suspension of a teacher. See ADMINISTRATIVE TRIBUNAL.

BONA FIDE: Latin "in good faith"; genuine, without any element of fraud or dishonesty.

BURDEN OF PROOF: The duty imposed on a party to an action of proving to the court certain matters of fact to the required level of proof.

BY A PREPONDERANCE OF THE EVIDENCE: The civil burden of proof. See BALANCE OF PROBABILITIES.

BY-LAWS: Statutory law enacted by lower governments or agencies, usually municipal governments or school boards.

CASE: An action or suit.

CASE LAW: The body of law developed from custom and judicial precedent embodied in the decisions which courts have made in resolving disputes, as distinguished from statutes and constitutions. Often referred to as "the ancient unwritten law of England." Also called COMMON LAW.

CAUSA CAUSANS: The immediate cause; the last link in a chain of causation.

CAUSE OF ACTION: A set of facts which will cause a court to grant relief, and therefore entitles a person to initiate and prosecute a lawsuit.

CHATTEL: Personal property; any tangible or moveable object.

CHARTER OF RIGHTS AND FREEDOMS: A bill of rights entrenched in the Canadian Constitution which guarantees fundamental freedoms, legal rights, democratic rights, mobility rights, equality rights, and language rights.

CIRCUMSTANTIAL EVIDENCE: Indirect evidence; facts providing reasonable grounds for inferring the existence of other facts.

CITATION: A formal reference to a published judgment, statute or other legal authority.

CIVIL CASE: Every lawsuit other than a criminal proceeding. Most civil cases involve a lawsuit brought by one person against another and usually concern money damages. A lawsuit that deals with private or civil matters.

CIVIL REMEDY: The remedy which an injured party has against the party who committed the injury, as distinguished from criminal proceedings by which the wrongdoer is made to expiate the injury done to society. A civil remedy may be monetary damages or some other type of remedy depending upon the nature of the case.

CIVIL RIGHTS: Fundamental freedoms and rights guaranteed by the constitution.

CLASS ACTION: A lawsuit brought on behalf of a group of persons similarly situated who all seek the same remedy.

CODIFIED LAW: The laws of a province or country that are recorded in written form.

COMMON LAW: See CASE LAW.

COMPARATIVE NEGLIGENCE: Where the negligence of both the plaintiff and the defendant is taken into account in awarding damages. See CONTRIBUTORY NEGLIGENCE.

CONDITIONAL DISCHARGE: A judicial disposition of a criminal case wherein the accused is found guilty of an offence but is discharged upon certain conditions. If the conditions are fulfilled then the accused is deemed in law not to have been convicted of the offence.

CONSTITUTION: The rules and laws, written or unwritten, that establish and order the political, legal and governmental structure of a state.

CONTRIBUTORY NEGLIGENCE: The failure to exercise care by a plaintiff, which contributes to his injury for which another is partly or mainly responsible. Damages are reduced proportionately by the contribution of the plaintiff to his own injury.

CONVERSION: The illegal appropriation to one's own use of the property of another.

COPYRIGHT: The right of ownership and right to reproduce an original literary, artistic or musical work granted to the creator of such work.

CORPOREAL PROPERTY: A tangible property which has substance and can be detected by one of the senses.

CORROBORATE: To support or confirm evidence by further evidence from another source.

DAMAGES: Money awarded by a court in a civil action as compensation for an injury or wrong suffered by the plaintiff. They are classed as:
(1) Punitive (exemplary) – In excess of the actual damage, but intended as a punishment of the defendant and to deter others.
(2) Special (liquidated) – Actual pecuniary loss or out of pocket expenses.
(3) General (unliquidated) – Monetary damages to compensate for actual losses not consisting of pecuniary loss e.g. physical injury.
(4) Nominal – A small amount awarded where the plaintiff has proved his case but the court is of the opinion that he has not suffered any real or serious damage.

DE FACTO: In fact; actual; a situation that exists in fact whether or not it is lawful. See DE JURE.

DEFAMATION: Injuring a person's character or reputation by false or malicious statements. This includes both libel and slander.

DEFAULT JUDGEMENT: Judgement for the plaintiff when the defendant fails to appear or file an answer within the given time.

DEFENDANT: The person against whom a legal action in brought. The party defending or denying a claim.

DE JURE: By right; lawful; a situation that exists as a matter of law whether or not it exists in fact.

DE NOVO (Latin): New; over again.

DICTA: Statement by a judge concerning a point of law not necessary for the decision of the case in which it is made.

DISCHARGE: See ABSOLUTE DISCHARGE and CONDITIONAL DISCHARGE.

DUE PROCESS OF LAW: The principles of justice which limit a government's power to deprive a person of his civil rights.

DUTY OF CARE: A concept in tort law used to indicate the standard of legal duty that one person owes to another.

ENACTMENT: Something that has been enacted by a legislature; a statute or part thereof.

ESTOPPEL: Being stopped from proving something (even if true) in court because of something said or done before that shows the opposite.

EX PARTE: With only one side present; an 'ex parte' judicial proceeding involves only one party without notice to, or contestation by, any person adversely affected.

EX REL: On behalf of; when a case is titled *Rex rel. Doe v. Roe*, it means that the state is bringing a lawsuit against Roe on behalf of Doe.

EXCLUSIONARY RULE: The rule that prevents illegally obtained evidence from being admitted in a criminal case.

EXPUNGE: Blot out. For example, a court order requesting that a student's record be expunged of any references to disciplinary action during such and such a period means that the references are to be "wiped off the books."

GRATUITOUS PASSENGER: An automobile passenger who has not given any type of compensation to the driver in exchange for the ride.

GRIEVANCE: In labour law, an injustice or wrong serving as grounds for complaint.

GUARDIAN: Someone legally appointed to care for the person and property of another who is not competent to act for himself, such as a minor or mentally incompetent person.

HABEAS CORPUS: A prerogative writ directed to a person who holds another in custody commanding him to produce that person (have the body) before the court and show cause for the detention.

HEARING: The presentation of evidence or argument before a court or quasi-judicial tribunal.

HEARSAY: Second-hand evidence; evidence of facts not in the personal knowledge of the witness, but a repetition of what others said. Hearsay is generally not allowed as evidence although there are many exceptions.

HOLDING: The ratio decidendi of a case; the rule of law in a case; that part of the judge's written opinion that applies the law to the facts of the case and about which can be said "the case means no more and no less than this."

IN CAMERA: In chambers; in a judge's private office; a hearing in court with all spectators excluded.

INCORPOREAL PROPERTY: Property which is intangible or not material in nature, i.e. it cannot be seen or touched. Copyright and patent rights are examples of this type of property.

INDICTMENT: A formal written charge of the commission of a crime presented in court.

INFANT: A minor; a person not legally able to act on his own behalf because he has not attained the age of majority which is usually 18.

INFERIOR COURT: A court of lower status; in Canada usually refers to provincial courts.

INFORMATION: A formal accusation or complaint under oath, charging someone with the commission of a criminal offence.

INFORMED CONSENT: A person's agreement to allow something to happen (such as surgery) that is based on a full disclosure of facts needed to make the decision intelligently.

INFRINGEMENT: A trespass upon a right particularly used in copyright cases.

INJUNCTION: A court order requiring the person to whom it is addressed to refrain from or cease doing some specific action.

IN LOCO PARENTIS: In the place of the parent; acting as a parent with respect to the care, supervision, and discipline of a child not the person's own.

IN RE: In the matter of; this is a prefix to the name of a case often used when a child is involved. For example, *In re Mary Smith* might be the title of a child neglect proceeding even though it is really against the parents.

INTENT: Design; resolve; determination; the state of mind in which an act is done. To render an act criminal, a wrongful intent must exist, but this intent may be presumed, if the necessary and probable results of the act were harmful, and the act was deliberately committed. See MENS REA.

INTER ALIA: Among other things; usually used when what is being mentioned is only part of what there is.

INTRA VIRES: Within their powers. Used in constitutional law to denote acts that are within the legislative powers of the body performing such acts. See ULTRA VIRES.

INVITEE: One who comes onto another's property with an express or implied invitation to do so.

JUDICIAL NOTICE: The recognition by a judge that certain commonly known and indisputable facts are true even though they have not been presented as evidence.

JUDICIAL REVIEW: The review by a court of a decision of an administrative tribunal or an inferior court to determine if the hearing was procedurally correct.

JURISDICTION: The extent of a court's authority to hear a case; also the geographical area within which a court has the right and power to operate. Original jurisdiction means that the court will be the first to hear the case; appellate jurisdiction means that the court reviews cases on appeal from lower court rulings.

JUSTICE: The title of a judge of a Supreme or Appellate Court.

LAST CLEAR CHANCE: In negligence law, the last obvious opportunity to avoid an injury. The person with the last clear chance will usually be held responsible in damages for the injury.

LEADING CASE: A precedent that has been so often followed as to establish a principle of law.

LEGAL PROCESS: The course of proceedings in a civil or criminal case.

LEGISLATION: Law enacted by a government.

LIABILITY: The responsibility for payment of damages resulting from negligence.

LIBEL: A defamatory statement published in a permanent form such as writing, pictures or film.

LICENSEE: A person who enters onto another's property with permission although not with an invitation.

LIMITATION PERIOD: A fixed period of time during which a law suit must be started if it is ever to be heard. The period varies for different types of action. See STATUTE OF LIMITATIONS.

LITIGANT: A person engaged in a law suit.

LITIGATE: To carry on a lawsuit.

MAGISTRATE: A judge of a provincial court.

MALA FIDES: Bad faith; malice. The opposite of BONA FIDES.

MALFEASANCE: The doing of an unlawful act.

MALPRACTICE: Professional misconduct; negligent conduct in the performance of professional duties.

MENS REA: "The guilty mind"; criminal intent; evil intent. The mental element in a criminal offence e.g. intention or recklessness as to consequence, which, together with the ACTUS REUS make up the commission of the crime. Mens rea is an essential element in most offences and must be proved. MINOR: See INFANT.

MINORITY: The status of a person who is of less that full age

MISDIRECTION: An error in law made by a judge in instructing a trial jury.

MISFEASANCE: The improper performance of a legal act.

MISTAKE: An act done or omitted, by reason of ignorance of law or facts, which a person would not have committed if he had rightly understood the law or facts. Mistake of fact is a good defence; mistake of law is not.

MISTRIAL: Descriptive of a trial at which an event occurs which causes the judge to terminate the proceedings because he believes that a fair verdict cannot be obtained on account of that event or the declaration following a jury's inability to reach a verdict.

MITIGATION: Reduction of damages or of punishment. Circumstances which do not amount to an excuse or defence may nevertheless properly be considered in mitigation of the punishment or the damages.

MODUS OPERANDI: Manner of operation.

MORAL TURPITUDE: Behaviour contrary to the accepted rules of propriety; immorality.

MOTION: A request made by a lawyer that a judge take certain action, such as dismissing a case.

NEGLIGENCE: The culpable failure to use ordinary care in performing a positive duty. The essential elements in a negligence action are the existence of a legal duty, a breach of that duty and consequent injury..

NEXT FRIEND: A person who acts for a minor or insane person in a legal action.

NOMINAL DAMAGES: See DAMAGES.

NONFEASANCE: The failure to perform an act required by law.

NON-SUIT: A judgment against the plaintiff, when he fails to prove his case, or neglects to appear at the trial.

NUISANCE: Actions which annoy or harm other persons. Private nuisance occurs, e.g. when one person uses his property so as to damage another's or interfere with his quiet enjoyment of it. Public nuisance is interference with the enjoyment of the whole community e.g. obstructing a highway.

NULLITY: An act or proceeding that is regarded as not having taken place.

OBITER DICTUM (Latin): A "saying by the way"; unnecessary words in an opinion. An opinion or statement about the law which is incidental, not essential, to the decision of the case.

OCCUPIER'S LIABILITY: The responsibility of an owner or possessor of property for accidents happening thereon to others.

ORDER-IN-COUNCIL: An order of the government made when exercising a law-making power granted to it by statute. See REGULATION.

ORDINANCE: The term applied to a municipality's legislative enactments or those of a territorial government. Similar to a statute. See BY-LAW.

PARENS PATRIAE: The historical right of all governments to take care of persons under their jurisdiction, particularly minors and incapacitated persons.

PENAL STATUTE: Legislative acts which prohibit particular behaviour, and impose a penalty for the commission of it, e.g. the Criminal Code.

PER CURIAM: By the court. It denotes an opinion of the whole court as opposed to an opinion of a single judge.

PER SE: Of itself; taken alone.

PETITIONER: One who initiates a proceeding by way of a petition to the court and requests some relief be granted on his behalf; a plaintiff. When the terminology "petitioner" is used, the one against whom the petitioner is requesting relief is referred to as the respondent.

PLAINTIFF: One who initiates a lawsuit; the party bringing suit.

PLEADINGS: The formal written statements of each party in an action. These include a Statement of Claim, Statement of Defence, and Counterclaim among others. The pleadings are not evidence but merely allegations of fact which the party making them must prove at the trial.

PRECEDENT: A court decision on a question of law that gives authority or direction on how to decide a similar question of law in a later case with similar facts. See STARE DECISIS.

PRELIMINARY HEARING: A hearing to determine whether there is sufficient evidence to require the indictment of an accused.

PRESUMPTION: An inference drawn from probable reasoning. In law, a person is usually presumed to have intended the consequences of his actions and no proof of actual intent is required.

PRIMA FACIE: "At first view"; clear on the face of it; a fact that will be considered to be true unless disproved by contrary evidence. For example, a prima facie case is a case that will win unless the other side comes forward with evidence to dispute it.

PRIVILEGE: A defence to a defamation action that the statement made was made under circumstances whereby it is not actionable.

PROBABLE CAUSE: Reasonable cause under the circumstances.

PROBATION: A judicial decision to allow a convicted person to go free under supervision and in accordance with certain terms.

PROCEDURAL LAW: The laws relating to the mode of proceeding in a civil or criminal case including the laws of evidence, rules of limitation and the formal steps to be taken in each case.

PROMISE TO APPEAR: A promise given by an accused after arrest that he will appear in court to answer the charge at a specified date.

PROSECUTE: To proceed against a person in a criminal action.

PROXIMATE CAUSE: The cause that actually leads to an injury; the one event without which the injury could not have taken place.

PUNITIVE DAMAGES: See DAMAGES.

QUANTUM MERUIT: As much as it merited – what he has earned.

QUASI-JUDICIAL: The case-deciding function of an administrative agency following its own procedure and rules of natural justice as distinct from a judicial decision of the courts following strict legal procedure.

QUASH: to annul; set aside; make void.

RATIO DECIDENDI: The reason for a decision. The principle of law that a case establishes. See HOLDING.

RE: In the matter of. See IN RE.

REASONABLE DOUBT: The degree of doubt as to the guilt of an accused which requires a verdict of not guilty. See BEYOND A REASONABLE DOUBT.

RECOGNIZANCE: A bond given by a person before a court binding that person to do or not to do something, such as to appear in court at a certain time, or to keep the peace.

REGULATIONS: Subordinate legislation enacted by a government through an Order-in-Council under statutory authority for the purpose of carrying out the statute in question.

REMEDY: The legal means to declare or enforce a right or to redress a wrong.

REMOTENESS: Distance, a lack of connection between a wrong done someone and the injury he suffered. If damage is too remote the injured party cannot recover for it from the wrongdoer.

RES JUDICATA: A thing decided. Thus, if a court decides a case, the matter is settled and no new lawsuit on the same subject may be brought by the persons involved.

RES IPSA LOQUITUR: The thing speaks for itself; a doctrine in the law of negligence, when the court holds that no further proof of negligence is needed than the incident itself, i.e. it could not have happened if there had been no negligence.

RESPONDENT: One who makes an answer in a legal appellate proceeding or a proceeding commenced by petition or notice of motion. This term is frequently used in appellate and divorce cases, rather than the more customary term, defendant.

RESTITUTIO IN INTEGRUM: The restitution of the parties to their original positions.

RESTRAINING ORDER: A temporary order of the court to preserve the status quo pending a full hearing of a dispute, to prevent immediate and irreparable injury.

REVERSE: To set aside, for example, an appellate court can reverse the decision of a lower court.

SIC (Latin): Literally; so; in this manner. Used in citing a quotation containing an error to indicate that the error was in the original material.

SINE DIE: Without a day i.e. indefinitely.

SINE QUA NON: A thing or condition that is indispensable.

SLANDER: Defamation in a non-permanent form; oral defamation; the speaking of false and malicious words that injure another person's reputation, business, or property rights.

SOVEREIGN IMMUNITY: The government's freedom from being sued for money damages without its consent.

STARE DECISIS: "Let the decision stand"; a legal rule that when a court has decided a case by applying a legal principle to a set of facts, that court should stick by that principle and apply it to all later cases with clearly similar facts unless there is a good reason not to. This rule helps promote fairness and reliability in judicial decision-making and is inherent in the common law system.

STATUTE: A law passed by a provincial or federal legislative body.

STATUTE OF LIMITATIONS: A statute that sets forth the time period within which litigation may be commenced in a particular cause of action.

STAY OF PROCEEDINGS: The suspension of a lawsuit. In criminal proceedings this can be for an indefinite time; it is done at the request of the prosecutor when there is insufficient evidence for conviction. In civil matters it occurs when the plaintiff does not have the right, at present, to sue.

SUB. NOM: Under the name.

SUBROGATION: Substitution of one person for another so that certain rights which attach to one person now attach to another. In insurance matters, where an insurance company pays money to its insured it will be subrogated to that person's rights to take action against the person occasioning the loss.

SUBSTANTIVE LAW: The law determining the legal rights of the parties to an action as opposed to the PROCEDURAL LAW for the conduct of the action.

SUI GENERIS: Of its own kind; unique; one of a kind.

SUIT: A civil action; litigation.

SUMMARY CONVICTION OFFENCE: Crimes of a less serious nature which are tried by a magistrate without a jury.

TORT: Any one of various private injuries or wrongs which are recognized by the law e.g. trespass, assault, libel, false imprisonment, conversion. Damages are usually awarded to the injured party.

TORT FEASOR: Wrongdoer; a person who commits a tort.

TRESPASSER: A person who enters onto another's property without any authorization or legal right.

TRIAL COURT: The court in which a case is originally tried, as distinct from higher courts to which the case might be appealed.

ULTRA VIRES: Beyond their powers. In constitutional law it denotes actions which are outside of the legislative authority of the government purporting to do so. For example it would be ultra vires for the federal government to make legislation pertaining to education as that is exclusively a provincial matter.

UNWRITTEN LAW: See CASE LAW.

VENUE: The locale where a case is to be tried. Where several courts may have jurisdiction, venue may be set at the court most convenient for the parties. If venue is not properly set originally, it may be changed later.

VICARIOUS LIABILITY: The responsibility of one person through the wrongful act of another.

VOID: Of no legal effect; a nullity

VOIDABLE: Capable of being rescinded.

VOLENS: Consenting.

VOLENTI NON FIT INJURIA: That to which a man consents cannot be an injury. A defence in tort law asserting that the plaintiff consented to the damage done or elected to take the risk with full knowledge of the nature and extent of the risk.

VOLUNTARY ASSUMPTION OF RISK: See VOLENTI NON FIT INJURIA.

WRIT OF SUMMONS: A process issued by a court at the request of a plaintiff to give the person sued notice of the claim made against him.

WRONGDOER: A person committing an injury, injustice or crime.

1. *Abbotsford School District 34 Board of School Trustees* v. *Shewan and Shewan* (1986) 70 B.C.L.R. 40. p. 358

2. *Adams* v. *Board of School Commissioners for the City of Halifax* [1951] 2 D.L.R. 816. p. 232

3. *Andrews* v. *Hopkins* [1932] 3 D.L.R. 459. p. 196

4. *Anns* v. *Merton London Borough Council* [1977] 2 W.L.R. 1024. p. 289

5. *Attorney General of British Columbia* v. *Board of School Trustees of School District 65* (Cowichan) (1985) 63 B.C.L.R. 130. p. 350

6. *B.M.* v. *State of Montana* 649 P.2d 425 (1982). p. 286

7. *Bales* v. *Board of School Trustees, School District 26 [Central Okanagan]* (1984) 8 Admin. L. R. 202. p. 288

8. *Barnes* v. *Hampshire County Council* [1969] 3 All E.R. 746. p. 248

9. *Beaumont* v. *Surrey County Council* (1968) L.G.R. 580. p. 233

10. *Beauparlant et al.* v. *The Appleby Separate School Trustees et al.* [1955] O.W.N. 286. p. 228

11. *Beckwith and Allen* v. *Colchester-East Hants Amalgamated School Board* (1977) 23 N.S.R.2d 268. p. 180

12. *Board of Education for the City of Toronto* v. *Higgs* [1960] S.C.R. 174. pp. 233, 250

13. *Board of Education of the City of New York* v. *Allen* (1959) 160 N.E.2d 60. p. 19

14. *Board of School Trustees of School District No. 37 (Delta)* v. *Vaselenak* (1977) 82 D.L.R. (3d) 509. p. 181

15. *Board of School Trustees, School District No. 39 (Vancouver)* v. *John Doe*, unreported B.C. Board of Reference decision August 28, 1979. p. 182

16. *Board of School Trustees, School District No. 13 (Kettle Valley)* v. *John Doe*, unreported B.C. Board of Reference decision, May, 1980. p. 183

17. *Boivin* v. *Glenavon School District* [1937] 2 W.W.R. 170. p. 267

18. *Boryszko et al* v. *Board of Education of the City of Toronto et al.* (1963) 35 D.L.R. (2d) 529. p. 265

19. *Brault* v. *Commissaires D'Ecoles De Ste. Bridge* [1951] R.L. 479. p. 200

20. *Brisson* v. *Lafontaine* (1864) L.C.J. 173. p. 195

21. *Brost* v. *Board of School Trustees of Eastern Irrigation School Division No. 44* [1955] 3 D.L.R. 159. p. 267

22. *Brown* v. *Board of Education* 347 U.S. 463 (1954). p.11

23. *Butterworth et al.* v. *Collegiate Institute Board of Ottawa* [1940] 3 D.L.R. 466. p. 237

24. *Caldwell* v. *Stuart et al.* [1984] 2 S.C.R. 603. p. 345

25. *Campeau* v. *R.* (1951) 103 C.C.C. 355. p. 113

26. *Carmarthenshire County Council* v. *Lewis* [1955] A.C. 549. p. 247

27. *Carriere et al.* v. *Board of Gravelbourg School District No. 2244 of Saskatchewan* [1977] 5 W.W.R. 517. p. 212

28. *Casagrande* v. *Hinton Roman Catholic Separate School District No. 155* (1987) 51 Alta L.R. (2d) 349. p. 347

29. *Chase* v. *R.* (1984) 40 C.R. (3d) 282. p. 126

30. *Chicoine* v. *Ryerson Polytechnical Institute* (1985) 15 Admin L. R. 261. p. 295

31. *Chilvers* v. *London County Council et al.* (1916) 80 J.P. 246. p. 249

32. *Ching* v. *Surrey County Council* [1910] 1 K.B. 736. p. 263

33. *Choukalos* v. *The Board of Trustees of St. Albert Protestant Separate School District No. 6* unreported. p. 319

34. *Cleary* v. *Booth* [1893] 1 Q.B. 465. p. 112

35. *Crits* v. *Sylveser* [1956] O.R. 132 aff'd [1956] S.C.R. 991. p. 276

36. *Cropp* v. *Potashville School Unit No. 25* (1977) 4 C.C.L.T. 12. p. 264

37. *Cromer* v. *B. C. Teacher's Federation* [1984] B.C.D. Civ. 4031-01. p. 351

38. *Cuisenaire* v. *Reed* [1963] V.R. 719. p. 94

39. *Cuisenaire* v. *South West Imports Limited* [1969] S.C.R. 208. pp. 94, 101

40. *D.* v. *Nat. Society for the Prevention of Cruelty to Children,* [1978] A.C. 171, [1977] 1 All E.R. 589. p. 141

41. *DeKoning et al.* v. *Boychuk* (1951) 2 W.W.R. (N.S.) 251. p. 230

42. *Doe* v. *Board of Education of Montgomery County,* 453 A.2d 814 (1982). p. 282

43. *Donald* v. *Hamilton Board of Education* [1944] 4 D.L.R. 227; [1945] 3 D.L.R. 424. p. 312

44. *Donohue* v. *Copiague Union Free School District,* 391 N.E. 2d 1352 (1979). p. 279

45. *D.S.W.* v. *Fairbanks North Star Borough School District,* 628 P.2d 554 (1981). p. 283

46. *Duncan* v. *Ladysmith School Trustees* [1930] 3 W.W.R. 175. p. 225

47. *Durham* v. *North Oxford Public School Board* [1960] O.R. 320. p. 263

48. *Dyer* v. *Board of School Commissioners for the City of Halifax* (1956) 2 D.L.R. (2d) 394. p. 232

49. *Dziwenka et al.* v. *The Queen in Right of Alberta et al.* (1971) 25 D.L.R. (3d) 12. p. 221

50. *Eaton et al.* v. *Lasuta et al.* (1977) 2 C.C.L.T. 38. p. 235

51. *Edmondson* v. *Board of Trustees for the Moose Jaw School District No. 1* (1920) 55 D.L.R. 563. p. 267

52. *Ellis* v. *Board of Trustees for Moose Jaw Public School District* [1946] 2 D.L.R. 697. p. 232

53. *Emerson* v. *Melancthon School Trustees* [1904] O.W.N. 12. p. 212

54. *Epperson* v. *Arkansas* (1969) 393 U.S. 97. p. 19

55. *Fitzgerald* v. *Northcote* (1865) 176 E.R. 734 p. 198

56. *Fryer* v. *Salford Corporation* [1937] 1 All E.R. 617. p. 227

57. *G.H. et al* v. *Board of Education of Shamrock School Division No. 38 of Saskatchewan,* [1987] 3 W.W.R. 270. p. 325

58. *Gadowsky* v. *The School Committee of the County of Two Hills, No. 21* (1980) 1 C.H.R.R. D/184. p. 357

59. *Gard* v. *Board of School Trustees of Duncan* [1946] 2 D.L.R. 441. p. 244

60. *Gelles-Widmer Company* v. *Milton Bradley Company et al.* 136 U.S.P.Q. 240. p. 101

61. *George et al.* v. *Board of School Trustees, School District 70 (Port Alberni)* [1987] 3 A.C.W.S. (3d) 361. p. 246

62. *Gibbs* v. *Barking Corporation* [1936] 1 All E.R. 115. p. 237

63. *Glass* v. *Warner* (1979) 17 A.R. 315. p. 181

64. *Goslett* v. *Garme* [1897] 13 T.L.R. 391. p. 203

65. *Foss* v. *Lopez* [1975] U.S. 565. p. 330

66. *Greater Victoria Sch. Dist. 61 Bd. of Sch. Trustees* v. *Smith,* unreported. p. 362

67. *Hall et al.* v. *Thompson et al.* [1952] O.W.N. 133. p. 235

68. *Helm* v. *Professional Children's School* 431 N.Y.S.2d 247 (1980). p. 284

69. *Herring* v. *Boyle* (1834) 149 E.R. 1126. p. 198

70. *Hoar* v. *Board of School Trustees, District 68 (Nanaimo) and Haynes* [1984] 6 W.W.R. 143. pp. 223, 292

71. *Hoffman* v. *Board of Education,* 400 N.E. 2d 317 (1979). p. 280

72. *Hollands* v. *Canterbury County Council* (1966), Kentish Gazette, September 30 and October 28. pp. 200, 287

73. *Hulme* v. *Marshall* [1887] J.P. 136. p. 204

74. *Hunter* v. *Johnson* (1884) 13 Q.B. 225. p. 199

75. *Hunter* v. *Board of Education of Montgomery County* (1982) 439 A.2d 582. pp. 199, 282

76. *Hutt et al.* v. *Governors of Haileybury College et al.* (1888) 4 T.L.R. 623. p. 322

77. *Iancu* v. *Simcoe County Board of Education* (1983) 4 C.H.R.R. D/1203. p. 356

78. *Ingraham* v. *Wright* 430 U.S. 651 (1977). p. 116

79. *James* v. *River East School Division No. 9* (1976) 64 D.L.R. (3d) 338. pp. 225, 291

80. *Jamieson et al.* v. *Attorney-General of British Columbia* (1971) 21 D.L.R. (3d) 313. p. 352

81. *Johnson* v. *Sampson 208 N.W. 814 (1926). p. 201*

82. *Jones et al.* v. *London County Council* (1932) 48 T.L.R. 577. p. 234

83. *Jones* v. *R.* (1987) 73 A.R. 133. pp. 317

84. *Keegstra* v. *Board of Education of the County of Lacombe # 14* (1983) 45 A.R. 348. p. 354

85. *Koch* v. *Stone Farm School District* [1940] 2 D.L.R. 602. p. 231

86. *Lamarche* v. *L'Orignal Separate School Trustees* [1956] O.W.N. 686. p. 267

87. *Lamphier* v. *Phipos* (1838) 8 C. & P. 475. p. 276

88. *Landeros* v. *Flood* 131 Cal. Rptr. 69 (1976). p. 135

89. *Lapensee et al.* v. *Ottawa Day Nursery Inc. et al.* [1986] C.C.L.T. 129. p. 261

90. *Lefebvre* v. *La Congregation des Petits Freres De Ste-Marie* [1890] M.L.R. 6 S.C. 430. p. 195

91. *Loney* v. *Toronto Board of Education* (1926) 30 O.W.N. 75. p. 201

92. *Loughran* v. *Flanders* 470 F. Supp. 110 (1979). p. 284

93. *MacKell* v. *Ottawa Separate School Trustees* (1914) 18 D.L.R. 475. p. 18

94. *Magnusson et al.* v. *Board of the Nipawin School Unit No. 61 of Saskatchewan* (1975) 60 D.L.R. (3d) 572. p. 262

95. *Mallett* v. *Clarke* (1968) 70 D.L.R. (2d) 67. p. 204

96. *Mansell* v. *Griffin* [1908] 1 K.B. 168. pp. 196, 197

97. *Mattinson et al.* v. *Wonnacott et al.* (1975) 59 D.L.R. (3d) 18. p. 246

98. *McCue et al.* v. *The Board of Education for the Borough of Etobicoke et al.* (reported in The Canadian School Executive, October, 1983 p. 30). p. 250

99. *McGonegal* v. *Gray* [1952] S.C.R. 274. p. 227

100. *McIntyre* v. *McBean* (1856) 13 U.C.Q.B. 534. p. 204

101. *McKay* v. *Board of Govan School Unit No. 29* (1967) 62 D.L.R. (2d) 503 rev'd (1968) 68 D.L.R. (2d) 519, [1968] S.C.R. 589. pp. 243, 290

102. *Moodejonge et al.* v. *Huron County Board of Education et al.* (1972) 25 D.L.R. (3d) 661. p. 229

103. *Moore* v. *Vanderloo* 386 N.W.2d 108 (1986). p. 285

104. *Moorhouse* v. *University of New South Wales* (1974) 23 F.L.R. 112. p. 97

105. *Murdock* v. *Richards* [1954] 1 D.L.R. 766. p. 196

106. *Murray et al.* v. *The Board of Education of the City of Belleville* [1943] 1 D.L.R. 494. p. 237

107. *Myers et al.* v. *Peel County Board of Education et al.* (1981) 123 D.L.R. (3d) 1. p. 241

108. *Ness* v. *Independent School District of Sioux City* 298 N.W. 855. p. 202

109. *New Jersey* v. *T.L.O.* 105 S. Ct. 733. p. 170

110. *North Vancouver Sch. Dist. 44 Bd. of Sch. Trustees* v. *Machado-Holsti*, unreported. p. 362

111. *O'Brien* v. *Procureur General de Quebec* [1961] S.C.R. 184. p. 225

112. *Offierski v, Peterborough Board of Education* (1980) 1 C.H.R.R. D/30. p. 355

113. *Paladino* v. *Adelphi University* (1982) 454 N.Y.S.2d 868. pp. 18, 284

114. *Park* v. *Chessin* (1976) 387 N.Y.S.2d 204. p. 295

115. *Patterson* v. *Vancouver Board of School Trustees* [1929] 3 D.L.R. 33. p. 261

116. *Peace River North Sch. Dist. 60 Bd. of Sch. Trustees* v. *Olson* unreported. p. 360

117. *Pearson* v. *Vancouver Board of School Trustees et al.* [1941] 3 W.W.R. 874. p. 261

118. *Peter W.* v. *San Francisco Unified School District*, 131 Cal. Rptr. 854 (1976). p. 278

119. *Phillips* v. *Regina Public School District No. 4 Board of Education et al.* (1976) 1 C.C.L.T. 197. p. 264

120. *Pierce* v. *Board of Education of the City of Chicago*, 370 N.E.2d 535 (1977). p. 283

121. *Pierce* v. *Society of Sisters of Holy Names* (1925) 268 U.S. 510. p. 19

122. *Piszel* v. *Board of Education for Etobicoke et al.* (1977) 77 D.L.R. (3d) 52. p. 236

123. *Pook et al.v. Ernesttown Public School Trustees* [1944] 4 D.L.R. 268. p. 262

124. *Portelance et al.* v. *Board of Trustees of R. C. Separate School. S.S. No. 5* (1962) 32 D.L.R. (2d) 337. p. 264

125. *Poulton et al.* v. *Notre Dame College et al* (1975) 60 D.L.R. (3d) 501. p. 250

126. *Price* v. *Wilkins* (1888) 58 L.T.R. 680. p. 198

127. *R.* v. *A.B.*, (1986) 26 C.C.C.(3d) 17. p. 166

128. *R.* v. *A.F.G.* [1985] B.C.W.L.D. 997. p. 168

129. *R.* v. *Baptiste and Baptiste* (1980) 61 C.C.C. (2d) 438. p. 115

130. *R* v. *B.C.W.* (1986) 27 C.C.C. (3d) 481. p. 160

131. *R.* v. *Bick* [1979] 3 W.C.B. 287. p. 114

132. *R.* v. *Burko* [1968] 3 D.L.R. (3d) 330. p. 324

133. *R.* v. *Cook* (1983) 37 R.F.L. (2d) 93. p. 130

134. *R.* v. *C.J.M.* (1986) 29 C.C.C.(3d) 569. p. 169

135. *R.* v. *Dimmell* (1981) 55 C.C.C. (2d) 239. p. 115

136. *R.* v. *Dupperon* (1984) 16 C.C.C. (3d)453. p. 115

137. *R.* v. *E and F* (1981) 61 C.C.C. (2d) 287. p. 125

138. *R.* v. *G.* (1985) 20 C.C.C.(3d) 289. p. 168

139. *R.* v. *G.P.S.* (1985) 24 C.C.C. (3d) 61. pp. 160, 161, 162, 168

140. *R.* v. *Gaul* (1904) 36 N.S.R. 504. p. 113

141. *R.* v. *H.* (1985) 22 C.C.C. (3d) 144. pp. 157, 167, 311

142. *R.* v. *Haberstock* [1971] 1 C.C.C. (2d) 433. p. 114

143. *R.* v. *Hopley* (1860) 2 F & F 202. p. 112

144. *R.* v. *J.M.G.* (1986) 33 D.L.R. (4th) 277. pp. 170, 311

145. *R.* v. *Kanhai* [1981] 9 Sask. R. 181. p. 114

146. *R.* v. *Metcalfe* (1927) 49 C.C.C. 260. p. 109

147. *R.* v. *P.B.* (1984) 44 C.R. (3d) 24. pp. 168, 169

148. *R.* v. *Popen* (1981) 60 C.C.C. (2d) 232. p. 127

149. *R.* v. *Robinson* (1899) 7 C.C.C. 52. p. 113

150. *R.* v. *Sarwer-Foner* (1979) 8 R.F.L. (2d) 342. p. 137

151. *R.* v. *Stachula* (1984) 40 R.F.L. (2d) 184. pp. 122, 133

152. *R.* v. *Tutton* (1985) 14 W.C.B. 10. p. 127

153. *R.* v. *W.W.W.* (1985) 20 C.C.C.(3d) 214. p. 157

154. *R.* v. *Zinck* (1910) 67 C.C.C. 114. p. 113

155. *Re Board of Governors of the University of Saskatchewan et al.* (1976) 66 D.L.R. (3d) 561. p. 355

156. *Re Busche and Nova Scotia Teacher's Union* (1975) 62 D.L.R. (3d) 330. p. 352

157. *Re Etobicoke Board of Education and Ontario Secondary School Teachers' Federation, District 12* (1981) 2 L.A.C. 265. p. 182

158. *Re Essex County Roman Catholic Separate School Board and Porter et al.* (1978) 89 D.L.R. (3d) 445. p. 348

159. *Re Essex Roman Catholic Separate School Board and Tremblay-Webster et al.* (1983) 142 D.L.R. (3d) 479. p. 349

160. *Re Essex County Roman Catholic Separate School Board and OECSTA and Kersey* (unreported) 1982. p. 349

161. *Re Infant* (1981) 32 B.C.L.R. 20. p. 141

162. *Re Peace River North Sch. Dist. 60 Bd. of Sch. Trustees and Stockman,* (unreported) p. 360

163. *Re Theriault* (1980) 29 N.B.R. (2d) 42. p. 46

164. *Re Zylberberg et al. and Director of Education of Sudbury Board of Education* (1986) 25 C.R.R. 193. p. 313

165. *Raison* v. *Board of School Trustees, School District No. 45.* (unreported) p. 205

166. *Ralph* v. *London County Council* (1947) 111 J.P. 246. p. 266

167. *Ramsden* v. *Hamilton Board of Education* [1942] 1 D.L.R. 770. p. 220

168. *Revelstoke Sch. Dist. 19 Bd. of Sch. Trustees* v. *Malpass,* unreported. p. 362

169. *Rosenberg* v. *Board of Education of the City of New York* (1949) 92 N.Y.S.2d 344. p. 18

170. *Ruman* v. *Board of Trustees of Lethbridge School District* [1943] 3 W.W.R. 340. p. 312

171. *Ryan* v. *Fildes* [1938] 3 All E.R. 517. p. 197

172. *Saumer* v. *Quebec* [1953] 2 S.C.R. 299 at 324. p. 16

173. *Schade et al.* v. *Winnipeg School District No. 1* et al. (1959) 28 W.W.R. 577. p. 265

174. *School Division of Assiniboine South No.3* v. *Hoffer et al.* (1972) 21 D.L.R. 608. p. 227

175. *Scoffield et al.* v. *Public School Board of Section No. 20, North York* [1942] O.W.N. 458. p. 230

176. *Shrimpton* v. *Hertfordshire County Council* (1911) 104 L.T. 145. p. 245

177. *Sirois et al.* v. *L'Association des Enseignants Francophones du Nouveau-Brunswick (AEFNB) et al.* (1984) 8 D.L.R (4th) 279. p. 213

178. *Smerkinich* v. *Newport Corporation* (1912) 76 J.P. 454. p. 220

179. *Smith* v. *Alameda City Social Services Agency,* 153 Cal. Rptr. 712 (1979). p. 281

180. *Smith* v. *Horizon Aero Sports Ltd.* (1981) 130 D.L.R. (3d) 97. p. 292

181. *Smith* v. *Martin et al.,* [1911] 2 K.B. 775 at 784. p. 321

182. *Snow* v. *State of New York* 469 N.Y.S.2d 959 (1983). p. 285

183. *Snow* v. *The Eaton Centre Ltd.* (1983) 70 C.P.R. (2d) 105 (Ont. High Ct.). p. 92

184. *Sombach et al.* v. *Board of Trustees of Regina R. C. Separate High School District of Saskatchewan* (1969) 9 D.L.R. (3d) 707, aff'd (1970) 18 D.L.R. (3d) 207. p. 266

185. *Spiers* v. *Warrington Corporation* [1954] 1 Q.B. 61. p. 320

186. *Stack* v. *Roman Catholic School Board for St. John's* (1979) 99 D.L.R. (3d) 278. p. 349

187. *State ex rel. Kelley* v. *Ferguson* (1914) 144 N.W. 1039. p. 19

188. *Stevens* v. *Howlitt* (1969) 4 D.L.R. (3d) 50. p. 230

189. *Stevenson* v. *Toronto Board of Education* (1919) 46 O.L.R. 146. p. 251

190. *Storms* v. *School District of Winnipeg No. 1* (1963) 41 D.L.R. (2d) 216. p. 264

191. *Thornton, Tanner et al.* v. *Board of School Trustees of School District No. 57 (Prince George) et al.* [1976] 5 W.W.R. 240. pp. 238, 291

192. *Tinker* v. *Des Moines Independent Community School District* (1969) 393 U.S. 503. pp. 19, 310

193. *Tuli* v. *The Board of Trustees of the St. Albert Protestant Separate School District No. 6* (1987) 8 C.H.R.R. D/3906. p. 323

194. *Tyler et al.* v. *Bd. Trustees Ardath School District* [1935] 2 D.L.R. 814. p. 245

195. *University of London Press, Limited* v. *University Tutorial Press, Limited* [1916] 2 Ch. 601. p. 94

196. *Walton* v. *Vancouver Board of School Trustees* [1924] 2 D.L.R. 387. p. 243

197. *Ward* v. *Board of Blaine Lake* [1971] 4 W.W.R. 161. pp. 16, 321

198. *Williams* v. *Eady* (1893) 10 T.L.R. 41. pp. 208, 224, 239, 249

199. *Winnipeg School Division No. 1* v. *Doreen Maud Craton* (1985) 6 C.H.R.R. D/3014. p. 358

200. *Winnipeg Teachers' Association No. 1* v. *Winnipeg School Division No. 1* [1976] 1 W.W.R. 403. p. 230

201. *Wisconsin* v. *Yoder* (1972) 406 U.S. 205. p. 319

202. *Wray* v. *Essex County Council* [1936] 3 All E.R. 97. p. 249

203. *Wright* v. *Cheshire County Council* [1952] 2 All E.R. 789. p. 238

Index